D1260179

B&T 12/03
R4

JEFFERSON'S
WAR

JEFFERSON'S WAR

America's First War on Terror 1801–1805

JOSEPH WHEELAN

CARROLL & GRAF PUBLISHERS
NEW YORK

JEFFERSON'S WAR
AMERICA'S FIRST WAR ON TERROR 1801–1805

Carroll & Graf Publishers
An Imprint of Avalon Publishing Group Inc.
245 West 17th Street, 11th Floor
New York, NY 10011-5300

First Carroll & Graf Edition 2003
Second printing, September 2003

Library of Congress Cataloging-in-Publication Data is available.

ISBN: 0-7867-1232-5

Interior design by Paul Paddock
Printed in the United States of America
Distributed by Publishers Group West

For my wife, Pat, and our daughters, Sarah and Ann.

CONTENTS

CAST OF CHARACTERS

Americans

John Adams: Minister to England, Vice President, President

William Bainbridge: Captain of *Philadelphia, United States*

Joseph Bainbridge: Naval officer, William's younger brother

Samuel Barron: Fourth Mediterranean squadron commodore, 1804–5

James Barron: Naval officer, Samuel's brother

James Cathcart: Consul to Tripoli

Jonathan Cowdery: *Philadelphia* ship's surgeon, diarist

Richard Dale: First Mediterranean squadron commodore, 1801–2

George Davis: Chargé d'Affaires in Tunis, succeeding William Eaton; Consul to Tripoli after Cathcart

Stephen Decatur, Jr.: Naval officer

James Decatur: Naval officer, Stephen's younger brother

William Eaton: Consul to Tunis, naval agent

Albert Gallatin: Jefferson administration Treasury Secretary

John Jay: Confederation Foreign Secretary

Thomas Jefferson: Minister to France, Vice President, President

Henry Knox: Washington administration War Secretary

Tobias Lear: Consul General for Barbary, Consul to Algiers, succeeding Richard O'Brien

James Madison: Virginia congressman, Jefferson administration Secretary of State

Richard Valentine Morris: Second Mediterranean squadron commodore, 1802–3

Presley O'Bannon: Marine lieutenant

Richard O'Brien: Consul General for Barbary, Consul to Algiers

Edward Preble: Third Mediterranean squadron commodore, 1803–4

William Ray: *Philadelphia* Marine, diarist

John Rodgers: Naval officer and Fifth Mediterranean Squadron commodore, 1805–6

James Simpson: Consul to Morocco

Samuel Smith: Jefferson administration Navy Secretary

Robert Smith: Jefferson administration Navy Secretary, succeeding his brother
  Samuel

Barbary

Hadji Ali: Algerian Dey

Hassan Bey: Tripolitan general

Mustifa Bey: Governor of Derna

Sidi Mahomet Dghies: Tripolitan Foreign Secretary

Reis Hammida: Algerian admiral

Hamet Karamanli: Exiled Bashaw of Tripoli

Yusuf Karamanli: Bashaw of Tripoli, Hamet's younger brother

Ahmed Pasha Khorshid: Ottoman viceroy of Egypt

Soliman Ben Mahomet: Moroccan Emperor after Maulay Sulaiman

Sidi Soliman Melli Melli: Tunisian ambassador to United States

Sidi Muhammad ibn Abd Allah: Moroccan Emperor

Bobba Mustapha: Algerian Dey

Hamouda Pacha: Tunisian Bey

Hassan Pasha: Algerian Dey

Murad Reis (Peter Lisle): Grand Admiral of Tripoli, named after a 17th-century
  Algerian pirate

Maulay Muhammed: Moroccan Emperor, succeeding Sidi Muhammed

Hadgi Unis Ben Unis: Tunisian Bey's Sapitapa, or commercial agent

Europeans

Sir Alexander Ball: British governor of Malta

Citizen Beaussier: French Chargé d'Affaires in Tripoli

Lord Horatio Nelson: British admiral, Mediterranean fleet

Nicholas Nissen: Danish Consul in Tripoli

Mathurins: Catholic friar order that redeemed Barbary captives

SHIPS OF THE UNITED STATES MEDITERRANEAN SQUADRON, 1801–1806, AND THEIR COMMANDERS

Squadron 1, 1801–2

President, 44-gun frigate, Commodore Richard Dale

Philadelphia, 36-gun frigate, Captain Samuel Barron

Essex, 32-gun frigate, Captain William Bainbridge

Boston, 28-gun frigate, Captain Daniel McNeill

Enterprise, 12-gun schooner, Lieutenant Andrew Sterett

Squadron 2, 1802–3

Chesapeake, 36-gun frigate, Commodore Richard Valentine Morris

Constellation, 36-gun frigate, Captain Alexander Murray

New York, 36-gun frigate, Captain James Barron, Captain Isaac Chauncey

John Adams, 28-gun frigate, Captain John Rodgers

Boston, 28-gun frigate, Captain Daniel McNeill

Adams, 28-gun frigate, Captain Hugh Campbell

Enterprise, 12-gun schooner, Lieutenant Andrew Sterett, Lieutenant Isaac Hull

Squadron 3, 1803–4

Constitution, 44-gun frigate, Commodore Edward Preble

Philadelphia, 36-gun frigate, Captain William Bainbridge

John Adams, 28-gun frigate, Captain Isaac Chauncey

Siren, 16-gun brig, Lieutenant Charles Stewart

Scourge, 16-gun brig, Lieutenant John Dent, Midshipman Ralph Izard

Argus, 16-gun brig, Lieutenant Isaac Hull

Vixen, 12-gun schooner, Lieutenant John Smith

Nautilus, 12-gun schooner, Lieutenant Richard Somers

Enterprise, 12-gun schooner, Lieutenant Stephen Decatur, Jr.

Intrepid, 4-gun ketch, Lieutenant Stephen Decatur, Jr., Lieutenant Richard Somers

Squadron 4, 1804–5

President, 44-gun frigate, Commodore Samuel Barron
Constitution, 44-gun frigate, Captain Stephen Decatur, Jr., Captain John Rodgers
Congress, 36-gun frigate, Captain John Rodgers, Captain Stephen Decatur, Jr.
Essex, 32-gun frigate, Captain James Barron
John Adams, 28-gun frigate, Captain Isaac Chauncey
Siren, 16-gun brig, Lieutenant Charles Stewart
Argus, 16-gun brig, Lieutenant Isaac Hull
Vixen, 12-gun schooner, Lieutenant John Smith
Nautilus, 12-gun schooner, Lieutenant John Dent
Enterprise, 12-gun schooner, Lieutenant Thomas Robinson, Jr.
Hornet, 10-gun sloop, Lieutenant Samuel Evans

Squadron 5, 1805–6

Constitution, 44-gun frigate, Commodore John Rodgers
President, 44-gun frigate, Captain James Barron
Constellation, 36-gun frigate, Captain Hugh Campbell
Congress, 36-gun frigate, Captain Stephen Decatur, Jr.
Essex, 32-gun frigate, Lieutenant John Cox
John Adams, 28-gun frigate, Lieutenant John Shaw
Siren, 16-gun brig, Lieutenant Charles Stewart
Argus, 16-gun brig, Lieutenant Isaac Hull
Vixen, 12-gun schooner, Lieutenant John Smith
Nautilus, 12-gun schooner, Lieutenant John Dent
Enterprise, 12-gun schooner, Lieutenant Thomas Robinson, Jr., Lieutenant David Porter
Hornet, 10-gun sloop, Lieutenant Samuel Evans
Franklin, 8-gun sloop, Lieutenant Thomas Robinson, Jr.

The Super Frigates

United States, 44 guns, built in Philadelphia, launched July 1797
Constellation, 36 guns, built in Baltimore, launched September 1797
Constitution, 44 guns, built in Boston, launched July 1798
Congress, 36 guns, built in Portsmouth, N.H., launched August 1799
Chesapeake, 36 guns, built in Norfolk, launched December 1799
President, 44 guns, built in New York, launched April 1800

GLOSSARY

Aground—Resting on the bottom.

Aloft—Anywhere above deck, such as in the upper yards, rigging or masts.

Becalmed—Motionless because of lack of wind.

Blockade—Incoming and outgoing traffic barred from a port by a patrolling enemy squadron.

Board—Taking possession of an enemy ship by climbing onto her deck.

Bomb Vessel—Two-masted vessel armed with one or two mortars for bombardment.

Bow—The front of the ship.

Brig—Shorthand for "brigantine," a two-masted vessel. U.S. Navy brigs often were armed with 16 guns.

Broadside—Simultaneous firing of all guns on one side of a ship.

Cannon—Guns of medium and long range. They were denoted by the weight of shot fired: 9-pound, 12-pound, etc.

Careen—Turning a ship onto its side to make repairs to the other side, or to remove barnacles.

Carronade—A large-bore carriage gun, usually on the top deck, used at short range, sometimes to fire a shrapnel charge to kill enemy sailors.

Cat-O'-Nine-Tails—A device for flogging sailors, comprised of nine knotted lengths of rope.

Corsair—A Barbary Coast ship licensed by the government to conduct raids on enemy shipping.

Corvette—A fast, three-masted ship with one gun deck.

Cutlass—A saber with a curved blade used in naval hand-to-hand combat.

Dry-Dock—A basin whose water level can be raised and lowered at will so that vessels can be guided onto blocks, the water then drained, and the ships examined and repaired.

Felucca—A small Mediterranean coastal trading vessel, narrow-decked with one or two masts.

Fireship—Any vessel filled with combustibles and explosives and sailed among enemy shipping, where crewmen would light a long fuse giving them time to evacuate before the vessel exploded.

Frigate—A three-masted ship with 24 to 44 guns mounted on one or two gun decks. Swifter than the larger "ships of the line," yet with enough firepower to hold their own against ships up to 64 guns, frigates were the mainstay of the U.S. Navy during its early years.

Galley—Oar-powered warship of the pre-sail era, often crewed by slave rowers.

Grog—Water-diluted rum.

Gunboat—Small, lightly armed naval vessel suited for shallow-water operations.

Halyard—Rope for raising and lowering sails.

Handspike—Wooden tool for maneuvering ship guns.

Hold—Large, below-decks storage chamber for provisions and cargo.

Impressment—Forcible draft into naval service during wartime. British impressment of U.S. merchant seamen led to the War of 1812.

Ketch—Two-masted sailing vessel used for coastal trading or fishing.

Lateen—A four-sided sail of Arabic origin seen almost exclusively on Mediterranean vessels.

Merchantman—A merchant ship.

Midshipman—The bottom officer rating, followed in ascending rank by lieutenant, captain and commodore in the early U.S. Navy.

Mole—Breakwater that protects a harbor from the sea.

Muster Book—Shipboard book listing the names of everyone aboard.

Passport—A pass issued by the Barbary States to merchantmen from friendly nations, protecting them against capture by corsairs. During the U.S.-Tripolitan war, U.S. consuls issued passes to Barbary traders as a guaranty against capture by U.S. naval vessels.

Polacre—A two- or three-masted, lateen-sail Barbary vessel comparable in size to a Navy brig or small frigate, often employed as a corsair.

Port—Left side of a vessel, viewed from the rear.

Privateer—Privately owned ship authorized by a government to capture enemy shipping in time of war. Privateers were granted government "letters of marque" permitting them to take possession of enemy prizes. If the captured vessel were condemned in a "prize court," the captor crew was entitled to share in the value of the spoils.

Prize Court—Place where captured ships, or "prizes," were adjudicated and shares of condemned prizes awarded to captor crews.

Quarantine—A restriction placed on ships arriving from ports notorious for disease. A quarantined crew could not land until local health officials cleared them. Quarantines normally lasted no more than 40 days.

Quay—A manmade strip of land in a harbor where ships can load or unload cargo or passengers.

Schooner—A two-masted vessel typically carrying eight to 12 guns and slightly smaller than a brig.

Shoal—Shallows in an area of deeper water.

Ship Log—Official ship record book, updated daily with observations on navigation, weather, and occurrences.

Ships of the Line—Ships of 64 to 130 guns that carried sufficient firepower to take positions in the "line of battle," a formation from which an admiral could bring the utmost firepower to bear at one time.

Sloop—A small sailing vessel, often one-masted, usually with fewer than eight guns. The term sometimes is used generically to refer to small warships.

Spar Deck—The upper deck behind the main mast from which the captain commanded his ship.

Speaking Trumpet—A crude megaphone used by officers to shout orders and communicate with other ships.

Sprung Mast—Mast that has broken free of its fastenings and must either be repaired or replaced.

Squadron—A small number of warships under one commander.

Starboard—Right side of a vessel, viewed from the rear.

Stern—The rear of a ship.

Struck his Flag—Lowered the flag in surrender.

Tack—An oblique ship's maneuver enabling it to sail into the wind.

Watch—On shipboard, the 24 hours of the day were divided into five four-hour and two two-hour watches, with the crewmen assigned to a watch responsible for the ship's operation during that period.

Xebec—A three-masted Mediterranean vessel, similar to a polacre. Xebecs were often used as corsairs.

(Source: *The Oxford Companion to Ships and the Sea,* Peter Kemp, editor, Oxford University Press, 1976.)

AUTHOR'S NOTE

The spelling and syntactical irregularities that recur in the correspondence, diaries, and ships' logs cited in this book reflect the era preceding uniform U.S. educational standards. Eighteenth-century men with scant formal schooling often became naval officers, diplomats, and government officials, whose public and private utterances subsequently became part of history.

PROLOGUE

August 1, 1801

Lieutenant Andrew Sterett surveyed the horizon from the *Enterprise* quarterdeck. Curly-haired and fair, with a powerful, curved nose, his sideburns nearly reaching his chin, the fire-eating young U.S. Navy skipper was especially watching for the square sails and long prow of a Barbary corsair. But for the moment, he had to curb his eagerness for combat because the sparkling Mediterranean lay empty. Canvas rustled above him, where the *Enterprise*'s crew worked the topsails to catch the faint breeze. From the bow and aloft, Sterett's lookouts continued to scan for signs of sail.

The Barbary War was only two months old, and the U.S. squadron—Commodore Richard Dale's 44-gun *President*, two smaller frigates, and Sterett's lightly armed, fast schooner—had been in the Mediterranean scarcely a month. The U.S. warships had not yet seen action against the Tripolitan navy. But that would change on this day.

The *Enterprise* was sailing to Malta to fill its water casks and the *President's*, depleted during Commodore Dale's initial diplomatic visits to all four Barbary States and a week of cruising off Tripoli. Above the *Enterprise's* stern fluttered the British ensign; Sterett was following Navy Secretary Samuel Smith's orders to fly false colors, knowing the Tripolitan policy of avoiding enemy warships. With England and Tripoli at peace, the corsair captains wouldn't shy away from British ships; they might even draw near for a piece of news, and thus be lured into a fight the Americans would welcome.

The *Enterprise* was the third American ship by that name, and she would not be the last. Her two predecessors had served without distinction during the Revolutionary War. Not until World War II would there be another *Enterprise* whose colorful history would rival that of Sterett's 12-gun schooner. During the Quasi-War that had ended in 1800, she had captured nine French ships in the West Indies in just half a year, including *Le Flambeau,* which had nine 14-pounders and a crew of more than 100. Later, after she was reconfigured as a brig in 1811, the *Enterprise* would claim more glory during the War of 1812, followed by action against the pirate Jean Lafitte in the Gulf of Mexico. By then, she would have picked up the nickname "Lucky."

Cries from Sterett's lookouts announced they had sighted a ship. Poking over the horizon was a square-sail brig with a long, pointed bow—unmistakably a Barbary corsair. The *Enterprise's* gun crews and Marines raced to battle quarters.

Before the *Enterprise* had departed for Malta, Dale instructed Sterett to engage the enemy only if he thought he could win—a broad mandate for an aggressive young naval officer thirsty for glory. If he encountered and defeated a Tripolitan corsair while en route to Malta, "you will heave all his guns overboard, cut away his masts, and leave him in a situation that he can just make out to get into some port." If he met a corsair on the return trip, the prize was to be brought to the squadron. In other words, fresh water took priority.

When they drew within hailing distance of the new ship, Sterett and his officers saw that she was indeed a Tripolitan corsair, aptly named the *Tripoli*. The American officers counted fourteen open gun ports—two more guns than the *Enterprise*. The *Tripoli*'s captain, Rais Mahomet Rous, exchanged greetings with Sterett. Thinking he was speaking to a British officer because of the ensign swinging above the stern in the light breeze, Mahomet Rous revealed he was hunting American merchantmen.

The instant he uttered those words, events moved at a gallop. Sterett lowered the British ensign and raised the Stars and Stripes. Enterprise Marines opened fire from the deck and firing platforms aloft, their musket balls clattering like hail on the *Tripoli*'s deck. The startled corsair crew replied with a partial broadside.

It was 9:00 A.M., August 1, 1801. The first naval battle of the Barbary War had begun.

The *Enterprise* was outgunned by the *Tripoli,* but Sterett was confident of his men's abilities. A demanding skipper, Sterett had drilled the *Enterprise*'s gunners during the Atlantic crossing until they were fast and accurate. He also knew the Barbary corsairs had notoriously poor gunners; they preferred pistols and steel at close quarters to exchanging broadsides. Sterett was determined that gunnery would determine this battle's outcome.

The *Tripoli* edged closer for boarding, and the pirates crowded onto the long bow. The *Enterprise*'s Marines, commanded by

Lieutenant Enoch S. Lane, shot them down. Then, like a boxer, the *Enterprise* sidestepped and pummeled the Tripoli with its 6-pounders from 30 yards away.

Twice more the *Tripoli* tried to close with the *Enterprise* for boarding, with the same bloody result.

As the combatants' fire-belching guns flickered in the dense smoke like summer lightning, the *Enterprise*'s superior gunnery began to tell. The *Tripoli*'s decks soon were littered with dead and maimed soldiers and sailors lying beneath smashed, crazily tilted masts. The hull was torn with jagged holes above the waterline.

The *Tripoli* lowered her flag in surrender. The *Enterprise* gun crews rushed onto the top deck cheering, only to come under renewed fire from the *Tripoli,* which had only feigned capitulation.

Sterett ordered another broadside. The roaring cannon fire crashed through the *Tripoli*'s hull, spraying the gun crews with deadly splinters. The Marines in the *Enterprise*'s rigging and on deck shot at everything that moved on the *Tripoli*'s spar deck. The screams of the wounded pierced the thick gunsmoke in the lulls between cannonades.

Mahomet Rous struck his flag again, and again Sterett stopped firing. As the *Enterprise* drifted closer, up went the Tripolitan flag and the corsair's cannons commenced firing once more.

The livid Sterett ordered the *Enterprise* to stand off and batter the *Tripoli* with its cannons. When the flag came down a third time, he told his gunners to lower their cannons and smash the *Tripoli*'s hull at the waterline. Sink her, he commanded them.

Mahomet Rous threw his flag into the sea. He was finished.

Still suspicious, Sterett demanded that the captain or another officer come over in a boat.

But the Tripolitans were out of tricks. Their boats were wrecked, all their officers killed or wounded.

Lieutenant David Porter and a small crew rowed to the enemy ship and found the torn deck a charnel house of mangled bodies, body parts, human viscera, and blood.

"The carnage on board was dreadful," Sterett reported to Dale, "she having 30 men killed and 30 wounded, among the latter was the Captain and first Lieutenant. Her sails, masts and rigging were cut to pieces with 18 shot between wind and water."

Among the dead was the *Tripoli's* surgeon. While the *Enterprise's* doctor attended to the enemy wounded, Sterett's crew cut down the *Tripoli's* shattered masts and flung them overboard, along with the corsair's cannons, cannonballs, powder, muskets, swords, pistols, dirks, and pikes. The Americans raised a stubby makeshift mast and rigged it with a small sail. The wreck limped off toward Tripoli.

Sterett did a damage assessment of his own ship: At the end of a three-hour gunnery duel at pistol-shot range, or about 30 yards, "we have not had a man wounded, and we have sustained no material damage in our hull or rigging."

Not every battle of the Barbary War would end so well for U.S. forces, yet when it is remembered at all, the 1801–5 war with Tripoli is often recalled as a swashbuckling adventure bookended by America's two struggles with England. It is easily forgotten because it did not fit any template formed by later U.S. conflicts, waged for union, democracy, territory, or corporate avarice. Yet, in none of those latter-day struggles did principled American outrage and improvised, unorthodox tactics coalesce as they did in the Barbary War.

Then, in the wake of the 2001 terrorist attacks on Washington and New York, the United States found itself in a new war much like the one two centuries earlier. As will be seen, the war that President Thomas Jefferson, the U.S. Navy, and the Marine Corps waged against Moslem Tripoli—led by Edward Preble, William Eaton, Stephen Decatur, Jr., Andrew Sterett, and Presley O'Bannon—was not so different from today's war on terror. In truth, the Barbary War was America's first war on terror.

Separated by 200 years, the conflicts might at first seem to have little in common other than Moslem adversaries who targeted American civilians. The Barbary States wielded terror in the name of Islam for mercenary purposes, not to advance a political agenda, the goal of Al-Qaeda and its allies. Their depredations did not occur in New York or Washington, but in the Mediterranean and eastern Atlantic, against "infidel" civilian contractors transporting goods on sailing ships. Yet, it was terror nonetheless, prosecuted cynically in the name of Islamic "jihad," Al-Qaeda's pretext for hijacking jetliners and crashing them into highly visible symbols of U.S. power. America's response in 1801 was the same as today: "to repel force by force," as Jefferson put it succinctly.

Tripoli and its three Northwest Africa neighbors—Tunis, Algiers, and Morocco—had preyed on Christian Europe since the early 1600s. Their corsair fleets had relentlessly attacked, killed, maimed, and enslaved civilians on the high seas, robbing them of their ships and merchandise. The Barbary States coerced ransom and protection money from Europe and, in exchange, permitted the European powers to trade without interference in the western Mediterranean—until the next time the Barbary States unleashed their pirate fleets.

The European nations meekly signed the debasing treaties and scrupulously bribed the bashaws, beys, deys, and emperors with cash, weapons, and ships, while the Barbary States unscrupulously broke every agreement. Only upon the greatest provocation did Europe attempt to assert its right to an unmolested trade without payment. These sporadic naval expeditions sometimes met limited success, but never caused lasting change. In 1801 the Barbary terror, although creaky with age, still commanded payments from Europe equaling $5 million in today's currency.

The enigmatic Thomas Jefferson stood up to the pirate states with a small squadron a fraction the size of Europe's vast fleets. Within days of his inauguration as the third U.S. president, without congressional or public debate of any kind, Jefferson ordered four warships to sail to coastal Northwest Africa and blockade and attack any Barbary State that was at war with America. By the time the squadron reached the Mediterranean in early July 1801, Tripoli already had declared war.

While Jefferson's surprising action doesn't square with the conventional "pacifist" image of the third U.S. president, the fact is he was a complicated and sometimes vindictive man with a long memory. And he had not forgotten his frustrating meeting with a Tripolitan ambassador in London two decades earlier, or his failure to organize a European coalition to blockade the Northwest African states.

Jefferson's war pitted a modern republic with a free-trade, entrepreneurial creed against a medieval autocracy whose credo was piracy and terror. It matched an ostensibly Christian nation against an avowed Islamic one that professed to despise Christians. A disciplined naval force of "super frigates" faced a loosely organized fleet of pirate corsairs.

Yet both America and Tripoli shared a common belief in naval armament as a means of realizing their diverging ambitions. Jefferson was convinced that a strong navy—paradoxical considering his overall philosophy of a minimalist central government—was essential to a thriving foreign trade. Tripoli's bashaw, or ruler, Yusuf Karamanli, believed that with a strong navy, Tripoli could supplant Algiers as the preeminent Barbary naval power, and feast on the bustling commerce Jefferson envisioned.

Fought for strong principles by an idealistic new republic, the Barbary War was an audacious action for a constitutional government scarcely twelve years old and only twenty years removed from its war of independence. The war in North Africa marked the first time that U.S. troops planted the Stars and Stripes on a hostile foreign shore.

If the names of Preble, Decatur, Eaton, and Sterett spur any recognition at this remove of two centuries, they might conjure images of sideburned men in ruffled shirts and jackets, frozen in a pose of noble alertness, or a crimson-tinged battle scene with wooden sailing ships belching fire. Through the gray gunsmoke haze, shadowy minarets rise above a whitewashed Mediterranean port.

But those fading portraits do not begin to do justice to the flesh-and-blood fighting men or their war, unlike any America has fought—until today, in the shadow of the bloody terror attacks on the World Trade Center and the Pentagon. During the Barbary War, naval officers led nighttime commando missions into the heart of Tripoli's harbor to destroy the enemy's ability to continue the war—once with spectacular success, once with tragic consequences. Key intelligence was transmitted to naval leaders from inside the bashaw's own castle fortress by code and "invisible ink." Temporary alliances and native insurgents supplied equipment and manpower at critical times. And the indomitable William Eaton, a precursor of the twenty-first-century special-forces operative, cobbled together an army of mercenaries, insurgents, native troops, and Arab cavalry to launch a surprise invasion.

The Barbary War posed all the difficulties of waging a distant conflict against a wily enemy that wouldn't come out and fight: the need to find and operate from bases supplied by friendly nations; no ready reinforcements; a maddening lag in communications with Washington; and, as a consequence of the last, the constant threat of command inertia. But resourceful commanders overcame these obstacles and forced the enemy to draw upon all of his defensive capacity. The U.S. Navy and Marine Corps demonstrated that they were up to the challenges of a far-flung war and were the equal, ship-for-ship and man-for-man, of any nation—and indispensable to projecting U.S. power.

The first naval heroes of the nineteenth century emerged from the Barbary War, as did the practice of training young officers during limited wars for larger conflicts later. The Mediterranean squadron served as a "nursery" for the young naval officers who would fight the War of 1812. The first U.S. military monument, located at the U.S. Naval Academy behind Preble Hall, is dedicated to the six naval officers killed in the Barbary War.

The war shaped the Navy's expeditionary tradition and established the precedent of simultaneously using diplomacy and military force—in the words of Navy Secretary Robert Smith, "Holding out the olive Branch in one hand & displaying in the other the means of offensive operations"—to achieve limited objectives.

While the Barbary War resembles today's war on terror tactically and strategically, it resonates most deeply in its assertion of free trade, human rights, and freedom from tyranny and terror. To defend those principles, Jefferson was willing to send a largely untried squadron across the Atlantic to go to war with a people whose customs, history, and religion were alien to the early American experience.

In 1801 as in 2001, there was never any question that the reasons for fighting were worth the price. The United States did not hesitate to go to war for its closely held beliefs, as America's enemies have come to learn since 1775.

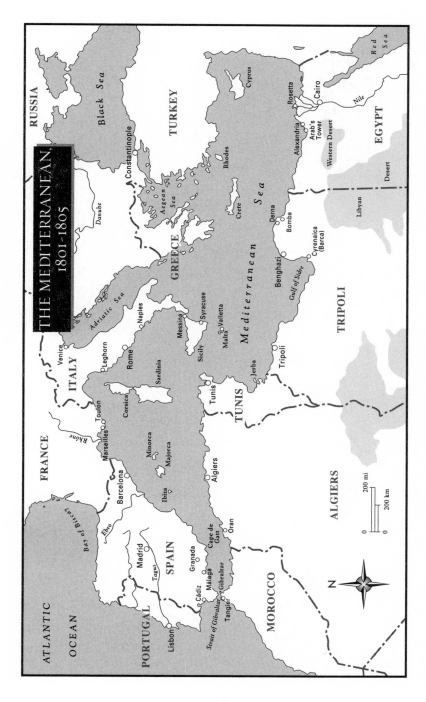

THE MEDITERRANEAN, 1801–1805

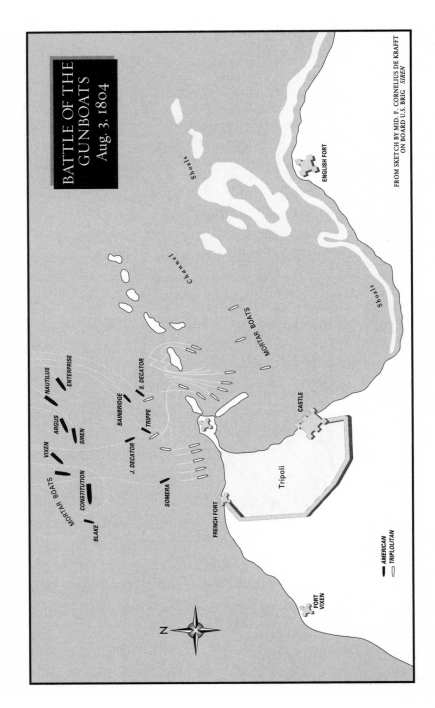

BATTLE OF THE
GUNBOATS
Aug. 3, 1804

FROM SKETCH BY MID. F. CORNELIUS DE KRAFFT
ON BOARD U.S. BRIG *SIREN*

ENGLISH FORT

Shoals

Shoals

Channel

MORTAR BOATS

NAUTILUS

ENTERPRISE

ARGUS

SIREN

VIXEN

BAINBRIDGE

S. DECATOR

MORTAR BOATS

CONSTITUTION

J. DECATOR

TRIPPE

CASTLE

BLAKE

SOMERA

Tripoli

FRENCH FORT

AMERICAN
TRIPOLITAN

FORT
VIXEN

N

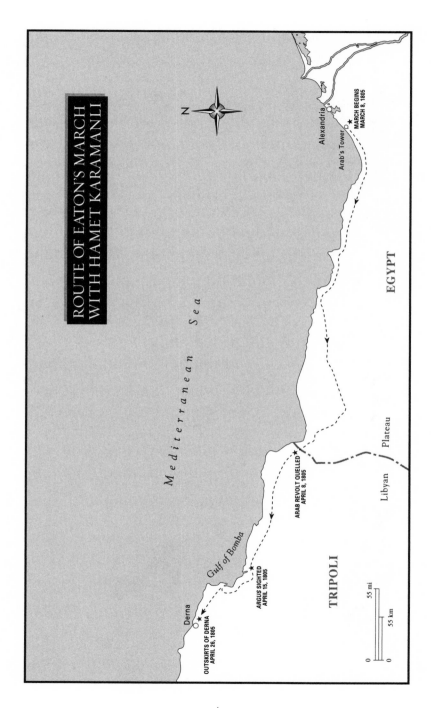

ROUTE OF EATON'S MARCH
WITH HAMET KARAMANLI

N

Mediterranean Sea

Alexandria
Arab's Tower
MARCH BEGINS
MARCH 8, 1805

EGYPT

Gulf of Bomba

Derna
OUTSKIRTS OF DERNA
APRIL 26, 1805

ARGUS SIGHTED
APRIL 15, 1805

ARAB REVOLT QUELLED
APRIL 8, 1805

Libyan Plateau

TRIPOLI

55 mi

55 km

0

0

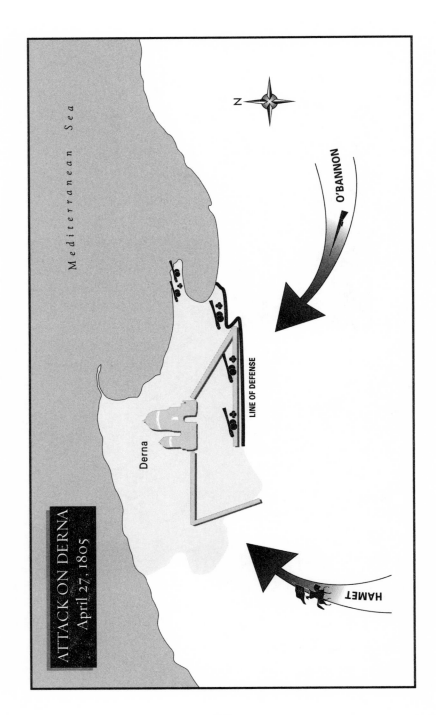

ATTACK ON DERNA
April 27, 1805

Mediterranean Sea

Derna

LINE OF DEFENSE

O'BANNON

HAMET

N

I

THE "PACIFIST" PRESIDENT

Washington, D.C., 1801

*The motives pleading for war rather than tribute are numerous and
honorable, those opposing them mean and short-sighted.*
—Thomas Jefferson to James Monroe, 1785

Nothing in Thomas Jefferson's inauguration speech
March 4 had foreshadowed his decision to embark the
United States on its first war on foreign soil, in Moslem Northwest Africa. The address's brief nod to foreign affairs was decidedly
unhawkish: "Peace, commerce & honest friendship with all
nations, entangling alliances with none." Jefferson was more
intent on healing the still-raw wounds of the unsurpassedly vituperous recent presidential campaign, celebrated by the victorious
Republicans as the "Revolution of 1800." "We are all federalists,
we are all republicans," he had declared in a soft voice that barely
carried beyond the front row of the Senate chamber; his aversion
to making speeches kept him off rostrums all but once during the
next eight years—the exception was his second inauguration.

The 1800 campaign was the summit of the virulent debate
between Republicans and Federalists that had raged throughout
the 1790s over government's role in completing the Revolution of

1776. The two most prominent surviving founding fathers, Vice President Jefferson and President John Adams, had found themselves in the vanguard of rival political parties with diverging philosophies on this all-important issue. The pendulum had swung away from Adams's Federalists in 1800, and the disgruntled president had left Washington on the 4:00 A.M. stage on Inauguration Day so he would not have to witness the ascent of his former friend to the office from which Adams had been sent packing.

The triumphant Jefferson wasn't going to waste words on foreign policy when his listeners were so anxious to hear him describe what his administration would be like. His election marked the new republic's first true regime change, unlike the succession by Washington's vice president and fellow Federalist, Adams. Jefferson pledged fealty to Republican ideals by presiding over "a wise and frugal Government, which shall restrain men from injuring one another, shall leave them otherwise free to regulate their own pursuits of industry and improvement, and shall not take from the mouth of labor the bread it has earned."

At no point did he mention his hardened resolve to smash "The Terror," shorthand for the long jihad waged in the Mediterranean and Atlantic by the Barbary States against Christian Europe, and now the United States. On this subject, Jefferson had long ago settled upon what he wished to do, and he wasn't in office three weeks before he acted. Without convening Congress or formally consulting his new cabinet, which was only slowly coming together in the raw new capital of only six months, on March 23 Jefferson issued the astonishing order to ready a squadron of warships to sail to the Mediterranean.

• • •

It might seem strange that Jefferson of all the founders—Jefferson, generally regarded as the most pacific of them—was poised to send the new U.S. Navy to war in the Mediterranean. Yet, since the 1780s, he had undeviatingly advocated defiance of the Barbary States, which had wrecked U.S. Mediterranean trade after the Revolutionary War and until the mid-1790s. Tripoli, Tunis, Algiers, and Morocco were old hands at state-sponsored terrorism. They had preyed for 200 years on European Christians, living off the loot snatched from coastal raids and ship seizures, and the protection money they were paid for not molesting shipping. Europe always had paid, sending punitive squadrons only when the losses cut too deep, and only to negotiate better extortion terms.

Jefferson fervently believed America had not thrown off one tyrant to bow to a lowlier one. "The motives pleading for war rather than tribute are numerous and honorable, those opposing them mean and short-sighted," he had written to James Monroe back in 1785. It was at about that time, when Jefferson was minister to France, that he had debated Adams, in those days his friend and counterpart in London, over whether it would be wiser to pay tribute to the Barbary States or to fight them. In words that resonate down to the present day, Jefferson had argued that force was the only sure antidote to terror. While Adams agreed in principle, he said the public wouldn't support a war. Adams advocated paying. America was unequipped to fight a war, he said, and paying tribute beat the alternative: forgoing a Mediterranean trade altogether.

But Jefferson and Adams were arguing a moot point; America's federal government had no money under the weak Articles of Confederation either for war or tribute. Consequently, there was just no Mediterranean trade. Jefferson tried unsuccessfully to form a confederation with Europe's smaller powers to blockade the Barbary States indefinitely. While serving as George Washington's secretary of state in the early 1790s, he urged Congress to build a navy to go to war against them. America instead negotiated treaties and arms-for-hostages deals with the Barbary States in the mid-1790s. By the time Jefferson became president, those treaties had cost more than $1 million.

In 1801, it appeared Jefferson had been right after all, for the treaties were unraveling. In the last months of the Adams administration, Tripoli issued an ultimatum threatening war in six months if it did not receive a new warship and a new treaty committing the United States to annual tribute. Tunis, Algiers, and Morocco also were unhappy because the gifts, armaments, and naval supplies the United States had promised them every year were late in arriving. The frustrated U.S. consuls had made excuses, pleaded with the rulers for extensions, and had tried to appease them with jewels, ships, cash, and gold. The consuls blamed the delays on the yellow fever epidemic in Philadelphia, moving the capital to Washington, the election. However, Jefferson didn't intend to make excuses, but to make war.

Two members of Jefferson's new cabinet were late arriving in Washington. James Madison, Jefferson's protégé, closest confidant and the new secretary of state, was delayed in Virginia settling the estate of his late father, who had died on February 27. The other late arrival was Albert Gallatin, the colorful, brilliant Geneva aristocrat whom Jefferson had named treasury secretary. Gallatin had commanded a regiment under Louis XVI in the French Revolution, and his face bore a vivid scar from a saber duel fought on horseback. It wasn't until early May that Madison was able to leave

Montpelier to assume his duties, and Gallatin didn't arrive until May 13. Jefferson convened the cabinet two days later to discuss the naval war for which he was readying a squadron at Norfolk and which was to sail in just two weeks.

"Shall the squadron now at Norfolk be ordered to cruise in the Mediterranean? What shall be the object of the cruise?" Jefferson asked his assembled cabinet members. While the orders already had been given, the president wanted to hear the views of his most trusted advisers.

They all agreed the squadron was needed to project American power and protect commercial interests in the Mediterranean. "The expedition should go forward openly to protect our commerce against the threatened hostilities of Tripoli," said War Secretary Henry Dearborn. Attorney General Levi Lincoln said the warships should take defensive measures if attacked, but should not hunt down and destroy the enemy. Madison, Gallatin, and Acting Navy Secretary Samuel Smith argued for hot pursuit into enemy harbors.

Gallatin broached the ticklish matter of congressional approval, which hadn't been sought. With Congress in recess, it would take weeks to assemble the House and Senate, even in an emergency. Gallatin personally thought it unnecessary. If a nation declared war on the United States, didn't the Constitution authorize the president to direct the public force? And Smith asserted that the president not only had the authority, but was "bound to apply the public force" to defend the republic.

The United States must announce its intentions at the outset, Madison urged. Jefferson agreed that American resolve would be "openly declared to every nation." He would write Tripoli's ruler, the bashaw, a letter stating why he was sending a squadron against the bashaw's nation. "All concur in the expediency of cruise," Jefferson scrawled in his meeting notes.

The Jefferson administration didn't know it, for news crossed the Atlantic only as fast as sailing ships, but Tripoli had already declared war on the United States. On May 14, the day before the cabinet meeting, the bashaw had delivered the declaration in Barbary's usual blunt manner: Soldiers marched to the U.S. consulate in Tripoli and chopped down the flagpole where the Stars and Stripes flew.

It was a propitious time for the United States to settle its Mediterranean affairs. America's undeclared three-year "Quasi-War" with France had ended only recently, and England and France were poised to resume their seemingly unending war. Against France, America had surprised many close observers by proving to be extremely proficient in waging naval warfare. The Quasi-War, fought almost entirely in the West Indies, accelerated the early development of the U.S. Navy and Marine Corps. The Navy now floated more than thirty ships, a signal achievement considering there had been no U.S. Navy five years before. But its strength would soon be whittled down, for Adams had signed a law in his last hours as president ordering every naval ship sold— all but thirteen frigates. Six were to be kept in active service, the other seven dry-docked.

This suited Jefferson, as thrifty with public money as he was spendthrift with his own, despite his habit of meticulously recording every purchase in his journals. He and other Republicans wanted to "shrink" the federal government after a decade of growth under Washington and Adams and pay off the $83 million national debt. This was the core of the Republican prescription for restoring the fading "Spirit of '76," that romantic vision of a peaceful rural society much like the one to which Cincinnatus returned after saving Rome, whose hallmark would be freedom from government interference. It was the antithesis of the Hamiltonian philosophy subscribed to by Washington and Adams that postulated a powerful central government and an emphasis on commercial manufacturing. Small wonder Republicans heralded Jefferson's victory which, they believed, would undo the evils of federalism. Yet for all that, Jefferson and the Republicans grudgingly conceded a central government's utility in one respect: conducting foreign policy. The new United States must speak with one voice—and not as a gaggle of states—to the world to be a prosperous trading nation. A navy, even a diminished one, would guarantee that that voice was listened to.

It would have been difficult to find more dissimilar nations than the United States and the four Barbary States in 1801. Except for its Native American population and a small percentage of Jews, the United States was solidly Christian, while the North African regencies were just as solidly Moslem—and openly hostile toward Christians. The new American republic was a laboratory of Enlightenment ideals, especially freedom, openness, and rationality; the Barbary Powers were medieval, closed, tyrannical, and corrupt. The United States was a new land, perched on the edge of a largely unexplored wilderness; Barbary—the name is derived from the Latin *barbarus* and Greek *barbaros,* ancient appellations for foreigners—was a burial ground for Greeks, Romans, Phoenicians, Carthaginians, Byzantines, Goths, Christians, and Moslems. While America dreamed of global markets for its growing profusion of products, the Barbary rulers' narrow aims hadn't changed in centuries: to invoke the Koran to extort money from Christian nations.

"Jihad" is derived from the word "jahada," meaning "to strive." The Koran exhorts Moslems to strive to purify themselves spiritually and promote Islam in the world. The first is a battle fought and won within the heart by overcoming temptation, and the second is achieved by doing right in the world. In early Koran interpretations, jihad was nonviolent; the believer conquered his urges and peacefully disseminated Islam's tenets throughout the world. War was permitted only in self-defense. As Islam exploded into a religion of conquest and contended with Christian Europe for territory during the Crusades, jihad took on a new meaning: It became a holy war to impose Moslem hegemony over non-believers.

Jihad's new interpretation became accepted practice in the Moslem world, regulated by a few simple rules. It could not be waged against other Moslem nations. It had to be authorized by an Islamic state's spiritual leader. Infidels must be forewarned, and offered the opportunity to remain autonomous, if they agreed to pay a tax. Their refusal to pay permitted jihad to be declared, and any captives taken from ships or in battle could be enslaved and ransomed. The Barbary States stuck to this template in their dealings with America and Europe, while blithely ignoring the Koran's many other strictures on war. Acting as their nations' temporal and religious leaders, the bashaws, deys, beys, and emperors decided when their corsairs would hunt the European merchant ships in the Mediterranean and Atlantic. They chose their enemies and fixed the price of ephemeral peace.

II

THE DREADFUL CORSAIRS

"Yield dogs, yield!"
—Barbary pirates' exhortation before boarding European
merchant ships

The seeds of the Barbary States' long jihad against Christian Europe and, later, America were planted by Queen Isabella and King Ferdinand of Spain in 1492, the year they sponsored Christopher Columbus's expedition into the Atlantic to find a western passage to India. The royal couple had grand ambitions for Spain, wishing to bring the entire peninsula under Christian rule. That meant finally crushing the Moors, the descendants of the Islamic conquerors of Iberia in 711.

The Moors were the progeny of invading Arab Moslems and of the North African Berbers whose origins predate the historical record, receding into the primordial mists millennia before Christ. Moslem cavalry pouring out of seventh-century Arabia reached Alexandria in 642 and began embarking on increasingly longer and larger expeditions into the Maghrib, the "land of sunset"— the vast arid region stretching from Egypt to the Atlantic, more than 2,000 miles. In the oceanic sand dunes and craggy hills, the Arabs met and conquered North Africa's indigenous Berber tribes in bloody clash after sharp, bloody clash, advancing west inexorably. Many Berbers converted to Islam and became staunch Arab allies who assisted in later conquests. By 707, the invaders and their auxiliaries occupied coastal North Africa from the Red Sea to the Atlantic.

During one expedition into the wild, barren land, Arab General Hassan ibn al-Nu'man al-Ghassani happened upon what remained of Carthage, the Phoenicians' once-mighty outpost and, later, the capital of the Carthaginian Empire. In 698, it was little more than ruins, occupied by ragged, starving bands living in squalor beside a large gulf. Hassan, a practical, energetic man, envisioned a new city closer to the head of the gulf; it would be better protected from the sea and from the rovers hunting easy plunder. It also would be perfectly situated for a shipyard. The city that he built became Tunis. Even as it went up, shipwrights began building a fleet of galleys, the oared ships that had carried merchants, adventurers, and conquerors along the Mediterranean shores for millennia. As the eighth century began, the first Barbary corsairs weighed anchor in Tunis to capture the merchant vessels of European Christians and sack Mediterranean coastal towns.

Before long, the Moslem conquerors were eyeing the towering landmass across the narrow straits from Morocco. The Moslem general, Tarik, gathered an invasion fleet to carry his assault troops across the short stretch of open water to Iberia, the onetime western province of the empires of Phoenicia, Carthage, and Rome. Iberia was a fabled land of silver and gold mines, fertile farmland and rich cities. For nearly 200 years, the Visigoths, one of the German warrior tribes that had overrun the crumbling

Roman Empire and its far-flung provinces, had prospered there, but now the Islamic juggernaut was at their door.

In 711, Tarik and 7,000 Moslem Berbers alighted from troop transports onto the rock that would bear Tarik's name—Gebal-Tarik, or Gibraltar. King Roderick summoned his Visigoth warriors to defend their land. The Moslems crushed the larger German army in one day, at Guadalete.

The Moors, as the amalgam of invading Moslem Berbers and later Arab arrivals would become known, prospered in Spain as no people had before or has since. Seville, Cordova, and Granada blossomed into densely populated, prosperous cities where Moslems, Christians, and Jews lived together in harmony. Women enjoyed more freedom and opportunity than they would anywhere else in Europe or the Islamic world for 500 years. As did Moorish males, they attended primary schools, where they learned to read, write, and recite the Koran before being instructed in a trade. Some went on to the universities to study mathematics, astronomy, philosophy, botany, medicine, and law. Literacy soared. Cordova alone boasted seventy libraries that held more than 500,000 books. (In 1800, U.S. libraries held only one tenth that number.) Advanced Moorish trade and agriculture practices created massive wealth and a food surplus that fed a growing urban populace. The Moors filled the cities with marble palaces, graced with their trademark double-horseshoe arches, and with gilded ceilings and doors inlaid with precious jewels.

But Christian power, formerly confined to the northern mountain fastnesses, expanded in the fourteenth and fifteenth centuries, and the Moors' territories contracted. Isabella and Ferdinand's marriage united Castile and Aragon. The Moors retreated to Andalusia.

• • •

In 1491, at the urging of Catholic clergy, Ferdinand and Isabella laid siege to Granada, Andalusia's capital. It fell on November 25. The cardinals and bishops beseeched the monarchs to expel the infidel Moors from Spain altogether. The Moors had tolerated Christendom when they were ascendant, but the Christian Inquisition harbored no reciprocal emotion. Cardinal Ximenes de Cisneros and his bishops and monsignors soon convinced Isabella to take a hard line and give the defeated Moors of Granada a choice: baptism or exile. It was the same choice Ferdinand and Isabella would give Spain's unbaptized Jews six months hence, with the result that over 100,000 eventually became exiles. Most Granadan Moors, however, preferred baptism to banishment; by professing a surface conformity, they could preserve their home and family, while secretly practicing the old faith as before—as many of the "converso" Jews did—although Ximenes made it difficult for them to do so, shutting down all the mosques and burning Moorish manuscripts. But the rural Moors were more uncompromising, stubbornly refusing to give up their faith or abandon their holdings. They dug into the fertile hills south of the city, bracing for the worst. It soon came: Ferdinand sent the Spanish army into action against them. The outnumbered rebels surrendered in 1492.

Thousands of exiled Moors who had spurned baptism loaded their possessions onto carts and their own backs and streamed into the port cities under the condemning eyes of the Spanish authorities. The Moors' forced dispossession began a century of banishments and exile. While a few refugees found sanctuary in Italy, most retraced Tarik's historic journey, in reverse, across the straits to

North Africa—to Barbary, where they were welcomed by their Moslem brethren.

Wanting to avenge their banishment by the Spanish, the Moors found their way to the Barbary shipyards, where their thirst for revenge met a kindred spirit among the corsair captains, always ready to go raiding. Soon more of the long-bowed corsairs than ever plowed the western Mediterranean on raids against coastal Spain. The Moors' former countrymen, the ones who professed a false allegiance to Christianity, helped guide them to Christian loot and captives. The "little war" against Spain had begun.

The escalating raids alarmed Isabella to the extent that she began contemplating a military expedition against Barbary. She sent spies to find which points were vulnerable to attack, but died in 1504 before mapping an invasion plan. The more cautious Ferdinand favored a containment policy while he concentrated on expanding Spanish trade with Italy. Meanwhile, the Moors' hatred of Spain festered in the Barbary ports.

The Spanish cardinals and bishops would settle for nothing less than the extirpation of every last crumb of Moorish culture. With some justification, Spanish Christians believed the Moriscos, as the surviving Moors who had submitted to baptism were now called, constituted a "fifth column" in the deadly struggle between the Islamic Ottoman Empire and Christian Europe that had begun in earnest with the Crusades. Spain clamped down on them. The clergy wasn't fooled by their baptismal-font conversions. They pressured Ferdinand's grandson and successor, Charles V, to issue an edict requiring the Moriscos to speak only Spanish and to abandon their native costumes, their Moslem names, and their public baths. Moslems, Jews, heretics, and nonbelievers of every stripe all would soon experience far worse treatment as the Inquisition honed its inhuman instruments of persecution and torture, such as the rack and stake, but this was how it began in Spain, with intolerance of cultural diversity. Charles signed the edict, but it was his son, Philip II, who carried it out. In 1567, Philip ordered the Moorish baths pulled down, as well as a host of other punitive measures intended to eradicate Morisco culture. The next year, the Moriscos rebelled. War swept Andalusia. The Morisco rebels made the Sierra Nevada Mountains their headquarters. The Spanish exulted in the opportunity to destroy the Moors.

Given command of the Spanish forces was Philip's gifted twenty-two-year-old half brother, Don Juan of Austria. Destined for renown at the epic naval battle of Lepanto in 1571, Don Juan ruthlessly clamped down on the Moriscos, soldiers and civilians alike. Spanish troops burned homes and farms, massacred women and children. The Moriscos retaliated in kind. But by May 1570, the Moriscos were finished. Fifty thousand were enslaved, or exiled to North Africa.

The remaining Moriscos began leaving Spain in large numbers, seeing that they, too, would be driven out eventually. The emigration continued for decades more. Between 1492 and 1610, three million Moors left or were forced into exile from Spain, settling mainly in Algiers, but also in Tunis, Morocco, and Tripoli.

Barbary swelled with new naval recruits eager to make war on Christendom, which had deprived them of their country, homes, and livelihoods. By the early seventeenth century, the Barbary corsairs were raiding every western Mediterranean Christian shore with impunity and roving the Atlantic as far north as Iceland.

• • •

Before the pirate ships took aim on Europe, the theater of the long war between the Ottoman and Holy Roman empires shifted from the gates of Vienna to the western Mediterranean. The Ottomans had been invited into Algiers in the sixteenth century to drive out the Spanish troops sent by Ferdinand and Cardinal Ximenes to stop the corsair raids. With a foothold in the region, Sultan Suleiman dreamed of an Ottoman-controlled sea from Gibraltar to the Levant. He combined his eastern Mediterranean fleet with the Barbary corsairs and set out to crush Christian resistance. Charles V, who besides being Spain's king was emperor of the Holy Roman Empire, met the Ottoman challenge with a Holy Roman coalition navy.

For fifty years, the behemoths struggled for naval dominance and struck at one another's western Mediterranean strongholds, with neither able to deliver a decisive blow. Charles's attempted invasion of Algiers in 1541 was wrecked by storms; Suleiman's assault on Malta in 1565 was stopped by the doughty Knights of St. John and timely reinforcements. Tunis changed hands several times. In 1571, the Holy Roman fleet commanded by Don Juan met the Ottoman navy at Lepanto in Greece's Gulf of Corinth in one of history's titanic naval battles, involving 542 ships and more than 150,000 troops and oarsmen. Spanish gunpowder and firearms carried the day, giving the Christians a seemingly momentous victory. But a year later, the Ottomans were at sea with an even larger fleet.

Matters closer to home began to absorb both imperial powers' energies. Spain had gone bankrupt and was trying to suppress the rebellious Dutch. Constantinople was convulsed by a power struggle after Suleiman's death, and the Ottomans faced a new threat from Persia. In 1580, the Holy Roman and Ottoman empires signed a truce. Christian and Ottoman war fleets disappeared from the western Mediterranean.

Washed up on the far shore of the global struggle between Christians and Moslems and filled with restless seamen, Barbary embarked on its golden era.

The shipyards of Tunis, Algiers, and Tripoli rang with cries of *"Allahu akbar!"*—God is great!—signifying the launching of yet another new corsair, a happy occasion calling for lamb's blood to be poured ceremoniously over the prow. The sanguinary ritual spoke to the fervent hope that the raiders soon would spill Christian blood.

Hundreds of English and Dutch pirates migrated to Barbary at the beginning of the seventeenth century. No longer needed in the king's service as privateers, they were exiled after merchants complained they were redirecting their attacks against English shipping. In Barbary, corsair privateer commissions awaited them from the ruling pashas. In Barbary, a pirate captain could grow rich, so long as he shared his loot with his crew and, of course, the pasha. While skilled seamen always were welcome in Barbary, the Europeans especially were, for they brought with them new technology: the sailing ship. Until then, the construction and operation of sailing ships were unknown in North Africa, which still employed galley ships propelled by slave oarsmen. The advent of the so-called "round ships" transformed the Barbary pirates into "The Terror."

The round ships needn't hug shorelines, nor haul 300 oarsmen and all of their food and water as the galleys did. With wind and canvas replacing the straining oar, sailing ships required comparatively few seamen, so they could be packed with fighting soldiers to overpower their victims quickly. Shipwrights adapted them to meet the pirates' special needs. The decks were built taller than European ships. They were made maneuverable and fast, with shallow drafts. The modifications suited them for coastal raiding, and for attacking and boarding merchant ships.

Coming upon a merchant vessel, the corsair would fire a broadside, while, from the tall upper deck, pirate soldiers raked the victim ship's decks with musketry. In the meantime, a large boarding party would mass on the ship's long bow, armed with muskets, swords, and pikes, knives clenched in their teeth. As trumpets blared, the boarders clashed their arms, shouting, "Yield, dogs, yield!" Often, that was enough to compel a surrender. It was usually over quickly either way, with the merchantman's crew stripped to their underwear, clapped in irons, and bound for Barbary's slave marts, where they would be sold like cattle. Coming into port, the corsairs fired celebratory salvos to announce their success.

Sail liberated the corsairs from the coastal waters and opened up new frontiers to loot and destroy. In large numbers, they passed through the Straits of Gibraltar into the Atlantic. Murad Reis, a legendary Algerian pirate captain, descended upon Lanzarote in the Canary Islands and took 300 prisoners, including the governor's family. Then he stood offshore so the captives' relatives could buy them back. In 1617, 800 raiders swept through Madeira and carried off 1,200 captives. A German renegade guided three Algerian ships to Denmark and Iceland in 1627, returning with 800 prisoners. Corsairs appeared off County Cork, Ireland, in 1631 and bore away 237 men, women, and children. Between 1613 and 1622, Algerian corsairs captured 447 Dutch ships. Four hundred English ships were taken in just four years, many right off the English coast. During six months in 1636, more than 1,000 Englishmen experienced the anguish of North African slavery. France wasn't spared, either. Between 1628 and 1634, eighty French ships and 1,331 men and women fell into the raiders' hands. Unsurprisingly, Europe experienced a serious shortage of ships and seamen.

But Spain suffered most. The Moriscos hadn't forgotten their expulsion and their losses; their hatred for the Spanish burned brightly.

The Spanish abetted it by expelling more than 250,000 Moriscos in 1609. In relentless retaliatory raids, the Moriscos and their Barbary allies wasted coastal towns and fields, carrying off loot and captives. Despite the pleas of the people, the Spanish government refused to divert significant numbers of warships to coastal defense from convoying supplies to the monarch's cousin Hapsburgs in Austria. Spanish coastal cities were thrown upon their own, largely ineffectual measures. Gibraltar's nine watchtowers manned by forty-two paid guards were not much of a deterrent and did little to allay the fear that gripped the people. In a 1614 letter to the king, Gibraltar's citizens said they never felt secure from the corsairs, "neither at night nor during the day, neither in bed nor at mealtimes, neither in the fields nor in our homes." Even when privateers licensed by the king attempted to interpose a barrier of armed ships between the raiders and Spain, the corsairs slipped through. Long stretches of coastline were abandoned, and commerce, community life, and fishing declined as the people moved away, or were slain or spirited away into captivity. Spain and Italy reported losses of 300,000 to 500,000 inhabitants each late in the seventeenth century—roughly 5 percent of their populations, comparable to losses today of 2 million to 3 million each. Spanish reformer Pedro Fernandez Navarrete said much of it was due to the loss of "those who, because of our neglect, are in slavery or captivity." Spain arguably never fully recovered from the habitual "climate of fear" from centuries of Barbary terror, retaining a vestigial xenophobia that it never has entirely shaken.

Europe's ruinous losses were the agencies of Barbary's unprecedented good fortune. In 1616 alone, the take exceeded 3 million livres—hundreds of millions of dollars in today's currency. The corsair chiefs lived like pashas, and the pashas like sultans. Algiers's population exceeded 100,000, making it one of the most populous cities on earth at the time. European pirates and Moriscos, Moslem and Jewish immigrants from the Levant, went on a spending binge, building palaces and stuffing them with loot and slaves. Wrote Diego de Haedo of his visit to Algiers in 1612: ". . . They have crammed most of the houses, the magazines, and all the shops of this Den of Thieves with gold, silver, pearls, amber, spices, drugs, silk, clothes, velvets, &c., whereby they have rendered this city the most opulent in the world: insomuch that the Turks call it, not without reason, their India, their Mexico, their Peru."

Algiers's lavish public baths had steam rooms, hot and cold water, and masseurs. After being kneaded and steamed, washed and dried, the sleek Algerian businessmen, corsair captains, and government officials might enjoy coffee or sherbet, and perhaps a pipe of opium. They went home to their nouveau riche palaces, decorated ostentatiously with mirrors from Venice; silks and velvets from Lyon and Genoa; Delft porcelains; carved Italian marble; Bohemian glass; and English clocks. Their worldly needs more than met, the new rich tried to secure their places in heaven as well. The Algiers skyline sprouted minarets as the corsair captains attempted to outdo one another's noblesse oblige with bigger and better mosques; the city soon had more than 100.

Admiral Ali Bitchnin, commander of Algiers's sixty-five corsairs, was the apotheosis of showy extravagance, with his two palaces in the city, a suburban villa, and several thousand slaves. He traveled with a large bodyguard. His sense of religious and civic obligation impelled him to build a mosque and a sumptuous public bath. The hazards of his busy trade, including the possibility of his own capture when he was kidnapping and robbing Christians, caused him to keep two captive Knights of St. John as human exchange currency at the ready.

There were many like Ali Bitchnin who believed in giving back to the community. Consequently, expensive, ornamented fountains, drinking troughs, and public latrines sprouted in every major city. With its pirate lucre, Tunis built a slave mart, the Berka, and repaired the Roman aqueduct at Carthage. Merchants prospered buying and selling corsair loot. Some of the wealth even reached the pockets of the lower classes. But for the most part, the peasants, craftsmen, and workers lived as simply and frugally as before.

An abundance of European slaves magnified the atmosphere of unbridled opulence; there were so many slaves that the middle and upper classes enjoyed unparalleled freedom from every sort of drudgery. Father Pierre Dan, one of the "Redemptionist" priests who negotiated ransoms for captives, estimated in 1634 that the city of Algiers alone was the unhappy home of 25,000 Christian slaves, mostly Spanish, Portuguese, and Italian. Europeans rightly feared captivity in Barbary as though it were death; it often was worse. As soon as they fell into the raiders' hands, the captives were stripped of their clothes, given rags to wear, and either were put in irons or made to work the ship. The pashas had their pick first. The youngest, handsomest male slaves were usually chosen as palace pages, and the prettiest women were sent to Constantinople as gifts to the sultan.

The rest were auctioned in the slave mart. Algiers's "zoco" was in the middle of the commercial district. Potential buyers examined the prisoners carefully, as they would any domestic animal they were considering purchasing. They checked over their teeth, walked them back and forth to see if they limped, poked and prodded them, made them jump, stripped them naked and felt their hands for calluses, a reliable indicator of their worth as manual laborers. Young boys and girls were prized above all, of course. For strictly pecuniary reasons, noblemen, army officers, and government officials also were valued highly, for they might be ransomed to their countrymen for a good price. Skilled workers were coveted, too, especially if their specialty happened to have anything to do with gunnery, seamanship, or shipbuilding.

The slave marts were stages for heart-wrenching scenes. Father Dan happened to witness an Irish family sold piecemeal into slavery, never to see one another again. Their inconsolable grief moved even hardened onlookers to tears. "It was a piteous sight to see them exposed for sale at Algiers, for when they parted the wife from the husband, and the father from the child; then, say I, they sell the husband here, and the wife there, tearing from her arms the daughter whom she cannot hope to see ever again."

Literature and the Redemptionist religious orders commonly depicted the Moslems as heartless, barbaric captors. True, some corsair captains made a practice of slicing off and collecting the noses and ears of their galley slaves. One reportedly bit off a Spanish slave's nose and ears for singing while he rowed. However, such atrocities were exceptions.

Christians usually were treated no worse than Moslem captives in Christian hands. It was in the owners' interests to keep slaves healthy for ransom or labor, although they rarely gave them much more than bare-minimum subsistence. To guarantee faithful service, slaves were loaded with chains weighing up to sixty pounds. At night, they were chained to stanchions or iron rings embedded in the floors of their squalid dungeons. "Our beds were nothing but rotten straw laid on the ground, and our coverlets peaces of old sailes full of millions of lice and fleas," wrote Sir Anthony Sherley, a seventeenth-century slave in Morocco. Ships docking in Algiers were required to remove their rudders and oars so would-be escapees wouldn't be tempted to commandeer them and sail to freedom.

Christian slaves toiled in the fields and vineyards, mined copper, carried water, chopped wood, took the place of four-legged beasts in the traces of carts and wagons, and quarried stone under extremely dangerous conditions. The fortunate few chosen as secretaries and interpreters, and the lucky ones employed as shipbuilders and carpenters—excellent, prestigious work—faced one immense drawback: They were so prized that their redemption often could not be purchased at any price. Surgeons were another valued class of worker, excused from all but professional duties. They wore three-corner hats and military clothing. Any captive who had ever sewn up a wound claimed to be a surgeon.

Seventeenth-century captives were largely spared the horrors of the galley ships, where before the advent of sail many Christian slaves ground out their days in abject misery. Chained naked to their rowing benches, six abreast, galley slaves pulled on a fifteen-foot oar as two boatswains with long, coiled whips paced a bridge overhead, watching for slackers. Sometimes they toiled twelve to twenty hours without rest—sleep was never really restful, for the slaves never slept stretched out full-length—with a sailor shoving wine-soaked bread into his mouth for sustenance. If they collapsed, they were flogged until they died or passed out and then were pitched overboard. For the pitiable galley slave, death might have come as a relief.

Among the slaves lacking special skills, a few lucky ones landed in good situations. One was Germaine Mouette, a privately owned French captive in Morocco from 1670 to 1681. Initially assigned to grind corn with a hand mill, Mouette found the work too arduous and deliberately ground the corn coarsely so that it was inedible. He was given easier work—watching over his master's young son. The boy became so attached to Mouette that before long the slave became a de facto family member. His ubiquitous twenty-five-pound chain was discarded and his diet improved radically from thin gruel and hard black bread to white bread, honey, and butter. Eventually ransomed, Mouette and his captors parted with tears and regrets.

While most captives were not as severely abused as the Redemptionists claimed in their dreadful accounts—which, after all, were intended to encourage donations to their ransom funds—cruelty was commonplace enough. At the rock quarries, slaves were harnessed to sleds and, under the lash of their "drivers," forced to drag huge boulders to the quays and shove them onto barges that hauled them to the harbor fortresses and breakwaters. Two thousand slaves built the Moroccan city of Meknes during the last

quarter of the seventeenth century; some were burned alive operating lime kilns. Slaves were bastinadoed—the soles of their feet
and their buttocks flailed with inch-thick sticks—flogged, half-
starved, tortured, burned, and skewered. As punishment for the
capital crime of killing a Moslem, a condemned Christian faced
the unspeakable fate of being cast from a parapet upon gleaming
hooks cruelly protruding from the city walls and, impaled, dying
a slow, agonizing death that could last for days.

Redemptionist priests like Father Dan of the Order of the Holy Trinity
and Redemption of Captives enabled many slaves to return to their
homes and avoid dying in chains. Jean de Matha founded the order
in 1199 to ransom Crusaders from the Moslems. Recognizing
Matha's good services, Pope Innocent III bestowed upon his order
the Convent of Saint Mathurin in Paris, and it became the order's
headquarters and shorthand name, the Mathurins, the name by
which the friars were known as they spread throughout France.
When they put down roots in Italy and Spain, they were called
Trinitarians. The friars raised ransom money in their parishes and
journeyed to North Africa with full purses to barter with the
Moslems for the return of the enslaved Christians.

The sight of the Redemptionists in their resplendent white
robes, emblazoned with blue-and-red crosses on their breasts to
signify the Holy Trinity, debarking in Algiers and Tunis cheered
the pashas and corsair captains. The well-meaning friars actually
helped preserve terrorism, kidnapping, and slavery as profitable
enterprises. In the sixteenth, seventeenth, and eighteenth centuries, the Redemptionists were a permanent feature of the Barbary landscape, like the forest of moored, square-sail pirate
corsairs and the frenzied slave marts. The pashas allowed the friars

to open prison hospitals staffed with nurses, cooks, and chaplains. Moslem slaveholders contributed to their upkeep so their slaves could receive good medical care. During eighty-two redemption missions between 1575 and 1769, friars bought the freedom of 15,500 captives. By no means were these the only redemptions; between 1520 and 1830, an average of 2,000–3,000 slaves were sold each year just in Algiers's zoco. The white slave trade was enormously profitable.

During the first half of the seventeenth century, Europe was absorbed by its own internal bloody religious and civil wars. No royal embassies were sent to treat with Constantinople; no expeditions were mounted; no appeals were made to free the slaves. While the Europeans pitted their warships against one another, the Barbary corsairs had free rein. The captives' countrymen bore the burden of paying what ransoms they could.

Europe futilely attempted to temper Barbary's attacks on its shipping by going to Constantinople to parley with the Ottoman sultan, who ostensibly controlled the regencies in Algiers, Tripoli, and Tunis (but not Morocco, never an Ottoman province). But the negotiations, even when concluded successfully, failed to scale back the depredations.

Then, in a radical departure, England opened direct negotiations with Algiers's pasha in 1622, in effect recognizing Algiers's autonomy from the Ottoman Empire and bypassing Constantinople. England had accurately assessed the drift in Ottoman–Barbary relations in recent decades. While the sultan continued as before to appoint the pashas of Tripoli and Algiers, increasingly those rulers operated independently, and Tunis began its own succession in 1591, when janissaries—Turkish soldiers—

revolted and put one of their own in power. It wasn't long before Tripoli and Algiers founded family dynasties.

England's 1622 treaty with Algiers forever changed the relationship between Europe and Barbary. Henceforth, Europe would bargain with the Barbary States as equals and not depend on Constantinople to force their compliance with treaties they scarcely even acknowledged. Other European nations lined up to sign treaties with Algiers and Tunis. Holland was first.

But even with a treaty, Dutch ships were still being seized by corsairs. Dutch officials sent a punitive squadron. Admiral Lambert appeared in Algiers's harbor in 1624 with several Algerian corsairs he had captured. He demanded the release of all Dutch captives and a new treaty, or he would hang the several hundred captive Algerian crewmen. The pasha and his officers refused, disbelieving that Lambert would carry out his threat. Lambert hanged all the captives from the ships' spars and sailed away, leaving Algerians convulsed with horror, shock, and lamentations. Soon Lambert's squadron reappeared with a fresh inventory of captured Algerian ships and their crews. When the admiral repeated his demands—and his threat—the Algerians released all their Dutch slaves and captured Dutch ships with alacrity, and signed a new treaty.

The Thirty Years' War ended in 1648, the year, too, that Holland won independence from Spain after eighty years of war. England, France, Spain, and Holland built towering new men-of-war of 100 guns or more for the next round of hostilities, and kept them in fighting trim by sending them to the Mediterranean when the corsair raids cut too deeply.

English Admiral Robert Blake reached Tunis in 1655 to negotiate at Oliver Cromwell's behest. England had recently beaten the Dutch navy and now was busy fighting Spain, which Tunis took as a signal to step up its seizures of English merchant ships. Should Tunis refuse to negotiate, Blake's orders were to "assault them either by land or sea and fight with, kill and slay all such persons as shall oppose you."

The Tunisians stated their bargaining position bluntly by firing on Blake's ships. Blake sailed to Porto Farina in the Gulf of Tunis to commit mayhem on the corsairs anchored beneath the fortress guns. "The Lord, being pleased to favor us with a gentle breeze which cast the smoke on them . . . facilitated our attack." Blake sank or burned nine Tunisian corsairs with heavy loss of life, at a cost of just 25 English killed and 40 wounded. From Tunis, Blake sailed to Algiers for further "talks." The sobering news of Blake's punitive attack on Tunis preceded him, and the pasha was delightfully conciliatory, eagerly reaffirming his nine-year-old treaty with England.

Blake's success inspired the other major powers to use force to discourage the unrelenting depredations on their shipping, but they discovered it acted as only a temporary brake on the attacks. Dutch Admiral Michiel de Ruyter, backed by a formidable fleet, dictated treaties to Tunis and Algiers in 1661 and liberated Christian prisoners. Ten years later, British Admiral Edward Spragg sailed burning ships—"fireships"—into the anchored Algerian squadron, destroying the cream of the fleet and killing 3,100 sailors. The shocking loss touched off a rebellion. The four janissary chiefs who had ruled Algiers for twelve years were assassinated, and a corsair captain was named the first "dey." He and his descendants ruled Algiers until France's invasion in 1830.

France was the next European power to retaliate against Algiers, whose dey had gone so far as to declare war. In 1682, Admiral Abraham Duquesne appeared off Algiers with orders to destroy the city, unleashing a terrific bombardment that killed 500 people and demolished 50 buildings. His orders executed, Duquesne sailed away without negotiating. The next year, he was back. He shelled the city again. Eager to avert further devastation, Dey Baba Hassen sent Duquesne a boatload of Algerians as hostages and offered to return hundreds of French slaves. But Duquesne wanted 700,000 livres in reparations for French shipping losses. Hassen said he didn't have the money.

One of the hostages delivered up by Hassen, Mezzo Morto, assured Duquesne that if he put him ashore he could convince Hassen to meet his terms. There was more to Morto's plan than what he told the French admiral, who sent Morto to the city in a boat to try his persuasion on the dey. The former hostage proved to be a dynamo of vaulting ambition. He rallied the corsair captains, assassinated Hassen, succeeded him as dey, and then threatened to kill all the French nationals in Algiers with cannon fire if Duquesne didn't stop the bombardment. Duquesne refused indignantly and ordered the fleet to resume its shelling.

Morto ordered Père Vacher, the vicar apostolic, to be tied to the mouth of a cannon. The vicar was blown to bits. Algiers's ramparts were also soon stained with the viscera of other French clergy and nationals. Unmoved by the slaughter, Duquesne continued the shelling, destroying more than 500 homes, several mosques, and a public bath. When Morto displayed a mulishness equal to Duquesne's and refused to sign a treaty, the French fleet just sailed away, leaving the French nationals' fate in their Algerian enemies' hands.

Five years of hostilities ensued between Algiers and France

without any resolution, and the French king Louis XIV sent
Admiral Jean d'Estrées to humble the Algerians. Upon reaching
the city, he found Morto still the ruler—and more recalcitrant
than ever on the subject of reparations. D'Estrées resumed the
bombardment Duquesne had suspended five years earlier. The
Algerians responded by blowing to bits with cannons the French
consul, the vicar general, and other Frenchmen. D'Estrées retaliated by executing Turkish captives and floating their bodies
ashore. With neither side willing to compromise, d'Estrées also
left without a treaty.

The punitive expeditions had no enduring effect on the Barbary
States' morale. No sooner would the European men-of-war leave
the western Mediterranean than new corsairs would be christened
with lambs' blood and sally forth in search of Christian prizes. A
sustained allied blockade such as Jefferson envisioned never
seemed to have occurred to Europe's leaders. "The Terror" became
an accepted hazard of conducting foreign trade, much like hurri-
canes and mutinies, desertions and accidents at sea.

Holland greatly aided Barbary's incremental shift to semi-
respectability by proposing a radical change in its relations with
Algiers: a "permanent" treaty with annual tribute. Holland was
weary of signing treaties that inevitably were broken, with a con-
sequent loss of men, ships, and cargo, followed by a retributive
counterstrike, and finally a new treaty to be broken later. It would
be more economical, the pragmatic Dutch reasoned, each year to
simply give the dey a cash "present" and "naval stores"—in other
words, the masts, cannon, gunpowder, swords, and muskets that
enabled the Algerians to continue extorting money from Europe.
Of course, the Barbary States didn't object to their extortion

racket's elevation to a line item in Holland's annual budget. In 1712 Holland sent Algiers $5,000, ten 24-pound cannons, 25 large masts, 450 barrels of gunpowder, 2,500 cannonballs, and 50 chests of gun barrels and swords—the very weapons of war that Barbary's rulers needed to extort even more money from Europe.

Austria, Venice, Naples, Hamburg, Sweden, Denmark, and the other small European trading nations lined up to sign similar treaties. Too weak to fend off the piratical raids on their shipping, they preferred the predictability of annual tribute to the random catastrophic losses inflicted by the corsairs. France and England were contemptuous, as they could afford to be, possessing the war fleets to sporadically compel the Barbary rulers' respect. Yet even they succumbed quietly to the temptation of buying long-term security with treaties sweetened by lavish presents, the occasional new warship, and plenty of cash.

The treaties enriched the rulers, but deprived the corsair crews of plunder and the freebooting, roving life they loved. Acutely aware that thousands of idle, brooding seamen, soldiers, and captains were the volatile ingredients of revolution, the rulers broke the treaties deliberately from time to time to keep the corsair crews busy and their captains in loot.

Algiers perfected the elaborate bit of de rigeur theater that came to attend the rupture of treaties. The dey would peremptorily send for the consul. Fearing the worst, the consul would dutifully present himself and receive a tongue-lashing over a trumped-up slight that the ruler would claim was tantamount to war. Of course, all the consul's efforts to repair the breach were doomed. Before long, soldiers would march out and chop down the consular flagpole, and out would go the corsairs to hunt down that nation's merchantmen. Denmark and Sweden, Russia, the two

Sicilies and Naples, Venice, and, later, the United States learned to read the signs. A new treaty with one meant another inevitably would find its flagpole on the ground.

By the end of the eighteenth century, the Barbary States were shadows of their former selves, surviving largely on their reputation. Algiers's population, thinned by plague and a stagnant economy, had dwindled in the 1780s to 30,000, one-third of the city's size 150 years earlier; the once-mighty pirate nation's corsair fleet had shrunk to just ten ships, some unseaworthy; and its slave population hovered around 1,000, a tiny fraction of the 25,000 who thronged Algiers in Father Pierre Dan's day.

Yet Europe continued to pay obeisance to the Barbary States' jihad protection racket as though the regencies' corsair fleets remained the scourge of old.

III

THE NEW NATION AND BARBARY

*When the hallowed months have slipped away, then fight associators
[idolators] wherever you may find them; take them and besiege them,
and waylay them at every outpost.*
—Koran, Surah 9:5

I n July 1785, John Adams settled his wife Abigail and their
daughter Nabby into a home on Grosvenor Square in
London's Mayfair, and optimistically took up his new duties as
minister to the Court of St. James. With Benjamin Franklin and
John Jay, Adams had negotiated the 1783 Peace of Paris, which
ended the Revolutionary War. He now harbored modest hopes of
wearing down British resistance to becoming a full-fledged trading
partner with its former colony. But it soon became painfully
apparent that he faced a nearly impossible task. The London
press's report of Adams's arrival was a harbinger of the reception he
would find. "An ambassador from America! Good heavens what a
sound!" it sniffed. England was in no mood to restore America to
favored trading status, even though the nations were natural commercial allies. The Revolution's wound to British pride was still
too raw to countenance a normal trade relationship. The cool, cor-
rect British diplomats kept the new American minister at arm's

length. Adams made his diplomatic rounds dutifully and wrote reports to Foreign Secretary Jay, without much hope of accomplishing anything.

So he must have been pleased when he learned in February 1786 that the new Tripoli ambassador was in London. Here was an opportunity finally to achieve *something*. Mediterranean affairs were increasingly occupying his attention and that of his Paris counterpart, Thomas Jefferson. In October 1784, a Moroccan corsair had captured the *Betsey* and her crew of ten American merchant seamen soon after she had sailed from Cadiz, Spain, for Philadelphia, her hold full of salt. Lateen corsair sails had appeared on the horizon, and it wasn't long before Captain James Erwin's brig was overtaken. Nine months later, Algerian corsairs operating in the Atlantic had captured the U.S. merchantmen *Dauphin* and *Maria* with twenty-one crewmen and passengers. "Our Sufferings are beyond our expressing or your conception," Richard O'Brien, the *Dauphin's* captain, wrote dolefully to Congress.

Jay already had instructed Adams and Jefferson to make treaties with the Barbary States, authorizing them to pay up to $80,000 in borrowed money from Holland, or wherever they could get credit for the customary presents. However, before the ministers entered any negotiations, they wanted to learn what the European nations were paying, and they almost surely took time to review their small store of facts about the Barbary States.

It was widely known among educated Americans that Tripoli, Tunis, Algiers, and Morocco were Moslem states and extorted tribute from Europe through terror. Less well known was the fact that Tripoli, Algiers, and Tunis were regencies of the Ottoman Empire, but Morocco was not. The three regencies were ostensibly under the rule of the sultan in Constantinople, but in truth they were virtually autonomous—and remained that way so long as they sent the sultan gifts periodically—and each regency had evolved its own succession. While the Barbary States, with Algiers historically predominant, presented a solid, menacing front to Christian Europe and America, they negotiated treaties independently, competed fiercely with one another and occasionally quarreled over territory, sometimes to the extent of going to war. And, confusingly, Algiers, Tunis, and Tripoli happened to be the names of the capital cities of their respective countries; Tangier was Morocco's capital.

At the end of their inquiry into European tributary payments, Jefferson and Adams knew only that the Dutch, Danes, Swedes, and Venetians all paid annual tribute—Venice in jewels and gold coins called sequins, and the others in naval stores and ammunition—but not how much. What would it cost for the United States to buy peace? The American diplomats didn't know. Consequently, by early 1786 the two ministers had not even attempted to open treaty negotiations with any of the Barbary States.

Thus, the Tripolitan ambassador's arrival presented a rare opportunity that Adams grasped resolutely. Making his embassy rounds one night in early 1786, Adams made a point of stopping at the Tripolitan's home. He intended only to leave his card and arrange a meeting later. To his surprise, he was immediately ushered before Ambassador Abdrahaman. The plenipotentiary welcomed Adams and begged him to join him by the fire.

The men warmed themselves at the fireplace, puffing on long-stemmed Turkish pipes that they smoked with the bowls resting on the carpet. "It is sufficient to say," Adams reported to Foreign Secretary Jay, "that his Excellency made many inquiries concerning America, the climate, soil, heat, cold, &c., and observed, 'it is a very great country, but *Tripoli is at war with it.*'" Adams protested that America wasn't ill disposed toward Tripoli, and neither nation had provoked the other. Abdrahaman patiently explained that that was beside the point. Provocation or no, America and Tripoli were at war, until they made peace. "His Excellency replied, that Turkey, Tripoli, Tunis, Algiers, and Morocco were the sovereigns of the Mediterranean; and that no nation could navigate that sea without a treaty of peace with them; that America must make such treaties with Tripoli first, then with Constantinople, then with Algiers and Morocco, as France, England, and all the other powers of Europe had done."

In 1786, the depressed U.S. economy could have used the stimulus of Mediterranean commerce. But with the Continental Navy disbanded and without treaties with Barbary, American merchants didn't dare risk it, even though they had hoped that reviving the pre-Revolution trade with Greece, Italy, and the Levant would compensate for the disappointing trading partners that England and France had turned out to be. They hadn't foreseen the consequences in the Mediterranean of throwing off the British yoke: Exposing themselves to the Barbary corsairs without the shield of British treaties and passports backed by Royal Navy guns, or U.S. treaties or guns, for that matter. Even with England's protection, there had been losses. In 1678, New York City churchgoers raised ransom money to free eleven American captives in Algiers. In 1698, during another New York collection to ransom more slaves, so many donations were made that the surplus helped pay for the erection of Trinity Church on Wall Street and Broadway. While at times even British passports were no safeguard against the Barbary rovers, they had enabled American merchants to conduct business in the Mediterranean for more than a century.

In the years leading to the Revolution, an average of 100 American ships transported 20,000 tons of goods annually to Mediterranean ports. Among the commodities traded there were Southern rice and lumber, grain and flour from the middle colonies, and New England rum and fish. Mediterranean markets consumed one-sixth of America's wheat exports and one-fourth of its exported fish. The Revolution dammed the stream of U.S. raw goods that flowed to the Mediterranean, and the postwar years were no better, with America lacking treaties. Richard Harrison, a Maryland merchant who was acting U.S. agent in Cadiz, urged Foreign Affairs Secretary Robert Livingston in 1783 to emphasize to Congress the importance of friendly relations with Barbary. "Our Commerce to Lisbon, this port & the Medeterranian must become very important, & these Freebooters will have in their power, & very probably in their Inclination, to molest it greatly." Harrison said England or France would never intervene with the Barbary States on America's behalf. "It is not [in] their Interest that our Navigation should become so extensive & free . . ." In that one sentence, Harrison had neatly summarized the other major obstacle blocking the path to a lucrative U.S. trade in the Mediterranean.

In 1782 Livingston had instructed Benjamin Franklin, then the U.S. minister in Paris, to make contact with representatives from the Barbary States. It was "a favorable moment for making ourselves known to them," he said, what with the Moroccan emperor's recent coolness toward Great Britain and France's unusual warmth toward the United States. But absorbed in Paris's pleasures, Franklin let the favorable moment pass without acting. No American envoys appeared in the Barbary states in 1783 or 1784.

With an entourage of robed attendants, Abdrahaman, the Tripolitan ambassador, swept into Adams's Grosvenor Square residence three days after their congenial fireside conversation. He had come for the express purpose of pressuring Adams to sign a peace treaty quickly. Having planted the idea during the initial meeting, Abdrahaman wanted to fan the embers. A treaty would enrich both Tripoli's bashaw and Abdrahaman himself. He warned that if America procrastinated, merchantmen and their crews might be seized, complicating treaty negotiations with tedious ransom discussions. And war must be avoided because it would be so terrible. "A war between Christian and Christian was mild, and prisoners, on either side, were treated with humanity; but a war between Turk and Christian was horrible, and prisoners were sold into slavery," Adams wrote, in reconstructing Abdrahaman's words for Jay. "Although he was himself a mussulman [Moslem], he must still say he thought it a very rigid law; but, as he could not alter it, he was desirous of preventing its operation, or, at least, of softening it, as far as his influence extended." The Tripolitan was pleased when Adams told him he had authority to negotiate a treaty, and as soon as he had departed, Adams dispatched a messenger to Jefferson in Paris, summoning him to a parley with Adams and Abdrahaman.

Shipbuilding, the whaling industry, and Southern agriculture suffered particularly during the grinding economic malaise following independence. The shipyards had built British ships before the war, but now were idled; the British were building their own ships at home. The whaling fleet had been nearly obliterated by the Royal Navy during the war. What's more, France and Britain were restricting whale and fish-product imports, ostensibly to cultivate their own maritime industries, but also to use the fisheries for training fresh seamen for the expected resumption of their unending war with each other.

Southern agriculture had not yet recovered from marauding British troops and the savage partisan war between loyalists and patriots. More than 50,000 slaves had slipped away during the fighting, many ending up in the disease-ridden refugee camps established by the British Army in the Southern colonies. There, they died by the thousands of smallpox and fever; Jefferson himself lost 27 of his slaves this way. With fewer slaves to harvest the tobacco and rice, planters cut back their acreage. Rice exports told the story: in 1770–73, a total of 277.1 million pounds; in 1783–86, just 128.3 million pounds.

But a worse brake on exports was Britain's unfriendly trade policy. Before the Revolution, colonial merchants had grown rich trading in the British West Indies. Now only American goods transported on English ships were admitted; goods on U.S. ships were turned away. Adams ambitiously proposed a new agreement that would have opened not only the British West Indies, but Canada, Nova Scotia, and Newfoundland to American products transported by American ships. The British were politely uninterested. Jefferson estimated British trade restrictions during the 1780s cost the United States 800 to 900 shiploads of goods, with a proportionate deficit in seamen, shipwrights, and shipbuilding.

High hopes were pinned on France, America's great war ally, becoming its great peacetime trade partner, obviating the need for more generous British agreements. The French, however, lacked the financial wherewithal to extend credit—a critical component that had never been a problem with English merchants. Without credit, U.S. merchants, lacking cash to make the purchases outright, were unable to buy finished goods in France to sell in America. A lesser impediment to a robust U.S.–French trade alliance was the American consumer's preference for English products, a consequence of long familiarity. There were other barriers as well: the high French protective trade tariffs, and French certainty that American merchants would only use the profits from any trade with France to pay off their debts to France's enemy, England.

Frustrated by the British and French, U.S. merchants pursued alternative markets in Asia and along the Baltic Sea. American tobacco, flour, and rum were prized in the chilly northern principalities, and the merchantmen returned from the Baltic laden with iron; duck cloth, a durable cotton fabric; and hemp. But the Baltic commerce was only modestly successful. China, however, fired American businessmen's imaginations with its potentially huge market. The trick was finding commodities the Chinese desired. The *Empress of China* cast off from Sandy Hook, New Jersey, in 1784 on its historic voyage to Canton bearing the shimmering hopes of businessmen who thought they had hit upon an ingenious solution to the conundrum of Chinese consumerism. The *Empress* was loaded with finished New England goods, which were bartered for furs in Vancouver and sandalwood in Hawaii. Chinese merchants snapped up their furs and sandalwood, encouraging U.S. merchants to expand their Oriental speculations to India and Indonesia. But for all their trouble the merchants were disappointed when their efforts scarcely dented the lost trade with Britain.

Jefferson reached the Adams home in the last damp, blustery

days of winter, his scientist's curiosity piqued by the prospect of meeting a Barbary "musselman" in the flesh. The novelty wore off quickly after the three ministers sat down together at Abdrahaman's home, and the Tripolitan gave them a matter-of-fact disquisition on temporary peace and "perpetual peace," and their respective costs. Temporary peace was good for one year, he said, and would cost 12,500 guineas, plus a 10 percent commission for Abdrahaman, or roughly $66,000 in all. Perpetual peace—supposedly everlasting, yet, as they all well knew, anything but that—was a bargain in the long run, he said. It would cost 30,000 guineas, plus the customary 10 percent commission, or a total of about $160,000. Abdrahaman reminded them politely that a state of war existed between their nations until America bought its peace. Jefferson and Adams were aghast at the figures he had quoted; Jay had authorized them to borrow only $80,000 for treaties with *all* the Barbary States. Abdrahaman went on to inform them that Tunis would demand a similar payment, but Algiers, the most powerful corsair regency, would probably expect more, plus ransom for the twenty-one captives from the *Maria* and *Dauphin*. He did not mention Morocco, the fourth Barbary State.

Adams and Jefferson argued vainly that America's basis for relations with other nations was the converse of Tripoli's: It regarded all nations as friends, and made war only upon provocation. How had the United States provoked Tripoli? they wanted to know. Abdrahaman said they didn't understand the fine points of Islamic jihad, as it was interpreted in Barbary. He proceeded to illuminate the ministers. "The Ambassador," Jefferson later wrote to Jay, "answered us that it was founded on the Laws of their Prophet, that it was written in their Koran, that all nations who should not have acknowledged their authority were sinners, that it was their right and duty to make war upon them wherever they could be found, and to make slaves of all they could take as Prisoners, and that every Musselman who should be slain in battle was sure to go to Paradise." The ambassador said the pirate crews were inspired to "the most desperate Valour and Enterprise" by the promise of a slave and an extra share of the loot to the first crewman to board an enemy ship. Merchant ship crews seldom resisted, and Jefferson said Abdrahaman "verily believed the Devil assisted his Countrymen, for they were almost always successful." Abdrahaman was paraphrasing the Koran's rules of engagement, as described in the 47th Surah: "Whenever you encounter the ones who disbelieve [during wartime], seize them by their necks until once you have subdued them, then tie them up as prisoners, either in order to release them later on, or also to ask for ransom, until war lays down her burdens." By first extending peace terms, impossible though they were, Abdrahaman also had satisfied his holy book's stipulation that Moslems must give enemies the option of war or peace before attacking, a commonly ignored preliminary.

After doing the arithmetic, Jefferson gloomily estimated the United States would have to pay more than $1.3 million to make peace with all the Barbary States and ransom the captives, which meant going to Amsterdam, hat in hand, to request a loan from the Dutch bankers, who usually were willing to extend credit to America. Jay, however, advised against it; it would be improvident to pile on more financial commitments when American credit was shaky as it was, with little to recommend it but the republic's glorious future, glimmering only faintly through the Revolution's miasmic aftermath.

• • •

Adams and Jefferson were fellow founders of the republic, still in the first, amiable phase of their long relationship, and virtually the only U.S. ministers empowered by Congress to negotiate treaties on America's behalf. Their responsibilities today would occupy hundreds of State Department employees. But in 1786, the United States, with slightly more than 3 million people, had a population scarcely equaling that of present-day Iowa or Connecticut. Its leaders were as well known to one another as members of an exclusive club. Because of the very recent experience of the Revolution, they typically presented a united front to the world, although at times they might disagree among themselves. Thus, no diplomatic meltdown occurred when Jefferson and Adams discovered that they disagreed over how to deal with the Barbary States. Friends since 1775, when they had served on the committee that drafted the Declaration of Independence, written by Jefferson and edited by his colleagues, Jefferson looked upon Adams, eight years his senior, as a mentor, and Adams regarded Jefferson as a protégé. They were in the habit of sharing their views, and agreed to do so now, in a series of candid letters—Adams the pragmatist favoring tribute, and Jefferson the idealist, war.

Adams observed that the loss of the Mediterranean trade would cost more than tribute, as would war. Therefore, tribute was preferable. In the best Enlightenment fashion, Adams set forth four propositions:

1. Peace could be purchased;
2. Without payment, there could be no peace in the Mediterranean;
3. No actions by Europe would either increase or lower peace's price; and

4. Delayed negotiations would drive up the price America would ultimately pay.

"From these premises, I conclude it to be the wisest for us to negotiate and pay the necessary sum without loss of time."

What did Jefferson think? Adams wanted to know. "If you admit them all, do you admit the conclusion? Perhaps you will say, fight them, though it should cost us a great sum to carry on the war, and although, at the end of it, we should have more money to pay as presents. If this is your sentiment, and you can persuade the southern States into it, I dare answer for it that all from Pennsylvania, inclusively northward, would not object. It would be a good occasion to begin a navy."

This last ringing phrase would resonate through the years. It was odd that the man who uttered it would commonly be mischaracterized as having opposed war with Barbary. Adams was certain America would win once it resolved to fight, "but the difficulty of bringing our people to agree upon it, has ever discouraged me. . . ." It was too bad there was no support for a war, because it would be "heroical and glorious" at a time when "the policy of Christendom has made cowards of all their sailors before the standard of Mahomet." Realistically, though, there was neither money nor public support for a war, Adams said, concluding that the immediate goal should be to restore the Mediterranean trade and nothing more; its absence was simply too costly. "At present we are sacrificing a million annually, to save one gift of 200,000 pounds. This is not good economy. We might, at this hour, have two hundred ships in the Mediterranean, whose freights alone would be worth 200,000 pounds, besides the influence upon the price of our produce."

Jefferson replied with one of the most eloquent letters that he ever wrote. "I acknowledge, I very early thought it would be best to effect a peace through the medium of war," he began. "Though it is a question with which we have nothing to do, yet as you propose some discussion of it, I shall trouble you with my reasons." He agreed with Adams's first three propositions. "As to the fourth, that the longer the negotiation is delayed, the larger will be the demand; this will depend on the intermediate captures: if they are many and rich, the price may be raised; if few and poor, it will be lessened."

A better policy would be to dictate peace through the expedient of war, through the agency of a navy. Jefferson gave six reasons, the first three reflecting his idealized vision of America:

1. Justice is in favor of this opinion.
2. Honor favors it.
3. It will procure us respect in Europe; and respect is a safeguard to interest.
4. It will arm the Federal head with the safest of all the instruments of coercion over its delinquent members, and prevent it from using what would be less safe. I think that so far, you go with me. But in the next steps, we shall differ.
5. I think it least expensive.

Jefferson then performed some dubious math. Building the 150-gun naval fleet he envisioned would cost 450,000 pounds sterling, and maintaining it, he claimed, 45,000 pounds annually—little more than what annual tribute might cost. America should build a small navy, war or no, to protect trade, he reasoned, and keeping it idle would still entail cost—fully half the price of having it patrol the western Mediterranean. Therefore, "we have a right to say that only twenty-two thousand and five hundred pounds sterling, per annum, should be charged to the Algerine war."

His sixth reason, "It will be as effectual," was predicated on his recollection that France once was able to dictate treaty terms to Algiers after a three-month blockade. The United States also could establish a blockade, aided by Naples and Portugal, and perhaps other nations as well.

Adams conceded there were excellent reasons for going to war with the Barbary States. "The resolution to fight them would raise the spirits and courage of our countrymen immediately, and we might obtain the glory of finally breaking up these nests of banditti." But while glory and fighting spirit were admirable ideals, they were too insubstantial to justify a war that would end only in a purchased peace, and that would harm America more than Barbary. "If We take a Vessell of theirs We get nothing but a bad Vessell fit only to burn, a few Guns and a few Barbarians, whom We may hang or enslave if We will, and the Unfeeling Tyrants whose Subjects they are will think no more of it, than if We had killed so many CatterPillars upon an Apple tree. When they take a Vessell of ours, they not only get a rich Prize, but they enslave the Men and if there is among them a Man of any Rank or Note they demand most exorbitant ransoms for them." Moreover, "congress will never, or at least not for years, take any such resolution, and in the mean time our trade and honor suffers beyond calculation. We ought not to fight them at all unless we determine to fight them forever. This thought, I fear, is too rugged for our people to bear." Adams saw all too well that their debate, stimulating as it might be, was of no consequence. ". . . I perceive that neither force nor money will be applied. Our States are so backward, that they will do nothing for some years."

Adams's words tellingly described the United States under the weak Articles of Confederation, which emphasized the sovereignty of individuals and states at the expense of the federal government. The Confederation government first had to obtain the approval of nine of the thirteen states before taking any important action. Nine states seldom agreed on anything, even foreign trade, which to a large extent was left up to the individual states, and with chaotic results: states vying with and undercutting one another to snatch foreign markets. The treasury was heavily in debt from the Revolutionary War. In 1785, the government sold the last Continental Navy warship, the *Alliance,* to pay off some of the debt. The Confederation Congress's sole tax, the postage stamp, paid for mail delivery only.

A navy couldn't very well be built with postage stamps.

America's dilemma in the Mediterranean was painfully clear in Philadelphia. George Washington voiced the leaders' frustration. "It seems almost Nugatory to dispute about the best mode of dealing with the Algarines when we have neither money to buy their friendship nor the means of punishing them for their depredations upon our people & trade," he wrote the Marquis de Lafayette in 1787. "If we could command the latter I should be clearly in sentiments with you and Mr. Jefferson, that chastisement would be more honorouble, and much to be preferred to the purchased friendship of these Barbarians—By me, who perhaps do not understand the policy by which the Maritime powers are actuated, it has ever been considered as reflecting the highest disgrace on them to become tributary to such a banditti, who might for half the sum that is paid them be exterminated from the Earth."

John Jay, too, longed to wage war on Algiers. "'I should not be angry,'" the French ambassador said the foreign secretary told him, "'if the Algerines came to burn some of our maritime Towns, in order to restore to the United States their former energy, which peace and Commerce have almost destroyed. War alone can bring together the various States, and give a new importance to Congress. . . .'" Jay also confided to Jefferson, "If we act properly, I shall not be very sorry for it. In my Opinion it may lay the Foundation for a Navy, and tend to draw us more closely into a foederal System."

Years before the Abdrahaman meeting, before the capture of the three American merchantmen by Morocco and Algiers, Jefferson had advocated building a navy to stand up to the Barbary States. As was to be his lifelong habit, Jefferson shared his ideas with his fellow Virginians, confidants and protégés, James Madison and James Monroe. "We ought to begin a naval power, if we mean to carry on our own commerce," he wrote to Madison in November 1784. "Can we begin it on a more honourable occasion or with a weaker foe? I am of opinion [John] Paul Jones with half a dozen frigates would totally destroy their commerce; not by attempting bombardments as the Mediterranean states do . . . but by constant cruising and cutting them to peices by peicemeal." He confided his private assay of the Barbary States' naval strength to Monroe. "These pyrates are contemptibly weak," he concluded. Morocco, he said, had four or five frigates of 18 or 20 guns. Tripoli floated a single frigate, and Tunis, three or four, every one of them "small & worthless." Algiers was more formidable with 16 ships carrying 22 to 52 guns. He was decidedly unimpressed with them all. ". . . the vessels of all these powers are wretched in the last degree, being mostly built of the discordant peices of other vessels which they take & pull asunder." War, as he would repeatedly declare, was the only currency besides bribes and tribute that the Barbary States respected. He neatly summarized his thoughts on the subject in a striking aphorism: "A coward is much more exposed to quarrels than a man of spirit."

Odd as it may seem, Morocco's seizure of the *Betsey* wasn't so much an act of war as a cry for attention. Emperor Sidi Muhammad ibn Abd Allah, arguably the mildest, wisest Barbary ruler at the time, had had a rooting interest in the upstart colonists during the Revolutionary War, a strange attitude for a monarch. For years, he had anticipated diplomatic relations with the American republic. Back in 1780, with the war's outcome by no means decided, the emperor had told U.S. consuls from Spain that if America won independence from England, he wished to sign a treaty. It was more than just a pecuniary interest; Sidi Muhammad genuinely wanted to be one of the first rulers to recognize the new nation.

Sidi Muhammad grew impatient when four years passed without a U.S. envoy arriving in Tangier. In 1784 he ordered his corsairs to seize American shipping, extremely scarce in the Mediterranean that year. The *Betsey* was taken in October. Alcaid Driss, the emperor's secretary, explained to William Carmichael, interim U.S. chargé d'affaires in Madrid, in December that America had brought the misfortune on itself by disregarding Sidi Muhammad. "It is not surprising then that he should use his rights, in such sort however that the Vessel with its Crew shall be returned provided that Congress thinks proper to send as soon as possible a Charge d'Affaires or Consul for the purpose of making peace with this August African Monarch." The emperor anticipated an envoy bearing generous gifts.

In the meantime, he impulsively displayed his benevolence toward America by sending the *Betsey's* crewmen to the Atlantic port of Mogadore and giving them the run of the city, instead of sending them into slavery. He also instructed his corsairs not to capture any more American merchant ships, but "to show them every favour, due to the most friendly powers; being fully determined to do much, when an opportunity offers." By July 1785 he had decided to release the *Betsey* and her crew, although no U.S. envoy had yet appeared in Tangier. Sidi Muhammad's long wait ended in 1786, with Thomas Barclay's arrival. The envoy and the emperor quickly concluded the best treaty America would make in Barbary in thirty years: $10,000 in presents and no annual tribute.

Algiers showed no compunction to deliver up the *Dauphin* and *Maria* and their twenty-one crewmen, so John Lamb, a Norwich, Connecticut, merchant and sea captain, was dispatched to ransom them. Ignorant of the dey's capacity for greed, Adams and Jefferson instructed Lamb to spend no more than $200 per man, laughably inadequate when it turned out Algiers wanted $3,000 each. Unsurprisingly, Lamb's mission was a disaster. With the report on his failed effort, Lamb passed along even more disturbing news: that Algiers had seized the ships possibly at the urging of Charles Logie, England's consul in Algiers. Lamb it turned out, hadn't been a paragon of diplomacy himself while in Algiers, but had ill-advisedly confided in Logie. Richard O'Brien, master of the *Dauphin* and a future U.S. consul to Algiers, wrote to Jefferson that Logie "I believe got all his [Lamb's] secrets from him." Moreover, he had also spoken with open contempt of France and Spain—in "the most vulgar language that it is with pain we see him so unworthy of this commission and the cloth he wore."

Britain's antipathy toward American trade in the Mediterranean was no secret. English businessmen liked to think of Algerian piracy as a cornerstone of their Mediterranean trade. "If there were no Algiers, England ought to build one," Adams had reported them saying in 1783. Lord Sheffield expanded on this theme in *Observations on the commerce of the American States* the same year. He shrewdly recognized the vital importance to Britain of the "carrying trade"—the ability to transport goods from all countries in English merchant ships—as well as the threat to it posed by America. For these reasons, the Algerian pirates were a godsend. "That the Barbary States are advantageous to the maritime powers is certain. If they were suppressed, the little States of Italy, &c. would have much more of the carrying trade." As for the Americans, Lord Sheffield believed that without Britain's navy as a bulwark, they were defenseless against the corsairs and must abandon any plans to establish a thriving Mediterranean trade, for, as he put it dismissively, ". . . they cannot pretend to a navy."

After Lamb's failure in Algiers, Jefferson appealed to the Mathurins, the Redemptionist order. They had recently ransomed 300 Frenchmen from Algiers at $500 apiece. The friars' success encouraged Jefferson in the wildly optimistic belief that they might be able to gain the American captives' freedom for $200, by acting as a disinterested third party. Willing to make the attempt, the Mathurins said the ploy had a slim chance of working only if the U.S. government pretended a complete lack of concern for the prisoners' welfare, and cut off the trickle of extra cash it was sending the consuls in Portugal and Spain who, in turn, had slipped it to the captives through the Spanish consul in Algiers. The money paid for extra clothing and food. When the payments stopped, the captives were forced back on a semistarvation diet and had to wear thin, ragged garments. They implored Congress, Jefferson, and Adams to resume the stipends.

The captives' renewed suffering was to no good purpose, for the Algerians were unwilling to lower their ransom price; slaves happened to be in scarce supply at the time. Jefferson raised the sum he was willing to pay to $550 per captive, but by then the situation had changed altogether. Amid the French Revolution's early rumblings, the Mathurins, fixtures in Barbary for nearly 200 years, recalled all the friars to France. Soon, the vast landholdings that had sustained the Mathurins' merciful enterprises through the centuries were confiscated, and the good friars were seen no more in North Africa.

For a public man, Thomas Jefferson was remarkably reticent and shrank from confrontations, letting Madison fight many of his battles for him while he watched from the wings. But when his ideals were affronted, Jefferson was capable of retaliating ruthlessly.

An example of Jefferson's capacity for vindictiveness occurred during the War for Independence, when Henry Hamilton, the British commander in Ohio and Kentucky, was captured by Virginia militiamen. The colonists hated Hamilton for reputedly buying scalps from Britain's Indian allies and encouraging them to commit atrocities. The militia brought him to Williamsburg in chains and before the Virginia governor, Thomas Jefferson.

Under the wartime rules, high-ranking officers commonly were paroled or exchanged. But Hamilton's actions so incensed Jefferson that he ignored custom and instead ordered him put in irons and denied visitors and even writing materials. Hamilton had surrendered to George Rogers Clark, the leader of the Virginia militia, only after Clark had agreed to certain conditions regarding his treatment. Jefferson refused to honor any of these terms. Threatened by the British with retaliation against American prisoners if Hamilton were not paroled, George Washington appealed to Jefferson—to no avail. Jefferson stubbornly refused to release Hamilton. He held him for a full year before finally paroling him, and only after forcing Hamilton to sign an agreement whose terms Hamilton disputed even as he put his name to it.

Jefferson displayed the same iron vindictiveness after his failure to ransom the *Maria* and *Dauphin* crews, casting about for ways to punish the Barbary States. Without his government's knowledge, he approached the smaller European nations with the idea of forming a confederation to blockade Algiers. Each nation would contribute either a vessel or cash and sit on a committee that would oversee the confederation's operations. Jefferson believed that with six frigates, half on duty at any given time, Algiers or any other Barbary State could be blockaded efficiently. There had never been a long-term naval coalition like this, but Jefferson was confident it would work, with its ships pouncing on Algerian corsairs when they left port and turning trading vessels away from Algiers. In his secret idealistic heart, Jefferson believed that such a permanent blockade not only would stop Algiers's attacks on European and U.S. shipping, but would bring about a gun-to-the-head sort of epiphany that would transform the pirate regency into an agrarian nation, possibly resembling the rural republican utopia he envisioned America becoming.

When he consulted the European ministers in Paris about a naval blockading confederation, he found them surprisingly supportive. Portugal, the Two Sicilies, Venice, Malta, Denmark, and Sweden all were interested, but one thing worried them: France.

Would France undermine the confederation? As they all well knew, France and England both wanted to suppress commercial competition in the Mediterranean. Jefferson took it upon himself to determine France's position, but in his own indirect way. While John Adams would have bluntly asked France's foreign minister, the Count de Vergennes, what France would do—and likely would have received an ambiguous or false reply—Jefferson was subtler: He laid out the confederation scheme for Vergennes and then asked him whether he thought *England* would interfere. England wouldn't dare, Vergennes declared. Satisfied by his response that France, too, would not stop the blockade, Jefferson now only needed to obtain the backing of his own government to launch the naval coalition.

Once again, he chose subtlety over directness. One of Jefferson's virtues was his willingness to let others advance his ideas—even take credit for them—if it improved their chances of being adopted. He placed the coalition proposal in the hands of the Marquis de Lafayette, America's great French ally and Revolutionary War hero. Jefferson chose Lafayette as the messenger because he feared that if he proposed the coalition to the Confederation Congress, too much would be made of his difference of opinion with Adams over Barbary, and that might overshadow the plan itself and wreck its chances. With Lafayette as the plan's advocate—and Lafayette always was willing to take a high-profile position on important issues—the proposal would stand or fall on its merits. Jefferson and Lafayette collaborated on a version to present to Congress.

Lafayette first presented the plan to George Washington, forthrightly addressing the Adams–Jefferson disagreement and neatly disposing of it. "There is betwen Mr. Jefferson and Mr. Adams a diversity of opinion respecting the Algerines. Adams thinks peace should be purchased from them, Mr. Jefferson finds it as cheap and more honourable to cruize against them. I incline to the latter opinion, and think it possible to form an alliance between the United States, Naples, Rome, Venice, Portugal and some other powers, each giving a sum of money not very large, whereby a common armement may distress the Algerines into any terms. Congress ought to give Mr. Jefferson and Adams ample powers to stipulate in their names for such a confederacy." Washington didn't stand in Lafayette's way. In 1787 Virginia formally proposed the coalition to Congress, recommending that Jefferson represent the United States.

Jay shot down the idea, and everyone knew he was right, even Jefferson. The Confederation government, he said, was far too feeble to participate in a federation, handcuffed by the requirement that nine states first approve every important action, and without authority to levy a tax to build a navy. That was the end of Jefferson's coalition against Algiers. As he put it, Congress "declined an engagement which they were conscious they could not fulfill with punctuality; and so it fell through."

IV

"A Good Occasion to Build

a Navy"

"I have got you, you Christian dogs, you shall eat stones."
—Algiers Dey Hassan Pasha, greeting American captives in 1793

At the dawn of the new constitutional government, Adams and Jefferson returned to a changed United States. The Constitution's ratification in 1788 promised better things for the United States, which had limped through the post-Revolution years under the anemic Confederation government with an empty treasury, no military force, and no taxation authority. All of that would change quickly. While neither Jefferson nor Adams was directly involved in drafting the new republic's framework—Hamilton and Madison were the unlikely collaborators who had seen to that—the government required the services of the two founders, and they sailed home across the Atlantic, Adams to become vice president and Jefferson to be secretary of state.

Nearly four million people lived in the United States in 1790. The most populous region lay south of the Potomac River, with 1.8 million inhabitants, inflated by hundreds of thousands of slaves; one slave equaled three-fifths of a white man under the census's bizarre calculus. One million people lived in New England, and 958,000 in the Middle Atlantic region.

The economic depression had ended, yet the economy remained flat. The new constitutional government had recently begun taxing distilled liquor and imports, but the taxes so far had produced only a trickle of revenue for the threadbare national treasury. Revolutionary War debt—$71 million in 1791, after all state and federal obligations were tallied—still hung over the government. Trade continued to lag behind pre-Revolution levels: U.S. exports totaled just $20.2 million in 1791, and imports $23 million. Wheat and corn were the top exports. Cotton, which would make the Southern planters rich in fifty years, scarcely registered as an export—just 3,135 bales were shipped in 1791.

Mediterranean trade in 1790 was no better than during the abysmal 1780s, when the United States had neither money nor a navy to forge diplomatic relations with Algiers, Tripoli, or Tunis. The sixteen surviving *Maria* and *Dauphin* crewmen—five had died from disease and mistreatment—were no nearer liberation from Algiers's dungeons, with negotiations stalled since Lamb's failed 1786 mission.

With Portugal at war with Algiers, U.S. shipping in the Atlantic was safe for the moment; Portuguese cruisers at Gibraltar barred Algerian corsairs from the Atlantic. But everyone knew that an Algiers-Portugal treaty would reopen the shipping lanes to Algerian depredations, imperiling America's nascent Atlantic trade. The dismal Mediterranean situation inspired no bold government initiatives, or brainstorms by the emerging generation of leaders, wholly absorbed with the business of launching the fledgling constitutional republic. Jefferson, however, was returning to America with an advanced international perspective from his five years in Europe, steadfast in his conviction that war was the only means to achieve a lasting, honorable peace with the Barbary States.

Jefferson never coveted Jay's foreign secretary position, or any job in George Washington's administration. He had sailed from France intending to settle his daughters in Virginia and then to return to France as minister, or, preferably, to retire from public life to his diverse, absorbing interests. At forty-six, he had spent half his life in public service and now craved the quiet of his farm and experimenting with crop rotation and hybrids; building, tearing down, and rebuilding Monticello, his lifelong passion; indulging his fascination with gadgets and tinkering; and adding to his massive library, which later, when he became strapped for cash, he would sell to the government. (It became the basis for the Library of Congress.) But Washington and Madison cajoled him into coming to Philadelphia to serve in Washington's Cabinet as secretary of state. After swallowing his disappointment, Jefferson attended to family matters in Virginia and then headed north to the capital city. At the very least, he would have a bully pulpit for urging action against the Barbary States. He used it for this purpose just weeks after joining the new administration.

The occasion was his December 30, 1790, message to Congress, in which he coolly analyzed the Mediterranean situation and the possible responses to Algiers's demand for $59,496 ransom for the *Maria* and *Dauphin* captives, who by then had been held for five years.

Besides being at war with the United States, Algiers also was in the midst of hostilities with Russia, Austria, Portugal, Naples, Sardinia, Genoa, and Malta, and was temporarily at peace with

France, Spain, England, Venice, Holland, Sweden, and Denmark. None had bought peace cheaply, Jefferson pointed out carefully. Spain's peace had cost a staggering $3 million to $5 million, plus $100,000 annual tribute; the ghosts of the exiled Moriscos must have shouted for joy. The treaties signed by the Dutch, Danes, Swedes, and Venetians committed each to yearly payments of $24,000 to $30,000, while Britain's "presents" to the Barbary rulers ran to $280,000 a year. It went without saying that those sums were beyond the cash-poor United States's resources.

He laid out the alternatives in the Mediterranean. For liberating the captives under the current circumstances, they boiled down to ransom or a prisoner exchange, but he added discouragingly that the Algerians often were loath to trade even one Christian for five or six Moors. The long-range policy options were more intriguing. The United States could risk trade in the Mediterranean without treaties and simply ransom future captives. It could buy peace through treaties and tribute. "For this, we have the example of rich and powerful nations, in this instance counting their interest more than their honor," he said scornfully.

He then dangled a third option, obviously his preference: "to repel force by force." He warned that once Portugal made peace with Algiers, the corsairs bottled up in the Mediterranean for five years would come after American Atlantic shipping. What would the United States do then, without a navy? A stable Mediterranean trade depended on America's beginning a navy, he said, estimating its initial cost at $400,000 and an annual expense of $125,000 to maintain it. Congress listened to Jefferson's message with little enthusiasm, although a Senate resolution was drafted to establish a navy when finances permitted. But the resolution died in committee.

Jefferson wracked his brain for creative ways to strike back at Barbary without going deeper into debt and came up with a scheme that would pay for itself while applying pressure on Algiers. His "Proposal to Use Force against the Barbary States" called for three frigates to be deployed against Algerian ships in the western Mediterranean. They also would capture Turkish and Greek vessels in the Levant, answering seizures with seizures. The Moslem captives would be sold in the slave mart in Malta, just as Christian captives were sold in Algiers—an interesting proposition from a man who favored eventual emancipation of all U.S. slaves (but not in his lifetime) and a ban on importing new slaves. The losses would impel the Ottoman sultan to pressure Algiers to make peace with the United States and release the hostages, Jefferson expostulated. The retaliatory attacks would command the Moslems' grudging respect and enable Americans to obtain a treaty without presents or tribute, while recovering the captives and their ships, and earning the regard of the other Barbary States. Jefferson warned that Congress must act swiftly before Algiers and Portugal made peace and Algerian corsairs poured into the Atlantic. His unconventional plan evoked no congressional response.

After Washington's second inauguration in 1793, Jefferson ardently wished to leave government and begin his postponed retreat into private life in Virginia. Washington persuaded him to hang on for six months while he sought a successor, but when fall arrived with no replacement in sight, his longing for a quiet rural retirement won out. Assured that his public life was over, Jefferson departed Philadelphia early in 1794 to immerse himself in the pursuits of a horticulturalist, scholar, inventor, architect, naturalist and philosopher.

• • •

A new dey ascended the Algerian throne. Hassan Pasha was the latest in a long line of despots who, nearly as often as they rose to power, were deposed bloodily. Richard O'Brien, captain of the captured *Dauphin,* wrote from his seven-year captivity that the timing was ideal for reopening negotiations. American leaders agreed that John Paul Jones, the iconic naval hero of the Revolutionary War, would be an ideal ambassador, commingling diplomacy and the suggestion of force. Jones had spent the previous three years in Russia as Catherine the Great's admiral, but now was barely scraping by in Paris. He accepted the mission. But before he could embark for Algiers, he died on July 18, 1792. The assignment next was entrusted to Thomas Barclay, who had negotiated the U.S. treaty with Morocco, but he, too, was carried away by illness before reaching Algiers. Finally the commission fell to David Humphreys, the minister to Portugal and Washington's aide during the war and his early presidency. Humphreys arrived in Algiers in the fall of 1793, just as catastrophe struck.

The British had been making trouble for the United States again. Logie, the London consul in Algiers who supposedly had urged the 1785 depredations that resulted in the loss of the *Maria* and *Dauphin,* had secretly persuaded the dey to make peace with Portugal, whom the British coveted as an ally against France. It also didn't hurt—at least from Britain's standpoint—that the removal of Portugal's Gibraltar blockade would severely damage American trade. Logie's machinations proceeded in such velvet silence that until the very last minute, even the Portuguese were unaware he was negotiating on their behalf. Yet when the treaty was presented to them as a fait accompli, costing a shocking $3 million, the Portuguese didn't blink. They signed it in October 1793, and the

Algerian corsairs streamed through the Straits of Gibraltar in search of American loot, lending credence to Richard O'Brien's wry observation about the Algerians: "Money is the God of Algiers and Mahomet their prophet."

News of the treaty rang like a fire bell in the U.S. consulates throughout Spain and Portugal. The consuls flashed word to merchantmen in Spanish and Portuguese ports of the imminent danger. But there was no way to warn ships already at sea that they were sailing into peril.

Its hold filled with flour, the *Polly* had cast off from Baltimore and sailed down the Chesapeake in September 1793. Passing the Virginia Capes, the brig, out of Newburyport, Maine, entered the Atlantic, bound for Cadiz. The Atlantic crossing was uneventful until October 25, when the *Polly* was 100 miles west of Cape St. Vincent, and Captain Samuel Bayley and his eight crewmen spotted a strange vessel. The British ensign fluttering over the stern eased their apprehensions. The English might stop and search the *Polly*, but not make her a prize—if the stranger really were British, for Algerian corsairs often sailed under false colors. The vessels drew closer, and the ship's captain and crew could be seen on deck wearing English-style clothing. The Americans relaxed their guard a fatal instant. Then armed men in turbans and robes boiled out onto the main deck. The *Polly* was caught. Algerian pirates swarmed over Bayley's ship, rifling clothing, trunks, and cargo holds. In minutes, the *Polly*'s crewmen were shivering on deck, stripped of their clothing. In their underwear, they were ordered around the deck and up into the chilly rigging to work the canvas.

When the Americans complained about their inconsiderate

treatment, they were rudely acquainted with the facts of their new life. The corsair captain, Rais Hudga Mahomet, said they were lucky to have been permitted underwear. "He answered in very abusive words that we might think ourselves well used that they did not take them," wrote crewman John Foss. "And he would teach us to work naked. And ordered us immediately to our duty."

Off the coasts of Spain and Portugal in the Atlantic, the corsairs had fallen upon American trading vessels like hungry lions. The reports filtering back to the consuls in Spain and Portugal were all bad. The captive ships included the *Hope* and *Minerva* from New York; the *Prudent* and *Minerva* of Philadelphia; the *George* of Rhode Island; the *Thomas,* a Newburyport vessel like the *Polly;* the *Olive Branch,* of Portsmouth, New Hampshire; the *Jane* of Haverhill, Massachusetts; the *Jay* of Colchester, Connecticut; the *Dispatch* of Petersburg, Virginia—counting the *Polly,* eleven ships with 104 crewmen, making 119 American prisoners of Algiers.

In Algiers's dungeons, the stunned prisoners encountered the survivors of the *Maria* and *Dauphin* and despaired. The fifteen remaining crewmen were rail-thin from their meager diet, broken in body and sometimes spirit, too. "All my hopes are blasted," wrote Samuel Calder, master of the *Joy,* "& whether ever I shall get away from this is entirely uncertain, indeed if I may judge by unfortunate Capt. O'Brien & Stevens who have been nine years here & most of their Crews are already Dead . . . we have no reason but to expect more."

But as the newcomers lost hope, the *Maria* and *Dauphin* survivors took heart as they scanned the fresh American faces. With so many of her countrymen in chains, America would surely act now.

• • •

Throughout December 1793, reports of the shocking losses, carried by the slow medium of ship and courier, trickled into Philadelphia, a city mourning its dead. Yellow fever had cut down 5,000 of the 30,000 inhabitants of the nation's capital. The epidemic began in the summer heat; by September, at least 200 people were dying every week. Believing that the fever was spread by contact, Philadelphians stopped shaking hands and walked in the middle of the streets. Businesses closed. "Everyone is getting out of the city who can," Jefferson wrote on September 11 before leaving for Monticello. The fever had struck down Alexander Hamilton, but he was recovering. President Washington had departed for Mount Vernon, War Secretary Henry Knox for Massachusetts. "When we shall reassemble again may perhaps depend on the course of this malady." Since antiquity, yellow fever and malaria [Latin for bad air] had been vaguely attributed to heavy, stifling air; consequently, Philadelphia's sultry summers were thought to be somehow responsible for the 1793 epidemic. It didn't abate until the November frosts. Doctors valiantly applied their well-meaning but bumbling treatments—bleeding and purging—in trying to save lives, unnecessarily ending some by sapping their patients' strength. Why such deadly outbreaks began or ended remained mysteries until the great discovery of the lowly mosquito's essential role more than a hundred years in the future.

When they reached Algiers, the American captives were crawling with lice, flea-beaten and filthy from their confinement in the verminous Algerian ship holds, where many were transferred after their own vessels were seized. They were herded by soldiers through Algiers's streets to the dey's palace. It was a demoralizing trek. "As we passed through the streets, our ears were stunned with the shouts, clapping of hands, and other acclamations of joy from the inhabitants, thanking God for their great success, and victories over so many Christian dogs, and unbelievers, which is the appellation they generally give to all christians," Foss, the *Polly* crewman, wrote in the remarkable *Journal of the Captivity and Sufferings of John Foss, Several Years a Prisoner in Algiers,* published in 1798. Hassan Pasha extinguished any lingering hopes of the prisoners receiving humane treatment with his chilling greeting: "I have got you, you Christian dogs, you shall eat stones."

Hassan's hard words were prophetic. The captives were organized into slave gangs that blasted and dragged huge rock slabs from the jagged mountains outside the city. Before dawn, their taskmasters rousted them from their miserable sleeping quarters on the damp ground in the city's prisons and distributed breakfast: a four-ounce loaf of black bread with a little vinegar—the thrice-daily ration—and marched them in columns to their soul-murdering workplace in the dusty mountains, each loaded with twenty-five-to forty-pound ankle chains to make escape impossible.

The prisoners used gunpowder to blast loose crushing stone slabs all week long, rolling them to the base of the mountains, where they collected in a heap. On Fridays, the Islamic day of rest, Moslem overseers indulged in sport at the Christian slaves' expense, forcing them to lift the slabs weighing twenty tons or more onto sledges, then harnessing the slaves like mules and driving them the two miles to the quay. The "drivers" flogged their crews in a race to reach the quay first with the most stones. It was a game for the Tripolitans, agony for the Americans. "They are continually beating the slaves with their sticks, and goading them with its end, in which is a small spear, not unlike an ox goad. . . .

If any one chance to faint, and fall down with fatigue, they generally beat them until they are able to rise again." The massive boulders were loaded at the quay onto barges and transported to the harbor mole, where more slaves dumped them as fill. Slaves did all of Algiers's heavy lifting. ". . . every article that is transported from one part of the Marine to another, or from the Marine to the city or from the city to the Marine or elsewhere must be carried by slaves, with poles upon their shoulders."

Of all the taskmasters, one named Sherief was the worst. Foss observed that he "never appeared to be in his element, except when he was cruelly punishing some christian captive." To the Americans' delight, cosmic justice was meted out to Sherief one day in April 1795. Sherief had taken twenty slaves to a city wall to remove a pile of boards, "and having beat several unmercifully without provocation; an American exclaimed in the English Language, which the Turk did not understand, 'God grant you may die, the first time you offer to abuse another man.'" With Sherief, that time wasn't long coming. Only a few minutes later, he swung his stick at a slave who hadn't moved fast enough. His intended blow was off the mark, and he was thrown off-balance. With satisfaction, Foss described what happened next. "His stick gave him such a sudden jerk, that he fell from the planks, between the planks, and was dashed to pieces."

The Americans' inhuman labors might have earned them their daily twelve ounces of bread, but not shelter for the night. They had to pay for that. If they didn't, they had to sleep on the ground in the bagnio's open courtyard, which was enclosed by the squalid, tiered rooms where the paying prisoners were allowed to sleep on the floor. Slaves caught sleeping indoors without paying were chained to a pillar every night until they did.

The Americans especially dreaded the end of Ramadan, a time of feasting for the Moslems—and near-starvation for the captives. During the monthlong Ramadan fast, the Moslems eschewed eating, smoking, or drinking between sunup and sundown. When it ended, they celebrated with two days of feasting. The captives were required to give their taskmasters presents and then were locked in the bagnio while the Moslems ate and drank. To underscore their lowly status as despised Christians, the slaves' meager daily ration was slashed from three tiny loaves to one.

The Algerians' "tenderest mercies toward Christian captives," Foss wrote, "are the most extreme cruelties; and who are taught by the Religion of Mahomet (if that can be called a Religion which leads men to the commission of such horrid and bloody deeds) to persecute all its opposers." While terrible indeed were Barbary's capital punishments, the base currency of discipline was the bastinado, painful but nonlethal. The prisoner's hands were tied behind him, and he was laid on his stomach. Loops attached to long poles were wrapped around his feet, which then were drawn up by the poles. When all was in readiness, the prisoner was beaten on the soles of his feet and his buttocks with inch-diameter poles, the number of lashes ranging from a dozen or two for mild or imagined infractions into the hundreds for serious offenses. Fourteen slaves caught attempting to escape from Algiers late in 1793 were each administered five hundred bastinados and loaded with fifty pounds of chain, attached to a seventy-pound weight. Bowed beneath their crushing burden, they ate, slept, and toiled in the quarry with the seventy pounds balanced on their shoulders. The breakout leader was beheaded, an arguably more humane punishment, and more merciful than the Moslems' array of other capital punishments reserved for Christians—

impalement, burning, or being flung onto the sharp hooks projecting from the city walls, to die in agony over days.

Moslems who committed capital crimes were usually strangled at a wall reserved for this purpose. They sat on the ground between two holes a neck-width apart. Rope was fed through one hole, around the victim's neck, and out the other hole. The executioner, seated on the other side of the wall, twisted the knotted rope ends around a stick until the victim died.

The massive Algerian raid prompted Congress for the first time to seriously consider establishing a navy, but the issue, as many like it in the future, divided representatives along geographical lines. Rural Southern Republicans opposed any foreign entanglements or standing military force, while Northern Federalists believed a navy was indispensable to a vigorous foreign trade. After lurking behind a dozen debates for a decade without breaking cover, the subject finally was out in the open in 1794. For the first time, nothing prevented Congress from acting. Tariff and whiskey tax revenues were streaming into the U.S. Treasury, and there was money for a navy if Congress elected to build one.

One measure above all was responsible for the improved revenue situation: the Merchant Marine Act of July 4, 1789, the so-called "second Declaration of Independence." Its 10 percent tariff differential favoring goods carried by American ships caused merchant tonnage to soar from 123,893 in 1789 to 529,471 in 1795. In 1789 only 17 percent of imports and 30 percent of exports were carried in U.S. ships; by 1795, U.S. ships carried 92 percent of imports and 88 percent of exports. Consequently, shipyards were booming up and down the East Coast. While U.S. ports were enjoying their first postcolonial boom, Eli Whitney was patenting the cotton gin, which soon would enable the South also to join in the prosperity.

Unlike Pearl Harbor in 1941 or the World Trade Center and Pentagon terror attacks sixty years later, Algiers's brazen piracy didn't cause the Republicans and Federalists to paper over their ideological differences. The Senate was 17–13 Federalist-controlled; the House, where the issue would be decided, was 57–48 Republican. As a result, even the question of naming a nine-man committee to make recommendations about a naval force resulted in a close House vote: 46–44 to proceed.

The navy debate began on Friday, February 7, 1794, when the committee chairman, Thomas Fitzsimons of Pennsylvania, read a resolution recommending a six-frigate naval force. The debate lasted a month, with James Madison, the Republicans' point man and Jefferson's closest confidant, leading the navy opponents, who were Southerners for the most part. Notably absent was Jefferson, who had resigned from Washington's Cabinet and left Philadelphia a month earlier with all his possessions, bound for Monticello and retirement—but only temporary retirement, as events would prove. His timely departure spared him the discomfort of having to choose between his Republican allies and a cherished project: building a navy.

Six frigates were too few, and yet the timetable for building them was too long to meet the current crisis, Madison argued. He proposed that the money for a navy instead be spent on a treaty with Algiers. He reasoned that the Algiers–Portugal truce likely would be broken before a U.S. navy was afloat, and, if negotiations with Algiers failed, America could use the treaty money to pay Portuguese warships to protect U.S. merchantmen.

Fitzsimons said it was presumptuous of Madison to so casually dismiss his committee's long and careful study of the issue. Algiers, he said, jeopardized all the recent advances in American trade, even its trade in commodities as prosaic as salt. Two million bushels of salt were imported from Europe each year, and if Algiers's warships curtailed that commerce, it would cost $1 more per bushel to import it from elsewhere, or $2 million—three times the $660,000 estimated cost of building a frigate navy. The similarly inflated cost of other commodities would ratchet the total severalfold, making a navy seem like a bargain by comparison. Benjamin Goodhue of Massachusetts attempted to knock down Madison's assertion that six frigates couldn't stand up to Algiers's navy; the committee, he said, had studied intelligence reports showing the force was adequate to the purpose. Fisher Ames of Massachusetts made alarmist predictions about what would happen if Congress failed to act. "Our commerce is on the point of being annihilated, and unless an armament is fitted out, we may very soon expect the Algerines on the coast of America."

The Republicans fell back to their second line of defense, the British question, another fault line between them and the Federalists, who wished to reestablish friendly relations with their former mother country. The Republicans, who with good reason distrusted Britain, favored closer ties with France, although the French Revolution's excesses were beginning to dampen the enthusiasm of even Francophiles. Britain, said John Nicholas of Virginia, not only had brokered the Algiers–Portugal truce, but had tried to discourage the Portuguese from convoying American merchantmen. Other Republicans warned that Britain would continue secretly to encourage Algiers to prey on American trade to prevent U.S. goods from reaching Britain's enemy, France. "Algiers was but the instrument, Britain was the cause," said William Giles of Virginia. Madison asserted that if America built a navy, Britain would urge Algiers to harass U.S. shipping. "In the same way that they give underhand assistance to the Indians, they would give it to the Algerines, rather than hazard an open war."

British interference was not well documented, argued Congressman William Vans Murray of Maryland, and it would be foolhardy for America to depend on Portugal for protection. "It would create a disgraceful dependence on a foreign power, and weaken the spirit of our marine; whereas, if you fit out frigates, you employ your money in nourishing the roots of your own industry; you encourage your own shipbuilding, lumber and victualing business." A U.S. squadron could blockade Gibraltar without fear of being confronted by Algiers's navy, because the corsairs "wanted plunder, not glory; when they discovered they had to get the first by hard fighting, they would listen to peace, accompanied by money."

The House passed the momentous Act to Provide a Naval Armament, 50–39, with congressmen from the rural South and West opposed and able at the last minute to attach an important amendment. Peace negotiations must be pursued with Algiers while shipbuilding went forward, and if a treaty were signed, construction must cease. President Washington signed the act into law on March 27, 1794. It allocated $688,888.82 for six frigates mounting at least 32 guns each.

War Secretary Henry Knox was a former artillery officer who had learned all that he knew about naval affairs from Plutarch's *Lives*. Now suddenly in charge of building a navy from scratch, he picked the brains of shipbuilders, businessmen, ship captains, and congressmen, and a vision of a fleet of "super frigates" began to take shape in his mind. The ships, Knox concluded, "should combine such qualities of strength, durability, swiftness of sailing, and force, as to render them equal, if not superior, to any frigate belonging to any of the European Powers." Given the job of designing the frigates and seeing them built was the esteemed shipbuilder Joshua Humphreys, who had designed the Continental Navy's 24-gun frigates at the age of twenty-four. Humphreys, who would become known as "the father of the U.S. Navy," was to be assisted by thirty-year-old Josiah Fox, who would transform Humphreys's ideas into blueprints that would guide the shipwrights in their work. Fox, a wealthy Englishman, had been traveling in America scouting timber for his family's shipyard when his extraordinary talent caught the attention of Knox and Humphreys. He enthusiastically accepted the challenge of helping build a navy from the ground up. Curiously, both Humphreys and Fox were Quakers.

Knox, Humphreys, and Fox were determined to build the best frigates in the world. Since the United States couldn't afford to match the imposing men-of-war of the first-rate European powers—mammoth two- and three-deck fighting ships with 64 guns or more—they reasoned that it was better to build ships swift enough to get out of their way, yet packing enough firepower to whip anything lesser. With only France possessing frigates in any number among the European powers, the United States could distinguish itself by building frigates unequaled anywhere in speed and firepower. Humphreys rhapsodized to Senator Robert Morris of Pennsylvania that the frigates "in blowing weather would be an overmatch for double-deck ships" and in light weather would be able to evade them. "No ship under sixty-four now afloat, but what must submit to them."

• • •

A decade had passed since the United States could claim to have a navy, but even during the Revolution, its warships were out-classed, outgunned, and outcaptained. They had contributed little to the war's outcome. Except for John Paul Jones's stunning vic-tory over the *Serapis,* and few other wartime exploits, the Conti-nental Navy had performed dismally. It had been launched with two armed merchant ships, two brigs, and a sloop, its crews filled out by press gangs. They sailed under the Grand Union flag, a knockoff of the British flag, until Congress adopted the Stars and Stripes in June 1777. The cobbled-together fleet and the small frigates Humphreys had designed all were sunk or captured—all but one of the thirty-five—while the British lost only five ships. At Yorktown, it was the French fleet that sealed off Chesapeake Bay. The last Continental warship, the *Alliance,* had been auc-tioned for $26,000 on August 5, 1785.

Knox parceled out the frigate–building among six shipyards from Portsmouth, New Hampshire, to Norfolk, Virginia—an early pork-barrel project benefiting the coastal states. He overconfidently pre-dicted the frigates would be completed by the end of 1795, underestimating the time needed by years. But the delays and cost overruns were of his own making. First, while spreading the work among six shipyards might have been politically shrewd, it compli-cated the logistics of bringing together all the materials to make a ship. Then Knox also made the frigates bigger, displacing 300 tons more than the ships Congress had authorized. Finally, he had insisted they be framed in live oak—not the typical white oak—because ships made of tough, durable live oak would last at least half a century instead of the usual dozen years or so. But that meant work crews would have to be sent to the sweltering Georgia Sea Islands to harvest the live oak. Malaria decimated them, and white replacement workers couldn't be found to brave the intense heat, humidity, fever, snakes, and bugs. Black slaves cut the live oak.

Humphreys and Fox first drew up blueprints for the three 44-gun frigates they intended to build: the *Constitution, President,* and *United States.* The other three warships would be smaller, 36-gun frigates: the *Constellation, Chesapeake,* and *Congress.* The *Constitution,* "Old Ironsides," built at 1,576 tons in Boston—and anchored there today, still a commissioned naval vessel—was built by Colonel George Claghorn, a Revolutionary War veteran, at Edmund Hartt's Boston shipyard, using Humphreys's design. Humphreys personally oversaw construction in Philadelphia of the *United States,* the first completed frigate, in July 1797. Forman Cheesman supervised the building of the *President* in New York. The *Congress* was built in Portsmouth, New Hampshire, and the *Constellation,* in Baltimore, by David Stoddert, under the watchful eye of Captain Thomas Truxtun, one of the early Navy's warriors who would bring the ship credit during the Quasi-War with France in the late 1790s. The unlucky *Chesapeake,* being built in Norfolk, was destined to be memorably surrendered twice: by Captain James Barron to the HMS *Leopard* in 1807, and six years later by Captain James Lawrence to the HMS *Shannon,* despite Lawrence's dying words to his crew: "Don't give up the ship."

The frigate builders looked across the Atlantic for inspiration, to France's powerful fleet. Not able to afford a navy like England's, the French, too, had chosen to build large frigates because they were cheaper and faster than the towering, heavily armed ships of the line with their three gundecks. Like the French ships, the American "super frigates" were copper-bottomed and on their two gundecks carried long guns that fired solid shot. Carronades were mounted on the spar deck, for clearing enemy decks with shrapnel. The long guns were standard on warships everywhere. Solid shot's chief purpose was smashing holes in enemy hulls and killing enemy gunners. A crude measure of cannon caliber was the weight of the shot that it fired; there were 36-pounders, 24-pounders, 18-pounders, 12-pounders, 9-pounders, and 6-pounders. The carronade was relatively new, named for the foundry in Carron, Scotland, that designed it in 1779. It was a light, maneuverable, short-barreled gun that could fire a large round or belch a cloud of wicked projectiles—nails, chain, odd metal bits—that eviscerated anyone in its path, or could shred an enemy's sails, leaving him dead in the water.

Copper bottoms repelled barnacles, increasing ship speed, and also made it unnecessary to "careen" the vessel—tip it on its side—every six months or so to scrape off barnacles and repair holes bored by toredo worms. The British Royal Navy sheathed all its warship bottoms in copper, starting with a crash program in 1778.

While they were built upon the French model, the frigates' operations followed the Royal Navy's worthy example. Americans copied English shipboard organization, discipline, and all manner of daily operations, down to the rum ration. The 44-gun super frigates were crewed by 356 seamen, and the 36-gun ships by 306 sailors. They enlisted for 12 months. Able-bodied seamen were paid $14 a month, and ordinary seamen received $10. While they earned less than merchant seamen, the sailors could share in booty during wartime. The typical American seaman was twenty-two. Often, he was English. Nearly half of the sailors came from the cities—at a time when America was only 5 percent urban. Each day, they stood at least one of the five four-hour watches and two

two-hour watches. They spent long hours scrubbing decks and brightwork, whitewashing ceiling planking, repairing rigging, patching small boats, and practicing gunnery.

There were rules for practically everything, and harsh consequences for breaking them. For serious infractions, miscreants were slapped in irons, put on bread-and-water rations—and, mostly, punished with the cat-o'-nine-tails. Less draconian punishments were meted out for lighter offenses. Quitting watch before relief arrived was punishable by three hours on the "spanker boom" and no rum ration for three days. Jutting over the ship's stern, the spanker could be a sickeningly rough ride in stormy weather.

David Humphreys and Joel Barlow opened negotiations with Algiers in 1795 as the frigate navy slowly came together. Humphreys and Barlow were former Yale classmates, Revolutionary War veterans, and, strangely enough, poets. Before becoming a diplomat and minister to Portugal, Humphreys had served as George Washington's secretary during the war and commanded a Connecticut regiment that in 1786 helped suppress Shays's Rebellion, a rural uprising over Massachusetts taxes. Barlow, who fought alongside Washington at Long Island, was a well-known literary and social figure. A third negotiator, Joseph Donaldson, Jr., worked alongside Barlow under Humphreys's direction. James Leander Cathcart, a prisoner since the *Maria* was captured in 1785 and the dey's secretary, served as mediator and translator.

The dey opened the parley by announcing that a treaty and ransom would cost the United States $2,247,000 cash and two frigates worth roughly $248,000. America could well afford it, the dey said, for hadn't a Spanish newspaper reported that U.S. exports totaled $28 million a year? Donaldson and Barlow hastened to assure the dey that was a gross exaggeration. Further meetings brought the price down. On December 22, 1794, Algiers and America struck a deal: $642,500 cash—about $10 million in today's dollars—for the captives' release; $21,600 worth of powder, shot, oak planking, and masts in annual tribute. The Americans sweetened the agreement by throwing in a 36-gun frigate, which would be called the *Crescent*. Thirty-four captives had died, but Algiers required ransom for them, too, although their bodies were not shipped home. Barlow borrowed the cash at high interest from Miciah Bacri, the dey's chief moneylender; Bacri simply drew the money from the national treasury and redeposited it. The eighty-five surviving prisoners shipped out on the unfittingly named *Fortune,* owned by Bacri.

The *Fortune* was one of the unluckiest freedom ships that ever sailed. No sooner had it left Algiers and entered the Mediterranean than plague erupted on board. It carried off Samuel Bayley, Foss's old captain on the *Polly,* leaving only four of the nine original *Polly* crewmen alive. The ship was placed in quarantine for eighty days in Marseilles, where the captives marked time until the plague had run its course and they were cleared to go ashore. Embarking again for Leghorn, Italy, the *Fortune* was stopped and boarded by the British, who robbed the captives of their clothing and money and claimed the ship for a prize. Barlow bitterly complained that the *Fortune* sailed under an American flag, and England could not simply appropriate U.S. property without cause; the British replied that the ship was Algerian, and they could do as they pleased. On top of everything else, Barlow later had to pay Bacri $40,000 for his ship.

Foss and some of the other captives transferred to another ship embarking for America that was even more ill-starred than the *Fortune*. A Spanish privateer captured her. After she was cleared in Barcelona, she was captured by a French privateer and released, seized by the British, and then by Spanish privateers again. Another Spanish privateer boarded her and stole all the provisions and clothing. After being captured and released once more by the British, the cursed ship finally reached America.

The Algerian treaty encouraged American diplomats to open negotiations with the other Barbary States. Hassan, momentarily pleased with the ransom and tribute he had gotten, helpfully supplied the American negotiators with supporting letters and cash advances. Moroccan Emperor Maulay Sulaiman, Sidi Muhammed's successor, quickly reratified the 1786 treaty after accepting a $20,000 gift. Tunis's treaty, signed in August 1797 for $107,000, contained no annual tribute, but required periodic gifts. Tripoli signed in January 1797 for $56,486 and no annual tribute. This agreement would begin to act on Bashaw Yusuf Karamanli like a sharp pebble in a shoe when he learned what Algiers and Tunis had gotten.

The diplomats shuttled back to Algiers, which was threatening war again because the promised naval stores were long overdue. Envoys placated the dey by announcing the United States would give him another 36-gun frigate. He was so happy that he placed orders for two more new American ships, promising cash on delivery. Peace might be at hand, but the United States had just spent nearly $1 million to secure it.

And it was just the beginning.

"WILL NOTHING ROUSE
MY COUNTRY?"

*There is but one language which can be held to these people, and
this is terror.*
—William Eaton, U.S. consul to Tunis

T
he Senate ratified the Algerian treaty on March 2, 1796,
and on March 15 President Washington unhappily
pointed out to Congress that the Naval Establishment Act obliged
him to stop work on the frigates. The prospect of a work stoppage
concerned him, he confessed, for "the loss which the public would
incur might be considerable, from the dissipation of workmen,
from certain works or operations being suddenly dropped or left
unfinished and from the derangement in the whole system." By
that, he meant the ironworks, shipyards, lumberyards, and
foundries employed in frigate building. Its loss might not "com-
port with the public interest." Another reason for Washington's
discomfiture was that every penny of the budgeted $688,888
already had been sunk into the frigates, plus another $400,000 in
overruns. If the frigate building were aborted with no issue, it
would be $1 million wasted. Seeing the point, the Senate overrode
the act's work-stoppage stipulation, authorizing completion of

two 44-gun frigates and one 36-gun frigate—the *United States,* the *Constitution,* and the *Constellation.*

A new threat arose—France, upset over the Jay Treaty negotiated with England in 1794. It angered France for what it did, and Republicans in America for what it didn't do.

Former Foreign Secretary John Jay had attempted to persuade the British to reopen the West Indies to unrestricted American trade—reprising Adams's 1780s mission. Many American commodities still were barred from West Indies ports, and no American ships were permitted to dock. The Jay Treaty's major achievement was obtaining most-favored-nation status for American ships trading in Britain, but it failed to loosen up West Indies trade and amazingly conceded to the British the right to seize U.S. goods bound for France. This wasn't a case of a bumpkin getting fleeced by slick London operators, but a shrewd bet by Washington and his advisers that when the half century of intermittent warfare between England and France ended—whenever that might be—England would be left standing, and not France. Also factored into their thinking was the feeling that America would have to fight England again one day, but that America's chances of surviving the British onslaught would improve with time; the Jay Treaty pushed back the inevitable war two decades. Knowing that the Republicans would be furious over Jay's yielding to the English over France, the Washington administration withheld the treaty's details from Congress. It wasn't until February 29, 1796, that the administration held its breath and grudgingly released the full treaty. Republicans exploded, accusing Federalists of appeasing America's old enemy.

France denounced the treaty, claiming it violated the

Franco–American alliance forged in 1778 at the height of the Revolutionary War. The French retaliated by adopting the same stance
toward American goods bound for Britain that the Jay Treaty
granted Britain in regard to France. French privateers began
seizing U.S. merchantmen in the West Indies. In just one year,
France captured more than 300 U.S. vessels.

Taking office in March 1797 as the second president, John Adams
had never disputed the wisdom of creating a U.S. Navy in his
exchange of views with Jefferson the decade before. He had agreed
with Jefferson that standing up to the Barbary States "would be a
good occasion to begin a navy." But with the Treasury empty and
full of misgivings about the American will to wage a distant foreign war, he had advised paying tribute. Now that the United
States had money and the beginnings of a navy, he aimed to use
both in the nation's defense against France. "A naval power, next
to the militia, is the natural defense of the United States," he told
Congress on May 16, 1797, but "the establishment of a permanent system of naval defense . . . can not be formed so speedily and
extensively as the present crisis demands." He asked Congress to
give him authority to arm merchantmen, to ready the three new
super frigates for sea duty, and to allocate funds to build more
warships.

Congress promptly granted him the authority to expand the
Navy and disbursed $392,512 for this purpose in March 1798, as
the ignominious details of the "XYZ Affair" began leaking out,
fanning animosity toward France to fever pitch. Elbridge Gerry,
John Marshall, and Charles C. Pinckney, sent to Paris on a peace
mission, had met three minor French officials—identified by
Adams in subsequent reports only as agents X, Y, and Z. The

French envoys haughtily announced negotiations were possible only if their foreign minister, Charles Maurice de Talleyrand, received a $250,000 gift and the United States loaned France $10 million. Pinckney's forceful reply, "No, no, not a sixpence," was inflated in the retelling into the ringing "Millions for defense, but not one cent for tribute," which became the national rallying cry of the day. Not long afterward, a French privateer sank a British ship in Charleston harbor, a flagrant violation of neutrality.

By the time Adams finally laid all the details of the XYZ Affair before the Federalist-controlled Congress, legislators were ready to act. Congress's pent-up hostility toward France over the 300 ship captures and the XYZ Affair burst forth in a torrent of legislation to stem the Jacobin threat. It changed the U.S. military and began America's transformation into a naval power. Congress created a Navy Department; authorized construction of twelve 22-gun ships, ten small vessels, and cannon foundries; approved twelve more ships of 20–24 guns each; suspended commerce with France and authorized seizure of French privateers "hovering" off the U.S. coast; sanctioned completion of the last of the original six frigates, the *President, Congress,* and *Chesapeake;* and authorized Adams to accept up to twenty-four warships built with money raised from the public during subscription drives. The drives were enormously successful, tapping into the rabid anti-French sentiment predominant in most areas. The Navy acquired the frigates *Essex* from Essex County, Massachusetts, the *John Adams* from Charleston, and the *Philadelphia* and the *New York* from the cities for which they were named. As an exclamation point to this flood of martial legislation, Congress created the U.S. Marine Corps on July 11, 1798. It was a second act for America's "soldiers of the sea," whose training and hierarchy mirrored the British Marines, crack shipboard and assault troops first organized in 1664. During the Revolutionary War, Continental Marines—perhaps 50 officers and 2,000 enlisted men altogether—had served on American warships through 1784, but they disbanded along with the rest of the Continental military establishment. Today, the Marine Corps observes as its birthday the date of the Continental Marine Corps' establishment: November 10, 1775.

Having acted decisively to defend the homeland's waters against the enemy without, Congress turned somewhat hysterically to quelling threats from within, a perilous business indeed, as latter-day defenders of the republic have found out in the twentieth and twenty-first centuries. Congress amended the Naturalization Act to extend the residency requirement for citizenship to fourteen years from five years. The new Alien Act empowered the president for two years to deport aliens he deemed dangerous, and the Alien Enemies Act permitted the arrest and deportation of male aliens from enemy nations. The Logan Act made it a high misdemeanor for U.S. citizens to parley with foreign powers without government sanction, a slap at Dr. George Logan's quixotic one-man mission to France. Then came the Sedition Act, the most dangerous of all: Any written or verbal criticism of the government, its policies, or officers could be prosecuted in federal court as a criminal libel. Outraged free-speech advocates poured into the streets of Philadelphia. Troops had to be called out to break up fights between Republicans and Federalists. The successful Federalist blitz proved to be a Pyrrhic victory; the backlash splintered the party and in 1800 cost the party the White House and control of Congress. It would never regain either.

The Lesser Antilles parenthetically close off the eastern Caribbean against the Atlantic in a sweeping curve from Puerto Rico to Venezuela. These tiny islands were the West's trading crossroad, where the raw goods of the Americas found their way into ships from Spain, France, England, Holland, and Portugal. It was where America and France fought their naval war, beginning in November 1798.

The 20-gun *Montezuma,* 18-gun *Norfolk,* and 14-gun *Retaliation* were cruising off Guadeloupe when they spotted two ships sailing west. The *Montezuma* and *Norfolk* took off in pursuit. The *Retaliation,* commanded by Lieutenant William Bainbridge, stayed behind to watch some unidentified ships off to the east that Bainbridge was sure were British. He was wrong; they were large French frigates—the 40-gun *L'Insurgente,* and the 44-gun *Voluntaire.* The French pounced, and Bainbridge struck his flag, surrendering—the first of the bad luck that would dog his naval career. When he was questioned by the French about the two ships they had seen with the *Retaliation,* Bainbridge exaggerated their size, and the French decided it would be unwise to pursue them.

U.S. warships were ordered to seize and destroy French commerce. Navy Secretary Stoddert dispatched twenty-one more, divided into four squadrons commanded by John Barry, Thomas Truxtun, Thomas Tingey, and Stephen Decatur, Sr., whose son would become one of the nineteenth century's first naval heroes. Two squadrons cruised in the Lesser Antilles and two near Cuba, hunting French merchantmen and convoying American merchantmen. Convoy duty could be enervating, especially for young naval officers craving combat, but the merchants welcomed the escorts. Besides protecting their investments, they brought down insurance rates, which had soared after the initial French seizures.

The war wasn't all convoys, though; sometimes American warships fought French warships. In the Leeward Islands in February 1799, Truxtun and his 36-gun *Constellation* encountered *L'Insurgente,* one of the ships that had forced Bainbridge to strike his colors. A gale had torn down the big French frigate's main topmast, and it had no choice but to stand and fight. Making the most of her relative immobility, Truxtun's gunners aimed withering cannon fire at *L'Insurgente*'s rigging and sails. The French fought back gamely. The battle became so intense that a fiery *Constellation* officer, Lieutenant Andrew Sterett, killed one of his own men for leaving his post. Sterett described the incident succinctly in a letter home: "One fellow I was obliged to run through the body with my sword, and so put an end to a coward." After resisting for an hour and a half, the French commander surrendered, with 29 killed and 41 wounded. Aside from the crewman slain for shirking, just 3 Americans were wounded. Sterett's rash act went unreported in the official account. In February 1800, Truxtun's *Constellation* fought a four-hour battle with *La Vengeance* that ended in a draw. While the *Constellation*'s carronades concentrated on *La Vengeance*'s deck and hull, the French shredded the *Constellation*'s rigging and took down her mainmast, then somehow managed to limp away.

The Quasi-War ended with the 1800 Treaty of Mortefontaine. France agreed to stop the illegal ship seizures and released the United States from the 1778 French–American alliance formed to fight Britain. The United States dropped its maritime damage claims. During the two-year undeclared war, France captured 159 U.S. merchantmen, but American ships recaptured 100 of them and seized 86 French merchant vessels. While there was no clear victor, the U.S. Navy gained confidence and experience and won nearly every engagement, while losing only the *Retaliation*. At the war's end, the Navy had 33 ships afloat, 17 coastal defense vessels and revenue cutters, and more than 5,000 officers and crewmen. Naval power advocates were thrilled that so much had been achieved so quickly. They were certain the U.S. Navy was on its way to great things.

"He was like a huge, shaggy beast, sitting on a low bench, with his hind legs gathered up like a tailor or like a bear," wrote U.S. consul William Eaton of his first meeting with Algiers's new dey, Bobba Mustapha. The new American consuls to the Barbary States had reluctantly removed their shoes before padding into the dey's throne room. "On our approach, he reached out his fore paw, which Consul O'Brien was obliged to kiss, and we—including four American ship captains—followed his example. The animal at that time seemed to be in a harmless mood. He grinned several times, but made very little noise."

The February 1799 audience was a courtesy call by the new American consuls in North Africa. Richard O'Brien, the former captain of the *Dauphin,* was the new consul general for the Barbary Coast and consul to Algiers, the regency that had enslaved him for eleven years. Eaton was assigned to Tunis and the task of placating Hamouda Pacha, who had been bey for one year. James Cathcart, another eleven-year survivor of Algiers's bagnio, was the Tripoli consul. Cathcart had mediated and translated during the Algiers–United States negotiations that resulted in the 1795 treaty with Bobba's predecessor, Hassan Pasha; Hassan had died in 1798.

O'Brien had arrived first and was on hand to welcome Cathcart and Eaton when the *Sophia* had docked at the quay in Algiers two weeks earlier. Cathcart and O'Brien disliked one another from their long years as fellow captives. (O'Brien had tried to block

Cathcart's appointment as Tripoli consul.) They were opposites in temperament, which might have been part of the problem. O'Brien was a composed man who tended to coolness, while Cathcart was a high-tempered former seaman of Irish lineage and limited education, but unlimited resourcefulness. While a captive in Algiers, Cathcart had made a handsome profit running a tavern in the prison while managing to work his way into the dey's confidence and becoming his secretary.

While Cathcart and O'Brien weren't happy to see one another, Bobba surely was cheered by the sight of the *Sophia*'s three consorts—the *Hassan Bashaw, Skjoldebrand,* and *Lela Eisha;* the former two were the brig and schooner he had ordered, and the latter was an appeasing gift from the United States for the delayed tributary naval stores. There should have been a fourth *Sophia* consort, but the *Hero,* loaded with overdue naval stores for Algiers, Tripoli, and Tunis, had been forced to turn back at Jamaica after springing a leak. The chronic delays already had begun to corrode America's relationship with the rulers of the three Barbary regencies. Bobba, however, was the least agitated of them, having recently received the brand-new *Crescent,* the frigate promised by the U.S. treaty, with its hold full of treasure: twenty-six barrels brimming with silver dollars, a last installment on the 1795 agreement. Together, ship and cargo were worth roughly $300,000.

The consuls' quayside salutations quickly faded as an imbroglio that had festered in the *Sophia*'s tight accommodations during the long ocean voyage suddenly erupted on the Algiers dock. Betsy Robeson, the twenty-year-old companion to Cathcart's new bride, the former Jane Woodside, announced she wanted to return to America and to have nothing more to do with the Cathcarts. The young woman appealed to O'Brien for protection until her return trip could be arranged. Whatever happened during the Atlantic crossing to alienate Miss Robeson remains a minor mystery. But Cathcart's propensity for crude language and his explosive verbal abusiveness likely contributed to Ms. Robeson's decision to sever relations, and there also might have been an unwelcome romantic overture. What happened next was abundantly clear: O'Brien's temporary guardianship over Miss Robeson blossomed into a blazing courtship. Six weeks later, Miss Robeson became Mrs. O'Brien. The strange affair permanently poisoned relations between Cathcart and O'Brien.

A divided American diplomatic mission was a poor footing upon which to begin establishing amity with the notoriously fractious Barbary States. While it was hardly ruinous, it would complicate matters for Eaton, suddenly thrust into the role of go-between.

Iconoclast and maverick, brilliant and mercurial, William Eaton was a most unique consul, destined for glory when he arrived in Barbary two weeks shy of his thirty-fourth birthday. Described in later years as a small Andrew Jackson because of his quick temper and pugnacity, Eaton was born in 1764, one of thirteen children of a Woodstock, Connecticut, farmer. As a child, Eaton was a voracious reader, and never was interested in farming. He said later in life that Plutarch's *Lives,* the book that had taught Henry Knox about naval warfare, had also influenced him powerfully. When he was 15, he enlisted in the Continental Army, where he spent an uneventful three years, never seeing action but rising to sergeant-major rank. After the War of Independence, he taught school for a few years and earned a bachelor of arts degree from Dartmouth College, where he showed an affinity for languages. His education completed, he became clerk of the Vermont House of Delegates. So far the arc of his life followed the conventional path of a bright patriot bound for modest achievements.

In the House of Delegates, Eaton's natural charm and gift for lobbying emerged, and he might have embarked on a comfortable political career had he not been restless, ambitious, and adventurous.

In 1792 Eaton rejoined the Army, accepting a captain's commission under Major General "Mad Anthony" Wayne. While training in Massachusetts, he met Eliza Danielson, the fortyish widow of Brigadier General Timothy Danielson, a Revolutionary War militia leader. They married, and he became the stepfather of two teenage children before he marched off with Wayne's army to campaign in the Ohio Valley against the Miami Indians.

The assignment was life-changing. For the first time, Eaton was able to observe firsthand a man he thought worthy of emulation. Eaton wrote of Wayne:

> He endured fatigue and hardship with a fortitude uncommon to men of his years. I have seen him in the most severe night of the winter of '94, sleep on the ground like his fellow soldier; and walk around his camp at four in the morning, with the vigilance of a sentinel. . . . When in danger, he is in his element; and never shows so good advantage as when leading a charge. His name is better in an action, or in an enemy's country, than a brigade of undisciplined levies.

Wayne assigned Eaton to the American Legion, an early special-operations unit. Eaton learned guerrilla warfare, rapid movement, living off the land, and Indian languages. He infiltrated the Miami villages and gathered intelligence. Perhaps recognizing a kindred spirit, Wayne promoted Eaton to deputy commander, and they became close friends. Wayne entrusted Fort Recovery to Eaton's charge while Wayne pursued the enemy into the forests, a sharp disappointment for Eaton. As things turned out, he had little time to brood; the Miami outmaneuvered Wayne and attacked Fort Recovery. For seven desperate hours, Eaton and his men repelled frenzied attacks by 500 Indians. Finally they gave up and melted back into the thick woods. Wayne gave Eaton permanent command of the fort as a reward, and this time Eaton missed the campaign's climactic battle—Wayne's victory at Fallen Timbers, which forced the Miamis' capitulation.

With hostilities ended in the Ohio Valley, the War Department assigned Eaton to Georgia. He patrolled the troubled Florida border, where the Spanish tried to keep the Indian tribes stirred up against the Georgians. Colonel Henry Gaither, Eaton's commander, grew to dislike Eaton. Perhaps he was jealous of Eaton's pipeline to War Secretary Timothy Pickering, with whom Eaton corresponded directly. He also might have been irritated by the Georgia legislature awarding Eaton land and honorary Georgia membership in appreciation for keeping peace along the St. Mary's River. Gaither court-martialed Eaton for insubordination and for allegedly selling government supplies to the Indians for personal gain. While Eaton was cleared of both charges, his Georgia assignment and Army career ended.

Eaton went to Philadelphia to wait for his officer's commission to expire. In what turned out to be a piece of career-making good luck, the government put him to work as a counterespionage agent. Eaton trapped and arrested a spy, then fed false information to the Spanish that resulted in a new, favorable treaty between Spain and the United States. The grateful Adams administration wanted to know how it could reward Eaton for his service, and he had a ready answer. In Georgia and while waiting out his commission in Philadelphia, he had developed a passion for the Arab world. He had read and reread the Koran and everything else he could find on Islam, the Mediterranean, and the Middle East. Dreaming of one day visiting the Levant, he even had taught himself some Arabic. He told the Adams administration he would be happy to be named consul to Tunis.

Eaton's jubilation at receiving his dream assignment faded quickly once he settled in at Tunis, where right away he began to renegotiate two annoying provisions of the 1797 treaty that the U.S. Senate had refused to approve. The first required the United States to send Tunis a barrel of gunpowder each time Tunis's fortress guns saluted an arriving American ship. Tunis was generous with its salutes, and gunpowder was expensive. The second provision was more serious: It allowed Tunis at any time to commandeer any U.S. merchantman, so long as paid what decided was a fair price. Eaton raised the treaty issues during his initial meeting with Hamouda Pacha, sending the bey into a rant about the delayed naval stores, which had been aboard the leaky *Hero,* and evoking a demand for more weapons and money, as well as a ship, which Eaton rejected. The *Hero*'s ruined cargo, being replaced in the United States, soured the relationship between Eaton and the bey for months.

Eaton managed to renegotiate the objectionable treaty provisions, excising the article permitting the Tunisians to commandeer U.S. merchantmen and compromising on the cannon salutes: A

Tunisian cannon salute still would require payment of a barrel of gunpowder, but could be answered by an American salute, for a similar payment. The salutes would cancel out one another. But the bey continued to badger Eaton about the delayed naval stores.

Eaton's outrage over the Barbary rulers' imperiousness soon began to boil over in his correspondence. The obsequiousness expected of the foreign consuls was particularly galling when he considered the caliber of the North African ruling class: "Not much shall be feared nor expected from a people whose principal ministers, principal merchants and principal generals consume day after day in the same company smoking tobacco and playing at chess," he wrote to Pickering. "While the citizens and soldiers are sauntering in rags, sleeping against walls, or praying away their lives under the shrines of departed saints—Such is the military, and such the industry of Barbary—yet to the shame of humanity they dictate terms to powerful nations!!!"

Eaton also disliked and distrusted Joseph Etienne Famin, the French trader who, at Joel Barlow's request, had midwifed the original U.S. treaty with Tunis. As Eaton built up his own network of contacts in Tunis, he became convinced Famin was systematically undercutting the United States with the bey and advising the bey's chief minister, the sapitapa, about how to squeeze more money from America.

Eaton initially tried to ignore and shun Famin, but fate set them on a trajectory toward collision. The master of the U.S. merchantman *Lizzie* one day complained to Eaton that Famin had solicited a $1,000 bribe from him, claiming he could help him circumvent the Tunisian taxes on his cargo. Eaton was certain that Famin would have kept the bribe money, informed the sapitapa that the *Lizzie* was cheating him on taxes, and gotten the master thrown in prison, thereby winning points with the dey. And Eaton would have had to use his own money to free him. As he and the *Lizzie*'s master walked through Tunis's streets together talking, Eaton's anger grew.

They unexpectedly encountered Famin, and Eaton confronted him with the *Lizzie* master's allegations. Famin told him to mind his own business. Eaton's quick temper flared. Snatching a whip from a mule-cart driver, he began horsewhipping Famin in the street, before a crowd of Tunisians. Bleeding and utterly humiliated, the Frenchman finally managed to crawl away on his hands and knees. He went straight to the sapitapa. The bey summoned Eaton and Famin to explain what had happened. The articulate Eaton was better prepared, even quoting Famin as having referred to the bey's prime minister and his officers as "thieves and robbers." The bey sent Famin away and invited Eaton to dine with him.

O'Brien and Cathcart believed that, with encouragement, the Barbary States gradually would embrace legitimate trade and abandon piracy. Eaton, however, was convinced Barbary would never change willingly. "The United States set out wrongly, and have proceeded so. . . . There is but one language which can be held to these people, and this is *terror.*" Congress must "send a force into these seas, at least to check the *insolence* of these scoundrels and to render *themselves* respectable." If America's elected officials would not resolve to fight Barbary, "I hope they will resolve at their next session to wrest the *quiverofarrows* from the left talon of the eagle, in their arms, and substitute a *fiddlebow* or a *segar* in *lieu.*"

O'Brien and Cathcart came around to Eaton's bleak view after a wearing, frustrating year of attempting to placate the dey and bashaw, respectively. The demands never ceased. For example,

Bobba Mustapha expected to be paid $20,000 in silver upon the appointment of a new consul. On his birthday, he looked forward to a gift of $17,000 in hard cash. And that amount was deemed a fitting present for his eldest son's birthday, too, and for each of the various Moslem holidays.

Eaton, whose fraying relationship with the bey was now punctuated by shouting matches, believed that France and England were instigating the trouble. He forwarded what evidence he could gather to Pickering. "I don't pray often, but on this occasion I pray devoutly that the armies of Europe may bleed each other till they faint with the loss of blood."

In the nick of time for Eaton, the repaired *Hero* arrived in Tunis in April 1800 with masts, gunpowder, cannons, and small arms. Tensions eased temporarily between Tunis and America. The bey, however, wished to be at war with some nation; his corsair crews were restless. The shadow fell on Denmark, whose treaty also pledged annual tribute of naval stores. Unfortunately for Denmark, its naval stores arrived after America's. The bey found them to be inferior and left them to rot on Tunis's docks. Tunisian soldiers chopped down the flagpole at the Danish consulate. Freshly armed with new American cannons, ammunition, and powder, Tunisian corsairs sailed into the Mediterranean to hunt Danish merchantmen, bagging eight, with cargo and crews worth millions of dollars. The Danish ship captains despaired over their heavy losses.

Eaton came to their rescue, buying six of the seized vessels on credit. He restored the ships to their captains at cost, his good deed earning him the Danish king's gratitude. But the Danes got the message delivered by the Tunisian corsairs and signed a new, more generous treaty in August 1800.

• • •

Eaton and O'Brien's troubles in Algiers and Tunis paled beside Cathcart's problems in Tripoli. Cathcart and Bashaw Yusuf Karamanli had never really established a rapport, and now their relations had become acrimonious and accusatory. While the Barbary States invariably presented a unified front to the Europeans and Americans, they nursed rivalries among themselves, and the bashaw was unhappy that America regarded Algiers as the preeminent Barbary power, when Yusuf believed his growing navy made Tripoli the equal of Algiers. Yusuf wanted a new treaty with the United States.

At Cathcart's first meeting with him, Yusuf had indifferently pushed aside the new consul's carefully chosen presents—a diamond-studded gold watch, diamond rings, handkerchiefs, and eight silver snuffboxes, among other choice items, valued at $3,000. Yusuf wanted to know where the naval stores and the brig were that America had promised. It was the first Cathcart had heard of a promised brig. Brian McDonough, British consul in Tripoli, informed Cathcart that O'Brien indeed had pledged to deliver a brig during the Tripolitan–U.S. treaty negotiations. When it became apparent to Yusuf that no amount of bullying was going to induce Cathcart to produce a brig and naval stores he did not have, Yusuf said he would settle for $18,000 cash for the brig and $25,000 for the naval stores. McDonough bargained the bashaw down to $18,000 for both, and Cathcart paid, borrowing at high interest from Yusuf's banker, Leon Farfara.

Some of Cathcart's problems with the bashaw were of his own making. When news of George Washington's death reached Barbary in 1800, O'Brien and Eaton wisely suppressed it. O'Brien went to the length of canvassing Algiers for American newspapers carrying the news and confiscating them. Eaton saluted Washington's passing with a black armband, but when the bey asked about it, he would say only that a friend had died. Both knew better than to furnish the rulers with any reason for demanding more gifts, which even a death could prompt. Cathcart, however, lowered the Tripoli consulate flag to half-staff. He instructed U.S. ships in Tripoli harbor to lower their flags, too, and to fire a 21-gun salute. When the bashaw discovered the reason, he demanded a $10,000 gift to help console him for Washington's death.

Yusuf complained unceasingly about his treaty to Cathcart and to anyone who would listen. In a letter to President Adams, he made the thinly veiled threat that Tripoli would remain at peace with America, "provided you are willing to treat us as you do the two other Regencies, without any difference being made between us." Parity meant a frigate like Algiers's 36-gun *Crescent*. It also meant a new treaty requiring America to pay annual tribute similar to what Algiers was receiving.

As Yusuf lobbied for better terms, he quietly allowed his corsairs to slip the leash. In July 1800, the 18-gun Tripolitan polacre *Tripolino*—a brig-size corsair—captured the New York brig *Catherine,* bound for Leghorn with a cargo valued at $50,000. The Tripolitan crew boarded, searched, and stripped the brig of everything of value, then brought it into Tripoli. It was intended as a strong warning only. Yusuf released the ship, crew, and cargo in October. But in unmistakable language, he said that if he did not get the treaty he wanted within six months, Tripoli would be at war with the United States. Cathcart grimly foresaw "the necessity of sending a sufficient force into this Sea to repel the Bashaw's demand. . . ."

• • •

William Bainbridge's *Retaliation* was the only American warship captured by the French during the Quasi-War, but Bainbridge's career had not suffered for it—he remained one of the infant Navy's foremost rising young officers. A lieutenant when he surrendered his flag to the *L'Insurgente* and *Voluntaire,* Bainbridge in 1800 was a captain, and the skipper of the 24-gun frigate *George Washington,* one of the merchantmen converted into warships during the hasty outfitting for the French war.

Bainbridge and the *George Washington* sailed into Algiers harbor in September 1800, the first Mediterranean port of call paid by a U.S. warship. The *George Washington's* cargo included gunpowder, sugar, coffee, and herring—and a late tribute payment for the dey. Bainbridge never dreamed what Bobba Mustapha had in store for him.

The dey had displeased the sultan by signing a treaty with France while the Turks were fighting Napoleon in Egypt and Syria. The sultan's unhappiness rightly made Bobba nervous, for while Algiers was arguably the supreme Barbary power, the Ottoman fleet and janissaries could easily crush Bobba's forces and depose him if it came to that. Bobba needed to placate the sultan. And that's where the *George Washington* and Bainbridge came into play.

After the diplomatic protocols had been observed, Bobba dropped his bombshell: He wanted Bainbridge to transport Bobba's presents and bribe money on the *George Washington* to the sultan in Constantinople. Deeply shocked, Bainbridge said he could never do that. No U.S. warship would serve as a delivery service for another nation, he said emphatically. Bobba delicately pointed out that the *George Washington* happened to be moored beneath the city's fortress cannons, which could blow the American frigate out of the water in minutes.

Bainbridge could see that escape was impossible. Rebuking himself bitterly for having brought his warship so close to the batteries, he acquiesced reluctantly to the dey's "request," displaying his knack of foreseeing the worst and giving up before it came to pass. He was certain that his submission to this affront to U.S. honor would doom his career.

The *George Washington* sailed for Constantinople on October 19, looking like Noah's ark. Besides its 130 crewmen, the frigate carried the Algerian ambassador and his suite of 100 attendants; 100 black slaves; 4 horses; 150 sheep; 25 cattle; 4 lions; 4 tigers; 4 antelope; 12 parrots; and money and regalia worth nearly $1 million. It also flew the Algerian flag—another indignity Bainbridge and his crew were forced to bear. Once they were out of sight of Algiers, Bainbridge lowered the Algerian colors and raised the Stars and Stripes. The menagerie staggered across the Mediterranean, the decks so crowded that crewmen were able to maneuver the ship only with difficulty.

The Americans took pleasure in tacking into the wind whenever the Moslems prostrated themselves facing east toward Mecca, as they were required to do five times a day. This forced the worshipers to change position incessantly so they always faced approximately east, toward Mecca. The constant shifting about was doubly irksome because they could never be entirely sure whether they were really facing east. They solved the problem by posting a Moslem beside the ship's compass to call out directions.

Bainbridge sailed through the Dardanelles, around the Golden Horn and into Constantinople with the dey's presents. The Turks had never seen the American flag before. It puzzled them at first, but they were impressed by its design. When they discovered that the frigate belonged to a mysterious new nation thousands of miles away, the sultan's officers rolled out the red carpet and gave Bainbridge and his officers the run of the exotic Ottoman capital. Bainbridge reciprocated their courtesies by inviting the Turkish officials to dinner on the *George Washington*. Throughout the meal, the Americans poured water from pitchers positioned at the corners of the table, explaining to their guests that each contained water from a different continent: Europe, Asia, Africa, and North America.

Two months after leaving Algiers, the *George Washington* returned, lighter, less congested, and bearing a chilly letter from the sultan demanding more money from Bobba within sixty days. Bainbridge wisely anchored far from the fortress cannons this time, so he could no longer be forced to serve as the dey's courier. When Bobba requested that the warship shuttle the additional tribute back to Constantinople and Bainbridge again refused, the dey was powerless to make him change his mind.

If Jefferson had misgivings about sending warships to the Mediterranean, they evaporated when he learned soon after taking office about the *George Washington*'s ordeal. "The sending to Constantinople [of] the national ship of war the *George Washington*, by force, under the Algerine flag, and for such a purpose, has deeply affected the sensibility, not only of the President, but of the people of the United States," Madison informed O'Brien. It demanded "a vindication of the national honor."

Eaton agreed wholeheartedly. He was astonished at Bainbridge's meek submission to Bobba's demands. "I would have lost the peace, and been empaled myself rather than yielded this concession. Nothing but blood can blot the impression. . . . Will nothing rouse my country?"

• • •

News of the *George Washington* incident flashed through the other Barbary regencies, with the unfortunate consequence that they became bolder in their own demands. Tunis's bey, Hamouda Pacha, told Eaton he wanted an American ship to carry Tunisian goods to Marseilles. Eaton reminded the bey that they had agreed to eliminate the treaty provision permitting him to commandeer U.S. ships. Eaton warned that if the dey persisted, he would order the ship to sail to America instead of Marseilles, and there the matter would be settled by the U.S. government. Eaton's threat deflated the bey's truculence to the point where he offered to pay $4,000 to use the merchant ship. Seeing that he had won, but needing to allow the bey to save face, Eaton accepted the offer. For all his griping about the bey, Eaton had to concede that Hamouda was more reasonable than Yusuf or Bobba Mustapha. "He seldom robs a man without first creating a pretext. He has some ideas of justice and [is] not wholly destitute of a sense of shame."

Bainbridge returned to the United States with letters from Cathcart, Eaton, and O'Brien—all urging that a naval force be sent to Barbary, all hinting at tendering their resignations. Particularly disheartening was Cathcart's portrayal of the grave situation developing in Tripoli, where the bashaw had become so openly hostile toward Cathcart that Eaton was asked to try parleying. But Yusuf denied Eaton an audience after he traveled to Tripoli and appeared at the palace. The rejection undoubtedly colored Eaton's unflattering first impression of the bashaw: "He was a large, vulgar beast, with filthy fingernails and a robe so spotted with spilt food and coffee that it was difficult to distinguish the original color of the garment." "He is a cur who can be disciplined only with the whip."

Bobba Mustapha wrote to the bashaw urging moderation. But his intercession really was only a pretext for extorting more presents from O'Brien, who was told the letter wouldn't be sent unless gifts were forthcoming. One of Bobba's officers helpfully supplied a list of what the dey had in mind: two pieces of muslin, two handkerchiefs, twelve finely woven pieces of cloth, two caftans, two pieces of Holland linen, thirty pounds of sugar, and a sack of coffee. The total came to $503. O'Brien dutifully went about gathering up the bribe, and then the dey threw in a last-minute request for a watch and ring. The dey sent the letter to the bashaw, but it did no good.

Cathcart knew Yusuf wasn't bluffing when he released the *Catherine* in October 1800 with the warning that he would be at war with America in six months if he didn't get a new warship and a new treaty. His foreboding deepened with each passing month. On January 3, 1801, he took the highly unusual step of issuing a warning to U.S. representatives throughout the western Mediterranean that Tripoli was poised to declare war. The catalyst was Sweden's new treaty, which meant Tripoli soon would need a new enemy. Sweden had agreed to pay $250,000 for peace and to ransom Swedish captives, plus $20,000 in annual tribute. The Swedes believed they had no choice if they wished to have an unmolested Mediterranean trade; of particular concern was the 3,000 tons of salt they imported from the region each year.

Cathcart's communiqué to the U.S. diplomats bristled with pessimism. "I have every reason to suppose the same terms will be demanded from the United States of America and that our fellow Citizens will be captured in order to ensure our compliance with the said degrading, humiliating and dishonorable terms."

Consuls and agents, he said, should inform U.S. merchant captains of the situation so they "may fly the impending danger."

VI

WAR AND EARLY TRIUMPH

*. . . Too long, for the honor of nations, have those Barbarians been suffered
to trample on the sacred faith of treaties, on the rights and
laws of human nature!*
—Thomas Jefferson, congratulatory letter to Lt. Andrew Sterett

Mediterranean peace was unraveling as Jefferson had predicted so astutely all those years ago when he argued for a naval force to break The Terror. In the early spring of 1801, Tripoli's corsairs were readying for war against America. The bashaw set the price of a new treaty at $225,000, plus $25,000 in annual tribute. It was a shocking sum compared to the $60,000 treaty of 1797, but not far out of line with what Yusuf was extorting from the European nations, testimony to the strides he had made in transforming Tripoli into a regional naval power.

With fierce single-mindedness Yusuf had pursued this goal since claiming the throne in 1795, a devotee of the axiom that a strong navy commands respect—and, in Barbary at least, respectable tribute from the Christian infidels. His more indolent father, Ali Pasha, had neglected the navy and left just three rickety warships for Yusuf when he seized the throne by treachery and murder. In two years, he had doubled his navy's size, thanks mainly to France's generosity. It was just the beginning. The Ottoman sultan expressed his pleasure with Yusuf's progress in 1797 by sending a 36-gun frigate and a 24-gun sloop, and, by 1800, Tripoli had eleven corsairs. Three years later, Yusuf's war fleet had expanded to nineteen warships, in addition to several skiffs and gunboats.

Tripoli's rapid rearmament enabled Yusuf to begin extorting higher tribute that, in turn, helped pay for more new warships. America's $60,000 treaty appeared embarrassingly paltry when compared with the sums Yusuf now commanded routinely: $100,000 each from Sweden, Denmark, and Sicilian Ragusa between 1797 and 1800; $80,000 in ransom and captured ship buybacks in 1799; in 1802 alone, $158,000 from Sweden, $40,000 each from Holland and Denmark, and $25,000 and a new ship from France. Small wonder that America's treaty chafed Yusuf and that he thought it was time for the United States to dig deeper.

Just as irritating was America's dismissive attitude. Four years after signing the treaty, the United States still owed $6,000. What's more, the consul promised by the treaty had arrived only in 1799, without a generous present or the promised ship. Clearly, the United States did not respect Tripoli.

More aggravating than the $60,000 and the sloppily kept promises was Article XII, inserted into the treaty by Richard O'Brien. It empowered Algiers to mediate any disputes between America and Tripoli, elevating Algiers to the status of Barbary power broker. This might have been palatable to Yusuf in 1797, but not by 1801. A constant reminder of this rebuke to Tripoli's national pride was the State Department's designation of the U.S. consul in Algiers, O'Brien, as "consul general," supervising the consuls in Tunis and Tripoli. None of this had escaped Yusuf's notice.

In letters to President Adams in April 1799 and May 1800, Yusuf demanded parity with Tunis and Algiers. He required deeds and not "empty words." In October 1800, when his corsairs released the *Catherine,* he had given the United States one more chance to display respect for Tripoli and its expanded navy with a commensurately generous new treaty. Time had nearly run out on his ultimatum by the time Jefferson took the presidential oath in March 1801.

The Jefferson administration made no attempt to mollify Yusuf or avert war. Yusuf and his fellow Barbary rulers regarded their faithless treaties and mercenary jihads as normal and just, and Europe certainly was accustomed to abrupt war declarations, kidnapping, and terror. But America's blood was still up after the Quasi-War, both in Washington and in embassies and consulates throughout the western Mediterranean.

Even as the squadron was being fitted out in Norfolk for action in Barbary, Eaton was grimly warning that if the United States capitulated to the bashaw's demands, it could expect to pay double to Tunis, and Algiers would insist on more than either Tripoli or Tunis. War was preferable. "If the United States will have a free commerce in this sea they must defend it: There is no alternative. The restless spirit of the marauders cannot be restrained."

Watching the situation darken from Madrid, Ambassador David Humphreys said a show of force would serve as a warning to the other Barbary States and raise America's reputation in Europe: ". . . it would strike with astonishment those who for a succession of Ages have submitted to the most humiliating indignities wantonly inflicted upon them by a handful of Banditti. . . ." It was time for the United States to show the Barbary States its talons. What was Tripoli to the fierce new republic that had so recently stood its ground against the European superpowers, England and France?

After the Jefferson Cabinet endorsed sending a squadron to Barbary, the president weighed whether to also obtain Congress's approval. His decision not to consult Congress established the president's authority to unilaterally send armed forces abroad. Jefferson's rationale was that Congress was in recess, and most members would not return to Washington, even if he called a special session. But the fact was that he believed he had authority to act alone: It was *his* prerogative to send warships to defend U.S. commerce. His advisers concurred, especially Treasury Secretary Albert Gallatin and Navy Secretary Samuel Smith, who said it was the president's duty to defend the nation if an enemy declared war. The United States embarked on its first distant foreign war without Congress even being informed, much less consulted.

Cathcart, his wife, and his young daughter embarked for Leghorn, Italy, ten days after Yusuf's soldiers cut down the consulate flagpole. As Cathcart well knew from history, legend, and what his own good sense told him, a Barbary diplomat's freedom, even his life, became subject to the caprices of the bashaw, bey, or dey when their countries went to war. And he wished to avoid returning to the bagnio at all costs now that he had a family. With relief, he watched Tripoli slip below the horizon. But unforeseen troubles awaited the Cathcarts.

Off Sicily, Tunisian pirates stopped and looted their ship, taking the Cathcarts' wine, fowl, vegetables, and fruit, and the captain's octant, chart, and only compass. The captain strenuously protested to the corsair chief, Reis Candioto, about the compass; they might wander lost for weeks without it. Candioto grudgingly gave him an old, battered French compass, and the resourceful Cathcart repaired it with paste and sealing wax so that they could navigate. When they finally reached Leghorn, the ship and all of its occupants were quarantined for twenty-five days because of the boarding.

While Cathcart and his family were enduring the extended quarantine, four U.S. warships were being readied for a long Mediterranean cruise: the 44-gun *President,* 36-gun *Philadelphia,* and 32-gun *Essex,* all frigates; and the 12-gun schooner *Enterprise.* Not yet informed of Tripoli's war declaration, Navy Secretary Smith had issued broad orders to cover all contingencies. The squadron was to appear before the Barbary capitals to project American power, and to serve as "a squadron of observation"—if Tripoli, Algiers, and Tunis all were at peace with the United States, which the squadron would not know until reaching Gibraltar. If any Barbary States were at war with America, "you will then distribute your force in such a manner, as your judgement shall direct, so as best to protect our commerce and chastise their insolence—by sinking, burning or destroying their ships and vessels wherever you shall find them." Convoy, blockade, and engage. Smith recommended that warships display false colors to trick the enemy into thinking they were neutrals and letting down their guard. It will "give you a fair chance of punishing them." The drumbeat of war resonated as well through Madison's instructions to Eaton, written May 20, five days after the Cabinet meeting: "It is hopeful that the contagion will not have spread either to Tunis or Algiers; but should one or both of them have followed the perfidious example, their corsairs will be equally repelled and punished."

America was alone in deploying its state-of-the-art frigate fleet—a good welterweight with a knockout punch—because war had been *threatened.* For centuries, England, France, Spain, and Holland had dispatched punitive naval expeditions to the western Mediterranean, but never in response to threats alone. Only when the pirate depredations crossed the threshold from acceptable to unacceptable losses did the European powers negotiate by cannon.

While natural U.S. pugnacity certainly played a large role in its unique response, prevalent attitudes toward Islam in 1801 also made it easy to vilify the Barbary States. European writers often held up Islam as an object lesson in the depravity that results from tyranny. Moslem absolutism, the literature said, discouraged reason and inquiry, learning and enterprise—the very engines of American invention. As examples, historians of the era liked to point to Egypt, once an oasis and now a burning desert due to Arab neglect; and to Turkey, where, as a consequence of Islamic obsession with religious worship and devaluation of learning, only one book had been printed during the entire eighteenth century.

And then there was the Moslems' supposed unrestrained sex, a flouting of the Puritan view of sex as a means of procreation and nothing else—and even of Benjamin Franklin's looser standard of sex for procreation and health. Polygamy and the fabled seraglio turned all of this on its ear; one could see that political and religious tyranny easily became sexual tyranny. Moreover, Europeans believed that segregating the sexes led to all sorts of abysmal vices, foremost among them homosexuality, the great taboo. This skewed picture of the Islamic world, shreds of which survive in the twenty-first century, contained just enough truth to resist contrary evidence. It was no wonder that Americans enthusiastically supported the naval expedition against Barbary when they finally learned about it.

There was another reason for the "cruise" besides striking a blow against the Barbary terror and Islamic tyranny: training seamen. "One great object expected from this Squadron is, the instruction of our young men: so that when their more active service shall hereafter be required, they may be capable of defending the honor of their Country." The inevitability of another war with England was gospel among America's leaders, as was the caveat that it should be postponed as long as possible, until the United States was strong enough to bear it. The cruise, Madison said, "will exercise our mariners and instruct our officers in the line of their service and in a sea, where more than any others, their services may be wanted. . . ." There was no better time than now, with America at peace with the great European powers. For good reason, the Mediterranean squadrons would become known as the "Nursery of the Navy."

The Quasi-War had proven that Americans were surprisingly well suited to the peculiar rhythm of naval warfare: months of monotony punctuated by bursts of intensive violence. Perhaps the high seas, like the oceans of prairie grass on the Great Plains, were a good fit for the blunt, restless American frontier spirit. The young lieutenants especially displayed a striking gift for explosive personal mayhem. They were men in their twenties, proficient with the sword and dirk, and able marksmen. The best, like Andrew Sterett, James Lawrence, Richard Somers, and Stephen Decatur, Jr., seemed to exult in personal combat. Sterett was said to have boasted that aboard the *Constellation,* where he had impaled the balking sailor, "We would put a man to death for even looking pale on board this ship." Indeed, it later developed during the War of 1812 that the Barbary War's junior officers would command famous ships and fight great battles.

Even as the Mediterranean squadron took on provisions for its war cruise, Jefferson and Gallatin chopped at the budget and the Navy's fleet. While the one action might seem to have undermined the other, Jefferson and his officers were confident they could do both. The president certainly was unwilling to turn his back on the war he had contemplated for nearly twenty years. Yet, in his inaugural speech, Jefferson had promised Republican frugality. President Adams helped him toward this goal with his last-minute flurry of bill signings, which included the momentous Naval Reduction Act. Even while readying the squadron for war in Barbary, Jefferson didn't flinch from carrying out the act's requirements, ordering the sale of all but 13 frigates, 7 to be laid up. The Reduction Act also slashed the naval officer ranks from 28 captains, 7 masters commandant, 110 lieutenants and 354 midshipmen to just 9 captains, 36 lieutenants, and 150 midshipmen. When Jefferson and Gallatin were finished, they estimated the annual savings to be $500,000. Encouraged by their success, they began cutting federal spending elsewhere, paring the entire annual federal budget to $2.3 million, less than half the previous year's, which left $7.3 million in projected revenues for debt service and reduction.

The naval cutbacks affected the important appointment of a Mediterranean squadron commodore. The unanimous choice was Captain Thomas Truxtun, the *Constellation*'s rugged captain during her Quasi-War victories. Truxtun's proven aggressiveness persuaded Jefferson, Navy Secretary Smith and Secretary of State Madison to select him over Richard Dale, his senior on the captains' roster because of his longer service. Truxtun, however, wanted Smith to appoint a flag captain—a naval captain who would command his flagship, the *President*, while Truxtun devoted all his attention to running the squadron. But this was impossible; no captain less senior than Truxtun was available to serve under him, and protocol forbade his commanding a more senior captain. Smith informed him that his request could not be met and that he would have to command both his flagship and the squadron. Truxtun declined. Command of the Mediterranean squadron instead fell to Dale, who did not object to the dual command.

The squadron mobilized rapidly, passing the Virginia Capes on June 2, 1801, and entering the Atlantic. When it was safely at sea and past the reach of a swift recall, Jefferson formally informed Congressman Wilson Cary Nicholas of its mission. Lest the squadron's dispatch be mistaken for a policy shift regarding all the Barbary regencies, Jefferson added that his administration planned to send Algiers its overdue naval stores. The three-year delay, the president said, wasn't due to "any want of the treasury"—a dig at the Adams administration. Yet he made it clear he didn't believe for a moment that the shipments would buy America peace. "We have taken these steps towards supplying the deficiencies of our predecessors merely in obedience to the law; being convinced it is money thrown away, and there is no end to the demand of these powers, nor security in their promises." The president attempted to massage any bruised feelings over his failure to consult Congress with a belated nod to its authority: "The real alternative before us is whether to abandon the Mediterranean or to keep up a cruise in it, perhaps in rotation with other powers who would join us as soon as there is peace. But this Congress must decide."

The squadron was in experienced hands even if they weren't Truxtun's. Dale had made his reputation as a fighting naval officer during the Revolutionary War. Captured three times by the British and having escaped once, he had served under John Paul Jones on the *Bonhomme Richard*. During the epic victory over the HMS *Serapis* on September 23, 1779, off Flamborough Head, Dale, then a twenty-three-year-old lieutenant, was the first American to board the enemy ship, swinging onto the spar deck on a rope. As a reward for valor, Jones awarded him a gold-mounted sword that Louis XVI had given him. When the U.S. Navy recalled Dale to active duty, he was making a good living as master of a West Indies merchantman.

From the quarterdeck of his flagship, the *President,* the shy, moody commodore directed the squadron's four ships with a caution that belied the reckless courage he had displayed as a firebrand lieutenant. Either age had mellowed him, or his Revolutionary War exploits had spent what boldness he had once possessed. Dale's subordinate commanders included Captain Samuel Barron of the *Philadelphia,* destined for a future commodoreship; Captain William Bainbridge of the *Essex,* former commander of the unlucky *Retaliation* and the ill-starred *George Washington;* and Lieutenant Andrew Sterett of the *Enterprise.*

The four ships together mounted 124 guns, giving them at least parity with Tripoli's navy. They were crewed by more than 1,000 men, including about half of the U.S. Marine Corps, which in its fourth year numbered fewer than 350 men. Already friction had

arisen between the naval officers and the Marines, who eschewed
nautical duties and on each ship operated under a separate command structure. The Marines' independent spirit grated on the
ships' officers.

Bad weather slowed the squadron's Atlantic crossing. The *Enterprise,* much faster than the three larger, heavier frigates, had to
keep trimming her sails to allow the other three to keep pace. Dale
gave Sterett permission to sail ahead. The *Enterprise* reached
Gibraltar on June 26 to find the Mediterranean jittery over the
renewed fighting between Britain and France—the same global
war they had been waging sporadically since 1744. British warships came and went from Gibraltar, and the two combatant
nations wrung the Mediterranean ports dry of provisions.

Three days after Sterett's arrival, the *Meshuda,* the 28-gun flagship of Tripoli's grand admiral, Murad Reis, and a 14-gun
Tripolitan brig sailed into Gibraltar Bay. Evidently unobserved,
Sterett kept a close watch on them until the *President, Essex,*
and *Philadelphia* arrived on July 2. Their appearance caught
Murad Reis off guard. Suddenly the Tripoli navy's admiral and his
best warships were mousetrapped at Gibraltar.

Murad Reis was actually the former Scotsman Peter Lisle, captured by Tripolitan corsairs five years earlier while a deckhand on
the American schooner *Betsey.* The former *Betsey* was now the
Meshuda, his flagship, and Lisle had "turned Turk"—converted to
Islam. Islam prohibits Moslems from enslaving other Moslems, so
Lisle's conversion exempted him from slavery and opened up fields
of opportunity. His conversion was by no means cosmetic, seeing
the lengths to which he took it during his long, illustrious career in
Tripoli. He adopted the name of the famous sixteenth-century

Algerian pirate, Murad Reis, who had kidnapped the family of the Canary Islands governor. The second Murad Reis became a prosperous corsair captain and married the bashaw's daughter. His trusted position in the family and skill as a mariner enabled him to advance rapidly to Tripoli's grand admiral.

Without delay, Dale sought a meeting with Murad Reis, intending to learn whether Tripoli was at war with America. Above the stern of the *Meshuda,* Murad Reis displayed the colors of the nations whose ships he had captured, ranked according to the regard in which the admiral held them. The American flag fluttered beneath all the flags, even the pennant of Naples, the weakest and least-respected maritime Mediterranean nation. It was a testimony to how much Murad despised the United States.

He cheerfully lied to Dale about how matters stood between Tripoli and America. No, he told Dale, so far as he knew, their respective nations were at peace.

Dale learned the truth while making the rounds at Gibraltar, and he resolved not to let Murad get away. The commodore posted the *Philadelphia* outside Gibraltar to take the Tripolitan ships if they tried to sail away. Taking the rest of the squadron, Dale cruised to Algiers and Tunis, hoping a combination of diplomacy, cold cash, and naval might would persuade the rulers to wait patiently a little longer for the naval stores they were supposed to have received in 1798. Dale gave Bobba Mustapha $30,000 cash and promised that the *George Washington* soon would bring naval stores, cloth, linen, and at least one cash tribute payment. In Tunis, Dale told the bey his overdue regalia was being prepared for shipment.

The *President* and *Enterprise* sailed on to Tripoli, while the *Essex* began escorting U.S. merchantmen through the dangerous western Mediterranean. The two warships anchored July 25 out-side Tripoli harbor. Dale sent a courier in a boat to deliver a letter to the bashaw. "The Squadron under my command will do Every Thing in there power to take and distroy the Corsairs and other Vessels belonging to your Excellency," he wrote. In a more concil-iatory tone, he said it was a shame America and Tripoli could not be at peace, because aboard the *President* he had a letter of friend-ship from President Jefferson and a $10,000 cash gift. Yusuf need only send a boat with a message rescinding his war declaration to receive both. Three days passed with no response from the bashaw. Then, a boat made its way across the harbor to the *President,* bearing a messenger with Yusuf's defiant answer: He had good reason for declaring war. Dale's reply pointed out that Article XII of the 1797 treaty required disputes to be mediated by Algiers. He added that it wasn't too late to make peace, for the president was not yet aware of Tripoli's war declaration. But by bringing up Article XII, Dale had blundered upon the very reason Tripoli had gone to war in the first place: America's recognition of Algiers as the predominant Barbary power, entitled to a better treaty than Tripoli. After this communiqué was sent to the palace, there were no more messages from the bashaw.

Dale's diplomacy failed, but his officers and men got their first look at the enemy stronghold. Tripoli rose broodingly from the sparkling waters of its crescent harbor. "The shore along is low & sandy, dangerous approaching it in thick weather or night, the marks to know Tripoli by at a distance are the two woody hills on the back of it," Bainbridge observed when his *Essex* crew viewed Tripoli from afar some weeks later. Bainbridge, who would come to know Tripoli all too well, was unimpressed by the sight. "The town has a mean appearance, it looks little better than a Village. Their fortifications appear to cover a good deal of ground it shows but few guns & apparently is slightly built."

In 1801 the city of Tripoli had 30,000 Moslem and 2,000 Jewish inhabitants, a fraction of the Tripoli regency's population of roughly 1 million. It was blessed with a hospitable climate, with most days sunny and the air clear. A rocky reef shielded the city from the winter storms. Flowering hibiscus, olives, and palms, sweet jasmine and oleander flourished along the narrow belt of fertile land hugging the coastline. In the countryside, the cultivated fields yielded pomegranates, aloes, tobacco, millet, barley, and watermelons weighing up to 100 pounds. The city itself was a warren of white flat-topped homes hugging narrow, winding streets. Slaves did all the heavy work. Moslem men prayed five times daily and conducted business leisurely under shady trees and in the dim recesses of their shops in their white robes and burnooses while drinking thick black coffee. They ate, smoked, slept, and spent time with their wives and children and entertained themselves with horse- and ostrich-racing and cockfighting.

The bashaw and his ancestors had wielded power in Tripoli since 1711. Hamet the Great founded the Karamanli dynasty by slaughtering the Turkish garrison and then leading a conquering army against the tribal Berbers who occupied the parched accordion hills outside Tripoli and the sandy wastes beyond. After he had subdued them, Hamet smoothed over matters with the Ottoman sultan, whose Tripolitan janissaries lay in fresh graves. This was seldom a problem so long as recognition of the sultan's suzerainty was accompanied by lavish gifts. Evidently, Hamet paid proper obeisance; the sultan recognized Hamet as Tripoli's legitimate ruler. During his long reign, Hamet expanded Tripoli's borders eastward and added the oases to the south, controlling the North African caravan routes. So thoroughly did Hamet cement his power that he occupied the throne long past his prime, until he was blind and had lost much of his authority. In 1745 he killed himself and was succeeded by his son Mohammed and, after him, Mohammed's son Ali.

When it came time for Ali to name a successor, logically enough he chose Hassan, his eldest son. Yusuf, the ambitious, conniving third son and only twenty at the time, enlisted the middle brother, Hamet, in a plot against Hassan. In front of his mother in the royal palace one day in 1790, Yusuf shot Hassan twice. Then, to make sure Hassan would die, he and his coconspirators stabbed his dying brother up to a hundred times. Public outrage over the coup forced Yusuf to name Hamet the bashaw and to remain in the background.

This arrangement didn't suit Yusuf for long. He led a revolt and besieged Hamet in the capital city for two years while their father, Ali, vacillated, first supporting one son and then switching allegiance to the other. The chaotic situation didn't escape the notice of an opportunistic Turkish freebooter named Ali Borghul, who had been watching the civil war from Egypt. In 1793 he suddenly appeared at Tripoli at the head of an army of Turkish mercenaries. He captured the city without firing a shot. Had Borghul been satisfied with this conquest, he might have enjoyed a long tenure, but instead he decided also to seize the island of Jerba—a Tunisian possession. Tunis promptly became a staunch ally of Yusuf's, enabling him to return to Tripoli with a patriotic army, vowing to free his people from the invader's yoke. By 1795 Borghul was ousted, and Yusuf and Hamet were back in power, Hamet as bashaw, and Yusuf nominally in charge of maritime affairs.

One day while Hamet was traveling in the countryside, Yusuf made his move. When Hamet returned on July 11, 1795, the city gates were closed to him, and his wife and five children had become Yusuf's prisoners. Hamet went into exile in Tunis. A few years later, he made the acquaintance of William Eaton, the new U.S. consul. They became friends and then allies.

From his Tunisian consulate, on July 23, 1801, Eaton sent a circular letter to U.S. agents and consuls throughout Europe announcing that the U.S. squadron was blockading Tripoli and asking them to inform the European powers. At this point, the blockade consisted of the *President* and the *Enterprise* cruising off the Tripoli coast. The *Essex* was busy escorting U.S. merchantmen, while the *Philadelphia* lurked off Gibraltar, waiting for the *Meshuda* and her consort to emerge. The Tripolitan warships, however, didn't budge from their anchorage.

But Murad Reis and his 366 crewmen on the *Meshuda* were growing desperate. The British Gibraltar government, friendlier toward American warships than Tripolitan cruisers, was refusing him provisions, and the hungry crew of the *Meshuda's* 14-gun companion brig had mutinied and gone ashore. There they broke into a bakery and ate the sweepings. Murad unbent his cruisers' sails and threatened the crew of a moored Ragusean ship with war on their Sicilian province if they didn't take the Tripolitans across the Strait to North Africa. The Raguseans reluctantly ferried them to Morocco. Murad, happily rid of his rebellious crew, took a separate passage on a British merchant ship to Malta in November. Soon he was back in Tripoli. Only after the Tripolitans had left Gibraltar did the *Philadelphia's* officers learn that they had abandoned their ships.

• • •

Commodore Richard Dale's first inkling that a ship from his squadron had decisively beaten a Tripolitan warship in battle was when his flagship, the *President,* encountered a hulk drifting toward North Africa under a dwarfish, tattered sail. When hailed by the Americans, the wounded captain said they were Tunisians. His 14-gun cruiser, he said, had been shot up by a 24-gun French corvette off Malta. Dale gave him a compass and let him go, certain the ship was Tripolitan, not Tunisian.

It wasn't long before his suspicions were confirmed by Lieutenant Andrew Sterett, upon his return on the *Enterprise* with fresh water from Malta. Sterett excitedly described his schooner's smashing victory on August 1 over the *Tripoli.* During a three-hour gunnery battle on the high seas, the *Enterprise* had coolly emasculated her adversary, despite the *Tripoli's* two-gun advantage over Sterett's ship. When it was over, thirty Tripolitan dead littered the enemy cruiser's decks, her masts were smashed, and her sails were shredded, while the Americans had sustained no casualties and no ship damage. After attending to the thirty wounded Tripolitans, who included all the ship's officers, the Americans had erected a stubby sail and sent the *Tripoli* on her way back to port. This was the very hulk that Dale had encountered.

With the aid of the compass supplied by Dale, the *Tripoli's* wounded captain, Mahomet Rous, and the surviving crew members managed to reach the city of Tripoli. News of the shattering defeat spread quickly through the narrow streets and cafés, finally arriving in the palace.

The furious bashaw ordered Mahomet Rous mounted backward on a jackass. With sheep entrails draped around his neck, he was paraded through the city streets and jeered and hooted by his countrymen. Then he was punished with 500 bastinados.

From Washington to Naples, Americans toasted the *Enterprise*'s brutal dismemberment of the *Tripoli*. Sterett was awarded a ceremonial sword and recommended for promotion to captain; the Enterprise's ninety-four Navy crewmen and Marines received a month's extra wages.

The victory inspired a play, *The Tripoli Prize, or American Tars on an English Shore*. New York audiences loudly cheered its debut in November 1802, although reviewer Washington Irving derided its implausible story line: A storm blows the *Enterprise* and *Tripoli* from the Mediterranean to the English Channel, where the American captain's son falls in love with an English girl, but then realizes after a climactic sea battle that duty comes before love.

In a congratulatory letter, Jefferson warmly noted that Sterett had "first taught our countrymen that they were more than equal to the pirates of the Mediterranean," and affirmed his steadfast determination to rid the Mediterranean of The Terror:

> Too long, for the honor of nations, have those Barbarians been suffered to trample on the sacred faith of treaties, on the rights and laws of human nature! You have shown to your countrymen that the enemy cannot meet bravery and skill united. In proving to them that our past condescensions were from a love of peace, not a dread of them, you have deserved well of your country, and have merited the high esteem and consideration of which I have now the pleasure of assuring you.

Sterett's promotion, however, ran aground on the Naval Reduction Act, which had left the Navy only nine captaincies, all filled at the moment. Before the war ended, Sterett would unhappily resign from the Navy when Stephen Decatur, Jr. was promoted to captain ahead of him.

The *Enterprise* skipper's bitter disappointment might have been the first instance of dashed expectations by American fighting men in Barbary, but it certainly would not be the last.

Nor would this be the last time the Barbary War's combatants would try to gain an advantage over one another by feigning surrender and flying false colors—ploys as old and new as war itself. As commanders well know, deception and surprise can win battles against a more numerous or better-armed enemy. Americans and Tripolitans would both use trickery when it suited them.

VII

THE WAR THAT WASN'T

Government may as well send quaker meeting-houses to float this sea . . .
—William Eaton

"We find it is all a puff! We see how you carry on the war with Tripoli!"
—Tunisian minister assessing U.S. lack of aggression to William Eaton

For the next two years, the Mediterranean squadron scrupulously avoided Tripoli harbor. Commodore Dale and his successor, Richard Valentine Morris, gave many reasons for their dilatoriness: It was too late in the season for offensive operations, they lacked the warships to be successful, they were too busy convoying. When they weren't convoying or blockading, they were shuttling mail, food, and water. Wheat, guns, and corsairs leaked through the porous blockade. After watching this purposeful busyness for a year and a half, Yusuf and Murad Reis concluded that the United States was just another mercantile nation, like Sweden, Denmark, and Naples, that could be bullied into paying tribute. This wasn't the outcome Jefferson had envisioned when he set out to chastise the North African regencies.

Dale perversely interpreted his orders to mean he couldn't attack Tripoli, but only *defend* U.S. interests and capture enemy corsairs at sea. So, instead of gathering his meager force for a climactic battle in Tripoli harbor, he dispersed it. The *Essex* convoyed merchantmen; the *President* and *Enterprise* blockaded; and the *Philadelphia* waited outside Gibraltar Bay for Murad to show. Dale complained there weren't enough ships for a proper blockade, much less to confront Tripoli. An effective blockade would require two frigates, two sloops of war, and a small bomb vessel to shell the town. In that assessment, he was remarkably accurate, but it evidently never occurred to him that he might bring his entire squadron before Tripoli, beard the bashaw, and end the war.

In truth, his heart was never in the cruise. By October, just three months into his cruise, he was talking of suspending the blockade and going home. "I don't expect there will be any great Necessity of your being at sea this Winter," he wrote to Barron. The Tripolitan corsairs stayed in port during the stormy months between October and March. "You will take a look now and then into Tripoli, to let that fellow see and know that you are on the look out for him." Between convoy duty and occasionally appearing off Tripoli to keep up the appearance of a blockade, the weeks would fly "until you are releaved by some Ship of the next Squadron that is to come out, which I suppose to be soon. . . ." Dale made plans to depart for home in early December, even though his deployment supposedly was for a full year.

While overly modest about his squadron's prospects, Dale was ebullient about his successor's, provided he was permitted to attack Tripoli—the commodore tenaciously clung to his belief that he was not—and if he were given enough vessels to prevail. As early as August 1801, only a month after reaching Gibraltar, he was predicting that his successor, presumably with more ships than he, would pressure Tripoli, "and now and then heave a few shells into the Town," until the bashaw sued for peace the following summer. "There never was, nor will there be again, for some time to come so favourable an opportunity for the United States to Establish a lasting reputation, for its flag in those seas." And without a drop of irony, he declared that his squadron already had proven to the world "what the Government of the United States can do."

A combination of winter gales, paperwork, and bad luck spoiled Dale's December leave-taking, and 1802 still found him in the western Mediterranean. En route to Toulon to have the *President*'s bottom checked for wormholes and rot, the Port Mahon harbor pilot ran the flagship onto a rock. Then Dale and his crew were quarantined for fifteen days.

If not a fighting commander, Dale was certainly efficient. He kept his squadron humming with paperwork and errands, and he was impatient with sloppy subordinates. Captain Daniel McNeill, whose frigate *Boston* had joined the squadron after delivering the new U.S. ambassador to France, was the opposite: administratively loose, but combative. Inevitably, the men clashed. McNeill gave Dale ample cause. To avoid quarantine in Toulon, McNeill had told the French authorities he had been to no other ports recently, when he had been to several. Dale rebuked McNeill angrily when he found out. Before the memory of that lapse of integrity had faded, McNeill was in trouble again. He sailed from Malaga minus three lieutenants, the ship's purser, and three other crewmen—all still ashore. As though to compensate for leaving Malaga with too few crewmen, at Toulon he sailed with three French officers and the *President*'s parson. They had come aboard for supper, overstayed, and awakened the next morning to find themselves under sail. "I hope you will be more particular in your enquirys on Board, when you are about to sail from any place," Dale fumed at McNeill. "You can have but little idea what trouble and displeasure it gives, and the consequence of leaving Officers behind, and taking, Officers of other Nations away contrary to their expectations." He asked Robert Smith, the new Navy secretary, to cashier McNeill.

But before his recall, McNeill revealed his virtues as a vigorous, able blockader, capturing four Tunisian coastal vessels trying to smuggle grain and oil to Tripoli. He then joined Swedish blockaders in repelling a squadron of Tripolitan corsairs and shot away the mast of a Tripolitan gunboat in Tripoli harbor. His solo accomplishments exceeded the rest of the squadron's combined achievements, chief of which was the capture of a Greek ship off Tripoli with twenty-one Tripolitan soldiers, fourteen merchants, five women, and a child.

Thinking ahead to when a future squadron might seriously prosecute the war, Dale generously freed the prisoners in Tripoli, thinking he was ensuring a reciprocal gesture in the event Tripoli captured Americans in the future. Then, as though having second thoughts about appearing too soft, Dale asked Nicholas Nissen, the Danish consul in Tripoli and a loyal American friend, to inform the bashaw, "He is much mistaken in the character of the Americans, if he thinks they are to be Frighten'd. They love peace, but it must be an Honorable one. . . ." Unimpressed by either Dale's bluster or his generosity, Yusuf deemed the forty-one freed captives would be worth the release of exactly six Americans. The remainder of Dale's tame cruise furnished no opportunities to find out whether the bashaw would honor the pledge.

• • •

Richard Valentine Morris wasn't a seasoned combat officer like Dale or Truxtun, but Thomas Jefferson owed much to his family. Richard's brother, Lewis Robert Morris, was a Vermont congressman when the cliffhanger 1800 presidential election, which culminated in an Electoral College tie between Jefferson and Aaron Burr, came before the U.S. House for resolution. Over the tense days of congressional balloting, resulting in tie after tie, Morris steadily voted for Burr, keeping the Vermont delegation's vote split evenly between Burr and Jefferson. But on the thirty-sixth ballot, Morris abruptly abstained, swinging Vermont to Jefferson and handing him the presidency. While no conclusive evidence suggests that Morris's selection as commodore was a quid pro quo, it may well have been.

Morris evidently anticipated an uneventful tour of duty in the Mediterranean. He brought along his wife, his baby son Gerard, and the family maid, Sal. In the late eighteenth and early nineteenth centuries, wives and paramours often accompanied officers to sea, but seldom on warships bound for a war zone. As a consequence of his bringing his family, Morris's ship became known as a "happy" ship and not a "tight" one, and his own personal comfort became more important to him than his mission. Navy Secretary Smith had been only too happy to grant Mrs. Morris permission to sail with her husband. "Immediately upon receiving it," Smith informed the commodore in April 1802, "I wrote to her complying with her request." Smith's eagerness to please very possibly stemmed from the fact that his first choice for the job—Truxtun again—had backed out at the last minute.

Truxtun had accepted the appointment initially, but, as the squadron's sailing date neared, he revived his old complaint, the one that had caused him to refuse command a year earlier: He wanted a captain to command his flagship so he could devote himself exclusively to squadron operations. It was a reasonable request: freed from daily management of a frigate and its 300 men, he could dedicate himself wholly to prosecuting the war. But the rest of his request wasn't so reasonable: unless his stipulation were granted, he would resign from the Navy. Smith disliked ultimatums from his captains. "The condition, Sir, is impossible," he shot back. No extra captains were available because of the Navy's force reduction. "As this must have been known to you—I cannot but consider your notification as absolute."

Truxtun was out of the Navy.

Morris's squadron assembled piecemeal at Gibraltar. The 36-gun *Constellation*, commanded by Captain Alexander Murray, arrived on April 28; the 36-gun *Chesapeake* under Morris came in on May 25; and the 28-gun *Adams*, under Captain Hugh Campbell, on July 21. Morris's other ships—the *Enterprise*, with Sterett still in charge, and the *Boston*—were already there.

Gibraltar vibrated with rumors of war, between France and England, and, at various times, between America and each of the Barbary States. The bashaw was sending five corsairs into the Mediterranean in defiance of the blockade. Algiers had sent twelve corsairs against Portugal and already had captured a frigate, boarding it so quickly the crew hadn't had time to unlock the ship's arms lockers. Forced to fight with handspikes, seventy-two Portuguese crewmen died before the ship was surrendered.

Moroccan Emperor Soliman Ben Mahomet was pestering U.S. consul James Simpson for a passport for the *Meshuda*, which was still penned up at Gibraltar. Without a passport issued by an American consul, the *Meshuda*, as a onetime Tripolitan cruiser of uncertain ownership, could be seized by U.S. warships as a prize the instant it left Gibraltar. Throughout the Tripolitan war, merchants from all the noncombatant North African nations routinely obtained passports from their American consuls to avoid having their vessels boarded by suspicous U.S. naval officers and searched for wartime contraband. But since the Moroccan emperor neither explained how the *Meshuda* had become Morocco's, nor what its business would be as a merchant ship, he did not receive a U.S. passport.

During the American squadron's Atlantic crossing, the *Chesapeake*'s mainmast came loose just four days out of Hampton Roads. Carpenters discovered 3-inch-deep rot and defective spars, but managed to stabilize the mast so the *Chesapeake* was able to continue her voyage. Between the impaired mast and poorly packed ballast and cargo, however, the crossing was anything but smooth. "I never was at Sea in so uneasy a Ship, in fact it was with the greatest difficulty we saved our masts from rolling over the side." After the flagship limped into Gibraltar, the British assisted with repairs.

The *Adams* brought Morris's orders to Gibraltar, and they couldn't have been clearer. The commodore was to collect Cathcart at Leghorn and appear before Tripoli with the entire squadron. "Holding out the olive Branch in one hand & displaying in the other the means of offensive operations, may produce a peaceful disposition towards us in the mind of the Bashaw, and essentially contribute to our obtaining an advantageous treaty with him." Cathcart had similar instructions from Madison—accompany the squadron to Tripoli and open negotiations with the bashaw, but let him make the first overture, so "awe inspired by a display of our force" could have its effect. Don't buy a peace,

Madison warned. "To buy a peace of Tripoli, is to bid for War with Tunis. . . ." Seldom have such forthright instructions been so utterly disregarded.

The Moroccan emperor's irritation over the blockaded *Meshuda* mounted. Soliman now announced defiantly that he would violate the U.S. blockade by bringing the *Meshuda* and her consort to Tangier, loading them with grain and then sailing to Tripoli. Certain the emperor intended merely to hand over the warships to Tripoli, Consul Simpson patiently tried to explain that a blockade's purpose was to keep *all* ships from entering an enemy port, but Soliman stubbornly insisted on the passports for the *Meshuda* and the brig. Simpson knew Moroccan corsairs could begin attacking American shipping at any moment if Soliman wasn't given the passports. He asked Morris, whose authority exceeded his when it came to the blockade, to permit him to issue them, in hopes of averting the unending trouble that would result from captured ships and prisoners, but Morris refused starchily. To no one's surprise, except possibly Morris's, the emperor banished Simpson from Tangier and, on June 19, 1802, declared war on the United States.

Morris notified the Navy secretary he would need more ships to fight both Morocco and Tripoli, but no sooner had he done so than the Moroccan emperor, Soliman, began backpedaling, possibly after considering that it might be unwise to antagonize a nation with five warships so close at hand when he lacked a credible fleet. He invited Simpson to return to Tangier. Simpson silkily reminded the emperor that the United States was sending him 100 gun carriages soon as a gift, and the touch of customary obeisance did the trick—Soliman called off the war, even if he hadn't altogether given up on the *Meshuda*. Moroccan crews soon were spotted in Gibraltar readying it and the brig for sea. Morris put a watch on them, wondering how he could legitimately stop the two ships from leaving, for they clearly belonged to Morocco now. The commodore reluctantly instructed Simpson to issue the passports.

Slow communication between Washington and the Mediterranean kept the two chronically out of step. Handwritten letters and reports crossed the Atlantic on sailing ships in one to three months, depending on whether the trip was "downhill"—sailor vernacular for America to Europe, a one-month voyage—or "uphill," against the prevailing westerlies, from Europe to America, which could take up to three months. The Navy Department sent the *John Adams*—a 28-gun frigate like her sister ship, the *Adams*—and *New York* to the Mediterranean upon receiving Morris's appeal for more ships to fight Morocco, and canceled the shipment of 100 gun carriages for Morocco. But by then, Soliman had called off the war. So the gun carriages didn't arrive as Simpson had promised, and another year went by before they did. When they finally showed up, the goodwill gesture was largely wasted because of the emperor's vexation over the delay. The *John Adams* and *New York* reached the Mediterranean just as Jefferson, Smith, and Madison learned that Soliman had canceled the war.

Even though they were not needed against Morocco, Jefferson decided to keep the two additional warships in the Mediterranean. The president's staunch belief in a navy's utility had evolved into a philosophy of perpetual naval preparedness. Belying his unyielding opposition to a strong central government, he wanted to build even more ships, and was working with architect Benjamin Latrobe on a blueprint for a roofed dry-dock at Washington Navy Yard where decommissioned warships could be warehoused "in a state of perfect preservation and without expence." Idle ships would be hoisted out of the water to keep the organism-rich harbor waters from eating away their bottoms, and placed under roofs out of the wet weather that rotted and warped masts and decks. Congress, which supported Jefferson's financial austerity policies without sharing his enthusiasm for naval preparedness, flinched at the dry-dock's $417,276 cost, and the plan died.

No sooner had the Moroccan crisis subsided than Tripoli snatched an American merchantman. Two corsairs had slipped through the blockade in early June, as the American merchant ship *Franklin* sailed unescorted from Marseilles for St. Thomas with wine, oil, soaps, perfume, and hats. Before the *Franklin* reached Gibraltar, on June 17, 1802, the corsairs overtook and seized her, with seven crewmen and two passengers. The *Franklin's* captain, Andrew Morris, and his crewmen owned the unhappy distinction of having become Tripoli's first U.S. prisoners of war.

Firing cannon salutes, the corsairs brazenly paraded the *Franklin* through the blockade, manned by the *Constellation* and a Swedish frigate, and into Tripoli harbor, as Morris fumed over his countrymen's inaction. The Tripolitans marched the crew through the city streets past shouting Moslem crowds, jubilant at the sight of captive Christians—a raucous scene that might have been reprised from 1793, 1785, or even 1635. English and French consuls swung into action and quickly gained the release of three crewmen who were British nationals and the two passengers who were French. But Captain Morris and three American crewmen remained captives.

The absence of a U.S. consul in Tripoli hampered efforts to gain their release, although William Eaton did what he could from

Tunis. Eaton tried to open a parley with Murad Reis when he appeared in Tunis, but Murad wouldn't negotiate or permit Eaton to visit the captives.

Algiers intervened unexpectedly. Bobba Mustapha reminded Yusuf that in 1801 he had promised one day to release six Americans when Dale had freed the forty-one prisoners from the captured Greek ship. If any proof was needed of Algiers's continued preeminence among the Barbary regencies, Bobba's intercession and Yusuf's response supplied it. On October 11, the freed American captives suddenly showed up in Algiers. Yusuf, however, couldn't resist levying a small ransom, agreement or no; after all, these were American Christians, and Tripoli was at war with their country. Richard O'Brien, the U.S. consul general in Algiers, paid the bashaw the $6,500 he demanded.

Richard Morris might have wrung an honorable peace from the bashaw had he sailed swiftly to Tripoli with Cathcart and negotiated at cannon's mouth—in other words, followed orders. He did not, even with Navy Secretary Robert Smith prodding him to act in a letter reaching him while he lingered at Gibraltar in the summer of 1802. "Let me at this time urge you to use every exertion to terminate the affair with Tripoli and to prevent a rupture with any of the other Barbary Powers."

Instead, the commodore began to display the indolence that would become the signature of his command. Two and a half months passed before he managed to pry himself away from Gibraltar and the balls and banquets, and the many opportunities to rub elbows with admirals, aristocrats, and diplomats. On August 18, 1802, Morris and the *Chesapeake* finally sailed from Gibraltar. He did not make for Tripoli, but leisurely escorted U.S.

merchantmen in a happy ramble along the southern European coast, touching at many pleasant ports—Malaga, Toulon, and Marseilles—and arriving on October 12 in Leghorn, where he met Richard Cathcart.

With winter approaching, Morris was loath to forsake Italy's amenities to cross to Tripoli. It was so late in the season, he wrote to Smith on October 15 in his first report since reaching the Mediterranean, "to render it impossible to appear off Tripoli before January." Morris confided to Cathcart that he wouldn't undertake a major operation against Tripoli until May or June.

It was a missed opportunity for securing favorable peace terms. Reports from Tripoli suggested the bashaw was open to negotiations. O'Brien had learned the bashaw would settle for $60,000 in cash and $10,000 in presents. For another $30,000, Algiers would mediate. When all the other bribes were paid, the treaty would cost $120,000. O'Brien was confident that it could be signed for less. Yusuf's openness to a negotiated peace was by no means a testament to the effectiveness of Morris's blockade. "This year has proved a great deal richer in grains than ever could be expected, so that the Blockade from that Side neither seems to be of much Service. . . ," Nicholas Nissen, the Danish consul in Tripoli, had reported to Eaton in July. The bashaw's amenability to talks more likely was due to concern over the U.S. military buildup.

But the propitious moment passed without Morris's acting. Sweden made peace with Tripoli for $150,000, plus an $8,000 consular present and $8,000 in annual tribute. The new treaty removed any pressure on Tripoli to negotiate with the United States, now its only enemy. With the rich harvest, Sweden's cash, and gifts of $40,000 and an 18-gun cruiser from France, the bashaw was confident he could fight a war, endure a blockade, or thwart any coup attempt.

The commodore and the "commodoress," as Mrs. Morris was now known among the *Chesapeake*'s crew, dallied in Leghorn nearly a month. In his journals and letters, Henry Wadsworth, a midshipman on the *Chesapeake,* displayed the family gift for composition that would reach its zenith in his nephew and namesake, Henry Wadsworth Longfellow. Young Wadsworth thought highly of Mrs. Morris, describing her as an avid reader who was particularly knowledgeable about geography and history. Yet he couldn't resist a wry dig at her looks, noting that "her person is not beautiful, or even handsome, but she looks very well in a veil." She was not the only woman aboard the *Chesapeake;* the boatswain, carpenter, corporal, and the captain of the forecastle all brought their wives, too. The forecastle captain's wife, Mrs. James Low, gave birth to a boy in the boatswain's storeroom.

Morris's lethargic cruise left the squadron's officers and men with plenty of time to get into trouble—chiefly, by drinking and dueling. During the long layover in Leghorn, Marine Captain James McKnight was killed by Navy Lieutenant Richard H. L. Lawson after a simmering feud between the two *Constellation* officers culminated in McKnight, a seasoned duelist, challenging Lawson. Dueling among American officers was a lethal byproduct of Europe's Romantic Age, when a gentleman's honor was more important than life itself. It was so widespread during the early nineteenth century that two-thirds as many U.S. naval officers died on the "field of honor" as were killed in battle. Lawson, who had never dueled, proposed three paces, counting on the brief distance to negate McKnight's experience. McKnight's second denounced Lawson as "an assassin" for suggesting such a ridiculously short distance, Lawson called McKnight a coward, and they finally agreed on two pistol shots each at six paces. If both remained standing and their honor still craved satisfaction, they would fight on with cutlasses until it was.

They trooped ashore. McKnight and Lawson stepped off their six paces, turned and fired simultaneously. McKnight missed, but Lawson's bullet struck McKnight in the chest, piercing his heart and killing him instantly. Marine Captain Daniel Carmick and other witnesses carried the body to the American Hotel, where they were staying. The staff, anxious to spare the other guests a grisly spectacle, turned the officers away, telling them Leghorn's coroner needed to conduct a postmortem to determine the cause of death, but they wouldn't permit it at the hotel. The Americans lugged McKnight to the cemetery, laid him on a raised grave marker, and sent for the coroner.

The coroner was a by-the-book bureaucrat. Carmick watched in horror as he cut out McKnight's heart. He asked Carmick to vouch that the ball indeed had passed through it, then began the grotesque hunt for the pistol ball. Carmick protested the dismemberment of his friend, but the coroner and other city officials were not to be dissuaded. Carmick stalked off in disgust. "I left them up to their Armpitts in blood," he reported to Marine Commandant William Burrows.

Murray, the *Constellation*'s aged, nearly deaf commander, had been unaware of the feud that had gone on right under his nose until McKnight's death came to his attention. He displayed his violent disapproval of dueling by arresting Lawson for murder and forbidding military honors at McKnight's burial. Murray and

Morris also both boycotted the service. Carmick wrote to Burrows, "I thought he [Murray] was rather unreasonable in desiring that there be inscribed on his Tombstone; 'That he had fallen victim to a false idea of Honor.'" McKnight was buried near the gravesite of the British satirist Tobias Smollett, who died in Leghorn in 1771 after finishing his epistolary novel, *The Expedition of Humphrey Clinker.*

Before the squadron left Leghorn, there was another tragedy. Carmick was returning to his ship with Lieutenant Sterett when some crewmen tried to catch the boat as it was pulling out. Sterett refused to wait for them, deciding to teach the sailors a lesson on promptness. They appropriated a barge. It overturned in the harbor's chop, and four sailors drowned.

The squadron idled in Livonine for a pleasant spell. At length it weighed anchor for Naples, with Wadsworth writing contentedly, "Yesterday we left Livonine with as much pleasure as we enter'd it, for 20, or 30 days will generally satiate us with any place."

Another duel caused an international incident. At Malta, where the *New York* had put in to wait out a storm, Midshipman Joseph Bainbridge, the younger brother of Captain William Bainbridge, was on liberty in Valletta when he had a run-in with a Mr. Cochran, secretary to Malta's governor, Sir Alexander Ball. Cochran tried to pick a fight with the American to impress his British officer companions. After being taunted and jostled repeatedly, Bainbridge finally flattened Cochran. The governor's secretary threw down a challenge. Concerned about Bainbridge's inexperience, Lieutenant Stephen Decatur, Jr., Bainbridge's shipmate and an experienced duelist—he would die in a duel in 1820 with the *New York's* current commander, Captain James Barron—volunteered as Bainbridge's second. Decatur demanded that the duel be fought at four paces. The men exchanged first shots. Cochran missed his, and Bainbridge blew off Cochran's hat. The men reloaded and fired again. This time Bainbridge was dead accurate: Cochran "reciev'd the ball in his head and instantly died," wrote Wadsworth. Alexander Ball, furious over losing his secretary, ordered Barron to turn over Bainbridge and Decatur to Maltese authorities for prosecution. Barron ignored the demand. The *New York* sailed with Bainbridge and Decatur. A Navy investigation exonerated the two, but they were sent home.

While Morris rambled among the western Mediterranean's friendly ports, support for the war was growing back home. Congress empowered the president to prosecute the war without declaring it formally. This was at Madison's urging; he believed the Tripoli war was too distant for effective congressional oversight. Congress also authorized armed vessels to make prizes of Tripolitan ships and, if needed, the commissioning of privateers. Navy enlistments were extended from one year to two.

Early in 1803, Navy Secretary Smith asked Congress for $96,000 for four warships of 14 to 16 guns, and $12,000 for eight gunboats. Naval officers and consuls had complained for a year and a half that the super frigates' deeper drafts hamstrung them as blockaders; they could not pursue shore-hugging small craft into the shallow harbors divoting the Tripolitan coast. Schooners, sloops, and gunboats were needed to chase blockade runners right into their hideouts. Eager to show its support, Congress gave Smith $50,000 to build up to fifteen gunboats, and granted his $96,000 request for the small ships. Construction of the four warships began immediately.

The Navy Department also began standardizing the operation of its ships, officers, and men, issuing new rules covering everything from uniforms to discipline, shipboard duties to shipboard menus. The fleet's diet left much to be desired when measured against later standards. Smith recommended a ration heavy on protein, carbohydrates, and liquor, with occasional vegetables to ward off scurvy:

Sunday: One and a half pounds of beef, one-half pound flour or Indian meal, 14 ounces bread, one-half pint spirits, one-half pint molasses.

Monday: One pound pork, 14 ounces bread, one-half pint spirits, one-half pint peas.

Tuesday: One and a half pounds beef, one pound potatoes, 14 ounces bread, two ounces butter, one-half pint spirits.

Wednesday: One pound pork, 14 ounces bread, two ounces cheese, one-half pint spirits, one-half pint rice.

Thursday: One a half pounds beef, one pound potatoes, one-half pound flour or Indian meal, 14 ounces bread, one-half pint spirits.

Friday: One-half pound flour or Indian meal, 14 ounces bread, two ounces butter, one-half pint spirits, one-half pint molasses, one pint rice.

Saturday: One pound pork, 14 ounces bread, one-half pint spirits, one-half pint peas, one-half pint vinegar.

Eaton was bitterly disappointed that Commodore Morris was rapidly proving himself no improvement over Dale. He chafed over the squadron's inactivity, grumbling to Madison, "Government may as well send quaker meeting-houses to float this sea. . . ." He also was angry with Murray of the *Constellation* for having refused to reprovision the *Gloria* at Gibraltar, stripping her of the privateer commission Eaton had awarded her, and even impressing some of her seamen into service on the *Constellation*. "I beleive you will find you were unauthorized in employing the Ship Gloria on Public account," Murray had written Eaton. Eaton happened to own the *Gloria* and had armed her at his own expense with the profits from a trading business he and Cathcart operated on the side. It was accepted practice for American consuls to operate private businesses while representing U.S. interests. Certain consulships, such as those in the West Indies, were particularly coveted because of their opportunities for accumulating great personal wealth. Eaton had some justification for making his own ship a privateer: He used the *Gloria* to deliver and pick up consular mail at Gibraltar, because the squadron's warships so rarely stopped in Tunis—over the previous six months, only McNeill had called, and just once. Murray's high-handedness angered Eaton and revealed his unhappy tendency never to forget a slight.

Yet Eaton was right about the Mediterranean squadron, whose lackadaisical performance made the Barbary consuls' jobs all the more difficult. The flimsy blockade and the commodores' fussy care in avoiding a direct confrontation with the bashaw forced the American consuls in Tunis, Algiers, and Morocco to compensate with a "paper blockade"—refusing to issue passports to any vessels going to Tripoli from their regencies. All of them had been pressured to issue the passports, even threatened. Tunis's bey had even ridiculed Eaton over the tepid blockade and the unwarlike Dale and Morris. As a former Army captain who knew how to fight and brimmed with ideas about how to bring Tripoli to heel, Eaton could only react with impotent fury to the barbs, painfully aware that the war was being prosecuted lamely. "Our operations of the last and present year produce nothing in effect but additional enemies and national contempt. . . . The Minister [of Tunis] puffs a whistle in my face, and says; 'We find it is all a puff! We see how you carry on the war with Tripoli!' " The United States risked disgrace, its citizens "dragged to Slavery and goaded to a lingering death under the bastinade of merciless robbers." Worse, America would have to buy peace "on the terms of an unprincipled, overbearing Bashaw of a wretched dog-kennel." "If America can yield to this, and look the world in the face without a blush, let her blot the stars from her escutcheon and viel with sack-cloth the sun of her former glory. . . ." Broke and ill, he wanted to go home. His post was "intolerable abuse and personal vexation," to no lasting purpose. He had wasted four years in Tunis.

All the consuls were unhappy, even Cathcart in his exile in Leghorn, far from any Barbary ruler. A Barbary consul, he groused, had to put up with humiliation, isolation, threats to life and limb, and "every species of insolence & degradation that a fertile brain'd Mohammetan can invent to render the life of a christian superlatively miserable . . . one moment menaced with chains, the next with death & damnation, in a state of constant vigilance concern & perplexity. . . ."

"Nothing of importance transpired in this quarter," Morris was able to report complacently to the Navy secretary in November. During the winter of 1802–3, he enjoyed the British social swirl in Malta for several weeks. Finally, in February 1803, he weighed anchor for Tripoli, even though he no longer had seven ships to parade in front of the bashaw; three were headed home. It didn't matter, for when he reached Tripoli, the weather was too stormy for maneuver or blockade.

Morris returned to Malta's pleasures.

VIII

FRUSTRATION

Though a fly in a man's throat cannot kill him, it will make him vomit.
—Tunis's sapitapa

Twelve months pass'd after I enter'd the Straits before I saw Tripoly.
—U.S. Midshipman Henry Wadsworth

aton's relationship with Hamouda Pacha deteriorated. They argued more frequently, and their quarrels at times threatened to explode into open enmity. But for the time being, expensive, gaudy gifts put off the day of reckoning. Morris's squadron delivered gifts to Hamouda worth $43,300: six rifles, their stocks, solid-gold barrels and gold-embossed locks embroidered with battle-axes, pikes, swords, fifes, drums, and bows and arrows. Each rifle came with a matched pair of gold-embossed pistols, jewels, and expensive cloth.

The bloom of goodwill fostered by the gift giving faded quickly. The bey instructed Eaton to issue him passports so he could trade with Tripoli, the very issue that had led to Morocco's war declaration. Hamouda believed Tunis had the right to trade with whomever it pleased, blockade or no. Of course, Eaton refused. The fiery argument that ensued ended with the bey's ordering Eaton to collect his belongings and leave Tunis. Eaton retaliated by refusing to issue any passports at all, to any Tunisian corsair, no matter what its destination. When tempers finally cooled, the bey sent the sapitapa, his commercial agent Hadgi Unis Ben Unis, to Eaton to try to patch up their tattered relationship. Unis did a poor job. He told Eaton the bey really didn't want war with the United States, only a more amenable consul. He said Tunis wasn't awed by America; if it came to war, his nation would lay up its large cruisers and send out small ships to harry U.S. shipping. "Though a fly in a man's throat cannot kill him, it will make him vomit," he told Eaton.

The brief rapprochement drew to a quick end when the bey demanded that the United States give him a new brig of war, a demand made "in the uniform spirit of insolence which Christians tolerate in these Regencies," Eaton reported disgustedly. It wasn't long before the brig of war grew into a 36-gun frigate. When Eaton refused to relay the request, the bey wrote to Jefferson directly. The frigate, he said, would "add to the high esteem I have for your nation, and would more and more cement the ties of our friendship." While the bey was making his pitch for the frigate, Unis, the sapitapa, was busy claiming he had been promised a gold-mounted, double-barreled fowling piece. "It is false," Eaton wrote to Madison.

The steady accretion of grievances reached critical mass on January 15, 1803, when the *Enterprise* captured the Tunisian imperial ship *Paulina* as it attempted to run the blockade. The *Paulina's* protesting captain, Lucca Radich, insisted he had intended only to drop passengers in Tripoli; the ship's cargo was destined for the island of Jerba, which belonged to Tunis. Eaton derided Radich's sophistry, noting that most ship captains, rather than violate the blockade, also would have dropped the passengers at Jerba, from where they could have reached Tripoli by land without difficulty. Eaton said the ship should go to the prize court in Gibraltar, which would determine whether the vessel was a valid war prize or an improper seizure.

The bey threatened war if the *Paulina* and its cargo were not restored and damages paid: "I will indemnify myself in a shorter and more certain way. You know I am at war with Naples and Genoa; I will order my corsairs to make reprisals on your merchant vessels entering those parts.'" Eaton sent an urgent appeal to Morris in Malta to come to Tunis immediately, and to bring Cathcart with him.

Obeying Eaton's summons, Morris brought the *Chesapeake, New York,* and *John Adams* into Tunis harbor on February 22. It was the commodore's first cruise in force to a Barbary port since his arrival in the western Mediterranean nine months earlier. Unmoved by the sight of the three frigates, the bey sent Morris a letter repeating his threat of war if the *Paulina* were not handed over to him. After huddling with Morris and Cathcart, Eaton joined them and Captain John Rodgers of the *John Adams* in a parley at the palace with the bey and sapitapa. Morris insisted the *Paulina* go to prize court, and the bey demanded immediate adjudication. Morris capitulated quickly. He brought the *Paulina's* manifest to the next meeting, and the American and Tunisian officials went over it line by line. It turned out the Tunisians had a legitimate grievance; much of the cargo was not the contraband the Americans had believed it carried. Unis pressed his advantage by demanding more money for items not listed on the manifest. Morris conceded the Tunisians everything. Satisfied the crisis was past, he prepared to leave Tunis.

But everything *wasn't* settled. Soldiers blocked the Americans when they reached the quay. Unis handed Morris a bill for $34,000, the amount that he said Eaton owed him and that Eaton supposedly had promised that Morris would pay when the squadron arrived. Unis announced that Morris would be detained until the bill was paid. The soldiers marched Morris, Eaton, Rodgers, and Cathcart back to house arrest in the consulate, with Eaton strenuously denying having made such a promise and protesting their treatment. Morris angrily blamed Eaton.

Yet it was true Eaton had borrowed $22,000 from Unis—to send to Hamet Karamanli, with whom Eaton had entered into a partnership to depose his brother Yusuf, the bashaw of Tripoli. Eaton had promised to repay the loan with money he expected from the U.S. government on the next frigate reaching Tunis. Eaton had added to his debt by borrowing to prop up his faltering shipping business, which traded between Tunis and Italy, where the underemployed Cathcart acted as his agent and kept him informed on the market for North African products—primarily wheat and oil. It was an initially profitable business that had experienced recent setbacks as a result of the U.S. blockade of Tripoli, which had turned Tunisian merchants against the enterprise. The debts to Unis had kept mounting up. Eaton also borrowed to underwrite the quixotic ransom of a Sardinian countess, the ineffably lovely Maria Anna Porcile, saving the young beauty from the seraglio of Tunisian Prime Minister Mustapha Coggia. Eaton's gallantry was wasted on the girl's miserly father, who refused to repay Eaton. The girl and her mother remained at Eaton's home, a consolation for the lonely consul, whose wife and family were back in Massachusetts.

At their meeting with Hamouda the next day, March 5, 1803,

Morris announced he would pay Eaton's debt from ship funds. But his gracious submission was buried under an avalanche of pent-up grievances between Eaton and the bey and his officials. The torrent of vituperation was unleashed when Eaton, still exasperated about Unis's mild distortion of his repayment promise, asked the bey if he had ever known him to be deceitful. The bey responded, "The consul is a man of good heart, but wrong head. He is too obstinant and too violent for me."

This and all the accumulated aggravations of his consulship loosened Eaton's tongue. "No wonder my head is bad when I am surrounded by so many impostors," Eaton shouted, and then accused the bey's officials of robbing him of his property. His outburst amazed and infuriated the bey and his ministers.

Cathcart reported what happened next: "'You are mad,' says the Minister. 'Yes, you are Mad' stuttered the bashaw in a Phrenzy, at the same time curling his Whiskers . . . 'I will turn you out of my Kingdom; tell the Commodore,' said he, 'this man is mad . . . I won't permit him to remain here.' 'I thank you,' Eaton replied, 'I long wanted to go away.'"

But his debt had to be paid before the Americans could leave. Eaton found a buyer for the *Gloria,* collecting $7,000, and scraped up $5,000 more by selling off some of his belongings. Morris made up the difference with $22,000 from the *Chesapeake's* purse. He appointed Dr. George Davis, the *Chesapeake's* surgeon, as temporary consul, and retired to his cabin, a bit dazed by the tumultuous events. The commodore sent the bey a note claiming he was too ill to present Davis in person, but offered his "respects."

Morris's mild reaction to the bey's outrageous provocations—the detention, the peremptory expulsion of a U.S. consul—mortified Cathcart no end. "Had I commanded the United States Squadron in place of sending this letter I would have sent him a copy of my protest against him for the insult my country suffer'd in my person for this overt act of violence & inform'd him that I should only wait the orders of my government to redress the grievance." Eaton, who had sparked the entire incident, was equally indignant. "It is unprecedented even in the history of Barbary outrage."

The disastrous meeting inspired the notoriously uncommunicative Morris to write his third letter in ten months to the Navy secretary. Had he known he would be held liable for Eaton's debts, he never would have gone ashore, he complained. He suggested Eaton had conspired with Unis to force the U.S. government to pay his personal debts. Foreshadowing his fate as squadron leader, Morris's letter crossed a testy communiqué from Smith upbraiding him for his long silence. "I presume it would be superfluous to remind You of the absolute necessity of your writing frequently and keeping us informed of all your movements."

Morris sailed to Algiers next. Madison and Smith wanted him to offer Bobba Mustapha $30,000 cash in lieu of the naval stores America still owed him. Things went no better than they had in Tunis. The dey refused the $30,000; he needed weapons and naval stores—not cash—to outfit his corsairs for jihad. Morris then introduced Cathcart as the new U.S. consul general succeeding Richard O'Brien. Bobba, who had stated flatly to Jefferson months earlier that he would reject Cathcart if he were named consul in Algiers, now did so. "His character does not Suit us as we know wherever he had remained that he has created difficulties and brought on a war." The snub prompted Cathcart to snidely suggest to Madison that he persuade O'Brien to stay on in Algiers, because he "is literally the echo of the Jewish Sanhedrim who are the Creatures of the Dey." Time and distance hadn't diminished Cathcart's hatred of O'Brien.

The two Mediterranean squadrons' accumulated disappointments and failures at last attracted the censorious scrutiny of Jefferson and his officials. With the federal budget shaping up, they were free to devote more attention to the Tripoli war. And now they wondered why it was dragging on without any decisive action. Eaton and Murray, now back in Washington, filled the ears of Jefferson and his Cabinet members with complaints about Morris's leisurely cruise. Fearing the Barbary States would perceive America to be weak and ineffectual, Jefferson, Madison, and Smith decided to send another force to the Mediterranean that would include the new brigs and schooners nearing completion in Philadelphia, Baltimore, and Boston. Given sailing orders were the 16-gun brig *Siren,* commanded by Lieutenant Charles Stewart; the 12-gun schooner *Vixen,* under Lieutenant John Smith; and the 16-gun brig *Argus,* skippered by Lieutenant Stephen Decatur, Jr., the first command in what would become a celebrated career. Lieutenant Richard Somers was ordered to take charge of the 12-gun *Nautilus,* a Baltimore merchant ship, and convert it to a schooner. Stewart, Decatur, and Somers, inseparable friends since they were children in Philadelphia, would make their marks in the Mediterranean.

Dale, the Navy's senior captain, was named squadron commander again. Navy Secretary Smith evidently never entertained second thoughts about Dale's uninspired leadership of the first squadron, and neither did Dale, who thought he deserved a promotion to admiral. Weary of his senior officers' demands, Smith reminded Dale frostily there was no such rank in the Navy and then read him the riot act: ". . . from the tenor of your letter, I perceive that it is also necessary to state to you, that no Officer of the Navy can consistently be allowed to decline at his will & pleasure a service to which he may be ordered by the President." Dale's resignation was accepted promptly.

Edward Preble got the command instead, a lucky break for the feisty Preble and the Navy. Preble, who had had to refuse commissions in the two earlier squadrons because of stomach ailments, was sufficiently recovered to serve, and he did not levy conditions. He was ordered to refit the 44-gun *Constitution* as his flagship. He found her rotting in Boston Harbor and spent much of the summer of 1803 making repairs. The *Constitution,* four schooners and brigs, the *Enterprise,* and the 36-gun *Philadelphia* gave Preble command of two frigates and five smaller ships. His appointment as commodore was dated May 14, 1803, exactly two years from the day that the bashaw's soldiers chopped down the U.S. consulate flagpole.

Unaware that he was about to be replaced, Morris at last decided to bring the squadron before Tripoli, after first changing flagships—moving to the *New York* and sending the *Chesapeake* back to the United States. Over Cathcart's protests that only he was authorized to negotiate a treaty with Tripoli, Morris put him on the *Adams* to Leghorn with a vague promise to summon him if needed. Actually, Morris intended to handle negotiations himself.

The first of the misfortunes and miscues that would pursue Morris during the remainder of his cruise now beset him. While the *New York* was crossing the western Mediterranean, a massive explosion in a storeroom killed 14 officers and men, blew down bulkheads, and ignited a roaring fire that crept toward the magazines and barrels of gunpowder, threatening the annihilation of the ship and her company. Working feverishly side by side, officers and crew fought the blaze with wet blankets and water buckets, teetering on the edge of an inferno. The ship was saved after an hour-and-a-half battle, inspired by Lieutenants David Porter's and Isaac Chauncey's desperate acts of bravery in the smoky belowdeck passageways, where they stopped the fire from spreading to the powder magazines.

The remnants of Morris's squadron assembled off Tripoli in May 1803. "Twelve months pass'd after I enter'd the Straits before I saw Tripoly," Wadsworth noted drily. "The *Chesapeak* return'd to America without seeing her enemies' Port." But now, the frigates *New York, John Adams* and *Adams,* and the schooner *Enterprise* were all blockading Tripoli. It was the largest display of U.S. naval power in two years of war.

Captain John Rodgers, commander of the *John Adams,* had made a name for himself as a bold officer during the Quasi-War, but his reputation as a fighting man even then was well established. It was helped along by an incident in England in 1796 involving the infamous Sir Banastre Tarleton, the ruthless cavalry commander whose raids in the Carolinas made him one of the most hated British commanders of the Revolutionary War. While dining at a Liverpool hotel, Rodgers spied a rowdy crowd swarming the streets, carrying on its shoulders Tarleton, then a major general running for re-election to Parliament. The procession was led by a man bearing a banner depicting Tarleton on horseback, dispersing a crowd of Americans, with a trampled American flag beneath the hooves of his horse. Provoked by the insult to his flag, Rodgers dashed impulsively into the street and struck the banner bearer. Then he retrieved his pistols from his room and confronted Tarleton in front of his supporters. Tarleton coolly claimed to be unaware of the banner and invited Rodgers to his campaign headquarters, where Tarleton laid the matter to rest by agreeing to destroy the offending banner. The episode ended on a high note for Rodgers, whose bold impetuosity along with Tarleton's gracious concession made him an instant hero among Tarleton's supporters. They hoisted Rodgers onto their shoulders and paraded him through the streets as they had Tarleton before.

Rodgers displayed the same tigerish streak while cruising off Tripoli on May 13. Spotting a 28-gun warship racing for Tripoli harbor, he cut her off before she could reach the sanctuary and boarded her. It was the *Meshuda,* Murad Reis's old flagship, now a vessel belonging to Morocco, the same ship that had compelled Morocco to declare war on the United States. As Simpson had predicted months earlier, the *Meshuda* was being used to aid Tripoli; she was packed with guns, cutlasses, hemp, and other contraband. Twenty crewmen were Tripolitans. As Morris later put it to Simpson, Morocco's elaborate show of taking ownership of the *Meshuda* "appears to be a detestable fraud."

Days later, the *Enterprise* spotted a felucca, a small coastal vessel, hugging the Tripoli shoreline, but before Isaac Hull's schooner could reach her, the crew brought her to shore. Hull armed a raiding party, but delayed giving the order to attack, needing the commodore's permission as well as the *New York's* supporting fire. By the time Morris arrived, Tripolitan cavalry had massed and the element of surprise was long gone. With the horse troops waiting outside the range of the *New York's* guns, but positioned to repel any raid,

Morris scuttled the mission. The *Enterprise* then attempted to shoot the felucca full of holes and sink her, but failed. The *Enterprise* and *New York* departed, and the felucca's red flag kept flying.

Five days after the felucca's beaching, the blockaders spotted nine gunboats and a small ship five miles west of Tripoli. As the *John Adams, New York,* and *Enterprise* converged for attack, the enemy vessels darted into a harbor and anchored. In two years, the squadron had never operated as a single entity, either in maneuvers or actual combat. But now the opportunity suddenly was at hand for a telling blow to be struck—if only the American cruisers could operate in concert. It was late in the day, and the setting sun perfectly backlit the sails of the U.S. ships, making them easy targets for shore fire, if the Tripolitans had been inclined to open up. Fortunately for the Americans, they didn't. Morris positioned his three ships abreast and sailed closer to shore. The wind died, and the Americans began to pay for their failure to practice maneuvers together. Drifting into one another's path, the ships fired broadsides at the moored gunboats and the shore. Morris tried to sort out the mess by shifting the *John Adams* in front of the *New York* and *Enterprise,* but all that did was enable Rodgers to fire on the gunboats, while preventing Morris and Hull from bringing their cannons to bear without hitting the *John Adams.* The warships slewed about awkwardly in the fading light.

The situation didn't improve with nightfall. "The moon shining against our sails & the light from our gun deck afforded them a sure mark at the distance of one mile," wrote Henry Wadsworth. But the Tripolitans were poor marksmen and timid defenders. Had they been Americans, "they would have rowed out & completely wrecked our three ships."

A few days later, the captain of a French sloop stopped by the *Enterprise* as it was leaving Tripoli reported that the shelling had killed three Tripolitans and wounded five others. Among the wounded was the bashaw's brother-in-law; he had lost his right arm.

Thirty-five miles northwest of Tripoli, the *Enterprise* spotted ten small ships in one of the many small bays that dimpled the Tripolitan coastline, and signaled the *New York* and *John Adams*. By 5:00 P.M. on June 1, the three warships were anchored a mile from the craft. They were feluccas, full of grain. Morris contacted their captains, and four of them met with him on the *New York*. They claimed they were Tunisians. More than a little skeptical, Morris gave them until midnight to bring their craft alongside the *New York*, or he would burn them.

With nightfall, more than 1,000 Tripolitan soldiers and cavalry massed on shore, racing their Arabian horses up and down the beach, waving muskets over their heads and showing off their equestrian skills. Lieutenant David Porter proposed a night attack on the grain ships. Morris rejected the plan, intending to abide by the midnight deadline he had set for the felucca captains to surrender their vessels. But he gave Porter permission to lead a reconnaissance sortie.

At 8:00 P.M., Porter, Wadsworth, and eight other volunteers climbed into two boats and in the moonlight quietly rowed to within pistol range of the feluccas. They could hear the crewmen talking. Before long, a Tripolitan sentry spotted the scouting party, and gunfire blazed from the beach. Returning fire, the Americans rowed hastily to a rock rising from the water, beyond musket range from shore. The excitement from the brief firefight and their freedom from the supervision of higher-ups put the young officers

151

and men in a lighthearted mood. Wadsworth clowned for them on the rock. "I stood on its summit & with my right hand extended towards heav'n took possession in the name of the United States," he wrote. At midnight, they rowed back to the *New York*. The feluccas hadn't budged from shore. The Americans would have to burn them.

Morris ordered an attack early the next morning. Fifty officers, sailors, and Marines boarded seven boats commanded by Porter as the bright morning sun winked off the turquoise water and the sandy beach in the distance. The landing force neared the shore under the ships' covering fire. Porter split his force, sending two manned boats loaded with combustibles to burn the feluccas and continuing to the beach with the other five.

The enemy had spent the night building defenses; the Tripolitans crouched behind makeshift barricades made of boat sails and yards, and behind rocks and hillocks bordering the beach. Cavalrymen milled on the sand.

The hour for battle had struck. The raiders waded ashore amid crackling small arms fire. Sailors and Marines had landed on Tripoli, the first U.S. amphibious landing on a hostile foreign shore.

A cavalryman on a superb black steed cut showy circles on the beach, flourishing his rifle, as the Americans and Tripolitans exchanged gunfire. The high-spirited horseman galloped close to the Americans—too close, presenting an inviting target. "Several took aim at him: he plunged forward fell & bit the dust," wrote Wadsworth, who was with the landing party. Cannon fire from the ships tore through the massing cavalry and foot soldiers.

The defenders, who numbered at least 1,000, now concentrated their rifle fire on the shore party, whose main purpose was to divert the Tripolitans' attention from the crews torching the feluccas. Fourteen Americans went down with wounds. Shot in both thighs, Porter continued to give orders. Before long, flames were shooting from the feluccas. The sailors and Marines on the beach scrambled back into their boats and pulled out. But they were too quick: The Tripolitans rushed in and were able to put out the fires before all the grain was alight. Despite his wounds, Porter begged Morris to allow him to return to finish the job. The commodore forbade him; it was too risky. The American squadron sailed away. The Tripolitans ran onto the beach, throwing handfuls of sand in the air defiantly.

Unimpressed by Morris' desultory skirmishes, Yusuf boasted to Nissen that if this was America's idea of war, he would demand $500,000 for peace. In the bashaw's mind, things could scarcely get any better. Tripoli had completed a rich harvest, the bashaw was loaded with cash from Sweden's treaty, and European goods arrived almost daily. "What a glorious blockade," Nissen remarked drily to Cathcart.

Having failed to awe the bashaw with American arms, Morris decided to try diplomacy. Sailing into Tripoli harbor with his squadron, Morris went ashore June 7 to open a parley with the bashaw's minister. The bashaw's terms weren't as stiff as Yusuf had told Nissen they would be, but they were plenty high: $200,000 for peace, $20,000 annual tribute, compensation for Tripoli's war expenses, and annual shipments of military and naval stores. Wadsworth, who accompanied Morris, reported that the commodore replied huffily to the proposed terms that "Were the Combined World to make the demand it would be treated with contempt. . . ." The bey's secretary took offense, "asking whether the com'r came on shore to laugh at him. . . ." The talks veered into shoal waters. With Morris still ashore, the bashaw lowered the white flag of truce, a signal for hostilities to resume. The commodore was perilously close to becoming the bashaw's prisoner—and might have, if the French consul hadn't interceded. He informed the bashaw's minister that he would guarantee Morris's honor, and that behind him stood Bonaparte and the might of France. Sobered by the invocation of the dreaded Napoleon, the bashaw and his officers reconsidered. The next morning, the white flag was run up the flag-pole again, and Morris returned unmolested to the *New York*.

Morris left Tripoli, never to return. He had pressing business in Malta—a new son. Mrs. Morris had given birth on June 9. Later in the month, still enjoying his family's company in Valletta, the commodore lifted the blockade altogether. Consul Davis had passed along an unsubstantiated report that Tunis and Algiers were merging their corsair fleets for possible war. Morris assumed that U.S. shipping would be their target, and he wanted all of his warships on hand in case he had to fight a new enemy. The *John Adams, Adams,* and *Enterprise* abandoned the Tripoli blockade and assembled at Malta with the rest of the squadron.

But Davis's report proved false.

Before quitting Tripoli, the squadron spotted a 22-gun Tripolitan polacre at anchor in a deep, narrow bay east of Tripoli. The *Enterprise* and *John Adams* moved in, lofting shells at it. The enemy crew abandoned ship. Rodgers was readying a boarding party when a boat was seen returning to the polacre with the captain and some crewmen. Rodgers resumed the shelling, and the polacre crewmen again prepared to abandon ship, firing broadsides to clear their cannons and striking their flag.

And then, without warning, the polacre exploded with an ear-splitting roar, shattering into thousands of pieces. Enemy troops on the beach collapsed with shrapnel wounds. Debris rained down on the harbor. The dazzled Americans watched as the polacre's main and mizzen masts rocketed 150 feet straight into the air—yards, shrouds, and stays fluttering. Rodgers's amazement jumps off the pages of his report to Morris: "The destruction of the before mentioned vessel, altho' awful, was one of the Grandest Spectacles I ever beheld.—After a Tremendous Explosion there appeared a Huge Column of smoke, with a pyramid of Fire darting Vertically through its Centre interspersed with Masts, Yards, Sails Rigging, different parts of the Hull & etc. and the vessel in an instant dashed to Attoms."

After assembling in Malta, the squadron cruised leisurely along the southern European coast. Morris' men were spoiling for a fight even if their commander wasn't. The *New York* pulled over a 6-gun galley, thinking she was Tripolitan. To the crew's disappointment, she was Tunisian. They let her go. Noted Wadsworth: "Had she been a Tripoline she would have been a prize for the Men were all hot for Battle, friends or foes.—The sight of a Turban soon enrages them." But there were few turbans at Messina, Naples, and Leghorn.

Elba, the island where Bonaparte would be exiled in eleven years, furnished unwelcome excitement. The trigger-happy French garrison fired on the *Adams*. Captain Hugh Campbell unwisely sent Lieutenant John Dent ashore to request an explanation, and the young officer was detained. The French commander arrogantly demanded compensation for each shot he had fired at the *Adams* before he would release Dent. Unlike the Tunisians, who had only wanted free gunpowder when they demanded a barrel for every cannon salute, the French wanted to slap the Americans in the face. With no other options but leaving Dent or recovering him by force and starting a war with France, Morris paid the bill angrily: 4 crowns, 6 francs. Wrote Wadsworth in his journal, "thro' his [Campbell's] damned foolishness our country is insulted & we pay for it too."

The *John Adams* convoyed merchantmen to Gibraltar, and the *Enterprise* went on a mail run to Malta. The *Adams* transported Cathcart from Leghorn to Tunis to become the new U.S. consul, succeeding Davis, and then joined the *John Adams* at Gibraltar.

Sailing on alone in the *New York,* Morris unexpectedly met the *Adams* again at Malaga. Campbell handed him a letter dated June 21 from the Navy secretary. "You will upon receipt of this consider yourself Suspended in the command of the Squadron on the Mediterranean Station and of the Frigate The *New York.*"

Rodgers was given temporary command of the squadron until Preble's arrival.

Jefferson had decided to recall Morris. Two years of inaction following Sterett's bloody defeat of the *Tripoli* had caused the president's initial enthusiasm for the war to congeal into icy frustration. Since 1784, he had longed to show Europe and Barbary that America was different, that it wouldn't bow to the haughty deys, beys, bashaws, and emperors, or tremble before their ragtag corsairs. For twenty years, he had wanted to chastise their insolence. After two years of war, he was no nearer that goal than when Commodore Dale had left the Virginia Capes in June 1801. The Mediterranean squadron convoyed; it did not fight. Jefferson was hearing that the blockade was little more than a fiction. If anything, the caution displayed by his two commodores had reassured the Barbary rulers that they had nothing to fear from

America. And Morris's long silence from the Mediterranean had only confirmed the president's suspicions that his commodore was nothing more than a timeserver.

Dissatisfaction with Morris had first spiked in March, when Eaton and Murray returned to Washington. Jefferson and his Cabinet listened to their complaints about the conduct of the war. Eaton had observed sourly to the U.S. House speaker that Morris "never burned an ounce of powder; except at a royal salute at Gibraltar in celebration of the birthday of his *British Majesty.*" The Cabinet met on April 8 to discuss Mediterranean affairs, but made no decision regarding Morris. Then, in May, Morris's so-called action plan had reached Washington. Its vagueness convinced Jefferson and his officers that Morris had to go. On June 16, the president asked Navy Secretary Robert Smith to bring the commodore home.

Morris was court-martialed. The panel of three fellow officers— Captains Samuel Barron and Hugh Campbell and Lieutenant John Cassin, superintendent of the Washington Navy Yard—and Judge Advocate Walter Jones, Jr. found Morris guilty of "inactive and dilatory conduct" in April 1804. Morris was faulted for leaving Tripoli unblockaded for months, for not appearing off Tripoli for an entire year, and for botching the few actions that he did direct. Morris's conduct, the panel concluded, had failed to enhance America's reputation. "This is to be ascribed, not to any deficiency in personal courage on the part of the commodore, but to his indolence and want of capacity." In his defense, Morris said he was proud that no U.S. property or citizens were captured on his watch. The court martial resulted in his dismissal from the Navy.

• • •

During Morris's last days in the Mediterranean, Algerian corsairs attacked a Royal Navy frigate off Malta. The British ship managed to escape into Valletta Harbor, where two British men-of-war and a frigate immediately put to sea, chased down the corsairs, and sank several of them.

Bobba Mustapha retaliated by ordering every English subject in Algiers imprisoned. When Lord Horatio Nelson, admiral of the Mediterranean fleet, learned of this, he sailed to Algiers harbor with seven frigates. Without preamble, the British warships opened fire on the city with shells and "hot shot" that ignited fires everywhere. With flames blossoming throughout his city and buildings crashing down, Bobba offered to negotiate. Nelson ignored the offer. The heavy bombardment continued, and damage began to mount exponentially. The panicked dey sent a second embassy urging a parley. Nelson responded this time—with demands of his own. The dey must free all the British prisoners, pay a fine, promise never to insult British honor again, and compensate British citizens for any losses. Bobba agreed to everything.

For anyone paying attention, it was a textbook demonstration of how to deal with a belligerent Barbary regency.

Eaton, for one, certainly would have appreciated Nelson's forceful action. In February 1803, he had written that it was "absolutely necessary that the United States should once, and at once, show themselves on the *Barbary,* and not European coast; and in a manner to make themselves known."

Heading the third U.S. squadron that would soon arrive in the western Mediterranean, Commodore Edward Preble likewise would have applauded Nelson's swift reprisal, as well as Eaton's prophetic words.

IX

THE *PHILADELPHIA* DISASTER

A just comparison of our situation, is one man tied to a stake attacked by
another with arms.—believe me that it cannot be fully concieved but by
those who may sadly experience.
—Captain William Bainbridge of the *Philadelphia,* in a letter
to U.S. Consul General Tobias Lear

October 31, 1803, 9:00 a.m.

The *Philadelphia's* lookouts sounded the alarm: An unidentified xebec, a Mediterranean ship the size of a small
frigate, was cruising near the shore east of Tripoli. The mystery
ship's sentinels spotted the Americans about the same time. The
xebec raised a Tripolitan ensign as it hastened westward for
Tripoli's harbor, staying close to shore.

At that moment, Captain William Bainbridge undoubtedly
regretted having sent the smaller, shallower-draft *Vixen* to Cape
Bon ten days earlier to chase a corsair that had slipped out of
Tripoli harbor and past the blockade. The schooner's departure
left Bainbridge and his 44-gun frigate cruising alone near the capital city.

Unwilling to let the xebec go, Bainbridge ordered the *Philadel-*
phia to give chase. The frigate's 307 men edged toward their rendezvous with destiny.

• • •

After commanding the *Essex* under Dale in 1801–2, Bainbridge had returned to the United States to supervise construction of light warships and had missed Morris's incompetent tenure. The *Vixen* was one of the new ships. So were two others with Preble off Morocco—the *Siren* and *Nautilus*. A fourth, the *Argus,* commanded by Lieutenant Stephen Decatur, Jr., was due to arrive soon in the western Mediterranean.

Preble had dispatched the *Philadelphia,* under Bainbridge, and the *Vixen,* commanded by Lieutenant John Smith, to Tripoli while he dealt with a new Moroccan crisis. The emperor was upset over the loss of *Meshuda* and her cargo of weapons and powder, captured by Rodgers while its captain tried to sneak through the Tripoli blockade. Soliman Ben Mahomet had bombarded Consul James Simpson with demands that the *Meshuda* be returned to him. The Moroccans had grown tired of Simpson's inaction, and when Preble reached Gibraltar, he discovered that Morocco was at war with the United States for the second time in as many years.

The commodore had teamed the *Philadelphia* with the *Vixen,* liking the pairing of muscle and mobility. Preble knew it was important to continue to project U.S. power at Tripoli despite the Morocco emergency. In mid-September, Nicholas Nissen, the Danish consul, had reported that he hadn't seen a U.S. warship in three months, and that all of Tripoli's cruisers were in the harbor: four ships of 8–14 guns and thirteen smaller craft, including six gunboats. It was an excellent time to blockade the enemy's port and trap his best ships inside the picket.

The *Philadelphia* and *Vixen* reached Tripoli on October 7 and cruised for nearly two weeks before parting company. Now, with the *Vixen* a day's sail away, Bainbridge and his officers studied the ship's charts, confident they could pick their way through Tripoli harbor's tricky shoals and reefs as they pursued the xebec.

Unfortunately for Bainbridge, Kaliusa Reef, a long, narrow sandbar four and half miles east of the city and a mile and a half from shore, didn't appear on any of the *Philadelphia's* charts.

Born a year before the Revolutionary War and the fourth son of Dr. Absalom Bainbridge, president of the New Jersey Medical Society, William Bainbridge never was interested in medicine. At an early age, he found another calling: the sea. Brawny and bold, young Bainbridge was a natural leader. He quelled a mutiny on a Holland-bound merchantman at eighteen, and four years later put down another shipboard insurrection in Bordeaux. While captain of the 4-gun merchantman *Hope,* he repelled an attack by an English schooner off St. John's, Newfoundland, and forced it to strike its flag. But later, when the *Hope* was boarded by officers from an English warship, Bainbridge could only watch helplessly as one of his seamen was impressed into the Royal Navy. He vowed to the English captain that he would impress an English sailor the first chance he got—and did so, announcing to the captain of the merchantman that he boarded who he was and why he was taking the sailor.

Bainbridge had risen rapidly to command in the U.S. Navy. He was a seasoned, dedicated skipper, but he was unlucky. His name was linked irrevocably with the surrender of the *Retaliation* in 1798 off Guadaloupe and with the ignominious *George Washington* episode, when he unwillingly became the dey's courier, delivering tribute and a menagerie of exotic animals and slaves to Constantinople. So deep was his shame afterward that he had sought—and obtained—an audience with President Jefferson so that he could explain personally what had happened. He evidently could be persuasive when he wished, for when the Navy was scaled back to just nine captains in 1801, Bainbridge was one of them, even though he was twenty-seventh in seniority. But while he had been vindicated in both instances, he was haunted by the specters of ruin and disgrace.

October 31, 1803, 11:00 A.M.

Bainbridge was unable to head off the xebec before it reached Tripoli, so he tried to bring the *Philadelphia* close enough to shell her. While his crew took depth soundings, he studied the charts to make sure he didn't shoal the frigate. He got within cannon range of the xebec at a safe depth of 42 feet—the *Philadelphia* drew 18½ feet forward and 20½ aft—and opened fire. After a thirty-minute cannonade at long range, Bainbridge broke off the action and turned the *Philadelphia* seaward.

And then, to the horror of the ship's company, a loud, grating sound arose from the frigate's hull—the sound of wood rubbing on packed sand and rocks. The crew was staggered by a sharp jolt. The *Philadelphia* had run aground.

A boat was lowered to take soundings. The news was bad. The frigate was stuck on rocks and a sandbar in 12 feet of water forward and 17 aft. The Americans were less than 5 miles east of Tripoli and 1½ miles from shore. They had to get off the reef.

In Tripoli harbor, enemy gunboats stirred to life. Singly and in pairs, they approached the American frigate cautiously, like hyenas circling a wounded lion. The *Philadelphia* crew fired their deck guns toward them. Soon, nine gunboats had assembled in a loose semicircle around the *Philadelphia,* careful to keep out of the range of the deadly 24-pounders.

Bainbridge saw that with the frigate not so badly shoaled aft as forward, he might lay all the sails back and try backing off the reef. But when he did this, nothing happened. He ordered the crew to start water in the hold, then pump it out, hoping the rapid shift in ballast would shake the frigate loose. It didn't. Three anchors were cut away from the bows; water casks were drained. All the guns were thrown overboard except the quarterdeck cannons. The *Philadelphia* remained on the sandbar.

Suddenly their predicament worsened. Wind and waves drove the *Philadelphia* higher on the shoal, and she tipped sickeningly to one side so that none of her cannons could be trained on the gunboats. In an attempt to utilize the deck guns, the crew cut away part of the stern, but when they fired the cannons, sparks set the stern on fire. Only the most desperate firefighting measures prevented the entire ship from being consumed. In a last attempt to jar loose the frigate, Bainbridge ordered the foremast cut away. When it fell, it carried away the main topgallant mast with it. Yet the ship didn't budge.

Seeing the *Philadelphia*'s guns rendered impotent, the Tripolitan gunboats drew closer and began to fire on the frigate. Shots whistled through the *Philadelphia*'s rigging and damaged her remaining masts.

At 4:00 P.M., after attempting every trick known to him that might conceivably break the sandbar's hold on the *Philadelphia*, Bainbridge met with his officers. Their situation was hopeless, they agreed unanimously. If they made a stand and fought, there would be unnecessary casualties. They had to surrender. "Some Fanatics may say that blowing the ship up would have been the proper result," bristled Bainbridge in his report to Preble, anticipating the disapproving second-guessing to come. "I never presumed to think

I had the liberty of putting to death the lives of 306 souls because they were placed under my command."

If the ship were going to be surrendered, Bainbridge wanted it handed over stripped of everything of value and sinking. Cannons, arms, and ammunition were dumped overboard. Carpenters bored holes in the ship's bottom. When seawater was pouring into the hold, Bainbridge gave the order for the *Philadelphia* to strike flag—the second surrender of a U.S. Navy vessel; Bainbridge was responsible for both. "Misfortune necessitates me to make a communication, the most distressing of my life," the demoralized Bainbridge would begin his report to Navy Secretary Smith.

The *Philadelphia* crewmen, who had expected to stand and fight, were astonished and angered by their officers' decision. The sailor manning the ensign halyards refused Bainbridge's order to lower the flag, even when threatened by an officer with being run through by a sword; a midshipman pushed the crewman aside and performed the disgraceful duty himself. The Stars and Stripes crept down the mast as crewmen "begged of the captain and officers to raise it again, preferring even death to slavery," bitterly recounted Marine Private William Ray in his *Horrors of Slavery: or the American Tars in Tripoli.*

Upon seeing the American flag come down, the gunboats ceased their shelling, and, for long minutes, nothing happened. It soon became apparent that the Tripolitans weren't about to board the *Philadelphia* without reassurances that the Americans wouldn't resist. Bainbridge sent an officer in a boat over to persuade the enemy that it was safe to take possession of his frigate.

Bainbridge mustered the crew on deck and lectured them about the unhappy fate to which he was consigning them as prisoners of war. They would be paid while they were in captivity, he told them. He urged them to hope for a speedy ransom. He counseled them to behave well. The practical-minded sailors and Marines raced to their sleeping quarters and rummaged through their sea chests, putting on as much clothing as possible, expecting to take it into captivity with them. They were a ludicrous sight when they reemerged on deck in three or four shirts and multiple pairs of trousers, pockets stuffed with cached food.

The Tripolitans finally gathered up the nerve to board the *Philadelphia.* Once assured of the crew's docility, they became rapacious, pillaging unrestrainedly as the Americans watched. Soon their eyes fell on the comically attired crew, and all the carefully hoarded clothing was ripped away. The greedy Tripolitans fell to fighting among themselves for loot. To restore order, the Moslem officers with their swords sliced off the hands of some of their own men. As the tide tipped the frigate farther onto her side and the sun dipped toward the horizon, the Tripolitans shoved the Americans into boats and at swords' point forced them to row to town. Nearing shore, they pushed the sailors and Marines into the surf and made them swim and wade the rest of the way. The American prisoners arrived in Tripoli shivering and wet.

Their captors herded them into the bashaw's castle, through a gantlet of armed janissaries and into a large room, where they stood soaking wet, wiping the janissaries' spittle from their faces. The bashaw himself received them. Seated on a small throne, Yusuf wore a white turban decorated with ribbons, and a blue silk robe embroidered with gold and tinsel. His belt glittered with diamonds and bore two gold-mounted pistols and a gold-hilted sword, with a chain and scabbard. "He counted us, viewed us with a smile, and appeared highly pleased with us," wrote Jonathan Cowdery, a *Philadelphia* surgeon's mate. The crew was marched to a large, chilly storage room in another part of the castle and ordered to clear it out. For the months to come, it was to be their home. They slept on sailcloth that they spread over the hard, uneven ground.

The officers and midshipmen were quartered in Cathcart's former consular home. During their first days of captivity, they were permitted to walk on the rooftop terrace overlooking the harbor. From this vantage point, they witnessed a melancholy sight the next day: the badly listing *Philadelphia* surrounded by boats, men carrying off armloads of clothing and goods. It wasn't long before Cowdery was noting, "We could see these robbers running about town, with our uniform coats and other clothing on."

An even more demoralizing sight greeted them on November 2: the *Philadelphia,* supposedly reefed and scuttled, floating placidly in Tripoli harbor, free of Kaliusa Reef. Spurred to uncharacteristic industry by the prospect of such a fine prize, the Tripolitans had plugged the holes the *Philadelphia*'s carpenters had bored dutifully in her bottom. Almost as a reward for the Tripolitans' arduous labors, the weather gods cooked up a gale from the west that raised the sea level, enabling the frigate to float off the rocks. Now added to the Americans' misery was the tormenting realization that had Bainbridge held out forty hours, they could have sailed away. Tripolitan divers even managed to salvage the ship's guns from the harbor bottom. The bashaw now possessed a fully equipped 44-gun frigate.

And Bainbridge didn't know it, since Kaliusa Reef did not appear on his charts, but only a few hundred yards beyond where the *Philadelphia* had reefed was a navigable passage through the sandbar. Had he waited a few minutes longer before attempting to turn seaward, he would have passed through unscathed. But the passage didn't show up on Bainbridge's charts, either.

• • •

News of the U.S. naval catastrophe rolled like thunder through Barbary and across the Atlantic to the United States, while in the cramped consular house Bainbridge vacillated miserably between self-recrimination and defensiveness. "Had I not sent the Schooner from us, the Accident might have been prevented," he wrote Preble, adding quickly that he dispatched the *Vixen* to Cape Bon to protect American commerce. Striking the reef, he told his commander, "was as unexpected to me as if it had happened in the middle of the Mediterranean Sea." He would have made a stand had there been any reason to hope for victory or relief, he reported to Preble. "I trust that a want of Courage can never be imputed where there is no chance of resistance. . . ." To U.S. Consul General Tobias Lear, Bainbridge wrote: "A just comparison of our situation, is one man tied to a stake attacked by another with arms. Believe me that it cannot be fully concieved but by those who may sadly experience."

Bainbridge confidently told Smith that he expected an official inquiry to exonerate him, but privately despaired, certain his record was irrevocably stained and his Navy career over. "I have zealously served my Country and strenuously endeavored to guard against accidents, but in spite of every effort misfortune has attended me through my Naval life. Gaudaloupe and Algiers have witnessed part of them, but Tripoli strikes the death blow to my future Prospects. . . ." Bainbridge's torment moved his officers to draft a statement supporting his conduct.

Busy convoying, Preble didn't learn of the disaster until November 24, when he hailed the British merchant ship *Amazon* off Sardinia and was given a sketchy account of what had happened. He instantly grasped its import. "This affair distresses me beyond description and very much deranges my plans of operation for the present. I fear our national character will sustain an injury with the Barbarians." It destroyed his hopes of ending the war the next spring. He feared that Tunis or Algiers would exploit the squadron's weakened state by raiding U.S. shipping. Bainbridge's quick surrender in no way squared with the commodore's warrior code. "Would to God, that the Officers and crew of the *Philadelphia,* had one and all, determined to prefer death to slavery; it is possible such a determination might save them from either." To his brother Henry Preble, he wrote that Bainbridge never would have lost his ship had he kept the *Vixen* close by. But while his first communications to his captive captain were brusque, Preble never blamed him for losing his ship, and later he did his best to bolster Bainbridge's low spirits. "I have not the smallest doubt, but that you have *all* done everything which you conceived could be done, to get the ship off . . . and I most sincerely regret, that your exertions were not attended with success. . . . You may rest assured, that in me you have a *friend,* whose exertions shall *never* be wanting in endeavours to relieve you. . . ." Preble promised to do everything possible to ease the crew's plight and obtain their freedom. "Keep up a good heart and for God's sake do not despair. Your situation is bad indeed but I hope ere long, it will be better."

It was nearly five months before the bad news reached Washington, because Joseph Pulis, the U.S. naval agent at Malta, had fallen into the habit of not shipping mail to the United States, either because of sloth or mental incapacity—it was never clear which. Preble discovered months' worth of mail piled up in Pulis's office when he visited him in February 1804. They included

Preble's letters to the Navy secretary and Bainbridge, and even unshipped clothing and provisions for the *Philadelphia* prisoners. In disgust, Preble appointed William Higgins to replace Pulis, whom he said spoke no English—Preble never stated his nationality—and "has no respectability attached to his character."

Jefferson's political enemies blamed the *Philadelphia's* capture on his tightfisted fiscal policies. The Federalist-leaning New York *Evening Post,* founded by Alexander Hamilton in 1801, called it "a practical lesson in Jefferson's economy." The administration's critics claimed that had enough ships been on blockade duty, the *Philadelphia* never would have been lost. Jefferson was willing to capitalize on their outrage to obtain more money for warships. "This accident renders it expedient to increase our force and enlarge our expences in the Mediterranean beyond what the last appropriation for the Naval service contemplated." Within a week, Congress authorized him to spend up to $1 million in unappropriated money from the Treasury to build two ships with up to 16 guns and to hire gunboats.

Of more far-reaching significance, Congress established a special "Mediterranean Fund," whose sole purpose was to underwrite the war. Until now, no revenue had been earmarked exclusively to fight Tripoli. Financed with a 2.5 percent tax on all imports, the "Fund" was to remain operational until three months after ratification of a Tripoli peace.

U.S. diplomats in Europe enlisted Napoleon's intercession with the bashaw and Czar Alexander I's with the Turkish Porte to obtain the *Philadelphia* crew's release. The ministers' resourceful actions only irritated Jefferson, touchy about seeking diplomatic favors when he was trying to earn Europe's respect. "I have never been so mortified as to the conduct of our foreign functionaries," he raged to Madison. "They appear to have supposed that we were all lost now, without resource: and they have hawked us in *forma pauperis* begging alms at every court in Europe."

For months, Jefferson had been losing faith in the Navy's ability to chasten Tripoli and had all but abandoned his single-minded quest for a winner's peace. He was impatient to end the war, and willing to settle for less than complete victory if it couldn't be won soon. So while the president hoped Preble would soon appear off Tripoli and beat "their town about their ears," he was prepared to negotiate a peace with the bashaw if Preble failed.

The disheartening Dale and Morris squadrons had greatly diminished Jefferson's high hopes of winning a peace at no cost. On May 8, 1803, he had convened his Cabinet and asked, "Shall we buy peace with Tripoli?" The Cabinet, whose optimism had similarly been deflated by the squadron's lackadaisical perform-ance, responded unanimously, Yes. Upon learning of the *Philadel-phia's* loss, Jefferson had hedged his bets yet again by ordering preparations for a fourth Mediterranean squadron.

Tobias Lear, the former private secretary and close friend of George Washington, was the new Barbary consul general. He had crossed the Atlantic on the *Constitution* with Preble. Besides being instructed to parley with Yusuf if possible, he was loaded with $43,000 cash to buy the biennial and consular presents for Algiers's dey and to satisfy a $15,000 debt with Miciah Bacri, the dey's chief moneylender. And Tunis also would need Lear's attention, for it had no U.S. consul; Cathcart, shunned by the bashaw and dey, also had been rejected by Tunis's bey. He would soon resign. But, unexpectedly, it was Morocco that absorbed Lear and Preble's energies from the instant they touched at Gibraltar.

• • •

Two days after reaching the Mediterranean, Bainbridge had stumbled upon Morocco's war plans, possibly averting a full-blown war. Off Cape de Gatt on August 26, 1803, the *Philadelphia* had hailed the *Mirboha,* a 22-gun Moroccan cruiser. Oddly, or so it had struck Bainbridge, an American brig was keeping the *Mirboha* company. The *Celia,* claimed the *Mirboha's* commander, Ibrahim Lubarez, had decided to sail with him to Spain. He claimed that he had boarded, but had not detained her.

After this brief interview over open water, conducted in the typical fashion with speaking trumpets, Bainbridge was even more suspicious. He sent a lieutenant to the *Mirboha* to check for prisoners. Lubarez wouldn't allow him to come aboard. Now certain that Lubarez was lying, Bainbridge dispatched a boatload of armed men, and the *Mirboha* captain permitted them to board his ship. Belowdeck, they found the *Celia's* captain, Richard Bowen, and several crewmen—held as prisoners. Bowen's Boston ship had been captured nine days earlier 25 miles east of Malaga. When Bainbridge demanded to know by whose authority Lubarez had seized the American brig, the Moslem captain showed him unsigned orders that he said were issued by Tangier Governor Hashash Alcayde. The orders listed the nations whose ships Lubarez was authorized to capture. Leading off the enemies' list was "the Americans." After liberating the *Celia* and her crew, Bainbridge made the *Mirboha* a prize and Lubarez and his men prisoners.

The emperor deeply resented Rodgers's seizure of the *Meshuda* and America's refusal to return the ship and crew. James Simpson, the U.S. consul in Morocco, had predicted that Soliman Ben Mahomet would abandon diplomacy for aggression and warned on August 15 that two Moroccan frigates had sailed with sealed orders, most likely instructing them to hunt U.S. merchantmen. Bainbridge had spoiled Morocco's plan to force the *Meshuda's* release by retaking an American ship and its captor. The United States now possessed two Moroccan vessels instead of one.

Morocco was only one of a host of problems that beset Preble upon his arrival in Barbary. Algiers's dey was demanding brass cannons, Tunis was still clamoring for a frigate, and both were petulantly threatening war in so many words if their wishes were thwarted. And then there was waspish relationship with Rodgers, the interim commodore whom Preble was supposed to relieve. Enmity sprang up right away between the two strong-willed men over a petty issue: Preble flying the commodore's pennant on the *Constitution*. Rodgers objected to it. Preble informed Rodgers icily that the pennant's purpose was not to give offense to Rodgers, but to identify the ship as the squadron commander's vessel. He quoted pedantically from his orders naming him squadron commander. Rodgers shot back that while he wasn't offended personally by the pennant, "my feelings as an *officer* has been most sensibly injured." Then he came to the nub of the matter—that since Rodgers's commission as a naval officer preceded Preble's, he was senior to him, and not even the government could sanction Preble's showing disrespect for Rodgers. After their tempers cooled, the captains managed to conduct a proper, but chilly, professional relationship that carried them through until Rodgers's departure a few months later.

Alerted by Bainbridge to Morocco's hostile intentions, Preble sent the *Argus* and *Enterprise* to cruise off Morocco and warn away U.S.

merchantmen. Preble hovered off Tangier, awaiting Emperor Soliman Ben Mahomet's return from a tour of the countryside. It took weeks. The large imperial entourage traveled slowly, and river flooding slowed them further. Meanwhile, the almost-war with Morocco simmered, threatening to burst into a shooting war any day. The American merchantman *Hannah* and her crew were captured at Mogadore. Officers from the *Constitution* boarded the 30-gun Moroccan cruiser *Maimona* off the Spanish coast. Preble and Lear suspected she was hunting American merchantmen, although her captain presented a valid passport and claimed he was only sailing to Lisbon from Sallee, Morocco. Preble let him go.

Finally, the emperor arrived in the capital on October 4 with 2,500 cavalry, attendants, one of his lives, and his brother. Preble and the *Constitution* sailed into Tangier harbor the next day with the *New York, John Adams,* and *Nautilus,* and anchored in front of Tangier's fortress in a display of naval prowess. Preble made a show of clearing his ships for action. The squadron's guns were primed, and the crews kept at quarters all night. The emperor's troops reciprocated with their own martial show. More than 10,000 Moorish cavalry lined the beach for two and a half miles, turned toward the Americans in the harbor, then performed a facing maneuver and marched into Tangier, firing volleys as the emperor's band played a march. Tangier's fortress and the *Constitution* thundered cannon salutes at one another. The delighted emperor, taking in the dazzling panorama through his telescope, ordered ten bullocks, twenty sheep, four dozen fowl, and other provisions sent aboard the U.S. ships as a goodwill gesture. Preble, Lear, and two midshipmen went ashore to parley. Midshipman Ralph Izard was struck by the unpretentiousness of the emperor and his suite. He was "a small man, wrapped up in a woollen haik or cloak sitting upon the stone steps of an old castle in the middle of the streets, surrounded by a guard of very ill looking blacks with their [fire]arms covered with cloth to prevent rusting."

The negotiations proceeded smoothly. The emperor suspended hostilities immediately, and Preble and Lear agreed to release the *Mirboha* and *Meshuda.* Soliman then reratified the 1797 treaty made by his father, Maulay Sulaiman. He blamed the "misunder-standing" on his Tangier governor. As the two nations formalized the agreement on October 11, the emperor reminded Preble and Lear that he had not yet received the 100 gun carriages that Simpson had promised him a year earlier. They assured him they were on the way. The emperor had heard that before, but, in fact, the carriages really were en route to Morocco this time, although their arrival occasioned some disappointment. Many were built for 12-pound ordnance while Morocco's was nearly all 18- and 24-pound. All were designed for sea service, when they were wanted for fortress use. And each carriage came with just one wooden handspike for maneuvering the gun, instead of the usual two. When Simpson purchased additional handspikes, the gift was pronounced satisfactory.

Back in Tripoli's crumbling, verminous dungeons, the *Philadel-phia* crewmen suffered the indignities of their first days of cap-tivity in quiet misery. The morning after the surrender, a "frightful hag" appeared in the crew's quarters. Revered by the Tripolitans as a prophetess and sorceress, the old woman supposedly had pre-dicted the *Philadelphia's* shoaling and capture, then had made it happen with her incantations. The Americans shifted uneasily under her hard, appraising gaze, fearing the worst. She pointed to a black crewman, and he was led away—not to be punished or executed, but to become a cook for the castle's Mamelukes, although his mates didn't know that then. The captives were left to their hunger pangs and vain attempts to ward off the castle's chilly dampness. Exploitative Neapolitan vendors visited them next, peddling lagby—a whiskeylike liquor made from dates—at exorbitant prices, cheating them a second time when he made change.

Murad Reis made the trip to the dungeon to gloat over the Americans he hated so much. Was Bainbridge a coward, or was he a traitor? Tripoli's grand admiral wanted to know. When the crewmen replied that he was neither, Murad sneered, "Who with a frigate of 44 guns, and 300 men, would strike his colours to one solitary gunboat, must surely be one or the other." He said his men would never have tried to board the *Philadelphia,* and the wind eventually would have carried her off the sandbar.

While the crewmen received only subsistence rations from their captors—each day, two 12-ounce loaves of black barley bread, coarse and full of straw and chaff, and three-quarters of a gill (about 4 ounces) of oil; and every two weeks, a little beef or pork—they learned to sell the bread on the streets, at least during the more liberal periods of their captivity when they were permitted to leave the castle in groups. With the money they received for the bread, they bought enough vegetables at the market to feed three men. Organizing small mess teams, they made vegetable soup and ate it with the bread and oil they didn't sell. They improved their sleeping arrangements by making hammocklike rope beds that they hung from hooks they had anchored in the prison walls.

Tripolitan foremen called "drivers" abused the weary, undernourished men with whips and sticks to make them work hard every day. The fortunate few with skills valued by their captors built gunboats and bored cannon. But the rest carried pig iron, powder, and mortar for repairing the castle walls, toiled in the inhumane rock quarries, and were set to work at even more impossible tasks. Three days before Christmas 1803, the drivers marched 150 prisoners to the harbor to raise an old wreck buried to her scuppers in sand. From sunup until early afternoon they labored in frigid water up to their armpits. "The chilling waves almost congealed our blood, to flow no more," William Ray wrote. "The Turks seemed more than ordinarily cruel, exulting in our sufferings. We were kept in the water from sunrise until about two o'clock, before we had a mouthful to eat, or were permitted to sun ourselves." That night, they were forced to sleep on the ground in their wet clothes. Many of the captives became ill. Ray privately despaired over the ceaseless misery. "With such usage life became insupportable, and every night when I laid my head on the earth to sleep, I most sincerely prayed that I might never experience the horrors of another morning."

Even without a modern media serving up constant reminders of their agonizing plight, the *Philadelphia* captives were in their countrymen's thoughts and their prayers. John Greenleaf Whittier's sympathetic description of the captives in "Derne," although written after the war, reflects American sentiment at the time:

> Rough-bearded men, whose far-off wives,
> Wear out with grief their lonely lives;
> And youth, still flashing from his eyes
> The clear blue of New England skies,
> A treasured lock of whose soft hair
> Now wakes some sorrowing mother's prayer;

Or, worn upon some maiden breast,
Stirs with the loving heart's unrest!

John Morrison, a twenty-seven-year-old crewman, was mortally injured while loading timber into a wagon and carried on a litter to town. In the Americans' dungeon, he "lay three days in the most excruciating pain." An Algerian with supposed medical expertise examined him. When he was finished, he claimed nothing was wrong with Morrison and called him a shirker. Ray recounted what happened next. "He went to the dying man, told him to rise, called him an infidel and a dog, and struck him several times with his cane. How our men burned to immolate the ferocious villain." After three days, death ended Morrison's suffering.

"Behave like Americans, be firm and do not despair, the time of your liberations is not far distant," Preble wrote the crew. ". . . obstinately persist in your rights of being treated as prisoners and not as Slaves." But the Americans were in Tripoli now, and Tripolitans not infrequently treated their own people worse than they did the Americans. It was a land of absolutes: absolute power, the absolute authority of law, the absolutes of Islam. There were masters and slaves, freemen and captives. Justice was meted out with expeditious severity, as Ray was able to attest after witnessing capital punishment, Tripoli-style. A janissary cut off the victim's left hand and right foot with an ax shaped like a half moon, and then the victim's raw, twitching stumps were dipped in boiling pitch. He was dragged screaming out of the city and left to die in agony outside the gates.

The *Philadelphia*'s officers routinely were granted comforts and leisure the crewmen only could dream of. During their early captivity, they lived in Cathcart's old consular home. It was cramped, but no dungeon, and immeasurably superior to their men's quarters in the damp storeroom. The officers were excused from all manual labor. They were permitted to walk into town or the countryside, six at a time. They ate better food, too—none of the coarse black bread on which their men subsisted. Typically, they had two eggs and a piece of bread with rainwater for breakfast and supper, and beef or camel and sometimes boiled cabbage with rainwater for dinner. Nissen augmented their ration by bringing them pomegranates, dates, and oranges. They passed the time writing, and reading books that had been plundered from the ship and that they had bought back on the street, and others loaned them by Nissen. Besides availing themselves of their little library, the midshipmen attended classes in mathematics, navigation, and tactics, taught by their officers. "We have lost all relish for dainties except books which we are supplied with," Bainbridge reported. "Our prison represents a College of Students."

Because of their rank, Bainbridge and Cowdery, the surgeon, enjoyed the best treatment of all. The captain even was invited to a celebration of the end of Ramadan. He and Lieutenant David Porter were served sherbet and coffee, and conversed with the bashaw and his family and officers. Then they shared a similar repast with the prime minister, followed by tea, coffee, sherbet, cakes, and fruits with the foreign minister, Sidi Mohammed Dghies, a kind man who mediated the Americans' disputes with their captors.

Cowdery was drafted into Yusuf's service as the royal physician after treating the bashaw for blindness in one eye—unsuccessfully, it turned out; blindness was a relatively common curse of the Barbary Coast, due to the sun, blowing sand, biting insects, and improper care. With happier results, Cowdery attended to the bashaw's eleven-month-old son, who was suffering from an unspecified illness. When the boy recovered fully, a grateful Yusuf rewarded Cowdery by lending him a horse and servant so he could visit the royal gardens two miles from the capital city.

The crewmen's desperate misery pushed them into rash acts. After a month of captivity, a sailor cut his own throat. He didn't die; the Tripolitans interceded before he could finish the job. One hundred forty English-born crewmen signed a petition to Lord Nelson asking that he claim them as British subjects so they could go free. Marine First Lieutenant John Johnson reported to Commandant William Burrows that Nelson's ". . . Answer was, if he done anything in the Business, it would be to have the Rascels all hung. . . ." Five crewmen "turned Turk," which automatically freed them from captivity and excused them from hard labor. The first convert was John Wilson, the *Philadelphia*'s coxswain. He wasted no time making trouble for his former shipmates, telling the bashaw he had seen Bainbridge throw nineteen boxes of dollars and a bag of gold overboard before surrendering the *Philadelphia*. Bainbridge denied it. The bashaw threatened to flog Bainbridge's servant if the captain didn't tell him the truth. Bainbridge convinced him Wilson was lying, and Yusuf released the servant unharmed. Wilson became one of the captives' most abusive overseers.

X

A DARING COUNTERSTROKE

The most bold and daring act of the age.
—Horatio Nelson

Preble and the Mediterranean diplomats sprang into action to meet the American prisoners' emergency needs. The Danish consul, Nicholas Nissen, America's only dependable friend in Tripoli, supplied extra food, clothing, books, and bedding, and served as a conduit for money, clothing, and goods shipped by U.S. consuls and Preble's agents. From Leghorn, Cathcart arranged for $3,000 to be sent to distribute among the prisoners. Lear opened an account in Tunis, authorizing Bainbridge to draw up to $10,000 from it. O'Brien, still in Algiers but with no official capacity, sent Bainbridge $2,000 in a box by Spanish ship. Charles Pinkney, a minister in Madrid, arranged with French and British agents to supply the prisoners with up to $4,000. Preble instructed William Higgins on Malta to buy whatever the captives needed, and to send Bainbridge regular stipends.

From the officers' prison in the U.S. consul's former home,

Bainbridge was able to communicate with Preble, although his letters were scrutinized—as was all American correspondence—by Tripolitan censors, to ensure that intelligence harmful to Tripoli did not make it onto the neutral vessels that carried American correspondence to and from Tripoli. Determined to slip the information past the censors anyway, Bainbridge looked for ways to conceal intelligence in his letters to the commodore. He first tried embedding codes and ciphers in otherwise innocent letters, and this worked until the Tripolitan censors became suspicious when they couldn't make sense of some of his letters and showed them to the bashaw. Yusuf ordered the censors to hold up any correspondence that wasn't written clearly. Bainbridge had to invent a new method.

He never revealed how he hit upon "sympathetic ink," the "invisible ink" of spy and detective fiction. After experimenting with milk and diluted lemon and lime juice, Bainbridge determined that lime juice was the most reliable medium. In early 1804 he began sending Preble intelligence written in "sympathetic ink" on the envelopes in which Nissen brought books to the officers, and between the lines of his routine letters to Preble. The censors' eyes discerned nothing unusual when they scanned Nissen's plain envelopes or read Bainbridge's reports to Preble. But when warmed over a flame, the envelopes and letters yielded their secrets as if by magic.

Nearly simultaneously, Preble, Bainbridge, and Lt. Stephan Decatur, Jr. independently proposed destroying the *Philadelphia* in Tripoli harbor, right under the bashaw's nose. Bainbridge suggested to Preble on December 5, 1803, that a disguised merchant ship could be sailed right up to the *Philadelphia,* and men hidden aboard could then destroy her. Surprise and stealth were paramount. He ruefully counseled against trying to sail the frigate out of the harbor "owing to the difficulty of the Channel." On December 10, at least a week before Preble would have received Bainbridge's letter, Preble himself was recommending the same bold action to Navy Secretary Smith. "I shall hazard much to destroy her—it will undoubtedly cost us many lives, but it must be done." Two decades later, when Decatur's widow was pressing a claim in Congress, Lieutenant Charles Stewart swore it was Decatur's idea; Decatur, he said, volunteered his schooner, the *Enterprise,* for the mission, but Preble did not want to risk one of his warships. He favored using a vessel whose loss would not matter, perhaps a captured enemy ship.

Tripoli's possession of the *Philadelphia* wasn't going to upset the western Mediterranean balance of power right away. A month after the frigate's capture, the bashaw was looking for a buyer, because he lacked trained seamen to crew her properly. U.S. consuls throughout Barbary were hearing that Yusuf might sell the frigate to Algiers or Tunis. But it made little difference to Preble whether the warship was put into service by Tripoli, Tunis, or Algiers. He well knew that America might find itself at war with any of them at any time. By mid-December, he had resolved to burn the *Philadelphia.* He methodically began gathering the tools for the mission.

Preble needed firsthand intelligence about Tripoli's harbor defenses, the *Philadelphia's* exact location, and the extent of the guard placed on her. While Bainbridge's intelligence was invaluable, Preble wanted to see the harbor for himself. Two days before Christmas 1803, he and Decatur sailed to the edge of the harbor and made a reconnaissance with telescopes. When Dale's squadron first called at Tripoli in 1801, the harbor forts scarcely mustered enough cannons to fire a proper salute. Preble and Decatur now counted 115 operable cannons on the parapets of the city's fortresses, testimony to Yusuf's progress in turning his regency into a first-class Barbary military power. Most importantly, Preble noted that the *Philadelphia* had been brought into the harbor within range of those guns. Clearly, to have any hope of succeeding, the mission would need to be executed with stealth, surprise, and speed.

While snooping around the edges of the harbor, Preble and Decatur had the good fortune to happen upon one of their mission's critical components, absent until this point: an expendable vessel to carry the commandos into Tripoli harbor. The *Mastico* was flying British colors when they intercepted her as she was leaving Tripoli, but the ketch was Tripolitan, with a Turkish master. The crew and passengers consisted of 7 Greeks, 4 Turks, 12 Tripolitan soldiers and officers, and 43 black slaves. The ship actually belonged to the bashaw; 23 of the slaves were intended as presents from Yusuf to the Turkish grand admiral in Constantinople. The other 20, belonging to Tripolitan merchants and ship's officers, were to be sold.

Under interrogation, a *Mastico* officer admitted having served on one of the gunboats that had harried the *Philadelphia* into surrendering. Preble's men searched the ketch, looking for loot from the *Philadelphia*. They turned up a sword and belt belonging to Lieutenant Porter, and a gold watch. "I believe from circumstances that not only the Tripoline Soldiers but the Turkish captain of this Vessel was active in boarding the *Philadelphia* and plundering the Officers," Preble wrote Bainbridge. He brought the ship and captives to Syracuse, his new operations base.

Preble had shifted the squadron's home from Gibraltar to what he believed was one of the best harbors in the Mediterranean. Meat, vegetables, fruit, candles, and rice were cheaper in Syracuse than even in the United States. Desertions had become a major problem in the squadron, but Syracuse afforded no hiding places, as did Gibraltar and Malta, where the British fleet always welcomed fugitive American sailors. Syracuse's inhabitants were friendly, and the government was grateful for the U.S. presence because it would keep away marauding Tripolitan corsairs. At no charge, it supplied moorings and warehouse space for storing boats and spars.

With custody of the 60 Turks, Tripolitans, and slaves from the *Mastico,* Preble believed his prospects for ransoming the *Philadelphia* captives at a reasonable cost had improved markedly. He also was certain the bashaw was hearing the rumors circulating throughout Barbary of his preparations for a summer offensive. Before the *Mastico*'s capture, Lear and O'Brien had quoted sums ranging to $500,000, based on comparisons of America's situation with other nations', and consultations with moneylenders in Algiers. Preble was sure the price had since dropped, and set out to learn what the bashaw was now demanding. Yusuf's agent at Malta laid out the new terms: swapping the 60 *Mastico* prisoners for 60 *Philadelphia* captives, paying $100,000 to free the 240 remaining captives (2 had died, 5 turned Turk), and giving the bashaw a schooner for the *Philadelphia.* The proposal tempted the commodore so far as to suggest giving the bashaw a bad schooner. But Preble decided that he could get even better terms by first attacking Tripoli.

· · ·

February 16, 1804

At twilight, the Americans and their Sicilian pilot, Salvador Catalano, scanned Tripoli harbor from the deck of the former *Mastico*, now the *Intrepid*. Scarcely visible nearby lay the *Intrepid's* shadowy companion. As the darkness deepened and the sliver of moon—shaped like the crescent on the Ottoman flag—spilled out a ghostly light to steer by, the ketch drifted into the silent harbor, headed for the largest ship. As they glided toward the big frigate, the Americans could see the outline of her bare topmasts, stripped of sails. Her lower yards lay on the gunwales. A few cruisers bobbed at anchor nearby in the gentle swell. The ketch, armed with only four cannons, appeared at first glance to be a typical Mediterranean trader. Decatur and the handful of men on deck with him all were outfitted in the loose-fitting garb of the region's natives. But belowdecks were hidden dozens of commandos, poised to pour from the passageways with knives and swords when given the command. Everyone knew tonight's password; it was easy enough to remember. The password was *"Philadelphia."*

Four future American naval heroes sailed on the *Intrepid:* Decatur, Lieutenant James Lawrence, and Midshipmen Thomas Macdonough and Charles Morris. All of them would forever be remembered for their deeds during the War of 1812, where Lawrence would lose his life on the *Chesapeake*. But this mission belonged to Decatur. He had mustered the seventy volunteers on the balky little ketch, led them through a weeklong gale off the coast that had tested the crew's mettle to its limit, and brought them safely into the enemy's harbor.

Who was the U.S. Navy's first bona fide hero, whose name would grace twenty American communities and several ships, who would die in a famous 1820 duel, and whose epitaph would read: "The pride of the Navy, the glory of the Republic"? Stephen Decatur, Jr. was born in 1779 in Worcester County, Maryland, where his parents had moved after the British occupied their home city, Philadelphia. He was the son of a U.S. naval officer and the grandson of Etienne Decatur, a French naval lieutenant who came to America to recover his health, married, and died, leaving an infant son. Etienne's son, Stephen Decatur, Sr., was a privateer captain during the Revolutionary War and a captain in the U.S. Navy during the Quasi-War, when he became responsible for the first capture of an enemy ship by a U.S. Navy vessel; near the mouth of Delaware Bay, he forced the French schooner *Le Croyable* to strike its flag. *Le Croyable* became the *Retaliation*, the ship Bainbridge surrendered in November 1798. In another irony, Captain Decatur, at the request of Philadelphia's citizens, became the first commander of the subscription frigate *Philadelphia*, the second ship Bainbridge surrendered and which Decatur's son now was intent on destroying.

Stephen Decatur, Jr. grew up in Philadelphia, where he spent his summers swimming in the Delaware River. He was a thin, sickly boy with curly black hair, dark eyes—and a racking cough. When he was eight, Stephen sailed to Bordeaux with his father, was cured of his cough by the sea air, and contracted a lifelong love of the sea. After attending the University of Pennsylvania for one year, he went to work for Gurney & Smith, the same company that employed his father as a merchant captain and that served as agents for the new U.S. Navy and its first frigate, the 44-gun *United States*, built by Joshua Humphreys. Decatur helped equip the *United States*, getting in on the ground floor of the Navy. When the frigate was completed, he rode it into the Delaware.

Then he joined its crew as a midshipman, with Richard Somers and Charles Stewart, schoolboy friends from Episcopal Academy. They sailed off to the Quasi-War under the legendary Captain John Barry.

By the time he arrived in the Mediterranean for the Barbary War—where he was later joined by a younger brother, Lieutenant James Decatur—Stephen Decatur was known for his dash, boldness, fearlessness, and coolness under fire. He was a noted duelist. He settled his first affair of honor in 1799 with an English merchant sailor, whom he shot in the hip, with Somers as his second. Later, he was Somers's second at one of the most bizarre duels ever fought. Decatur inadvertently started the trouble by calling his friend a "fool" while joking around at dinner one day. Somers accepted the jibe in the proper spirit, but the other junior officers did not; they snubbed Somers when he failed to take offense and challenge his old friend Decatur. The shunning so angered Somers that he decided to issue a challenge after all—to his hypercritical messmates, all six of them, one after the other. The first duelist shot him in the right arm, and the second winged him in the thigh, causing him to faint from loss of blood from the large-bore wound. Decatur urged his friend to give it up or to yield his place to him, but Somers refused, insisting on continuing from his seat on the floor, although he could not even hold his pistol firmly. With Decatur squatting beside him and steadying his pistol for him, Somers wounded the third officer, and there it ended.

In the Mediterranean, Decatur served under Bainbridge on the *Essex* in Dale's squadron and under Barron on the *New York* in Morris's. Before he was sent home as a result of Joseph Bainbridge's deadly duel with the Maltese governor's secretary, Decatur and Macdonough had an adventure in Syracuse one night, when three unfortunate robbers accosted them on the street. The trio quickly discovered they had picked two victims who happened to be armed with sharp swords and who exulted in combat. Decatur and Macdonough wounded two of the highwaymen, and Macdonough chased the third onto a rooftop. The cornered robber hurled himself to his death rather than face the lieutenant's bloodied sword.

The "secret expedition," as Preble called the clandestine mission, consisted of the *Intrepid,* with Decatur and his volunteers, supported by the 16-gun *Siren,* commanded by Decatur's friend, Lieutenant Charles Stewart. Decatur had assembled his *Enterprise* crew and requested volunteers for a mission. As a testament to the high esteem in which Decatur's men held their youthful commander, the entire ship's company had stepped forward. Stewart encountered the same reaction when he asked the *Siren's* crew for ten volunteers for an undisclosed operation.

In company with the *Siren,* the *Intrepid* left Syracuse on February 3 with 71 men: 12 officers and midshipmen, 5 of them from the *Constitution;* 50 seamen; 8 Marines; and the *Constitution's* pilot, Salvador Catalano. The *Siren's* crewmen were not told the purpose of their mission until they were at sea the next morning. They gave three loud cheers when they learned they were going to finally strike back at the bashaw. Midshipman Ralph Izard wrote proudly to his mother: "We shall astonish the Bashaw's weak mind with the noise of shot falling about his ears. Perhaps some shot more lucky than the rest may reach his heart & free our countrymen from Slavery."

Preble's instructions called for the *Intrepid* crew to board the *Philadelphia* and subdue the frigate's Tripolitan crew as quietly as possible—with cold steel. "It will be well in order to prevent alarm to carry all by the Sword." The assault force would set fire to the gunroom berths, cockpit storerooms, and the "birth deck," and then aim the 18-pound deck guns down the hatches and blow out the bottom. Boats from the *Siren* would roam the harbor, destroying targets of opportunity—any moored corsairs they happened upon—and then would cover the *Intrepid*'s withdrawal.

The strike force arrived off Tripoli on February 8 in heavy seas and wind. Catalano scouted the harbor alone in a small boat and returned shaking his head over the weather. If they went in, he said glumly, they would never come out again. Decatur postponed the mission as conditions worsened rapidly. Seas became so rough that the *Siren* was unable to weigh anchor; swinging capstan bars flattened and injured several crewmen when they attempted to do so. Daybreak found the *Siren* still struggling to weigh anchor in the wild, battering waves. Fearing discovery by the Tripolitans, Stewart finally ordered the anchor cut away. The ships went to sea to weather the gale. It lasted a week.

The *Intrepid* was small, frail, and a poor sailor in bad weather. Her officers and crew took turns on the ship's pumps as the craft bucked and shuddered in the towering seas. Accommodations were cramped and uncomfortable. When they weren't busy trying to keep the ketch afloat, all that the men were able to do was lie down—Decatur, the other officers, and the surgeon in the tiny cabin; six midshipmen and the pilot on a platform over the starboard water casks; and the eight Marines over the portside casks. The rest of the crew was hunkered down in the hold, shut off from light and air, among tumbling crates and scurrying rats. There was little to eat, as a consequence of having been provisioned with rotten beef. The most recent beef shipment had arrived at Syracuse in the "worst sort of fish barrels," with the pickling leaking and some beef already spoiled. Preble had disgustedly thrown most of it overboard. Yet some barrels evidently had made it onto the *Intrepid*. The commando crew was reduced to eating biscuits and water.

The storm finally subsided on February 15, and the ships approached Tripoli again. They missed the port in the dark that night, but at sunset the next day they stood just outside the harbor. The *Intrepid* slowly approached the mole, flying English colors, with Decatur and his men using weighted draglines to delay their arrival until after nightfall. The British consul raised the royal ensign on shore in welcome.

Another gale was coming from the north. To avoid being trapped in the harbor by the weather, Decatur launched the mission a half hour early. Decatur divided his force into teams, each assigned a specific task. Lieutenant Lawrence and Midshipmen Macdonough and Alexander Laws were to lead ten men to fire the berth deck and forward storeroom. Midshipman Morris and eight men were to set the cockpit and after storeroom ablaze. Midshipmen Izard and Rowe were to take fifteen men and hold the *Philadelphia's* deck against a counterattack. Midshipman Thomas Anderson of the *Siren* would cruise alongside the frigate in a boat and cut down any enemy crewmen trying to escape. Lieutenant Jonathan Thorn and Gunner William Hook would remain on the *Intrepid,* ready to send more powder and combustibles to the *Philadelphia* if needed. Also staying behind would be Surgeon's Mate Lewis Heerman and seven men, to guard the *Intrepid* in case of a surprise counterattack.

Preble had handpicked Catalano, his flagship's pilot, to guide the *Intrepid*. The thirty-two-year-old Sicilian knew Tripoli harbor's shoals, sandbars and tricky currents from his years of sailing merchant ships between Tripoli and Malta. Now, as the *Intrepid* drew within hailing distance of the *Philadelphia*, Catalano's presence paid double dividends. A voice in the darkness called out to him, in Barbary's lingua franca—a mix of Arabic, Berber, and Mediterranean dialects in which Catalano was fluent—to state his business. Replying in the same dialect, Catalano said he was a trader who had lost his anchors in a gale at Cape Mesurado. He asked permission to run a line to the *Philadelphia*.

It was 9:30 P.M.

As the ketch edged toward the stripped-down frigate, from their hiding places below deck, the crewmen could hear Catalano talking to the *Philadelphia* officer about the weather and the lost anchors. They fingered their swords and dirks nervously—only edged weapons would be used on this night—and double-checked the powder and combustibles to ensure they were ready to be fired quickly. They made sure they all had candles, which they would light after capturing the ship, to illuminate the places where they would set the fires.

The *Philadelphia's* officer on deck asked Catalano about the mysterious ship everyone in the harbor could see lurking offshore. The Sicilian had a ready answer—she was the *Transfer*, an overdue Tripolitan ship. That and his story about the lost anchors evidently satisfied the Tripolitan. He gave the *Intrepid* permission to moor beside the *Philadelphia* for the night. A boat crewed by *Intrepid* sailors disguised as Mediterranean merchant seamen tensely towed a rope from the ketch to the frigate, fearing discovery at any moment. When the rope was secured to the frigate's forechains, the *Intrepid's* deck hands hauled on it, bringing the ketch snug against the *Philadelphia*.

And then, from the darkness came the heart-stopping alarm the American sailors had all dreaded: "Americanos!"

Instantly, the *Philadelphia*'s gun ports swung open. The commandos could hear the tampions being knocked from the cannons.

"Board!" shouted Decatur. The shock force surged toward the frigate with Decatur leading. While leaping to the *Philadelphia*, Decatur slipped, and it was Morris who claimed the honor of being the first aboard, with Decatur and Laws close behind. The Americans swiftly formed a line across the deck and attacked the Tripolitans with swords and knives.

The enemy's bloodcurdling screams shattered the harbor's nighttime tranquillity. Within ten minutes, before the enemy crew could fire a single cannon, the deck was littered with dead Tripolitans. Some escaped by leaping overboard and casting off in a boat, which Lieutenant Anderson intercepted. His men killed several crewmen.

The *Philadelphia* was back in American hands.

Decatur fired a rocket, the prearranged signal to the *Siren* that he had seized the *Philadelphia*. The assault teams lit their candles and went to work burning the frigate.

If the screams didn't awaken them to the fact that they were under attack, the rocket and lit candles unmistakably did. The Tripolitans opened up with their fortress cannons. Crewmen from the two nearby corsairs, both within easy cannon-fire range, peppered the commandos with inaccurate small-arms fire, but the corsairs' cannons, which might have done real damage, inexplicably remained silent.

The *Philadelphia* went up so fast that the flames chased the boarders from below deck, shooting out of portholes and from the spar deck hatchways. The blaze arced into the rigging as the

Americans fled to the *Intrepid*, already beginning to pull away as tongues of fire leaped out at her.

Decatur was the last to leave. He looked around the burning deck one more time and flung himself into the *Intrepid's* rigging. As she swung away, a round from a shore battery whistled through her topgallant sail.

The attackers hastened to escape the harbor. In the two boats towing the ketch, the American crewmen strained at their oars, and the *Intrepid's* sweeps also dug deep into the water. The rowers watched flames hungrily lick up the *Philadelphia's* masts receding behind them. The frigate's guns, loaded for harbor defense, suddenly began firing themselves, and, almost as if making a last defiant gesture, she blasted a full broadside into the city.

Morris described the sight of the burning frigate as "magnificent"; the flames climbing the rigging and masts formed "columns of fire, which, meeting the tops, were reflected into beautiful capitals." A little later, the frigate's cables gave way and the dying hulk drifted under the bashaw's castle. It burned there all night long.

With seamless precision, the Americans had captured and destroyed a frigate in an enemy harbor, within range of 115 fortress guns and two warships, and escaped—all inside twenty-five minutes, with only one man slightly wounded. They had killed at least twenty enemy soldiers and taken one prisoner. The exploit would have embroidered the record of any commando unit, in any era.

Five miles away on the *Siren*, Stewart watched the *Philadelphia's* topmasts fall. He hadn't gotten into the fight. The *Intrepid's* early embarkation had thrown off the attack timetable. Thirty *Siren* crewmen in two boats had set off for the harbor, only to meet the

Intrepid as she was heading out to sea. They turned back without getting a chance to damage other enemy ships in the harbor. The two ships met off Tripoli about 1:00 A.M. and set sail together for Syracuse. At daybreak, they were 40 miles away from Tripoli, yet they still could see the light from the burning frigate. The *Philadelphia* burned to the waterline. Her ribs weren't found until 1903.

On February 19, lookouts at Syracuse announced the approach of two ships. The quarterdecks of all the squadron's vessels blossomed with field glasses scanning the horizon. To Preble's immense relief, it was the *Intrepid* and the *Siren*. Having received no messages from Stewart and Decatur since they had left Syracuse two weeks before, Preble was full of gnawing fears and questions. At least now they had safely returned. The commodore signaled impatiently, "Have you succeeded?"

"Yes," the *Siren* answered.

The commandos sailed triumphantly into Syracuse harbor to loud cheers from the crews of the *Constitution, Vixen,* and *Enterprise.* Stewart and Decatur wasted no time in boating to the *Constitution.* They reported to their commander that they had destroyed the *Philadelphia* without losing a single man. While Preble noted later that day in his memo book, with his customary terseness, "*Syren* and *Intrepid* arrived having executed my orders," he was more fulsome in his praise when reporting to Navy Secretary Smith: "Their conduct in the performance of the dangerous service assigned them, cannot be sufficiently estimated—It is beyond all praise."

The *Philadelphia's* destruction in Tripoli harbor electrified Europe and America. From the *Victory* off Toulon, Admiral Horatio Nelson called it "the most bold and daring act of the age." Pope

above: The U.S. Navy schooner *Enterprise* (right) defeats the Tripolitan warship *Tripoli*, on August 1, 1801, in the first battle of the Barbary War. (Naval Historical Center).
below: Lt. Andrew Sterrett, the *Enterprise* commander, was a demanding officer who once ran a seaman through with his sword for cowardice in battle. (Naval Historical Center).

top: The U.S. Navy frigate *Philadelphia* ran aground in Tripoli harbor on Oct. 31, 1803. The disaster gave Tripoli a frigate and 307 American prisoners. (Naval Historical Center).

above (left): Upon surrendering the *Philadelphia,* Capt. William Bainbridge owned the unhappy distinction of having commanded the only two U.S. naval vessels captured during wartime. (Naval Historical Center).

above (right): Commodore Edward Preble, the Barbary War's most effective American naval leader, was dismayed by the loss of the *Philadelphia,* but quickly set into motion plans for her destruction. (Naval Historical Center).

Boarding the Philadelphia.

above (left): Lt. Stephen Decatur's crew boards the *Philadelphia* before setting her ablaze under the enemy's nose on February 16, 1804. (Naval Historical Center).

above (right): Lt. Stephen Decatur led the daring mission to destroy the *Philadelphia*, becoming an international hero. (Naval Historical Center).

left: The *Philadelphia* burns in Tripoli harbor. (Naval Historical Center).

above: Commodore Preble's squadron enters Tripoli harbor on August 3, 1804, to destroy enemy shipping and fortifications in what became known as the Battle of the Gunboats. (Naval Historical Center).

right: Lt. Stephen Decatur's deadly struggle during the Battle of the Gunboats with the Mameluke captain who Decatur believed fatally wounded his brother, James. (Naval Historical Center).

above: The fireship *Intrepid* mysteriously exploded September 4, 1804, while on a mission to destroy shipping in Tripoli harbor, killing all 13 crewmen. It was America's last naval offensive of the war. (Naval Historical Center).

below: William Eaton, former U.S. Army captain and consul to Tunis, planned a surprise attack on eastern Tripoli in 1805 with the Tripolitan ruler's deposed brother, Hamet Karamanli. (Naval Historical Center).

above: William Eaton (right) and Hamet Karamanli (left) led an invasion force of U.S. marines, dissident Tripolitans, Arabs and European mercenaries 520 miles through the desert to the outskirts of Derna, Tripoli. (Naval Historical Center).

below: Marine Lt. Presley O'Bannon, William Eaton's most trusted officer, planted the Stars and Stripes atop the battlement at Derna, the first American flag-raising on hostile foreign soil. (Naval Historical Center).

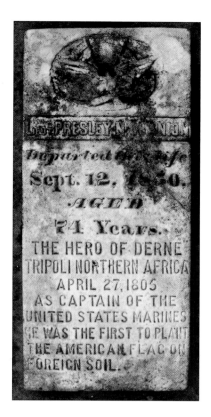

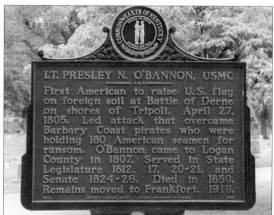

Lt. Presley O'Bannon's headstone and historical marker in a cemetery in Frankfort, Kentucky. (Photo by Walter Chisholm).

right: The Tripoli Memorial, the oldest U.S. military monument, dedicated to the six naval officers killed during the Barbary War. It stands behind Preble Hall at the U.S. Naval Academy in Annapolis, Maryland. (Photo by Brian Greenlee).

below: During a 1949 ceremony, markers were placed at the Tripoli gravesites of five *Intrepid* crewmen. Among those present were (l-r) Captain William Marshall, commander of the USS *Spokane;* Orpay Taft, U.S. consul to Tripoli; Rear Admiral Richard H. Cruzen, division commander; and Joseph Karamanli, Tripoli's mayor and a direct descendant of Yusuf Karamanli, the nation's ruler during the Barbary War. (Naval Historical Center).

Pius VII was moved to extol the actions of Decatur and his men: "The American commander, with a small force, and in a short space of time, has done more for the cause of Christianity than the most powerful nations of Christendom have done for ages!"

This was what Jefferson had longed for all these twenty years: to show the world the United States was different from the Old World, that it was a nation of dauntless men, that the ship that bore Decatur and his crew to glory was aptly named and embodied the new nation's spirit. He undoubtedly warmed to Consul George Davis's report of the reaction at Tunis: ". . . it is the only occurrence, which has forced them to view the American character with proper respect."

In America, Decatur quickly became the new Navy's most celebrated hero. He was promoted to captain over the heads of other, more senior lieutenants, making him at twenty-five the youngest naval officer to hold that rank. Congress commended Decatur formally, awarded him a sword, and rewarded him and his crew with two months' extra pay. A silent play written for the occasion, "Preparations for the Recapture of the Frigate *Philadelphia,*" began with the song "Hail Columbia," and ended with a procession honoring the *Intrepid* and her crew.

Francis Scott Key was moved to pen a song to the tune "To Anacreon in Heaven." "To Anacreon" was originally composed in the 1770s in Britain by John Stafford Smith for a London gentlemen's drinking club, the Anacreontic Society, to honor its namesake, Anacreon, the convivial bard of ancient Greece. In 1798, Tom Paine wrote different words to the music and called it "Adams and Liberty"; it was a hugely popular political song. Key's new, forgettable lyrics, which appear in his works under the simple title "Song," were sung at a banquet honoring the *Intrepid* crew. A decade later, the British attack on Fort McHenry inspired Key to write new lyrics to the old tune. He called it "The Star-Spangled Banner." One of the verses honoring America's Barbary heroes:

In conflict resistless, each toil they endur'd,
'Till their foes shrunk dismay'd from the war's desolation:
And pale beam'd the Crescent, its splendor obscur'd
By the light of the star-spangled flag of our nation,
    Where each flaming star
    Gleam'd a meteor of war,
And the turban'd head bowed to the terrible glare,
Now, mixed with the olive, the laurel shall wave,
And form a bright wreath for the brows of the brave.

Twenty years later, after both Preble and Decatur had died, the question that had long been debated by Navy men in ships' messes and harbor taverns suddenly captured the attention of Congress: Could the *Philadelphia* have been saved? Susan Decatur made the issue timely by filing a claim, as Stephen's widow, to government prize money for the *Philadelphia*. Her claim asserted that the frigate could have been taken intact, and that Stephen Decatur always believed that he could have towed the frigate out of the harbor. Salvador Catalano, the *Intrepid*'s pilot, also stated that he believed all along that she was salvageable, and had shared his opinion with Decatur moments before she was burned. But, he said, Preble's orders prevented them from making the attempt.

Other crew members, however, filed affidavits asserting that it would have been impossible to save the ship. Her sails were unrigged, there was no one to man her, and she was moored near two corsairs and within range of the fortress cannons.

Mediterranean diplomat M. M. Noah urged the government to pay Mrs. Decatur's claim, evidently as a gesture to a naval hero's widow, for he also pointed out that it didn't really matter whether the *Philadelphia* could have been saved or not; America made a stronger statement by burning her.

The night of the commando attack, the American captives were jarred awake by screaming, shouting, and the rumble of the bashaw's castle cannons. The commotion also awakened the *Philadelphia's* officers at the consul's house, where they flung open the windows facing the harbor and beheld the spectacle of flames swallowing their ship. How it came about remained a great mystery to them all until the next day.

At daybreak the next morning, the crewmen's keepers rushed into their prison and began beating everyone they could lay hands on, "hissing like serpents of hell." As the reason for their fury gradually dawned on the Americans, they could not contain their exultation. Their obvious high spirits over the bashaw's loss of his prize served as a goad to every Tripolitan they encountered. "Every boy we met in the streets would spit on us and pelt us with stones; our tasks were doubled, our bread withheld and every driver exercised cruelties tenfold more rigid and intolerable than before." Their captors withheld the twice-monthly ration of pork and beef and confined the American officers to their quarters. Cowdery, forbidden to could visit patients, observed, "The Turks appeared much disheartened at the loss of their frigate."

The bashaw, who had watched her burn from his castle, summoned country militia to the city, expecting a full-scale assault by American troops. The city ramparts were hastily repaired, but when the soldiers tried to mount cannons salvaged from the burned hulk, the gun carriages broke down and one of the guns exploded, killing and wounding five soldiers.

More guards were placed over all the captives, and the officers were summarily moved out of the relative comfort of the consul's home into the castle. Their new home was a large, smoky room illuminated by a single grated skylight. "I have seen the Sea four times in five months," Bainbridge grumbled to Preble in July 1804. "Close kept under lock & key."

Six weeks after the raid, Preble returned to Tripoli with the *Constitution* and *Siren* to find out whether the bashaw wished to parley. Yusuf was more intransigent than ever, refusing to exchange prisoners and demanding at least $500,000 for the captives and peace. One reason for the stiff terms was that the Tripolitans believed that Decatur and his commandos had massacred some of the *Philadelphia's* Tripolitan crew. Three bodies had washed up "covered with wounds," Tripoli's foreign minister, Sidi Mohammed Dghies, informed Bainbridge, asking, "How long has it been since Nations massacred their Prisoners?" The bashaw wanted to question the Tripolitan prisoner in U.S. custody.

Preble refused to bring the prisoner ashore and said Decatur had reported no massacre. The boarders had fought with edged weapons, and "people who handle dangerous weapons in War, must expect wounds and Death, but I shall never countenance or encourage wanton acts of Cruelty." Preble also declared that he would sooner sacrifice all the *Philadelphia* prisoners than submit to unfavorable terms. The bashaw forbade Preble to send clothing ashore for the captives; he said such items could only be landed in a neutral vessel.

Preble sailed away and resumed preparations for the summer attacks on Tripoli that he was planning.

XI

PREBLE'S FIGHTING SQUADRON

I find hand to hand is not childs play, 'tis kill or be killed.
—Captain Stephen Decatur, Jr., in a letter to Keith Spence, Philadelphia's purser and father of Midshipman Robert T. Spence

Around me lay arms, legs & trunks of Bodies, in the most mutilated state.
—Midshipman Robert T. Spence, in a letter to his mother

August 3, 1804 1:30 p.m.

Anxious to begin the attack, Commodore Edward Preble
scanned the old port of Tripoli through his spyglass from
the *Constitution's* quarterdeck. Fair weather had returned after a
week of gales. Now his squadron stood before the enemy capital,
ready for action. Months of preparation would come together this
day—for the bashaw as well as Preble. In Tripoli, gun crews
manned 115 cannon on the fortress walls, and 25,000 Tripolitan
soldiers recruited, trained, and massed for this contingency waited
in prepared positions to repel any amphibious landing. From
behind the two-mile-long arm of rocks and shoals protecting the
harbor waited the alert crews of twenty-four ships and gunboats
commanded by Grand Admiral Murad Reis.

The commanders of Preble's fifteen warships, gunboats, and
mortar boats watched the *Constitution* for the signal to deploy.
Preble sorely missed the *Philadelphia,* whose loss left him with just
one frigate, his flagship. Five frigates were on their way to the

199

Mediterranean, but he was unsure when they would arrive, and he couldn't delay any longer. The coming fall storms would foil his plans to use the six gunboats and two mortar vessels loaned him by Naples. They were ideal for maneuvering in shallow water, where the *Constitution* and the assembled squadron's six brigs and schooners dared not venture. But the gunboats were flat-bottomed and heavy, and did not row or sail well—they had had to be towed from Syracuse. They would be unusable in stormy seas. Each bomb vessel carried a 13-inch brass sea mortar—perfect for lofting shells over the fortresses and into the city. The gunboats were armed with long 24-pound bow guns. Preble's flotilla bobbing at anchor outside Tripoli's reef was manned by 1,060 Americans and Neapolitans.

Since taking command of the Mediterranean squadron in 1803, Preble had ached for the chance to cripple Tripoli's warmaking ability, "by destroying their vessels in port, if I cannot meet them at Sea." But as Dale and Morris also had recognized, Preble saw that he needed shallow-draft ships to draw close enough to the city to unleash a punishing bombardment. Cathcart had tried to procure gunboats from France, and, failing at that—French shipbuilders were absorbed in supplying Napoleon's navy—he proposed building them from scratch at Leghorn, and had sketched possible prototypes. But Preble had a better idea: Naples was hostile to Barbary, friendly to America, and expanding its navy, so why not borrow the gunboats from Naples? Prime Minister Sir John Acton informed Preble in May that Naples would be happy to lend the United States the floating batteries, and threw in six additional 24-pound guns. Preble mounted all six on the *Constitution*'s spar deck, giving her an impressive fifty guns. "They are fine Battering Cannon, and I expect will do good service," the commodore noted cheerfully. Acton also generously supplied 200 barrels of gunpowder, as well as muskets, pistols, and ninety-six Neapolitan sailors to help crew the vessels.

Preble's attempted diplomacy with Tripoli had failed. He had sent Richard O'Brien, the former consul general, into Tripoli on June 12 with authority to offer $40,000 in ransom, $10,000 in bribes, and a $10,000 gift for Yusuf whenever the new U.S. consul arrived. The bashaw spurned the peace bid and wouldn't even allow O'Brien to visit the *Philadelphia* prisoners. He grudgingly permitted him to send ashore clothing for them, then reversed himself and lowered the white truce flag before O'Brien could send the clothing; the British delivered the shipment weeks later. Preble sailed away vowing to "beat & distress his savage highness" into accepting his terms.

Preble and every consul in the region felt the sharp urgency of bringing the war to a head. At stake was America's reputation in Barbary. "It is from thence we are either to assume and support a National Character with these States;—or bow the neck and answer to the eternal cry of give," wrote George Davis from Tunis. Echoing Jefferson's long-held sentiments, Tobias Lear said the United States was "a Nation different from all others, we are now powerfull if we chuse to exert our strength."

It was a favorable moment for an attack on Tripoli. All was quiet in Algiers, and while Morocco and Tunis were complaining about the Tripoli blockade, they weren't going to do anything about it. Morocco again was badgering U.S. Consul James Simpson for a passport, this time so it could send wheat to Tripoli. Tunis was grousing over the *Philadelphia*'s destruction—Tripoli was supposed to have given the frigate to Tunis to settle debts—

and was clamoring again for a gift frigate. The bey also professed to be outraged over U.S. warships having fired on a small coastal trading vessel carrying earthenware from Jerba; the incident was of little consequence, with no one hurt and scarcely $100 in damage done. Davis predicted nothing would come of all this because Tunis had its hands full with its war against Naples, and because of the calming effect of Preble frequently appearing in Tunis harbor with the *Constitution*. Tunis was waiting to see what Preble did at Tripoli; Davis said it was imperative that Preble stagger Tripoli with the force of his attack and impress the other Barbary States. *"It must be dreadful to Barbary."*

Almost alone, Bainbridge was skeptical of Preble's chances of forcing peace upon Tripoli solely with naval force. From his castle prison, Bainbridge had had plenty of opportunity to observe the Tripolitans at close hand, and he was sure warships alone would not make the bashaw agree to a peace that didn't suit him. Tripoli was too well fortified to be beaten into submission by bombardment; its coastline was too pockmarked with bays for an effective blockade; and it had only a meager commercial trade to begin with, conducted by a few Jewish merchants whose interests were of little concern to the bashaw—and especially now, with the plentiful harvest. Bainbridge believed that only an amphibious attack by several thousand U.S. troops would force the bashaw to agree to peace on American terms, and that a landing force could easily capture the city and impose terms. While convinced that anything short of that would meet limited success and require a bought peace of some kind, Bainbridge recognized that a naval attack would serve one purpose: "A harassing bombardment will no doubt tend to make the terms more moderate. . . ."

• • •

August 3, 1804 2:30 P.M.

Signal flags shot up the *Constitution*'s halyards, ordering the squadron to commence fire. The bomb vessels began lobbing shells into Tripoli. Sheets of musket and cannon fire flashed from enemy ships and batteries, clattering on the American warships' masts and hulls and roiling the water among the mortar boats, gunboats, brigs, and schooners. The squadron replied with a thunderous cannonade, and the fight was on. Soon a curtain of blue-gray smoke hung over the bright waters. The *Philadelphia* prisoners listened anxiously to the ominous rumble of cannons coming from above their castle prison. Tripoli's streets were filled with running men. "Every Turk had his musket and other weapons, and wild disorder rang out from every arch." Extra guards suddenly appeared outside the captives' prison doors. The captives were driven to the castle magazine. Powder kegs weighing 100 pounds each were loaded on their backs, and they were forced to carry them at a jog, while being beaten by drivers, up to the castle batteries—a distance of three-quarters of a mile. Along the way, the riled townspeople threw stones at them and punched and slapped them, uttering "every insult and indignity that could be offered or endured."

Preble's gunboats split into two divisions of three gunboats each under Captain Stephen Decatur and Lieutenant Richard Somers, and attacked the Tripolitan gunboat fleet. In Somers's division were Lieutenant John Blake and Decatur's younger brother, Lieutenant James Decatur. Stephen Decatur led Lieutenants Joseph Bainbridge—whose older brother William was imprisoned less than a mile away—and John Trippe. As Stephen Decatur's formation advanced toward nine enemy gunboats through a curtain of grapeshot and musket balls, Bainbridge's lateen yard was shot away, and he couldn't steer his vessel and bring it alongside the enemy. So, from a distance, he harried the Tripolitans with cannon and musket fire, while Decatur, Trippe, and three dozen crewmen swarmed aboard two enemy craft. Decatur and twenty-four men cleared the decks of their prize in just ten minutes.

Trippe boarded another gunboat, and the two vessels suddenly drifted apart, leaving him and just ten men to face thirty-six enemy. Undaunted, Trippe's small force attacked with swords, pistols, pikes, and tomahawks. Trippe, small but well-proportioned, took on the enemy captain, an athletic man well over six feet tall. Before the battle, the Tripolitan had sworn on the Koran that he would "conquer or die," and now he fought both Trippe and Midshipman John D. Henley with abandon. Impressed by the captain's wild courage, the American officers exhorted him to surrender so they would not have to kill him. But the captain grimly fought on, ignoring his own wounds while slashing and stabbing Trippe with his scimitar eleven times in the head and chest. Reeling and bloody, Trippe saw an opening and desperately drove his sword into the Tripolitan, who fell and lay motionless on the deck. As Henley stepped over him, the captain suddenly gave a violent twist to Henley's ankle before going limp and expiring on the spot. For the rest of his days, Trippe shed tears whenever relating their epic struggle.

Somers's division bore in on the second gunboat formation. While Somers and his crew drove five enemy craft inside the protection of the rocks with grapeshot and musket fire, James Decatur attacked the largest enemy gunboat. It quickly struck its flag, but as Decatur boarded it, the treacherous captain raised a pistol and shot him in the head. As the shocked crewmen attended to their dying lieutenant, the enemy gunboat escaped.

The boat bearing the wounded James Decatur happened to cross paths with Stephen Decatur's gunboat. When Decatur learned how his brother had been wounded, he left his prize with Lieutenant Thorn, took eleven men, and went looking for the Tripolitan captain. He vowed to give no quarter, just as his brother's assailant hadn't. "I find hand to hand is not childs play, 'tis kill or be killed." Decatur overtook an enemy gunboat, and he led his tiny boarding party aboard. Decatur searched out the captain, a huge Mameluke. The captain lunged at Decatur with a pike. When Decatur swung his cutlass to block the blow, his sword shattered on the metal pike head, and the captain drove the pike into Decatur's chest. Decatur yanked it out before it caused mortal damage and flung it aside. The men wrestled on the deck. Decatur, smaller and quicker, emerged on top, just as a Tripolitan crewman swung a sword at his head. The blow might have ended Decatur's life had it landed. But Daniel Frazier, a Decatur crewman wounded in both arms, thrust his head into the sword's path and took the heavy, chopping blow on his own skull, sparing his captain. (Miraculously, Frazier survived.) The Mameluke flipped over Decatur, whipped out a short, curved knife, and stabbed down toward Decatur, who caught his wrist with his left hand before the Mameluke could sink the blade into his chest. As they struggled for the knife, with his other hand Decatur fumbled for the pistol that he kept in his pocket, managed to cock it, pointed it in the direction of the captain, and pulled the trigger. The captain slumped over, dead.

The captain's death took all the fight out of his crewmen, and they surrendered. While Decatur always believed he had avenged his brother's death—and Stewart agreed that he had—Preble and Somers thought the killer had gotten away on another gunboat.

As a souvenir of their epic hand-to-hand fight, Decatur kept a book of Arabic prayers and Koran passages that he found in the dead captain's pocket. (After her husband's death years later, Susan Decatur gave the book to the library at Catholic College in Georgetown, in the District of Columbia.)

The *Constitution* bombarded the forts and the city with 262 rounds of shot and shell, damaging buildings throughout the city and toppling a minaret. Five enemy gunboats and two galleys that had been held in reserve behind the rocks tried to flank the gunboats, and Preble swung his fifty guns on them. The storm of grapeshot stopped the sortie cold and inflicted heavy losses and "great havoc."

At 4:30 P.M., two hours after signaling the attack, Preble gave the signal to retire. The brigs, schooners, and boats towed away the gunboats, mortar boats, and their prizes under the *Constitution*'s covering fire. Preble took the bomb vessels in tow, and the squadron sailed out of the harbor.

The battle was over.

Decatur reported his captures to Preble, who was agitatedly pacing the *Constitution* quarterdeck, his uniform in shreds from a shot that had badly damaged a deck cannon during his ship's brisk shelling. Decatur announced that his division had taken three prizes. Preble, expecting more than three ship captures from the attack, spun around and seized him by the collar. "Aye, sir," he cried, shaking Decatur, "why did you not bring me out more?" The frustrated commodore stalked off to his cabin.

But when he learned later what had happened to Decatur's brother, Preble sent for the captain and apologized. He sent Decatur on the *Constitution*'s barge to bring James aboard the flagship. James died on the barge, propped in Midshipman Charles

Morris's lap. Decatur sat up with the body all night, remembering the happy times they had shared as boys. But at the burial at sea the next morning, Decatur was more proud than sad. To Morris, he confided, "I would rather see him there, than living with any cloud on his conduct."

The battle, a stunning demonstration of American fighting prowess, buoyed the spirits of the squadron's crewmen and officers. They had itched for a fight like this since Sterrett demolished the *Tripoli* nearly three years ago to the day. In the savage hand-to-hand fighting at which the Tripolitans supposedly excelled, the Americans had proven they were fiercer, better trained, and better led. "I always thought we could lick them their own way and give them two to one," said Decatur, and in unsurprising nineteenth-century fashion added, "Some of the Turks died like men, but much the greater number like women." Grateful as he and the other Americans were for the Neapolitans' help, Decatur was more amused than impressed by their battle demeanor. "While we fought they prayed."

Forty-four Tripolitans perished in the close-in fighting on the three captured ships, with thirty-five taken prisoner and twenty-six wounded, three later dying of their wounds. Gunfire killed and wounded many other enemy on other gunboats and the fortress batteries. James Decatur was the only American battle death; Trippe, Stephen Decatur, and a dozen others were treated for wounds. The squadron's rapid, accurate gunnery sank three enemy vessels and cleared the decks of several others. The Tripolitan gunners consistently fired high, hitting sails and rigging, never once hulling an American ship.

Besides the combat casualties, there was one other American

victim of the battle: Lieutenant John Blake. Blake's gunboat never closed with any enemy gunboats; it kept to the fringes of the action. His unhappy crew could only fire from a distance on the harbor and fortresses, but being where targets were fewest, their gunboat fired the fewest rounds. In an alert squadron such as Preble's, Blake's evasion was known to one and all within hours. Whispers of cowardice wafted through the squadron wardrooms. While Preble never reprimanded Blake officially, indignation among the officers reached such a pitch that Blake tendered his resignation as gunboat commander, rather "than to continue under a Suspicious Eye." Preble accepted the resignation without comment.

Stung by their losses, the Tripolitans uneasily watched the American squadron lingering just beyond the harbor, wondering when it would attack again. To soothe their apprehension, they ascribed the Americans' surprising violence in the recent battle to drunkenness and attempted to exorcise their fears by abusing the *Philadelphia* prisoners. They put them to work repairing fortress walls and replenishing the forts' powder from the castle magazine, abusing them constantly. "The infuriate Turks, wherever we met them, would strike, spit upon and stone us."

A few days after the gunboat battle, the squadron stopped a French privateer leaving the harbor, and after ascertaining that her papers were in order, Preble persuaded the captain to take ashore fourteen badly wounded Tripolitans. Preble's humane gesture did not evoke a commensurate action by the bashaw toward the American prisoners. "They did not abate their cruelties to us in consequence of it," Ray wrote. If anything, the beatings worsened, to the point where the Americans petitioned Yusuf's intercession.

He ordered the abuse stopped, but then impassively watched a guard flail a captive without intervening.

After a long day of patching up the victims of Preble's attack, Cowdery decided to no longer aid or comfort the enemy. Motivated primarily by patriotism, he also saw that with this turning into a real shooting war, he soon could be overwhelmed with Tripolitan casualties. But Cowdery had no stomach for the ugly confrontation with the bashaw that a blunt refusal to serve would necessitate. Two days after the attack, the ship's surgeon was asked to treat a soldier's shattered hand from a bursting blunderbuss. Cowdery took a dull knife and amputated all but one finger, then very deliberately dressed the wound "in a bungling manner."

Cowdery had accurately assayed Preble's character and intentions. The commodore was indeed relentless. His orders from Secretary Smith were virtually the same as Morris's had been: to blockade and "annoy the Enemy" and to work in concert with Lear to negotiate peace if possible. But Smith also had added, "The conduct for sometime past pursued by our squadron in the Mediterranean, has, unhappily, not been calculated to accomplish the object of government nor to make a just impression on the Enemy of our national character."

For the first time, Smith had chosen the right man to prosecute the war. Preble was determined either to force the bashaw to make a reasonable peace "or to destroy his city . . . I wish to close the war with the Barbarians by conduct which shall establish our naval character among them and make them have a respect for peace. . . ."

The commodore had kept up a steady blockade that snared a half dozen prizes, including the 16-gun brig *Transfer*, which he had converted into the U.S. warship *Scourge*. Twice during July there were sharp clashes between the Americans and Tripolitans. The *Siren* chased a small Tripolitan ship aground on July 7 and, with the *Vixen's* help, destroyed it with cannon fire during a skirmish with 1,000 enemy troops on the beach. A week later, another ship was chased and riddled after it was beached, but Tripolitan soldiers killed four Americans in one of the *Siren's* boats. The *Vixen* and *Siren* retaliated massively with cannon and small-arms fire, killing and wounding 150 Tripolitans. These harassing actions pleased the commodore, who had little use for the North Africans, whom he regarded as "a deep designing artfull treacherous sett of Villains and nothing will keep them so quiet as a respectable naval force near them." Now that he had gone to the trouble of procuring gunboats and mortar vessels and towing them to Tripoli from Sicily, Preble was in no hurry to leave.

After a turbulent early life, Preble was only beginning to mellow in his forty-second year. When he was fourteen, he had watched the British burn his home and half the town of Falmouth, Maine (it later became Portland), making a patriot of him. Later, he joined the Massachusetts State Navy, and was a midshipman on the 26-gun frigate *Protector* when it captured the *Admiral Duff* off Maine—and when the *Protector* was captured by the 44-gun *Roebuck* without a fight. The British threw the American crew into the notorious prison hulk *Jersey* in New York harbor. Preble's father pulled strings and arranged an exchange for his son, and he went back to sea as commander of the 12-gun Massachusetts Navy sloop *Winthrop*, harassing Loyalist cruisers operating out of Bagaduce, Maine, and capturing the *Merriam* in a daring raid at Penobscot Bay in 1782. During the last year of the war, he cruised to Bermuda and the West Indies, seizing naval prizes.

After the war, Preble made a comfortable living as a merchant captain, but he missed the naval service. He applied for a commission when Congress established the U.S. Navy in 1794, but didn't receive it until 1798, during the Quasi-War naval expansion. At thirty-seven, he was old for a lieutenancy, but he accepted. Displaying that he was a fighting commander, Preble earned a rapid promotion to captain. He then had the great luck of being given command of the 36-gun frigate *Essex,* leaving Newport, R.I., on an epic voyage to Batavia in the Dutch East Indies, from where he was to convoy eleven U.S. merchantmen home. The *Essex* was the first American warship to cross the equator, the first to show the flag in the East Indies, and the first to round the Cape of Good Hope twice. While it was a thrilling voyage of discovery, it exacted a heavy toll on Preble; he contracted malaria and a chronic stomach ailment, possibly ulcers, that shadowed him to a premature death and forced him to turn down commands in Dale's and Morris's squadrons.

A husky six-footer with hard, appraising, dark blue eyes, his fair skin bronzed by years at sea, Preble was known as a harsh disciplinarian and, at times, for being a violent man. As recently as 1799, criminal charges had been brought against him in Boston for striking a man in the head with a pistol. He avoided prosecution by paying $45 for medical bills; later, Preble sent the man another $200 when he discovered that he remained laid up months after the attack.

The *Constitution*'s crew disliked him at first. He was irritable and remote. He posted a Marine sentry at his cabin door, permitting only quarterdeck officers and a few others in to see him. His junior officers felt the lash of his sharp tongue whenever their performance failed to meet his high standards. Although it would have been of small consolation had his men known it, Preble was well aware that he needed to control his outbursts. In a letter to his close friend, War Secretary Henry Dearborn, he referred to advice Dearborn had given him previously on "the government of temper."

Temper was one thing, shipboard discipline another matter altogether. Unlike Morris, Preble ran a tight ship, where even profanity was prohibited and where crewmen were punished often and severely. Two or three *Constitution* crewmen languished in irons on any given day. Floggings were administered weekly, sometimes more frequently. For example, on October 4, 1803, five seamen each received 12 lashes for negligence and "perfect neglect of duty." On November 16, 1803, a Marine got 48 lashes for refusing duty, attempting to desert, and insubordination; a seaman was flogged 36 times for neglect of duty, drunkenness, and "insolence"; and another seaman was given 24 lashes for neglect of duty. Two weeks later, four seamen were whipped for drunkenness, with the ringleader getting 36 lashes for stealing the rum that caused their misbehavior. The next week, several more men were punished for drunkenness. Preble kept all the ships in his squadron on the same tight leash, demanding brief ports of call to keep the crewmen away from temptation and his warships at sea as much as possible.

Preble's strictness was arguably justified, given the reality of early nineteenth-century shipboard life—months of unremitting isolation and forced confinement with crewmen who often were thieves, murderers, and drunks. If officers did not punish rule breakers swiftly, their floating community of 350 might well erupt in chaos and ignominious mutiny—a commander's greatest hobgoblin; the mere whiff of insurrection had to be ruthlessly quashed. Thus, when Robert Quinn, a seaman on the *President*, circulated a letter complaining about the crew's treatment by officers in June 1804, he was court-martialed for inciting mutiny. For his sentence, his head and eyebrows were shaved, and burned into his forehead with a hot metal brand was the word MUTINEER. He was given 320 lashes, meted out on the various ships of the squadron, as an example to all. "It is to be sure most cruel punishment," remarked purser John Darby of the *John Adams*, "but the very existance of the Navy require it."

An often oppressive disciplinarian, extremely demanding, abrupt with subordinates, Preble might have been hated and feared by his men had he not awed them with his indomitable fighting spirit, which earned their lasting respect. They were won over during a memorable nighttime encounter with a strange ship off the Spanish coast soon after the *Constitution*'s arrival in the Mediterranean. The meeting took a decidedly sinister turn when the mystery warship refused to respond to repeated hails by Preble's flagship.

"I hail you for the last time," Preble announced through the trumpet. "If you do not answer I'll fire a shot into you."

A voice from the darkness said: "If you fire I will return a broadside."

Preble hotly replied that he would like to see him do it, and asked the ship's name. The voice said it was the 84-gun HMS *Donegal.* He ordered Preble to send over his boat.

This was too much. Preble said he'd "be damned" if he'd send a boat.

"Blow your matches, boys!" he shouted. A gasp went up from the gun deck, and the crews readied their cannons for firing.

A tense silence fell over the two ships. Then, the slap of

approaching oars could be heard—a boat from the mystery ship. A junior officer offered apologies and said his ship wasn't the HMS *Donegal* after all, but the 32-gun HMS *Maidstone*. The *Constitution* had caught her napping, and her captain had bluffed to try to buy time to get his crew to quarters. The bluff had very nearly snowballed into a tragedy for the *Maidstone*—because she had underestimated Preble's temper and courage.

From that day forward, Preble's men thought the "old man" was all right.

August 7, 1804, 2:30 P.M.

Four days after the gunboat battle, the squadron returned to Tripoli harbor. With his strike force reinforced by the three captured enemy gunboats, which had been easily converted to U.S. gunboats under the command of Lieutenants Thorn, William M. Crane, and James Caldwell, Preble hoped to lure Tripolitan warships away from the protective batteries and sink them.

The gunboats and the two bomb vessels took up positions opposite the western part of the city and began shelling the neighborhoods and streets. The six schooners and brigs bombarded a seven-gun battery guarding the area. Crews on fifteen enemy gunboats and galleys anchored beneath the city walls watched the lively duel between the batteries and ships as though it were a sporting event, making no move to engage the Americans.

And then, without warning, Gunboat 9, Lieutenant Caldwell's prize, exploded with a roar, spraying a wide area with splintered wood and metal and mangled body parts. A one-in-a-million direct hit on her magazine by an enemy battery had done it. Thousands of eyes watched anxiously as the smoke and debris cleared. When it did, to everyone's amazement a gun crew could be seen standing on a shard of floating deck, attending to a cannon, pieces of the vessel splashing into the water around them. The crew fired the gun once and reloaded it, but before they could fire again, their tiny platform began to sink. They gave one last cheer as they slipped beneath the waves, yet survived.

Midshipman Robert T. Spence, who was in charge of the gun, later recalled that he was aiming the loaded cannon when the gunboat blew up, flinging him straight into the air. When he came down, he landed next to the cannon and its dazed gunners, amid horrific carnage. Displaying superb presence of mind, he fired the gun. "Around me lay arms, legs & trunks of Bodies, in the most mutilated state." Among them was Caldwell, recognizable only by his uniform. His arms and legs were gone, his face mutilated. "He was not dead, although he sank instantly." Ten men died on Gunboat 9, including Caldwell and Midshipman John S. Dorsey. Six were wounded.

The American gunboats and bomb vessels kept up a steady fire, damaging buildings throughout the city. The bashaw hunkered down in a bombproof room deep in his castle, but was overcome by curiosity when he heard Gunboat 9 explode. He left his sanctuary only after a Moslem cleric took the precaution of placing a small piece of paper with scriptural quotations written on it atop the bashaw's head to guard him from danger.

The enemy gunboats never ventured away from the batteries as Preble had hoped. At 5:30 P.M., with the wind strengthening, Preble recalled the squadron. Besides the casualties on Gunboat 9, two other sailors were killed by enemy cannon fire. It was the costliest day of the war yet for the Americans.

That night, Captain Isaac Chauncey arrived off Tripoli on the frigate *John Adams* and handed Preble a letter informing him that he soon would be relieved of command of the squadron by Commodore Samuel Barron.

Preble gloomily set aside his carefully laid plans for destroying Tripoli's batteries and wrecking its gunboat fleet to await the arrival of Barron and his four frigates.

XII

A Destructive Scheme

I am convinced by what I have already seen, that we can reduce Tripoly to a heap of Ruins. . .
—Commodore Edward Preble, in a letter to Citizen Beaussier, French chargé d'affaires in Tripoli

.. . a vast stream of fire, which appear'd ascending to heaven.
—Midshipman Robert T. Spence, in a letter to his mother

Preble's fate was sealed by the *Philadelphia* surrender, which had spurred the Jefferson administration to send Commodore Barron and the additional frigates across the Atlantic. Only after the relief force was embarked did Jefferson and his Cabinet learn of the *Philadelphia's* destruction. Whenever Barron arrived, Preble would have to give up command of the squadron, for Preble was senior to only two other Navy captains—Isaac Chauncey and James Barron, who was sailing with his older brother. Commodore Barron and the other two captains in his squadron—Hugh Campbell and Preble's nemesis, John Rodgers—were senior to Preble.

Navy Secretary Smith tried to soften what he knew would be a heavy blow to Preble's pride: "You have fulfilled our highest expectations," he said, and his conduct had been honorable "and in all respects perfectly satisfactory to us." In a sense, this only made matters worse, for if Preble's conduct were so exemplary, why must he be relieved? Rather than quibble, Preble gave way gracefully. While he regretted that "our naval establishment is so limited as to deprive me of the means and glory of completely subduing the haughty tyrant of Tripoli, while in the chief command," he would do everything possible to assist his successor.

Noble words notwithstanding, Preble's pride was crushed, as his journal entries showed. ". . . how much my feelings are lacerated by this supercedure at the moment of Vicotry cannot be described and can be felt only by an Officer placed in my mortifying position." Not wanting others to think that he was being forced out for poor performance, he circulated Smith's letter among Sir Alexander Ball, the British governor of Malta, and his other Mediterranean contacts.

Yusuf rejected Cowdery's request to take some men and bury the twelve American sailors and officers whose bodies had washed ashore after the naval battle on August 7. Weeks later, when Cowdery was returning to the city from the bashaw's country palace, he came upon the remains "in a state of putrefaction. . . . They were scattered on the shore for miles, and were torn in pieces by dogs."

The days crept by without any sign of Barron. The *John Adams*, it turned out, had arrived with only eight serviceable guns, and, thus, was of no use to Preble, adding to his irritation over being superseded. Chauncey had stripped his ship so she could carry more provisions. He had transferred all but eight gun carriages to the *Congress* and *Constellation*, which were somewhere in the Atlantic with Barron's *President* and the *Essex*.

While Preble waited, he weighed resuming the attacks on Tripoli, but first decided to try to negotiate a ransom and peace, hoping to end the war one way or the other while still squadron commander. Since the failed parley in June, he had sent Bainbridge an invisible-ink message urging him to make the same $60,000 offer to the foreign secretary, Sidi Mohammed Dghies, and to see where it went. Dghies, however, said the bashaw would not negotiate with prisoners. Preble tried Citizen Beaussier, the French chargé d'affaires in Tripoli, as an intermediary. Preble and the American consuls were dubious about Beaussier's motives and sympathies, but he was willing to shuttle proposals and counterproposals back and forth, and he had Yusuf's ear.

Two days after the bombardment, Preble offered $80,000 to ransom the American captives and make peace, plus a $10,000 gift for the bashaw when the new U.S. consul took his station. Beaussier returned the following day with a counterproposal: $150,000. Impossible, Preble said. He did some saber rattling. "Perhaps after the next attack he [Yusuf] may be willing to accede to mine." But Preble evidently had second thoughts, and made a new offer on August 11: $100,000 for ransom and peace, $10,000 in gifts to the bashaw's officers and a $10,000 consular present. Yet he couldn't resist adding in an aside to Beaussier. "I am convinced by what I have already seen, that we can reduce Tripoly to a heap of Ruins: the destruction of Derna & Bengaza will follow, and the blockade be constantly continued, unless the present terms are accepted." The bashaw made no reply.

Preble reconnoitered the harbor on the 16-gun brig *Argus*. Every officer in the squadron, Preble included, adored the *Argus*. She was fast and trimly built, a mariner's delight. Stephen Decatur, Jr. had exulted in her handling during the Atlantic crossing. Isaac Hull, when he took her over from Decatur, had noted that she easily outsailed the *Siren,* a virtually identical ship. Preble had declared her to be "so fine a Vessel, and so well calculated and armed for the service" that he wanted to take her into Tripoli harbor. He did just that on his scouting run, but in his enjoyment of her maneuverability, he strayed within range of Tripoli's batteries. Enemy gunners opened up on the *Argus,* raking the copper off the bottom and hulling her with a round of heavy shot 3 feet above the water line. It hit right below where Preble was standing on the quarterdeck. He hastily ordered the *Argus* back to sea, and she limped out of the harbor.

With no sign yet of Barron, and the summer slipping away, Preble decided to resume the attacks on Tripoli and to continue them without letup until Barron arrived. Early on August 24, the squadron towed the gunboats and bomb vessels into position. At 2:00 A.M., they leisurely shelled the batteries and city until daylight. Preble called the effect "uncertain." Beaussier was blunter, describing the bombardment as "perfectly null—Not a single Bomb was thrown beyond the Forts. . . ."

Yet the nervous bashaw reinforced the city with 1,000 country militia, motley troops with rusty muskets, who liked to beckon and sing to the Americans to run their vessels aground.

Storms kept the squadron away from Tripoli, but as soon as the weather cleared, Preble led his warships and gunboats—the mortar boats were being repaired back in Syracuse—into the harbor. Their magazines were full of powder, shot, and shell, their decks cleared for action, and their crews eager to get in some licks at the bashaw's forces.

The gunboats anchored within pistol range of the bashaw's

castle, and at 3:00 A.M. on August 28 they began shelling the city, harbor boats, and batteries. This bombardment was livelier than the last. For three hours, the Americans blasted the enemy with hundreds of rounds of shot, grape, and canister, sinking a large ship and badly damaging several others. Four Tripolitan sailors were killed on a gunboat raked by grapeshot. The Tripolitans fired back furiously, shredding sails and rigging and sinking a cutter from the *John Adams,* killing three sailors.

Inside the city, shot and shells killed and maimed citizens and soldiers, forced gunners to abandon several batteries, damaged the sailors' prison, shattered the houses of the Spanish, Swedish, and Dutch consuls, and killed a camel. Bainbridge was nearly killed in his bed when a 36-pound cannonball crashed through the wall of his room, tearing off his bedclothes and burying him in stone and mortar. Fellow officers dug him out, bruised and nursing a wound on his right ankle that caused him to limp for months.

At daybreak, Preble brought the *Constitution* and her 50 guns close to the batteries, exposing her to the fire of 80 guns while the stately frigate poured 300 rounds of solid shot and 300 more of grapeshot and canister into the city, the batteries, and the bashaw's castle. The barrage lasted forty-five minutes, which must have seemed an eternity to the fortress gunners, showered with stone and dust after every salvo. They fired back gamely, but the *Constitution* was positioned so close to the walls that the Tripolitans could not depress their guns enough to hull it.

A few days later, blockading American ships stopped a Spanish vessel leaving Tripoli harbor. Her captain, who had been in Tripoli during the shelling, reported the attack had wreaked "great havoc and destruction" and killed "a vast number."

• • •

Carpenters and gunnery mates made repairs while Preble planned yet another attack. He was determined to smash the bashaw's forts and destroy his warships before Barron's squadron arrived. In possession of forty-two Tripolitan prisoners from the gunboat battle of August 3, Preble suggested a prisoner exchange. But Preble found the damage and casualties he had inflicted had only stiffened Yusuf's resolve. Beaussier reported that the bashaw had defiantly vowed "to encounter all your forces in Order that Europe & Africa may conceive a favorable opinion of his strength . & courage." The bashaw not only rejected Preble's prisoner exchange, Beaussier said, but now demanded $400,000 for ransom and peace, plus presents for himself and his officers. Preble answered the best way he knew: with another attack.

The squadron returned to Tripoli harbor on September 3 with six gunboats and the two repaired mortar boats in tow. At 3:30 P.M., they began throwing shells into the city, while the *Siren, Vixen, Argus, Nautilus,* and *Enterprise* poured a withering fire into enemy shipping in the harbor and one of the main fortresses, Fort English. A fusillade of cannon fire roared from the bashaw's castle, the mole, the crown, and the city's batteries.

The American fire smashed two Tripolitan gunboats in the harbor and destroyed the home of the bashaw's chief naval contractor in the city. The bombardment threw the city's inhabitants into "the utmost terror and distraction," observed Jonathan Cowdery, the captive *Philadelphia* surgeon. Yet for some reason—probably improperly set fuses—few shells landing in the city actually exploded. There were so many unexploded shells that the bashaw offered a bounty for every intact one brought to him.

To draw off some of the hot fire aimed at his warships and

gunboats, Preble once again sailed the *Constitution* close to the batteries and the bashaw's castle, cruising back and forth within range of scores of guns and flashing deadly broadside after broadside—eleven in all—into the castle, town, and batteries. The *Constitution* silenced one battery and heavily damaged buildings and homes, while shot and shell from seventy enemy guns splashed the water around her, the spray wetting her nearly to the lower yards. Cannon fire and grape shot tore through her sails, rigging, braces, bowlines, tacks, and lifts, but Preble kept her so close to the walls that no one could hull her. A little after 4:30, Preble gave the signal to withdraw. The Americans hadn't suffered a single casualty.

Preble's reckless sorties awed the bashaw's men, who thought Preble mad for parading the *Constitution* beneath the city's guns as he had, firing broadsides at the castle and city. "That he ever lived to return was ascribed, by them, to some superior agency's invisible protection."

The hard-bitten commodore set his crews to work the next morning making repairs, while he put into play a destructive scheme he had long contemplated: sending a fireship into the harbor and blowing it up among the enemy shipping. The *Intrepid,* which had served Decatur and his commandos well when they burned the *Philadelphia,* would be converted into a floating bomb. A small handpicked crew would sail her as close as possible to the enemy corsairs' moorings and the bashaw's castle, light a fuse, and row away in two fast boats before the ketch blew up.

An overabundance of officers and crewmen volunteered for the extremely dangerous commando raid. Preble picked Somers to lead it. His executive officer would be Lieutenant Henry Wadsworth. When Somers asked his *Nautilus* crew for volunteers, every man stepped forward. He carefully added that no one need enlist in the operation who was not prepared "to blow himself up, rather than be captured." No one backed out. Instead, his crew gave three cheers, and all of them begged for the privilege of lighting the fuse. "It was a glorious moment, and made an impression on the hearts of all witnessing it, never to be forgotten," wrote Midshipman Charles G. Ridgely.

The five attacks on Tripoli had turned Preble's young officers into seasoned combat leaders. Far more than his two predecessors, Preble had carried out former Navy Secretary Samuel Smith's instructions to train a new corps of naval officers. "One great object expected from this Squadron is, the instruction of our young men: so that when their more active service shall hereafter be required, they may be capable of defending the honor of their Country," Smith had written in 1801 when he sent Dale to Barbary at the head of the first Mediterranean squadron. Dale and Morris had convoyed and blockaded, but had not fought. Preble was waging a real war, and the young officers who served under him, forever known as "Preble's Boys," were absorbing the experience in their sinews.

"No place presents so good a nursery for them at present as the Mediterranean," Cathcart had observed. The Barbary War was not a crisis, but an opportunity, "the effects of which will be more visible in a few years." In the backs of the minds of American leaders—from Washington and Adams to Jefferson and Madison—had loomed the specter of war with England. Britain's sixty-year-old war with France had bought the United States precious time to prepare for the inevitable war with England they believed would come one day.

Tensions between the former mother country and her ex-colony were evident during Preble's cruise. In Malta in May, sailors from the HMS *Narcissus* had boarded an American prize and impressed three seamen, refusing to give them up when confronted by the officer in charge. The previous October, three American sailors had deserted at Gibraltar to the HMS *Medusa,* whose captain claimed they were British subjects and would not turn them over for arrest. A few days later, two *Constitution* seamen deserted to a British warship. Preble himself demanded their return, but the British captain would not comply; the deserters were British subjects, he said. He suggested that Preble should turn over all the British subjects in his squadron.

Preble's Boys would teach Great Britain to respect American sea power during the War of 1812. In Preble's hard, exacting school off Tripoli, they learned the art and science of naval warfare: Stephen Decatur, Charles Stewart, Isaac Hull, James Lawrence, Thomas Macdonough, John Trippe, Charles Morris, Joseph Bainbridge, David Porter, and Isaac Chauncey. A decade later, Hull, Bainbridge, and Stewart would take turns commanding the *Constitution;* Decatur would capture an English frigate; Chauncey would command the naval forces on Lake Champlain and the Great Lakes; and the rest would distinguish themselves as well. Even in 1803, Preble knew what he had: "many remarkable fine young men whose conduct promises great things to their Country." After he had spent some time schooling them, he reported proudly: "I have an excellent set of officers who dare do anything I order them to do." They now were poised to add another page to their résumé: sailing a fireship into the harbor under the bashaw's nose and blowing it up.

• • •

September 4, 1804, 8:00 P.M.

The commandos made their somber final arrangements in case they didn't return. The crewmen told their shipmates how their clothing should be apportioned, while Somers bade farewell to his friends Decatur, Stewart, and Joseph Bainbridge. Somers impulsively removed a ring and broke it into pieces that he handed around to them. They gave back the keepsakes, unwilling to jinx the mission. They shook hands and said they would see him soon. Then he was gone.

The *Argus, Vixen,* and *Nautilus* escorted the *Intrepid* as far as the reef. Midshipman Joseph Israel suddenly appeared alongside in a boat, bearing Preble's last-minute instructions and best wishes. Impulsively, he asked to remain on the fireship. Somers gave his consent, bringing the *Intrepid*'s complement to the unlucky number of thirteen.

The convoy watched the ketch enter the harbor. The commandos were supposed to fire a signal rocket after they lit the fuse and evacuated the vessel. The *Intrepid* was loaded for pyrotechnics: The magazine was packed with five tons of gunpowder in 100 barrels and 150 fused shells. The powder-train fuse was supposed to give the officers and ten crewmen—four from the *Nautilus,* six from the *Constitution*—fifteen minutes to row off a safe distance before the fireship exploded.

Anxiously, the squadron's officers, sailors, and Marines peered into the black harbor.

At 9:45, the fortress batteries suddenly opened fire.

Right on the heels of that, a massive explosion filled the sky with flaming shells soaring hundreds of feet over the water "like so many planets, a vast stream of fire, which appear'd ascending to heaven." The huge concussion from the blast echoed off the harbor's old stone walls and "awed their batteries into profound silence with astonishment," wrote Preble. The ensuing eerie silence was pierced by frightened shrieks from within the city, carrying miles across the water. The loud cries "informed us that the town was thrown into the greatest terror." Kettledrums beat the garrison soldiers to arms.

The squadron waited tensely for the signal rocket, for the slap of oars on water. The *Nautilus* showed a light to aid her shipmates, and the enemy batteries rained shot down all around the schooner. The crew paid the shelling no mind, instead suspending themselves with lighted lanterns from the sides of the ship until their heads nearly touched the water—to watch for signs of movement in the harbor. To signal her location, the *Constitution* began firing her guns and rockets every ten minutes. She didn't stop until 9:00 A.M. But there was no boat, no signal.

In the morning light, there was no sign of the *Intrepid* or her boats, only three damaged enemy gunboats being towed toward shore. The *Intrepid* had been blown to pieces, with no survivors.

The explosion caused little damage to Tripolitan shipping, and if any Tripolitans were killed, the captives never heard about it. They surely would have, for the city's Neapolitan captives, Jews, Greeks, and Maltese normally were quick to inform the Americans of every Tripolitan setback.

Without any basis in fact, Preble concluded in his official report that the *Intrepid* probably was surrounded suddenly by enemy gunboats and boarded and, true to their vow, Somers and the crew lit the fuse and blew themselves up, preferring "*death and the destruction of the enemy* to *captivity and torturing slavery. . . .*" However, this was only speculation. It is more likely that the *Intrepid* exploded by accident, or that her magazine sustained a direct hit from the city batteries. It will never be known for certain.

Over the next days, thirteen bodies torn beyond identification were found floating in the harbor or washed up on the shore. This time, the bashaw permitted Cowdery to bury the dead Americans properly. With the *Philadelphia*'s boatswain and some crewmen in attendance, he held a service and interred Somers, Wadsworth, Israel, and the ten sailors just east of the town wall.

The bashaw and his officers threw a feast in thanksgiving to Allah.

Dirty weather set in, and Preble sent the gunboats and bomb vessels back to Syracuse. Then Barron and his four frigates arrived. The new commodore assumed command of the squadron in a ceremony September 10 on the *President*.

A couple of days later, Preble chased down two strange ships that turned out to be carrying 16,000 bushels of wheat to Tripoli. The capture was Preble's last act as a fighting captain. He took the prizes to Malta and proudly turned over command of the *Constitution* to Captain Stephen Decatur, Jr., "whose merits eminently entitle him to so handsome a command."

Barron cruised off Tripoli with his impressive squadron for three weeks without going into action, then sailed to Malta and Syracuse for the winter.

Preble returned to America in triumph. President Jefferson took time from the celebration of his second inauguration to congratulate him. The commodore dined with James and Dolley Madison, called on former President John Adams at his home in Braintree, Massachusetts, sat for a portrait by Rembrandt Peale, and was feted at ceremonial dinners from Philadelphia to Portland. Congress struck a gold medal in his honor.

He was placed in charge of building nine gunboats. With Preble overseeing the work in New England with his usual rigor, the ships all were finished on time and launched in 1806 and 1807, a feat of organization and efficiency that seems incredible in the twenty-first century, when government contract work often drags on past deadline.

Preble's squadron had brought the war to the bashaw's city for the first time. In only a month, it inflicted more damage on Tripoli than during all of the three previous years. American shot, shell, and cold steel claimed the lives of hundreds of enemy soldiers and sailors, at a cost of thirty U.S. servicemen killed and twenty-four wounded. But as September 1804 ended, the *Philadelphia* crewmen in Tripoli's soul-killing dungeons now for eleven months, were no nearer liberation.

The squadron officers, led by Lieutenant David Porter, pooled their money to honor the six "Preble's Boys" killed during the battles in Tripoli harbor in August and September 1804. With $1,245 that they raised, they hired a Leghorn sculptor, John Charles Micali, to build a monument to the fallen junior officers. It was America's first military monument. Micali hewed the statues and pedestal from Italian marble. After the monument was completed in 1806, it was disassembled, packed into fifty-one cases at Leghorn, and shipped to the United States on the *Constitution*. First erected in the Washington Navy Yard, the monument was vandalized in August 1814 by marauding British troops who hacked at it with swords. It was repaired and moved outside the Capitol, where it resided more than forty years. In 1860 it was moved again, on the steamship *Anacostia,* to the new U.S. Naval Academy in Annapolis, Maryland. It stands today behind Preble Hall, home of the Naval Academy Museum. Its inscription reads: "To the Memory of Somers, Caldwell, Decatur, Wadsworth, Dorsey, Israel."

> *The love of glory inspired them*
> *Fame has crowned their deeds*
> *History records the event*
> *The children of Columbia admire*
> *And commerce laments their fall.*

In Portland, Maine, young Henry Wadsworth's grieving sister, Zilpah, and her husband, Stephen Longfellow, named their infant son Henry Wadsworth Longfellow. He grew up to become the most beloved American poet of his age. The Longfellows' next-door neighbor was Edward Preble.

In 1938, the State Department began an official inquiry into the *Intrepid* crew's remains. With singular energy, Mustafa Burchis, the Tripoli harbormaster, took it upon himself to locate them. He interviewed the descendants of families that had lived in Tripoli in September 1804, and studied journals, diaries, and records. He sent a report to the U.S. embassy in Rome, but it was burned with other embassy papers when war broke out in 1941. After the war ended, Burchis reconstructed his findings, which suggested the final resting place of at least some of the crew was the Protestant Cemetery, established by European and American consuls in 1830. In a corner of the old walled burial ground, near a cliff, Burchis and U.S. consular officials located five unmarked graves above the beach where the Americans' bodies reportedly had washed ashore.

In April 1949, the U.S. cruiser *Spokane* arrived in Tripoli harbor. No fortress guns fired on her. No Tripolitan gunboats sailed out to dispute the harbor. U.S. sailors and Marines and a British Army unit marched the half mile from the city to the cemetery, with a Scottish Cameron Highlanders band playing martial music. One of the fifty dignitaries in the solemn procession was Tripoli's mayor, Joseph Karamanli, a direct descendant of the bashaw.

Placed at each unmarked grave was a plaque reading, *"Here Lies an Unknown American Sailor Lost from the USS* Intrepid *in Tripoli Harbor 1804."*

As a U.S. Marine honor guard fired a rifle salute to the gallant commandos, a bugler played "Taps."

XIII

PLOTTING A REGIME CHANGE

Malta, November 18, 1804

I cannot but flatter myself that we may realize the success of our calculations on this coalition; and that you will have the glory of carrying the usurper a prisoner in Your Squadron to the United States.. . .
—William Eaton, in a letter to Commodore Samuel Barron

The *Argus* cast off from Malta's quarantine ground and slipped into the Mediterranean, headed to Levantine ports that never before had seen U.S. warships. Lieutenant Isaac Hull and his crew traveled under two sets of orders. The written orders described a routine convoy of American merchantmen from Alexandria or Smyrna to Malta; the oral ones promised adventure, and they were the operational ones, having come directly from Commodore Samuel Barron. Hull was to proceed to Egypt, as the cover orders stipulated, but with a special passenger, the versatile William Eaton, whom he was to lend every assistance on a top-secret mission: helping Hamet Karamanli assemble an insurgent army to overthrow his brother Yusuf. It was a quixotic assignment befitting Eaton's unique gifts and his metamorphosis from consul to Tunis to "Navy agent for the Barbary Regencies."

Eaton had lobbied furiously to return to Barbary with troops after his expulsion from Tunis in 1803. Upon his return to the

United States, Eaton had gone straight to Washington, even before going home to his wife Eliza after a four-year absence. There he had complained loudly about Morris's passivity while urging the Jefferson administration to commit troops against Tripoli. He made a special plea to the skeptical Cabinet, with only Navy Secretary Smith willing to give his unconditional support. "The Secretary of War [Henry Dearborn] believes it would be too great an effort and expense to send troops to Barbary, and thinks it both easier and cheaper to pay tribute to the savages, even if it should become necessary to double or treble our tribute payments," Eaton noted disgustedly before finally going home to Brimfield, Massachusetts. He soon was back in Washington. While the government would not commit troops, it would support an insurgency by Hamet Karamanli, the legitimate ruler of Tripoli.

This proposal was first suggested to Eaton in June 1801 by Richard Cathcart, the former consul to Tripoli. By September, Eaton was pitching it to Madison: "The subjects in general of the reigning bashaw are very discontented and ripe for revolt; they want nothing but confidence in the prospect of success." While tacitly approving the plan at the time, the secretary of state was squeamish about its underhandedness, possibly recalling the scheming of Spain, France, and England during America's colonial days. Such a conspiracy, he said, "does not accord with the general sentiments or views of the United States, to intermeddle in the domestic contests of other countries." But three years of war with Tripoli with no end in sight had made the scheme look appealing to Jefferson. He met privately with Eaton in June 1804, presumably to discuss the plan; there is no record of the meeting. However, Eaton afterward came into 1,000 War Department muskets and his new position in the Navy Department.

The administration's secretiveness and Smith's prudent instructions to Barron reeked of ambivalence: "We have no objection to you availing yourself of his co-operation with you against Tripoli—if you shall upon a full view of the subject after your arrival upon the Station, consider his co-operation expedient. The subject is committed entirely to your discretion." Should Barron decide to use Hamet, he would find "Mr. Eaton extremely useful to you." Similarly cautious were Madison's words to Consul General Lear. Madison permitted up to $20,000 to be spent on the Hamet project, but confessed to preferring continued attacks and blockading to the proposed joint operation with the former bashaw, "as the force under the orders of the Commodore is deemed sufficient for any exercise of coercion which the obstinacy of the Bashaw may demand."

The problem was the flaccid Hamet; he inspired confidence in no one. Thin, pale, and dull-eyed, with pockmarked cheeks, he lacked any personal charisma, and was inclined to every sort of self-indulgence, abetted by the dozens of sycophants in his traveling retinue. He had been an exile for nearly ten years, and few Tripolitans clamored for his return, remembering his singular ineffectiveness as bashaw and cognizant of the fact that in all that time he had been unable even to effect the release of his wife and children from his brother's custody. Among the many disaffected people in the countryside who complained of Yusuf's stiff tax levies to finance his war against America, scarcely anyone mentioned Hamet as a plausible alternative to his brother. Eaton had worked hard to build up Hamet's credibility, which Hamet had just as steadily undermined with his poor judgment. Most notably, he had moved to Tripoli's eastern provincial capital, Derna, at Yusuf's invitation, despite Eaton's warnings that the bashaw intended to have him killed. In July 1803 Hamet had to flee Derna into Egypt when Yusuf sent troops to kill him.

Eaton was aware of Hamet's failings and the good reasons for the government's tepidness toward the operation. But like Bainbridge, Eaton believed that only a ground campaign would force Yusuf to make an honorable peace. With Dearborn opposed to committing U.S. troops, Hamet represented the one hope of attacking Tripoli with a land force and America's winning peace on its terms. Because of his brief tenure as bashaw a decade earlier, Hamet still was familiar to Tripolitans, although not especially beloved. More importantly, Eaton believed Hamet would be loyal to the United States if it helped him snatch the throne from his brother Yusuf. Eaton said that organizing an expedition around Hamet was the difference between "taking a vicious horse by the heels" and having one with a bridle already in its mouth, its reins ready to seize. The expedition would be the capstone of Eaton's life.

After obtaining Jefferson's blessing for the Hamet alliance, Eaton dispatched his stepson, Eli Danielson, to Philadelphia and New York to withdraw money that Eaton had made in land speculation to augment whatever government funds he would get. Danielson purchased tents, saddles, and cooking gear, and Eaton ordered a scimitar from a New York smith, to be made of Toledo steel.

Eaton knew the Navy neither supported his plan nor him personally. Some of the Navy's antipathy toward him dated to Morris's detention in Tunis, for which Eaton still was blamed by naval officers. They also had closed ranks against Eaton because of his complaints about Captain Alexander Murray. Bainbridge, Murray, Morris, and Barron all disparaged Eaton's project at various times, although Murray came around after meeting Hamet on Malta. He even transported Hamet to his short-lived government position at Derna. Significantly, Preble, the most aggressive commodore to command the Mediterranean squadron, supported the plan, but he had now been superseded by Barron.

Eaton worked hard to win over Barron during their long Atlantic crossing on the *President*. The trouble wasn't just Eaton, it was Hamet's unsuitability, and it also was the Navy's secondary role. Barron initially refused to advance Eaton cash, arms, or ammunition, and turned Eaton down when he tried to raise money by seeking reimbursement for the ransom he had paid for Anna Maria Porcile. Eaton argued that he was owed the ransom money because the U.S. government had made him release her before he was able to collect from her father. Eaton complained to Smith that he had to get an advance on his salary—$1,000, nearly a full year's pay—so that he could hire mercenaries and buy provisions. "If my project succeed, the government will take the benefit of a *miracle*," he wrote exasperatedly to Smith, in a letter asking that a $50,000 fund be established at Malta for the operation. (It never was.) He vowed to personally fulfill the promises made to Hamet, even if his government did not. "If it fail, government sacrifices nothing; though my family may feel a sacrifice." While Barron eventually loosened the purse strings, it would never be enough to satisfy Eaton.

Yet Barron followed Smith's orders dutifully, although choosing to interpret them in the narrowest sense that obligated him to commit the fewest resources. Hull's verbal orders, which the lieutenant later recited in a sworn statement, stated that Hamet would receive the squadron's support at Derna or Benghazi, "and I will take the most effectual measures with the forces under my

Command for co-operating with him against the usurper, his brother; and for reestablishing him in the regency of Tripoli." But this was before Barron was laid low by a liver infection that nearly killed him and, consequently, fell under the spell of advisers such as Lear who opposed the government's support of Hamet and favored a quick, negotiated settlement with the bashaw.

Eaton, however, was determined to overcome all obstacles, formidable though they would be. To Preble, whom he admired for his bold attacks on Tripoli and whom he considered a friend, he described the result he hoped to effect through his alliance with Hamet. "How Glorious would be the exhibition to see our fellow citizens, in captivity at Tripoli, march in triumph from a dungeon to their tyrant's palace and display there the flag of the United States."

The *Argus* arrived at Alexandria on November 25, 1804, firing a 17-gun salute—the world's newest republic paying its first official visit to one of the oldest cities still extant. Founded in 332 B.C. by Alexander the Great, Alexandria had been ruled at various times by Greeks, Romans, Persians, Byzantines, Arabs, and Ottomans. The Americans gazed in wonder at the ancient and medieval buildings, mosques and homes ranged on the hills to the south of the harbor, and the city's 6,000 residents gazed back at the Americans with intense curiosity.

In the backwash of the Napoleonic wars, Egypt's 4 million inhabitants were convulsed in 1804 by civil war and anarchy. Napoleon's lightning invasion in 1798 was launched with the intent of adding a colony and providing a forward base for a campaign against British India. French troops quickly captured Alexandria and moved on to Cairo, defended by the Mamelukes, former Ottoman slaves of Kurdish, Turkish, and Circassian descent whose power in Egypt now rivaled the Ottomans. The Mamelukes fielded a formidable cavalry—"Let the Franks come; we shall crush them beneath our horses' hooves!" a Mameluke prince reportedly exclaimed—but they were overmatched against the French, whose artillery and firepower were decisive at the Battle of the Pyramids in 1798. The French took control of all of Egypt.

Then disaster struck on August 1, 1798, when the French fleet, anchored in Abukir Bay at Alexandria, was annihilated by Lord Horatio Nelson. With Napoleon and his army stranded and blockaded by the British fleet, the Turks readied invasion armies to reclaim Egypt. But the shrewd Napoleon thwarted them by launching a preemptive strike against Turkish forces massing in Syria and later wiping out a Turk army landed at Abukir Bay. Then, in 1799, he slipped away to France, leaving his army behind. The British and Turks regrouped. In 1801 they attacked and defeated the French. Turkey's sultan reasserted his sovereignty over Egypt, but in reality this only marked the commencement of a death struggle for supremacy between the Mamelukes and Ottomans that would last a decade. In the lawless countryside, rival armies and ragged bands of deserters and highwaymen pillaged and murdered without check. The only guarantors of safety were arms and numbers.

Into this chaotic mix waded Eaton and a handful of able men— Marine Lieutenant Presley O'Bannon, Richard Farquhar, Lieutenant Joshua Blake, Midshipman George Mann, Eaton's stepson, Eli Danielson, two seamen, and a Marine enlisted man. They had to find Hamet before there could be any march into the Tripoli regency 300 miles to the west, and they did not know where

Hamet was. The search party boarded a cutter at Alexandria and sailed to the mouth of the Nile River at Rosetta, about 20 miles northeast of Alexandria. While waiting for the tide to carry them into the Nile, they walked on a beach where French and British troops had fought in 1801. It was "covered with human Skeletons, ghastly monuments of the Savage influence of avarice and ambition on the human mind," observed Eaton.

They started up the Nile for Cairo, a river journey of more than 100 miles, hoping to learn from the Ottoman viceroy, Ahmed Pasha Khorshid, where Hamet might be. By this time, Eaton had seventeen well-armed men with him, thanks to the kindness of the British agent at Cairo, Major E. Misset, who had loaned Eaton his secretary and several men for the journey.

William Eaton arguably was America's first modern intelligence operative, as the appellation later would apply to agents who gathered information in hostile territory and then analyzed and acted on it. A striking blue-eyed man of slightly above average height, Eaton was both a thinking man and a man of action. Above all, he possessed the ability to concentrate his force on a single object. Well-educated and articulate, he was fluent in at least four Arabic dialects, all learned during his Barbary consulship. He also could speak four American Indian languages, and at Dartmouth had studied French, Latin, and Greek. His prodigious daily output of letters and journal entries rivaled any diplomat's. He also happened to be a crack rifle shot, could hit a target with a knife thrown from 80 feet, and was an expert with the scimitar, a weapon that had captivated him during his early days in Tunis; he had mastered the art of twirling it over his head—a trick few besides the janissaries of Constantinople could perform proficiently.

Eaton's affinity for indigenous people and knack for adapting to their environment would prove indispensable during the rigorous months ahead. These traits had made him a gifted scout and spy under General "Mad Anthony" Wayne in the Ohio country, when he donned buckskins and infiltrated the Miami Indian villages, and on the Spanish frontier in southeast Georgia—places where he had become adept at living off the land, engaging in guerrilla warfare and rapid movement. When Jefferson, Madison, and Smith approved Eaton's plan to restore Hamet to Tripoli's throne, it is unlikely that they realized to what extent success would depend on Eaton's abilities.

On the Nile, the Eaton party passed scenes worthy of Dante's pen—indiscriminate killings, villages ransacked so many times that nothing of the slightest value remained, and starving refugees. Bandits and armed deserters from the warring armies robbed one and all. "Egypt has no master," Eaton wrote to Sir Alexander Ball, the governor of Malta. "The Turkish soldiery, restrained by no discipline sieze with the hand of rapine, everything for which passion creates a desire," and the Mamelukes were no better. "Wild Arabs" roved the banks of the Nile, ready to pounce on the defenseless. They carefully avoided the well-armed Americans and British in Eaton's two boats, each equipped with a swivel-mounted gun. Along the way, Eaton's party hunted pigeons and fowl; if the sight of their arms didn't discourage the Arabs, the loud reports of gunfire certainly did. They reached Sabour as Arabs were driving off the villagers' herds; the day before, the same village had been plundered by 500 Albanian deserters from the Turkish army.

At Sabour, the people welcomed the sight of the Americans' red-and-blue uniforms and round hats. (The French wore triangular hats.) "They kissed our hands; and with prostrations to the ground and eyes inflamed with anguish implored English succor," Eaton wrote to Ball, suggesting the time for an English reoccupation might be at hand. In fact, everywhere they went, the people wanted to know if they were English and when they planned to return and restore order. Egyptians, Eaton said, preferred the English because they "*pay* for every thing; the French *pay nothing* and take everything—They don't like this kind of deliverers." Eaton impressed the natives with his rifle marksmanship by splitting an orange twice with three shots at 32 yards.

In Turkish-ruled Cairo, Eaton learned Hamet had joined the other side, the Mamelukes. No one knew exactly where he was. Moreover, his alliance with the rebels made a rendezvous awkward, with Turkish troops controlling the countryside between Cairo and the Mamelukes' strongholds to the south, and the Mameluke redoubts themselves under attack.

Cairo's viceroy, Khorshid, politely overlooked the fact that their ally had joined the enemy, and made the Americans welcome. Cairo, more populous (260,000) than anyplace most of the Americans had ever seen, put on a show for the visitors. They were escorted to the palace in a torchlight parade through the city. Spectators lined the road for a mile and a half, eager to see the men from the New World, who were accompanied by some of Khorshid's attendants and six splendidly liveried Arabian horses.

At the palace, Khorshid rose from an embroidered purple sofa with damask cushions to greet them ceremoniously. They drank coffee, smoked pipes, and ate sherbet while the viceroy peppered them with questions about the United States, its geography, government, and people. Eaton made the most of the situation, describing at length the customs of the American people and explaining that the Barbary War was being fought to vindicate U.S. rights. He compared the Barbary pirates and the Ottomans in a manner flattering to the Turks. Eaton said Americans and Turks were alike, and drew startling—but not necessarily accurate—parallels between Islam and the peculiar offshoot of Christianity he claimed Americans practiced: the worship of one God, with no unnecessary bloodshed.

With the ice broken by Eaton's flattery, the viceroy brought up the ticklish subject of Hamet. He had intended to honor his predecessor's promises to aid Hamet until his unfortunate alliance with the Mamelukes. Eaton, who knew that everything depended on the viceroy's support, interjected that "it was more like God to pardon than to punish a repenting enemy." His homage to the viceroy's godlike powers and his other flattery utterly disarmed Khorshid; he promised to send emissaries to locate Hamet and to permit Hamet to join Eaton and leave Egypt unmolested. It was a supreme diplomatic victory for Eaton. He cemented their relationship by announcing that he wished to name Dr. Francesco Mendrici, formerly the Tunis bey's doctor, to be the agent for the United States in Cairo. Khorshid certainly raised no objections; Mendrici happened to be his chief physician.

The viceroy's envoy traced Hamet to the Upper Egypt city of Miniet, where 3,000 besieged Mamelukes recently had thrown back 8,000 attacking Albanians and Turks. Eaton sent a letter suggesting that they meet in Rosetta, where Hamet could seek British protection.

Eaton impatiently awaited a response in Cairo, acutely aware that all of his hopes for driving Yusuf from power with a land expedition hinged on Hamet's reply. Would he join Eaton? Had he abandoned hopes of regaining his throne? Eaton knew that without his cooperation, there could be no insurgency, no invasion.

The reply, which came quickly, was all that Eaton had hoped for. After mildly rebuking Eaton for delaying, Hamet said he was leaving Miniet for the home of a sheik friend to begin preparing for the expedition. "Thus you must assist from the sea and I from the land, and God will aid us in establishing peace and tranquility."

A few days later brought another letter from Hamet: "I cannot but congratulate you and felicitate myself after so much apprehension doubt and solicitude, that we now calculate with certainty on the success of our expedition. . . ." He already was headed down the Nile to meet Eaton. Bring plenty of money, he said unnecessarily—Eaton well knew that money was everything in North Africa. "Do not think about money because the occasion demands heavy expenditure. It is a matter of making war, and war calls for money and men."

They agreed to rendezvous near Lake Fiaume, 190 miles from the Mediterranean coast and on the edge of Egypt's Western Desert. Eaton embarked from Alexandria at the head of a troop of mounted men consisting of Lieutenant Blake, Midshipman Mann, and twenty-three others. Less than halfway to Lake Fiaume, Turkish troops stopped them at their lines, the outermost frontier of Turk-controlled territory, and would not permit them to go on. Eaton and his men had no choice but to settle into Demanhour, governed tyrannically by the local Turkish army commander known as the Kerchief. Eaton went to work trying to win over the harsh, dour leader, flattering him for his troops' military bearing, and stating that he was undoubtedly a man of valor. Few could resist Eaton's charm for very long. Soon the Kerchief and Eaton were on excellent terms, and the Kerchief had no problem with Eaton's notifying Hamet that he was in Demanhour and inviting him to join him there.

While he waited, Eaton watched the Turkish troops drill, visited the Kerchief, and reconnoitered the village, whose inhabitants were as intensely curious about the Americans as they were about the villagers. Eaton began to notice a mournful-looking boy lurking around his lodgings. The boy shied away whenever Eaton invited him inside. Eaton made inquiries about him, and learned that the boy's father, a prominent, wealthy villager, had owned the house where Eaton was staying. But when the Turks came, they beheaded him and appropriated all of his property, including his home. The boy, five brothers and sisters, and their mother lived only a few doors down from Eaton. Softhearted when it came to women and children, Eaton gave the family all of the pocket money that he had. "The child kissed my hand; and wept! God, I thank thee that my children are Americans!" To his wife Eliza, he wrote: "There is more pleasure in being generous than rich . . . Man wants but little, and not that little long."

Unaccountably, the Kerchief cooled toward the Americans. Turkish guards suddenly appeared outside the Americans' quarters and accompanied them on their walks. Eaton tried to learn from the Kerchief the reason for the chill, but the leader was closed and suspicious. Finally, Eaton teased out the problem: The French consul was spreading it about Egypt that Eaton and his men were British spies who were using Hamet to aid the Mameluke rebels. It was believable enough, given the rumors already abroad that the British were secretly subsidizing the Mamelukes. Once again, the Americans had been caught in England and France's crossfire.

Eaton so thoroughly allayed the Kerchief's suspicions that when Hamet reached Demanhour on February 5 with his suite of 100 attendants, they were greeted by salutes from the Kerchief's honor guard. "Tents were pitched for the accommodation of his people, and provision made for their refreshment—the Bashaw sleeps tonight at the Kercheifs house, and tomorrow afternoon we depart for Alexandria. . . ." However, the French consul's slander damaged Hamet in Alexandria. The governor and admiral forbade him to set foot in the city, and refused to let him embark by ship from there.

The restrictions didn't matter. Hamet had decided to attack by land rather than by sea, wisely reasoning that if he sailed, he would have to depend on his followers making their way cross-country without his leadership. Most of them probably would never reach Derna. The decision resolved a host of problems that Lieutenant Isaac Hull had foreseen, chief among them being space; if even 100 of Hamet's force sailed to Derna on the *Argus,* there would have been no room for their provisions.

The expedition's audacity invested the sojourners' preparations with an electric quality. They would have to cross 460 miles of rocky, arid wasteland before Hull could resupply them at Bomba. Would they be able to carry enough food and water to last them until then? Would Hamet, as he claimed, be able to marshal support among the desert inhabitants, or would they only encounter hostile Bedouin tribes? Once the invaders reached Bomba, they would be only three days from Derna, Tripoli's second-largest city. And from Derna, it was but another 100 miles to Benghazi. If an attack on Benghazi succeeded, U.S. warships would carry the army the last 400 miles to Tripoli itself for the climactic assault.

Hamet camped at Arab's Tower, 30 miles west of Alexandria's

old port, while Eaton and O'Bannon went into Alexandria to recruit soldiers.

Hull had begun signing up mercenaries in the port city while Eaton was waiting in Demanhour for Hamet, but the jittery Turkish officials ordered him to hand over some Maltese whom he had recruited, then demanded that he stop altogether. Hull discharged everyone he had signed, closed his Alexandria house, and moved aboard the *Argus*. The French whisperings about Eaton's party really being British spies were damaging enough, but Yusuf made matters worse by sending an envoy to Alexandria to persuade the governor and admiral to stop Hamet from leaving Egypt. The envoy was remarkably frank with the governor. The bashaw, he said, feared that his people would rally to Hamet's standard, and he would have to flee or lose his head. Yusuf was weary of the war with America, the envoy said.

Yusuf's growing concern over his brother's movements was becoming increasingly evident in Tripoli as well. He "is now very attentive upon your transactions with his brother in Alexandria—a Camp is going against Derne ," Nissen, the Danish consul in Tripoli, wrote in sympathetic ink to Consul Davis in Tunis. Yusuf's agent in Malta, Gaetano Schembry, was urging the bashaw to intensify his ill-treatment of the *Philadelphia* prisoners to force America to agree to peace. Nissen warned in his secret message to Davis: ". . . you Sacrifice your prisoner's life here in case of success."

Even before Eaton's rendezvous with Hamet, gloom had pervaded the bashaw's castle over the protracted war. And then the 1804 grain harvest was so poor that in October, Yusuf had halted all grain sales—except to his household. This had precipitated a fierce argument with Murad Reis, his Scottish son-in-law, who had planned to buy barley in the market. Yusuf lost his temper with Murad—the grand admiral was drunk and insolent—and struck him and threw him in prison. Later, when tempers cooled, the bashaw released him and blamed their quarrel on a servant. The servant was punished with 500 bastinados. In November, Yusuf suffered an epileptic seizure. "His people thought he was possessed with the devil," wrote Cowdery. A marabout, a Moslem holy man, was summoned to drive the devil out; the seizure's abatement was ascribed to his incantations. In December, Yusuf presided over his son's marriage to Hamet's eldest daughter, a "very handsome" twelve-year-old.

While Hamet enlisted Arab supporters, Eaton and Lieutenant O'Bannon tramped the streets of Alexandria looking for European soldiers of fortune. Hull opened a $10,000 line of credit in Alexandria and had given Eaton $3,000 cash for recruitment expenses. Eaton spent it and an additional $3,000 before completing preparations for the expedition. Eaton estimated the expedition would cost at least $20,000, a bargain by any measure. Before parting with Hull, Eaton got another $7,000 advance and instructed Hull to have $7,000 more for him at Bomba. Eaton well knew that in North Africa, where only one's tribe and Islam commanded absolute loyalty, money was the third-best guarantor. "Cash will do much with the inhabitants of this Country; even those whom it will not engage to fight, will by it be engaged not to fight: With it we can pass generally."

A more diverse army probably never assembled under U.S. auspices. There were Greeks, Italians, Tripolitans, Egyptians, Frenchmen, Arabs, Americans, and British—eleven nationalities in all. Of the 400 or more expeditioners, just 10 were Americans: Eaton, Lieutenant O'Bannon, Marine Sergeant Arthur Campbell, 6 Marine privates, and Midshipman Paoli Peck from the *Argus*. Two Englishmen had signed on—Richard Farquhar and his brother Percival. (But only one Farquhar actually went on the expedition; it is unclear which, for Eaton referred to both as "Richard"; one of the Richards was turned out for embezzling $1,332.) Selim Comb, a Turk, was in charge of the 25 cannoneers, who had no cannons. Captain Luco Ulovix and a Lieutenant Constantine led 38 mixed European and Egyptian infantry, mostly Greeks. The rest consisted of Hamet and his 90 Tripolitan attendants, and up to 300 Arab cavalry and footmen under Sheiks il Taiib and Mahomet. Scores of horses, 107 camels, and some jackasses carried the food, water, and ammunition.

The ragtag army was a patchwork of clothing, uniforms, and military bearing, ranging from the unwavering discipline of the uniformed Marines to the irascible, erratic Arab cavalrymen, who were as apt to mutiny as to charge recklessly. As a former Army combat officer, Eaton clearly saw his little army's shortcomings and tried to remedy them. He needed 100 Marines, 100 stands of arms, cartridges, and two brass fieldpieces with trains and ammunition, he told Barron.

Of the motley band Eaton and O'Bannon scraped up in Alexandria, no one had a life story matching that of the incomparable Johan Eugene Leitensdorfer. He was the courier who had handed Hamet Eaton's message in Miniet urging the rendezvous in Rosetta. Leitensdorfer happened to be between engagements, a rarity for a man who lived on the run, over a lifetime in which he practiced thirty occupations, served in five armies, and married three women without a divorce. Eaton made Leitensdorfer one of his top officers.

Leitensdorfer was born Gervasso Prodasio Santuari near Trent in the Tyrol in October 1772. He studied for the priesthood, but found it wasn't for him. He quit, married, and went to work as a surveyor. Yet the ordinary workaday life did not suit him either, and he joined the Austrian army, acquiring the taste for adventure and the wanderlust that would dominate his life. He fought the Turks at Belgrade and the French at Mantua, where he deserted rather than be hanged for dueling. Changing his name to Carlo Hossando, he joined Napoleon's army. The French learned of his previous service in the enemy army and arrested him on suspicion of being a spy. He escaped from prison after drugging his guards with opium and fled to Switzerland, where he became Johan Eugene Leitensdorfer. His family sent him money, which he used to buy watches and jewelry, then peddled his wares throughout Spain and France.

Under his new name, he rejoined the French army in time for the invasion of Egypt in 1798. He assisted the French with their Egyptian agricultural and economic projects. When the British drove out the French three years later, he opened a coffeehouse, bought a home in Alexandria, and married a Coptic woman, while still married to his first wife in the Tyrol. His career as a coffeehouse proprietor lasted only until the British withdrew from Egypt in 1803. Once again feeling the pull of the religious life, he sailed to Messina and became a novice at a Capuchin monastery. But he found that he didn't want to be a friar, and soon became a street magician in Constantinople. Then he enlisted in the Turkish army and was sent back to Egypt. When the Mamelukes defeated his unit in battle, he deserted, hid among the Bedouins, and made his way back to Constantinople, where he converted to Islam, circumcised himself with his own razor, and became a dervish, adept at sorcery and tricks, with the new name of Murat Aga. He roamed the Black Sea's south shore, peddling excerpts from the Koran written on small slips of paper, which he sanctified by rubbing them against a shaved spot on top of his head.

While wandering rugged northern Turkey, Leitensdorfer encountered the bashaw of Trebizond, who had been struck blind. Claiming he could restore the bashaw's sight, Leitensdorfer blew caustic lime into his eyes and washed it out with milk, then started him on a "sweat cure." Midway through it, Leitensdorfer himself began to sweat, doubtless imagining what might happen to him if the cure didn't work. He decided not to wait around to find out and joined a caravan bound for Persia. Bandits overtook and robbed the travelers. While plundering the caravan, the chatty thieves informed them of the bashaw's miraculous recovery of his eyesight. Leitensdorfer hurried back to Trebizond to claim a rich reward, and then joined a Moslem pilgrimage to Mecca. At Jedda on the Red Sea, he met a Lord Gordon, a gentleman Scot who was on a tour, and became his interpreter. They traveled to Abyssinia and Nubia. Back in Cairo, Leitensdorfer quit Gordon, returned to Alexandria, separated from his second wife, and joined Eaton.

His adventures with Eaton were by no means the final chapter. He drifted to Palermo, married a third time, but couldn't settle down. So he sailed to the United States. He became a surveyor of public buildings in Washington, D.C., under Benjamin Latrobe. Later, as a watchman at the U.S. Capitol, he lived in a room in the north wing, cooking for himself, making shoes and maps, and catching birds. Congress awarded Leitensdorfer 320 acres in Missouri for his service with Eaton, and paid him a rate for each mile he traveled with the expedition. Later, a Viennese theater production about his incredible life drew large audiences.

Eaton drew up a formal agreement with Hamet titled "Convention between the United States of America and his Highness, Hamet, Caramanly , Bashaw of Tripoli." The remarkable document, written by Eaton, and signed and witnessed on February 23, 1805, in Alexandria, contained fourteen articles and an additional "secret" one that committed Hamet to handing over Yusuf and Murad Reis to Barron as surety of Hamet's fulfillment of the other pledges that he made.

In exchange for Eaton's supplying Hamet with arms and ships to restore him to the throne, Hamet agreed to a host of terms, all contingent on his becoming bashaw: releasing the *Philadelphia* captives without ransom; repaying the United States for its monetary support with the tribute he would collect from Denmark, Sweden, and the Batavian Republic; granting America most-favored-nation status; and henceforth levying no tribute on the United States. In other words, in gratitude for America's help, Hamet would end hostilities forever and treat America as an equal. The convention also made Eaton general and commander in chief of the invasion force collecting in Alexandria.

Sanguine about the expedition's prospects, Eaton boasted to Barron: "I cannot but flatter myself that we may realize the success of our calculations on this coalition; and that you will have the glory of carrying the usurper a prisoner in Your Squadron to the United States; and of releiving our fellow citizens from the chains of slavery without the degrading conditions of a ransom."

Turkish troops swooped down, snaring Hamet's servants on

March 2 as the last expedition provisions were being loaded onto a boat in Alexandria. Then they began advancing on Hamet's camp at the Arab's Tower. Panic broke out among Hamet and his attendants. Only Lieutenant O'Bannon's firm intervention prevented mass flight.

The reason for the surprise raid, Eaton noted with relief, was only a neglected bribe. "We found the impediments raised to us were occasioned by influence of the supervisor of the revenue, who had not yet been bought.—The day was spent in accommodating the affair."

Eaton joined Hamet at Arab's Tower. At 11:00 A.M. on March 8, 1805, the patchwork army began marching into the wasteland to the west.

XIV

AMERICA'S LAWRENCE

*From Alexandria to this place there is not a living stream, nor rivulet,
nor spring of water.*
—William Eaton, in his journal of the expedition

*Wherever General Eaton leads, we will follow. If he wants to march
us to hell, we'll gladly go there.. .. The General always knows what
to say and do, in any situation.*
—Lieutenant Presley O'Bannon, USMC, from
his account of the desert march

As befitted a commander in chief, William Eaton led the way in a flashy general's uniform with epaulets. With him were the Marines, also sharp in their blue and scarlet uniforms. The army's martial appearance then fell off sharply to a hodgepodge of uniforms and castoff raiment from an assortment of armies, and then descended even further to flowing Moslem robes, hats, turbans, and headdresses and drab European civilian attire. The expedition's officers and Arab cavalry traveled on horseback, while the rest of the army was afoot, their supplies carried on the backs of camels. The army trekked 15 miles during its first day on the march. It camped on a high bluff near the coast and found good water.

The army followed the curve of the Mediterranean shoreline westward, sometimes a day's march inland, sometimes closer to the sea. It was the same line of march followed by Alexander the Great 2,136 years before, and by previous and subsequent waves of conquerors and wayfarers from the Mediterranean and East: Berbers, Assyrians, Persians, Romans, Byzantines, and Arabs. During World War II, Rommel and Montgomery would duel along this 40-mile-wide corridor; their operations and supply officers would consult maps of Eaton's expedition.

The route threaded through arid country that compared favorably with the blazing ocean of sand a day's march south, but was by no means hospitable. In March and April, temperatures hovered between 90 and 100 degrees by day, and plunged to freezing at night. During the "winds of 50 days" during early spring, fine sand blew continually all day, sometimes rising on great whirlwinds that, when backlit by the sun, resembled moving pillars of fire. The gritty sand got into the eyes and mouth, into weapons and food. When the wind died, clouds of black flies appeared to torment the travelers.

To reach Derna 520 miles away, the sojourners must skirt the Qattara Depression, cross the Desert of Barca, a northern arm of the Libyan Desert, and ascend the rocky Libyan Plateau overlooking the coast. While the region's meager rainfall supported scruffy vegetation—wildly extravagant compared with the forbidding sands to the south—a journey through the dry country was survivable only if one knew where to find the water. Somehow Eaton always did. Lieutenant Presley O'Bannon noted with obvious admiration, "General Eaton's instincts are uncanny."

The Marines were unsure of Eaton at first because he wasn't one of them and was prone to grandiosity, which aroused the down-to-earth Marines' suspicions. However, the Marines soon became his staunchest allies. "Wherever General Eaton leads, we will follow," O'Bannon wrote. "If he wants to march us to hell, we'll gladly go there . . . The General always knows what to say and do, in any situation."

• • •

Two days into the march, the camel drivers and Arab footmen went on strike. They refused to take another step unless Eaton immediately paid them the money he had promised them at the end of the march: $11 per camel. It turned out that Sheik il Taiib had spread the rumor that the Christians intended to cheat them. Eaton refused to pay. The Arabs refused to march. Eaton ordered the Christians to start back for Alexandria, "threatning to abandon the expedition and their Bashaw, unless the march in advance proceeded immediately." The camel drivers relented.

Three days later, a courier rode up with the news that Derna had revolted. The governor reportedly was hiding in his castle, and the province awaited Hamet's triumphal arrival. The electrifying report launched a nearly tragic chain of events. The Arab cavalry fired their weapons into the air in celebration. Hearing the gunfire, the Arab footmen bringing up the rear with the baggage thought the caravan was being attacked by desert nomads. They instantly turned on their Christian escort, intending to kill and rob them in the confusion of the attack before the nomads reached the baggage train. A massacre was narrowly averted by the intervention of a single Arab who insisted they verify they were being attacked before commencing the slaughter. Cooler heads prevailed. The alleged Derna insurrection, it turned out, never occurred.

Chronic theft reached crisis proportions. Barley and provisions disappeared daily. Two days after the near-massacre, Arabs stole all the cheese and a musket, bayonet, and ammunition from the Marines' tent. Cheese was one thing, weapons another. Thereafter, the Marines safeguarded the muskets by sleeping on top of them.

The army sometimes came upon the faint traces of the region's ancient conquerors and inhabitants. They drew water from deep Roman wells and cisterns, and at the castle at Massou (now Matruh), they bathed in stone baths built for Cleopatra, and explored a valley dotted with the ruins of ancient gardens and mansions. The vestiges of the irrecoverable past deeply impressed the Americans. At a ruined ancient castle with an immense cistern, Eaton examined scattered, eroded grave markers bearing Turkish and Arabic inscriptions marking the final resting places of Islamic pilgrims, "expressive of little else than an ejaculation." One of Eaton's foreign officers found two copper coins "with Greek inscriptions but so effaced as not to be intelligible. . . ."

The brief interregnum ended with another outburst of fractious self-interest that threatened to destroy the expedition. The camel drivers again refused to continue, claiming Hamet had contracted with them to pack the caravan's provisions only to Massou—and hadn't paid them anything at the outset of the expedition, as Eaton had been led to believe. They were right; Hamet had made the partial deal and not told Eaton. Eaton promised them cash if they could travel two more days; he hoped to meet desert tribesmen by then and hire a fresh caravan. Eaton gave them his last $533 and $140 borrowed from his Christian soldiers. For the moment, it seemed to satisfy them. But during the night, most of them started back to Egypt. In the morning, only forty camels remained. Their drivers refused to go on, and then they deserted, too, the next day, March 20. At this unhappy juncture, Sheik il Taiib and some of the other chiefs announced they would not march farther until a courier was sent to Bomba to find out whether U.S. vessels had arrived with fresh provisions. A rumor made the rounds, further undermining the army's morale: that Yusuf had dispatched 800 cavalry and an infantry force to defend Derna, and that it had already passed Benghazi. This report proved mostly accurate.

Eaton responded to the refusals by stopping the Arabs' rations and threatening to order his Christian troops to occupy the castle and hold out against the Arabs until he could summon a U.S. relief force. The Arabs' resolve melted. Fifty drivers returned to the caravan with their dromedaries, and the column marched 13 miles to a plateau where they found good cistern water. The next day, they arrived at the desert Arabs' camp, and 80 mounted warriors joined Hamet, followed a few days later by 150 foot soldiers, with their families and movable goods.

The tribesmen thought the Americans "curiosities . . . [and] laughed at the oddity of our dress; gazed at our polished arms with astonishment:—at the same time they observed the greatest deference toward us as bore any distinctive marks of office." They offered to barter young gazelles and ostriches, but Eaton could offer only rice in exchange. The expedition moved on, its larder reduced to hard bread and rice. Water was scarcer, available only in rock cavities and cisterns now. "From Alexandria to this place there is not a living stream, nor rivulet, nor spring of water."

A fresh crisis arose. A report that Yusuf's cavalry was but a few days from Derna caused Hamet and the Arabs to announce they were abandoning the expedition. Eaton, resolute as always, again cut off their rations and met with the Arab chiefs and Hamet. "Despondency sat in every countenance." Hamet said he would continue, but Sheik il Taiib said he would not until he received assurances that the U.S. vessels were waiting at Bomba.

Until this point, Eaton had shown remarkable restraint in the face of the Arabs' continual complaints and threats, but now he exploded. "I could not but reproach that chief with want of courage and fidelity.—He had promised much and fulfilled nothing.—I regretted having been acquainted with him:—and should be well satisfied if he would put his menace in execution of returning to Egypt, provided he would not interfere with the dispositions of the other chiefs." Unaccustomed to being dressed down like this, the stunned sheik stormed from the meeting, "swearing by all the force of his religion to join us no more." Eaton stopped Hamet from sending an officer after il Taiib to paper over their breach.

The next day, March 27, the sheik left the expedition with half the Arabs. Eaton again rejected Hamet's pleas to send a messenger after them. "The services of that chief were due to us:—We had paid for them:—and he had pledged his faith to render them with fidelity." Hamet said he feared the sheik would now support Yusuf. "Let him do it," Eaton replied. "I like an open enemy better than a treacherous friend." However, the sheik had second thoughts and returned sheepishly. "You see the influence I have among these people!" he told Eaton, showing him he had brought back all of his men. "Yes," Eaton wrote in his journal, "and I see also the disgraceful use you make of it."

Hamet balked now. He retrieved the horses he had given to the expedition's officers, distributed them among his footmen, and drew off with the Arab cavalry. "Joseph Bashaw's forces had siezed on all his nerves." After reproaching Hamet for disloyalty and for flinching from adversity, Eaton marched off with the Europeans and the baggage. Two hours later, Hamet caught up with Eaton, full of praise for Eaton's firmness and claiming his irresolution had been only a show to appease his followers. Hamet might have overcome his fears temporarily, but the tribal Arabs who had joined the caravan were marching in the other direction to Egypt. Sheik il Taiib had persuaded them to desert. Hamet sent one of his officers, Hamet Gurgies, after them with a detachment, and he returned with the deserters a day later.

Sheiks il Taiib and Mahomet squabbled over $1,500 given them by Hamet, Mahomet swearing he would not continue until he got his money, and then departing with his men. Weary of the sheiks' querulousness and greed, Eaton spent the day visiting a desert tribe that lived in a nearby castle. The tribesmen examined with amazement the clothing, epaulets, arms, and spurs of the Americans and Europeans. "They were astonished that God should permit people to possess such riches who followed the religion of the devil!"

The expedition wasn't all hardships, threats, and thievery. The Arabs sometimes staged horsemanship exhibitions, and from O'Bannon's tent wafted the cheerful sound of a mountain fiddle. O'Bannon was a native of Faquier County in the Blue Ridge Mountain foothills of northern Virginia, and was married to the former Matilda Heard, the granddaughter of the great Revolutionary War hero, General Daniel Morgan, the victor at Cowpens. A Marine for four years, O'Bannon was twenty-nine, tough and resourceful. He believed in discipline. On the *Adams* at Gibraltar in 1802, he had expressed disgust with Captain Hugh Campbell's laxness, reporting to Marine Commandant William Burrows that he "has conducted himself in such a manner as to forfeit the respect of the Officers on Board his own Ship and I believe it extends to all who know him."

But O'Bannon had a fun-loving side that reflected his Irish ancestry, and whose outlet was his fiddle. "O'Bannon [is] one of the Happiest fellows Living," especially when performing for the Spanish ladies at Gibraltar, the same Campbell reported to Burrows. A favorite, whose strains could be heard coming from O'Bannon's tent on desert nights, was "Hogs in the Corn." He also played Irish jigs, and Private Bernard O'Brian sometimes danced to them.

Eaton's volcanic relationship with the Arab sheiks edged toward an explosion when a delegation of six sheiks demanded more food. The entire army was down to a daily rice ration. Delegation leader Sheik il Taiib warned Eaton that a mutiny was imminent unless he opened up the larder. Eaton ordered them out of his tent and threatened to execute Taiib if there were an uprising. Later, the sheik returned in a conciliatory mood that Eaton reciprocated. "I replied that I required nothing of him by way of reconciliation but truth, fidelity to the Bashaw, pacific conduct among the other chiefs, uniformity and perseverance in this conduct," Eaton wrote. "These he promised by an oath; and offered me his hand. . . ."

Meanwhile, Hamet was pursuing Sheik Mahomet, who had abandoned the expedition and was on his way back to Egypt. Absent several days, Hamet rode up with the sheik and his party on April 2 after riding 120 miles. The rare display of energy and force by Hamet pleased Eaton immensely. "He rode all night of the 31st and succeeding day in an uncomfortable fall of rain and chilly winds," Eaton wrote with avuncular pride, and "subsisted his party during the expedition on milk and dates which were occasionally brought him by the desert Arabs."

• • •

The expedition crossed Tripoli's border, and Eaton felt the need to proclaim his army's intentions to the Tripolitan people. He was keenly aware that if his message were properly presented, it might swing popular support to Hamet. This was crude psychological warfare. In the twentieth century, it would become an art and science, and U.S. psy-ops officers would leaflet Europe, Vietnam, Kuwait, and Iraq, urging the enemy to give up. But in 1805, psy-ops did not appear in warfare manuals; it was left to the initiative of individual officers. How Eaton came up with the idea isn't known for certain—perhaps from his infiltration of the Miami tribe, or when he matched wits with the Spanish on the Georgia–Florida frontier.

The proclamation began with Eaton playing the religious card that had worked so well with the Cairo viceroy. American Christianity, he said, was a peaceful religion, "the orthodox faith of Abraham," and thus a sister faith to Islam. With common ground established, he launched his attack on Yusuf. The bashaw was "a bloodthirsty scoundrel" who had killed one brother "even in his mother's arms," and had driven out his other brother, Hamet, while surrounding himself with "hypocrites" and "vagabonds." Yusuf, he said, had spurned America's peace overturns and attacked U.S. shipping with pirate ships commanded by

scoundrels who had just escaped from certain Christian countries to evade the punishment which their crimes merited . . .

He leads you into war with no advantage to you whatever. He does not hesitate to drench his shores with your blood, provided that he be able to gain money by it! Yes, he scoffs at your sufferings, saying: O what value are these Moors and these Arabs! They

261

are just beasts which belong to me, worth a great deal less than my camels and my asses . . .

God has stamped upon his forehead the mark of Cain, the first murderer . . . the end of his usurpation and of his cruelty approaches . . . The wrath of God has been aroused against the said Joussuf, the treacherous scoundrel.

The United States was committed to Hamet, "a just and merciful prince, who greatly loves his subjects" and who wished to return to the throne and bring peace to Tripoli.

Promising weapons, food, money, and soldiers to help the people of Tripoli overthrow Yusuf, Eaton pledged unwavering personal support: "I shall be always with you until the end of the war and even until you have achieved your glorious mission, in proof of our fidelity and our goodwill."

It isn't known how the proclamation was received in Tripoli, but the caravan attracted more desert Arabs now that Hamet was in his native land. By early April, there were 600 to 700 fighting men, with another 500 camp followers and Bedouin families.

Eaton's feud with the Arab sheiks reached a roaring climax on April 8, when they refused to budge from camp until a courier was sent to Bomba to determine whether Hull had arrived with food. Only six days' rice ration remained. Eaton argued that with Bomba that many days away, it would be foolhardy to use up their remaining food idly awaiting the courier's return; they then would have to march to Bomba anyway, and on empty stomachs. The sheiks were unmoved. "If they preferred famine to fatigue they might have the choice," Eaton told Hamet. He ordered their ration stopped.

Hamet now displayed his constitutional gutlessness by

announcing that he was turning back. The expedition's simmering tensions came to a full boil. The Arabs prepared to make a grab for the provisions. Eaton and O'Bannon mustered the Christian troops in front of the food tent with loaded muskets. The far more numerous Arabs advanced, stopping just yards away from the Christians' dressed ranks. For a full hour, the armed allies confronted one another with loaded guns and swords. Finally Hamet pitched his tent to show he was remaining with the expedition. He persuaded the Arabs to dismount.

Eaton then made a nearly fatal mistake. He gave the order for the Christian troops, still in ranks, to perform the manual of arms, evidently thinking this would be a good time for them to hold their daily practice. "The Christians are preparing to fire on us!" the Arabs shouted when they heard the clash of muskets. Two hundred mounted their horses and charged on the gallop, stopping at the last possible instant and withdrawing a short distance. Still on their horses, the Arabs pointed out all the Christian officers and aimed their weapons at them. "Fire!" they cried. But some of Hamet's officers bellowed simultaneously, "For God's sake do not fire! The Christians are our friends!" Miraculously, no one fired.

The Christians began to lose their nerve. Soon only Eaton, O'Bannon and his Marines, Peck, Richard Farquhar, Selim Aga, his lieutenants, and two Greek officers faced the mutinous Arabs. Eaton, unarmed, advanced toward Hamet, exhorting him to avert a slaughter. Dozens of Arab muskets were aimed at his chest. Hamet looked distracted. Eaton tried to address the cavalrymen, but they drowned him out with their shouts.

Eaton began to berate the Arabs in a loud voice and in their own tongue. He said they were "women" who were afraid of battle. "The General continued to revile them until I thought he would lose his voice," said O'Bannon. "Then, all at once, his manner changed, and now he sounded joyous." He shouted words of encouragement, and some of the Arabs cheered.

The standoff ended when several Arab chiefs and some of Hamet's lieutenants rode between the two sides with drawn sabers and drove back the Arabs. Eaton sternly pulled Hamet aside. Had he forgotten the expedition's purpose and that they were all supposed to be allies? "He relented:—called me his friend & protector:—said he was too soon heated:—and followed me to my tent, giving orders at the same time to his Arabs to disperse."

Later, O'Bannon scolded Eaton for rashly mingling with the mutinous Arabs while unarmed. With a laugh, Eaton raised the sleeves of his robe to reveal a pair of bone-handled throwing knives strapped to his wrists. "A slight tug at the handle of either knife would have brought the weapon instantly into his hand."

Eaton sent a fast courier ahead to Bomba to look for Hull while the army pushed on. Christians and Arabs alike were down to their last reserves of strength, subsisting on a daily cup of rice and a half-ration of water. Captain Selim Comb augmented their pinched diet with a wildcat: 5 feet long, sable color, with black ears and nose and a dark-brindled tail. His greyhound had chased it down in the desert. "It was cooked, and it eat very well." There was never enough water to slake their raging thirst. At one stop, the soldiers and camp followers crowded around a well of filthy water, jostling one another to wet their lips. The pushing caused a horse to tumble down the slope to the well, taking two people with him. Halting on April 9 at a cistern, the marchers found two dead men in the water, Moslem pilgrims murdered by bandits. "We were obliged nevertheless to use the water," observed Eaton.

Until O'Bannon stopped the practice, the hungry Marines cut the buttons from their dress uniforms and traded them with Arab women for food, and possibly sexual favors. The women strung the buttons into necklaces and wore them around their necks. Some of the foot soldiers and Bedouin families turned back for lack of adequate food. Hamet killed a pack camel for meat and traded another to the desert Arabs for sheep. He butchered and distributed the mutton to all the troops, now reduced to eating wild fennel and sorrel that they found in ravines, and to foraging for roots and wild vegetables.

Another mutiny flared over the rations. This time, it was the cannoneers. Eaton wearily prepared to quell it—just as the courier returned with news that he had sighted vessels at Bomba. "In an instant the face of everything changed from pensive gloom to inthusiastic gladness." New life was breathed into the expedition. The mutiny forgotten, the caravan pressed on.

At last they reached Bomba.

The empty bay mocked them. There were no ships, there was no one to meet them. The expedition succumbed to its accumulated disappointments and hunger. The bitter Arabs claimed that there had never been any resupply ships expected at Bomba, that the Christian leaders were "imposters and infidels;—and said we had drawn them into that situation with treacherous views." Powerless to stop it, Eaton watched the expedition breaking up before his eyes. The Arabs laid plans to depart the next morning, brushing aside Eaton's exhortation that they all press on to Derna. Despairing, Eaton and the Christians climbed a hill overlooking the harbor and lit signal fires. They stoked them all night, hoping that Hull was at sea nearby, and would see the fires and come to a rendezvous.

At daybreak on April 15, there still were no ships in sight. Eaton watched helplessly as the Arabs prepared to break camp and return to Egypt. The expedition appeared to be over. One of Hamet's servants climbed the signal hill for a last look at the Mediterranean—and spotted a sail in the distance. It was the *Argus*. Hull had seen the signal fires during the night. "Language is too poor to paint the joy and exultation which this messenger of life excited in every breast," wrote Eaton.

Hull had reached Bomba April 4, but, finding no one there, he had cruised to Cape Razatin, he told Eaton. Returning to Bomba and still finding no one, he sent a party ashore to determine whether Eaton had been there. When it couldn't find any evidence that he had, the *Argus* had lingered offshore, checking the bay periodically.

Eaton's army spent a restorative week encamped at Bomba. Food and provisions were plentiful. The *Argus* and *Hornet* sent ashore 30 hogsheads of bread; 30 barrels of peas; rice; three hogsheads of brandy and wine; 100 sacks of flour; 10 boxes of oil; a bale of cloth; and $7,000 for Eaton.

After crossing 460 miles of desert in five weeks, the army now faced the critical 60-mile push to Derna. The Americans and Arabs, Greeks and Turks, Tripolitans, and assorted Europeans knew this leg of the journey likely would end in a pitched battle from which they would emerge victorious, or in chains. The marchers rested and ate and drank their fill.

On April 23, they marched out of the parched land where they had spent the last forty-six days and into a wetter region of cultivated fields. Now that the army was in Tripoli, volunteers were joining daily, swelling the expedition's ranks to about 1,000 fighting men as the force advanced toward Derna. Before his men could act on the growing temptation to scavenge from the land, Hamet sent a herald crying throughout the camp: "He who fears God and feels attachment to Hamet Bashaw will be careful to destroy nothing. Let no one touch the growing harvest. He who transgresses this injunction shall lose his right hand!"

Yusuf's envoy to Alexandria had returned with intelligence about Eaton and Hamet's expedition. The bashaw had immediately acted to head them off, ordering his chief Mameluke, Hassan Bey, to lead an army toward Egypt to intercept and defeat Hamet. Yusuf had established a regular army only three years earlier, to thwart Hamet and subdue revolts in the interior. By the time Preble attacked Tripoli, the bashaw's army had swelled to 1,500 Turkish mercenaries, 12,000 Arab and Berber cavalry, and thousands of irregulars—25,000 troops in all for Tripoli's defense.

A tent was pitched on the castle battery and manned by sentries watching every night for invaders, while Yusuf stepped up his war preparations. Bainbridge and Eaton were right: Tripoli was vulnerable to land attack—and the bashaw knew this in his bones. As Hassan's army prepared for its long march—Derna was about 500 miles from Tripoli—the American prisoners were put to work hauling ammunition and food to the army's staging area. Displaying his growing fears of a coup, the bashaw locked up the relatives of his expedition's officers in the former U.S. consular house, to ensure the loyalty of Hassan's army. Before the troops departed, a marabout absolved the officers of their sins, according to surgeon Jonathan Cowdery, and assured them of victory.

Yusuf sent his son-in-law into the countryside to recruit more troops for Tripoli's defense. He returned empty-handed; the people wouldn't fight. Yusuf's levies had been too heavy, with women even stripped of their jewels. The Spanish consul, storing up good favor against the day Spain would find itself on Tripoli's enemy list, gave the bashaw a shipment of muskets.

Everyone was certain the city would be attacked in the summer, but Yusuf's women and children chose to remain in the castle rather than move to the family's country palace. "They said that if they must be taken, they would rather fall into the hands of the Americans than the Arabs," Cowdery noted wryly.

The increasingly flustered bashaw declared to Cowdery that if the Americans forced him to, or if they attacked Tripoli, he would put every American prisoner to death. A few days later, he asked Cowdery how many Marines the United States had. Ten thousand, the ship's surgeon replied. And troops? "Eighty thousand, said I, are in readiness to march to defend the country, at any moment; and one million of militia are also ready to fight for the liberty and rights of their countrymen!" The bashaw looked very somber.

As Eaton's expedition neared Derna, reports reached him that Derna's governor was fortifying the city and Yusuf's army was close by. The worried Arab chiefs conferred with Hamet into the night. Eaton was not invited to their consultations.

The next morning, April 26, Sheiks il Taiib and Mahomet announced they were turning around, and the Bedouins refused to strike their tents. The hours ticked away while Eaton argued with them, painfully aware of all the days lost because of the Arabs' intractability. Only a day's march from Derna, they risked losing the race to Yusuf's army.

Eaton cajoled, wheedled, and reproached, finally resorting to the unfailing expedient of cold cash. He promised the Arab chiefs $2,000 if they would resume the march. That got them moving again.

That afternoon, the fiftieth day of the desert march, Eaton's army reached the heights above Derna.

Eaton joined a cavalry patrol scouting the city. There was no sign of the bashaw's troops.

Unaware that Eaton's army was poised to strike at Tripoli's second-largest city, Jefferson and his officials had begun to doubt whether there would ever be an honorable peace with Tripoli. It couldn't be said that the U.S. government had stinted on committing resources; the $555,862 appropriated for Commodore Dale's tiny squadron in 1801 had tripled in four years and now sustained twelve ships crewed by 2,000 men. Nor was the problem the blockade or the convoys. The blockade pinched Tripoli at times, and the convoys had denied enemy corsairs a single American prize since the capture of the *Franklin* in June 1802. On top of these pressures, the bashaw was having to foot the cost of maintaining a large army. But Barron's squadron, the largest naval force ever deployed by the United States, had not fired on Tripoli in eight months and, without the threat of attack, Yusuf felt no compunction to sue for peace. Frustrated U.S. leaders, including the recently reelected Jefferson, were ready to trim down the Mediterranean squadron to a skeletal blockading force.

In the bashaw's castle beside Tripoli's harbor, the *Philadelphia* crewmen tried to keep up their spirits, even though they had seen nothing in seven long months to kindle any new hope of liberation; since Preble's departure the previous September, American warships had only blockaded Tripoli, without once going on the attack. During their seventeen months of captivity, five crewmen had died, and five had converted to Islam and no longer lived in confinement. The remaining 297, officers and men alike, ate and slept in dank, ill-lit dungeons in Yusuf's castle. Their treatment was no better than before, with the work gangs roughly turned out at first light each morning for hard labor.

In the lavish castle rooms reserved for the bashaw, Yusuf and his officials disparaged America's naval war and blockade. If he had three frigates, Yusuf boasted to Cowdery, Tripoli could blockade America as effectively as the Americans had invested Tripolitan ports. "He said he could do it as easily as a frigate and schooner could blockade Tripoli!" Only Preble's August 3 attack had really shaken the Tripolitans, Nissen said, and "the damage done is absolutely of no consequence," although a stray musket ball had starred a mirror right where Nissen had been standing in his home minutes before. Nissen recommended to Barron that he concentrate on blockading Tripoli's eastern ports, where gunpowder was being smuggled from the Levant.

Despite the bashaw's boastful talk, the war had drawn down his treasury, forcing him to impose levies that had made his countrymen outside the capital resentful. Yusuf also had borrowed from his neighbors. He owed Tunis $120,000, and his plan to use the *Philadelphia* as partial payment was consumed in the flames of Stephen Decatur's incendiaries. The bashaw was counting on America tiring of the war and paying for peace. All of these factors, and Eaton's presence outside Derna, made April 1805 an excellent time for a decisive naval offensive. A two-pronged attack combining Eaton's army and Barron's fleet would surely force Yusuf to sign any treaty that would allow him to keep his throne.

This was what Secretary of State Madison and Navy Secretary Smith had had in mind when they instructed Barron and Consul General Lear to apply military force until America could dictate peace terms. Barron would blockade and "annoy the Enemy," Smith said, until "it is conceived that no doubt whatever can exist of your coercing Tripoli to a Treaty upon our own Terms." Lear then could negotiate a treaty "without any price or pecuniary concession whatever," as Madison put it, with the only permissible expenditure being for the captives' ransom, up to $500 each, minus trades. Should "adverse events or circumstances . . . which are not foreseen here" intervene, and Lear judged "a pecuniary sacrifice preferable to a protraction of the war," he might pay for peace, but only as a last resort.

Jefferson was readier to cut his losses in Barbary than Smith's and Madison's instructions to Lear and Barron indicated. The orders were drafted after a Cabinet meeting on January 8, 1805, at which Jefferson and his advisers resolved to send "new instructions not to give a dollar for peace," but "if the enterprise in the spring does not produce peace & delivery of prisoners, ransom them." Jefferson, however, confided in a letter in March to a longtime Virginia friend, Judge John Tyler, that he intended to scale back America's commitment to the war even more. If Barron failed to dictate a peace by the end of the summer, he planned to reduce the Mediterranean squadron to a three-ship blockading force to protect U.S. shipping. A continual blockade was better than a bought peace, the president said, and would cost no more than annual tribute. Whatever the outcome, he would never pay tribute to Tripoli because it would invite fresh demands from the other Barbary States. Jefferson believed the United States already had shown the tributary European powers how "to emancipate themselves from that degrading yoke. Should we produce such a revolution there, we shall be amply rewarded for what we have done."

Jefferson's candid letter did not mention Eaton's clandestine mission.

Despite all the hopes riding on Barron's cruise, and Tripoli's vulnerability to a joint land–sea attack, Barron's squadron would not be going on the offensive soon. The commodore was fighting for his life in his Syracuse sickbed. Afflicted with liver disease soon after reaching the Mediterranean in the late summer of 1804, by November Barron had made Captain John Rodgers, his second in command, responsible for the squadron's day-to-day operations. Barron retained overall command of the squadron, optimistically thinking he would turn the corner any week. But his health collapsed. On November 14, Midshipman Henry Allen reported, "It will soon be determined whether he lives or not." By December 27, Barron could not hold a pen to write a letter. In January, 1805, he hovered near death. Barely surviving that crisis, he remained so weak that his secretary wrote many of his letters for him. April found him still unable to return to his ship.

Lear's influence over Barron and the squadron's operations waxed with Barron's waning health. At a distance of 200 years, his motives are unclear, although they most likely included a strong dose of ambition mingled with the belief that diplomacy should conclude the war. Lear had spent his adult life amid the republic's founders and the towering events attending its birth, but never as a participant. He was George Washington's close friend and represented him in business affairs. After Washington died in 1799, Lear became a diplomat, but at forty-three he had not yet made his mark or his fortune, and hoped to do so in Barbary.

Whatever his motives, Lear openly criticized Eaton's scheme to build an insurgency around Hamet Karamanli and drive his brother Yusuf from Tripoli. ". . . I should place much more confidence in the continuance of a peace with the present Bashaw, if he is well beaten into it, then I should with the other, if he should be placed on the throne by our means."

Tobias Lear had been Barbary's consul general for nearly two years. In his portrait from that time, he appears as an oval-faced man with large, intelligent eyes and a pointed nose, clad in an army officer's coat, with a sedentary man's double chin. Lear often signed his correspondence "Colonel Lear," proud of the rank Washington had given him during the Quasi-War with France. Washington, picked to command American ground forces, had named Lear his chief aide. Washington's army never took the field because the French didn't send an army to North America; the Quasi-War was fought at sea. Lear, however, signed his correspondence with his titular rank for the rest of his days.

He had devoted nearly his entire adult life to America's first family. In May 1786 the twenty-four-year-old Harvard graduate became George Washington's personal secretary and moved to Mount Vernon. Over the years, he became more of a family member than employee, particularly after making two of Washington's nieces his second and third wives, after his first died in Philadelphia's 1793 yellow-fever epidemic. As Washington's personal secretary, he handled correspondence, kept the family books, tutored the children, attended to Washington's varied business interests, and dined every day with the family. He followed Washington to New York and Philadelphia when he became president.

At the beginning of Washington's second term, Lear struck out on his own, hoping to make a fortune through business and land speculation in the new capital city being built on the Potomac. He continued to act as Washington's business agent and sent him letters full of shrewd observations whenever he traveled. He also served as a director of the Potomack Company, organized by Washington and other businessmen to make the Potomac River a commercial pipeline to the heartland.

In December 1799, when the ex-president was dying of pneumonia at Mount Vernon, it was Lear who held his hand as he uttered his last words. (Washington told him not to put him in his burial vault until he had been dead three days, just for good measure.) Washington's will granted Lear rent-free tenancy for life at Walnut Hill Farm at Mount Vernon.

Yet, during all his years with George Washington, the repository of all the early United States' hopes, Lear was an observer, not a participant. Only once had he been a central player in his own right, and it had not redounded to his credit. Lear was blamed for the sensational disappearance of all the correspondence between Washington and Jefferson from 1797 until Washington's death two years later.

This was significant because Washington and Jefferson, fellow Virginians and Revolution patriots and friends for twenty years, had quarreled bitterly in 1797 and had exchanged several sharp letters. The disappearance of the copies undoubtedly made of Washington's letters to Jefferson and Jefferson's replies to Washington—while they were in Lear's possession—erased all traces of their angry exchange. Of course, none of the letters turned up among Jefferson's papers because Jefferson's indiscretion had caused the rupture in their friendship in the first place, and the letters would have reflected poorly on him.

Jefferson, as did all Republicans, had vilified the Jay Treaty as a dirty piece of bootlicking by Anglophile Federalists. But unfortunately, Jefferson also vented his unhappiness in a blistering letter to Philip Mazzei, a former Monticello neighbor who had moved back to his native Italy. Through circuitous means, the letter unexpectedly found its way into print in the United States, and a storm erupted. The catalyst was Jefferson's thinly veiled reference to Washington, already a national icon, in the line, "men who were Samsons in the field & Solomons in the council, but who have had their heads shorn by the harlot England."

Jefferson was disconcerted by the letter's publication, and Washington was furious. The breach that opened up between the two old friends wasn't helped by the accusations that flew in a subsequent exchange of heated letters. Only one survived Washington's death. In it, Washington expressed outrage over the "grossest and most invidious misrepresentations" of his administration's actions.

John Marshall, the first U.S. Supreme Court chief justice and the era's leading Federalist, discovered the strange gap in the men's correspondence when he took possession of Washington's papers in early 1801—from Lear, who had them to himself for a year. (Marshall based his masterful, four-volume Washington biography on these papers.) Lear said nothing to Marshall about the gap. Later, however, he acknowledged to Alexander Hamilton and others that he had destroyed letters Washington would never have wished to be made public.

But Lear might have acted for more selfish reasons than concern for Washington's posterity. In *The Checkered Career of Tobias Lear,* historian Ray Brighton suggests there might have been a quid pro quo between Lear and Jefferson, who was running for president when Lear had possession of the papers. Publication of the letters very likely would have cost Jefferson the election, which he only managed to win on the thirty-sixth ballot in the U.S. House, after an Electoral College tie with Aaron Burr.

Lear and Jefferson had been friends since Jefferson's years in Washington's Cabinet, and Lear privately agreed with Jefferson's Republican views. He also needed a job that paid well, for his unlucky business speculation in the new capital had plunged him deeply into debt.

While it will never be known whether Lear and Jefferson had an agreement about the letters, Jefferson and Madison made sure Lear had a government job for the rest of his short, eventful life. (In 1814 Lear saved the Army's records when the British burned Washington. Two years later, he committed suicide.)

Within weeks of Jefferson's inauguration, Lear was appointed to his first job: consul to Santo Domingo. This was a coveted post, because opportunities abounded for getting rich in the West Indies trade. But Lear happened to arrive during the tumultuous aftermath of a slave rebellion and was expelled months later when French troops invaded.

As consul general for the Barbary States, he had hoped to establish a reputation and accumulate wealth, but the war had afforded him a chance for neither.

Early in 1805, Lear temporarily moved from Algiers to Malta so he could be close to Tripoli if an opportunity arose for a parley. He was eager to negotiate a peace, no matter what Eaton and Hamet accomplished. The shortest distance to his goal was through Barron, who lay helplessly ill in Syracuse. Lear shuttled between Malta and Syracuse, making sure nothing—such as a naval offensive—upset his plan for a diplomatic settlement. He also systematically undermined Hamet's credibility with Barron. Eaton had so favorably impressed the commodore during their Atlantic crossing that at the beginning of 1805, Barron had pledged to cooperate with Eaton and Hamet and to restore Hamet as bashaw. Lear, aware that if their desert expedition dethroned Yusuf his own efforts would inevitably become expendable, or, at best, secondary, inexorably turned the commodore against Hamet and Eaton.

He had to tread carefully because he didn't want to come across to Barron as a crank, and because no one really knew what the president had agreed to when he met with Eaton the previous year. So he took cover in others' opinions, such as those of Nissen, who assayed the damage caused by Preble's attacks as "very inconsiderable." And there was Bainbridge, who in his letters from captivity clearly opposed any action that would jeopardize his crew's safety or extend its captivity. Bainbridge also thought little of Eaton's expedition, or of Hamet, a "poor effeminate refugee . . . who had not spirit enough to retain his situation when placed in it," and who had "wandered an Exile far from Country, Wife & Children for more than 8 years without disturbing the Regency of Tripoli." Bainbridge, who had plenty of idle time to ponder the Tripoli situation, had concluded that blockading was futile. As he saw it, America had three options: bombard Tripoli and seek terms immediately; capture the city with an army; or "abandon us entirely to the hard fate which serving our Country plunged us into."

Lear also pounced on Richard Farquhar's bitter complaints

about Eaton after Eaton expelled him from Alexandria for embezzling expedition funds. "He writes to the Commodore that Mr E. is a madman," Lear gleefully told Captain John Rodgers, a friend from his brief Santo Domingo consulship. "He has quarreled with the Ex-Bashaw &c &c &c, We are in daily expectation of more authentic accounts from that quarter; but I make no calculation in our favour from that source." Lear never identified the source, and nothing more came of the matter.

By the spring of 1805, as Eaton's expedition was pushing deep into eastern Tripoli, Barron was beginning to sound like Lear on the subject of Hamet: "I confess that my hopes from a Cooperation with him are less sanguine than they were." He attributed his changed outlook to recent information "from persons well acquainted with the Bashaw [Hamet] of his Character & Conduct." In other words, Lear. No report from Eaton had yet arrived to change Barron's thinking about the overland campaign. But Lear's influence over Barron—who, although invalided, still clung to his authority as regional commander to conduct the war as he saw fit—was nearly absolute after the commodore's long months of illness. Barron confessed to Lear that his newfound lack of confidence in Hamet, coupled with the expedition's cost and overly ambitious goals, "compel me to relinquish the plan."

Barron also anticipated every conceivable drawback and obstacle whenever he weighed bringing his naval force into action against Tripoli. An attack was ill-advised without gunboats, the only vessels that could safely navigate the shallow harbor, and he had been unable to procure any from Naples or Venice. He was unsure when ten being built in the United States would arrive. The enlistment period of Preble's squadron began expiring in early autumn, "an important period in our Arrangements." Three frigates needed refitting. Under the circumstances, Barron made no plans to bring his large squadron against Tripoli.

The situation was rich in its circuitous irony. With Barron disinclined to launch a naval attack, Lear had to depend on the very force he was trying so hard to discredit—Eaton and Hamet's army, encamped on the heights above Derna—to force Yusuf to sign an honorable peace for which Lear could then claim credit.

XV

DERNA AND PEACE

Derna, Saturday April 27, 1805

I shall see you tomorrow in a way of your choice.
—William Eaton in a letter to Mustifa Bey, governor of Derna

My head or yours.
—Mustifa Bey

Hidden in the sparsely wooded hills overlooking the city, Eaton, Hamet, and their officers studied the white buildings and palm trees fringing the harbor. With upwards of 10,000 inhabitants, Derna was Tripoli's second-largest city. Bananas, dates, grapes, melons, oranges, and plums flourished in the city's orchards and irrigated gardens, whose cultivation dated to the 1493 arrival of the Moors exiled from Spain. To the north, the Mediterranean's sparkling blue waters stretched to the horizon. Mussolini would call Derna "the pearl of the Mediterranean," but other visitors, immune to its charms, were oppressed by its isolation and the air of desolation bestowed by the endless sea and the nearby hills.

Derna was the administrative and military hub of Cyrenaica, Tripoli's distant eastern province and traditionally its most restive, as a result of its 500-mile remove from the capital across stretches of hostile territory. Its nomadic Berber and Bedouin tribesmen remained largely outside Yusuf's authority. Hundreds of them had rallied to Hamet's standard, swelling his ranks to 1,000 fighting men. Derna itself was only nominally in the bashaw's camp and just as liable to switch sides.

After Eaton, Hamet, and their army occupied the hills overlooking the provincial capital on April 26, Eaton scouted the enemy defenses with a small mounted force and gathered intelligence from dissident city chiefs. What he learned was not reassuring. The city was defended by at least 800 government troops, a shore battery of eight 9-pounders and a 10-inch howitzer on the terrace of the governor's palace. A third of the populace was firmly in Yusuf's camp, and most of them lived in the city's southeast district. They had fortified that area of the city by cutting firing ports in the walls of the homes. In the northeastern sector, defenders had thrown up breastworks tying in with the buildings. The chiefs warned Eaton that he would have difficulty dislodging the troops because they knew that if they held out, Yusuf's 1,200 cavalry and infantry would relieve them in a day or two. This information made Eaton eager to attack as soon as possible, but disheartened Hamet. "I thought the Bashaw wished himself back to Egypt," Eaton noted drily in his journal.

After reconnoitering Derna and seeing to his army's disposition for the night, Eaton joined Lieutenant Isaac Hull on the *Argus,* and they mapped out a battle plan for the next day. Eaton spent the night on the brig and awakened the following morning with the fatalistic thought that this day might well be his last. Before boating ashore to rejoin his army, he left instructions for doling out his personal effects in the event that he was killed in battle. Hull would get his cloak and smallsword; Captain James Barron, his Damascus saber; his stepson, Eli Danielson, his gold watch and chain; and Charles Wadsworth, his estate executor back in America, was to receive the rest.

Derna's defenders and the assault troops in the hills tensely watched Lieutenant John Dent maneuver the *Nautilus* close to shore east of Derna with the two 24-pound carronades Eaton had requested. They were landed at an awkward spot, at the foot of a sheer 20-foot-high rock. The cannoneers rigged a block and tackle, but inching just one of the carronades up the escarpment was so time-consuming that Eaton decided to leave the other one behind.

Mustifa Bey, Derna's governor, had spurned Eaton's one attempt to avoid battle. Eaton had offered Mustifa a position in Hamet's future government if he granted the expeditionary force passage through his city and permitted it to buy supplies. "I shall see you tomorrow in a way of your choice," Eaton wrote in closing. The messenger returned with the governor's answer, scrawled on Eaton's letter:

My head or yours
Mustifa

Eaton deployed his forces. All was in readiness.

At 1:30 P.M., the two armies began to pepper one another with small-arms and cannon fire. By 2:00, this overture had swelled to a roar along Derna's well-defended southeast corner, opposite which Lieutenant O'Bannon commanded the Marines, the sixty cannoneers and Greeks, and a couple of dozen Arab foot soldiers. Derna's harbor batteries fired at the three U.S. ships in the harbor.

Blue-gray smoke hung over the battlements and harbor. Hamet whirled off with his Arab cavalry to seize an old castle overlooking the southwest part of town.

The *Argus, Hornet,* and *Nautilus* drew themselves up 100 yards from the city and opened up with their 9-pounders, and over the next forty-five minutes silenced the waterside batteries, one by one. However, the gunners facing O'Bannon's men kept up a withering fire that drowned out Eaton's lone carronade that was firing shrapnel at the defenders. The heavy musket and cannon fire began to rattle Eaton's men. Then the carronade crew shot away the rammer, the long wooden stave for pushing shot, wad, and cartridge down the bore, and the gun fell silent. Raked by artillery and musket fire from hundreds of enemy troops, and with their one fieldpiece out of commission, O'Bannon's European and Arab foot soldiers were on the verge of bolting.

Eaton knew he must attack now or lose control of his men. He and O'Bannon exhorted the motley force of just over sixty men, clad in Marine Corps garb, scraps of uniforms from European armies, civilian clothing, and Arab robes, to follow them. Eaton's army surged across the open ground toward the walled city, bayonets flashing.

The defenders outnumbered the attackers ten to one and had the advantage of being able to fire from behind walls. But the brazen frontal assault threw them into a panic. They got off a ragged volley, abandoned their positions and beat a pell-mell retreat into the city. They stopped to fire from behind walls and palm trees, thinning the ranks of Eaton's assault troops. But Eaton's men kept coming. Suddenly Eaton clutched his left wrist and lagged behind, hit by a musket ball.

O'Bannon took charge, aided by Midshipman George Mann of

the *Argus*. The assault force cleared the batteries of enemy with bayonets and small-arms fire. O'Bannon and his Marines lowered the bashaw's ensign and ran up the American flag over the ramparts—the first time the Stars and Stripes was planted on a hostile foreign shore by U.S. troops. Cheers erupted from Eaton's men and the sailors on the three U.S. warships.

The Americans turned around the enemy's cannons, already loaded and primed, and opened fire on the retreating government soldiers running through the city streets. The warships joined in with supporting fire as Hamet's cavalry charged in from the opposite side, pinching the defenders between the two attacking forces. A little after 4:00 P.M., Hamet and his force burst into the governor's palace, and resistance ended.

While no work of military genius, the storming of Derna was the first decisive American victory of the Barbary War. It was a heavy blow to the bashaw's hopes for a quick, lucrative treaty, and an amazing personal triumph for Eaton. At the head of a mutinous army, Eaton had crossed 520 miles of forbidding desert and wrested Tripoli's second city from a large armed force waiting behind prepared fortifications, at a cost of just two dead—Marine Privates John Whitten and Edward Seward—and a dozen wounded, Eaton among them.

Derna made O'Bannon the U.S. Marine Corps's first hero. In years to come, the Marines' pivotal role at Derna would be immortalized by the anonymous lyricist who penned the words "to the shores of Tripoli," one of the two named battles in "The Marine's Hymn." O'Bannon later accepted a scimitar from Hamet as thanks, and it remains the model for the ceremonial sword still issued to Marine officers. Despite all the encomiums, O'Bannon resigned his commission two years later, frustrated over not being promoted to captain; the Marine Corps was authorized to have only four, and the slots all were filled. He moved to Kentucky, where he became a community leader and served in the legislature. He died on September 12, 1850. The headstone over his remains, moved by the state to Frankfort in 1920, misstates his rank but accords him the laurels he had earned: "The Hero of Derne Tripoli Northern Africa April 27, 1805. As Captain of the United States Marines He was the First to Plant the American Flag on Foreign Soil."

Mustifa, Derna's governor, was trapped in Derna by Eaton's and Hamet's converging forces. He hid in a mosque, then in a harem, the most sacrosanct of Moslem sanctuaries. His protector was a sheik who, coincidentally, had sheltered Hamet when Yusuf's troops had come after him two years before. Now the sheik just as stubbornly denied Hamet and Eaton access to Mustifa, claiming the prerogatives of a Moslem host. The sheik said a breach of hospitality would bring down the "vengeance of God" and "the odium of all mankind." Eaton threatened him with bombardment and menaced his home with fifty bayonet-wielding Christian troops. The sheik said he preferred bombs to God's chastisement. "Neither persuasion, bribes nor menace, could prevail on this venerable aged chief to permit the hospitality of his house to be violated," Eaton wrote wearily. Eaton knew that if he trespassed on the sheik's protection the entire city would turn against him. He was reduced to plotting ways to lure Mustifa into the open, hoping to capture and trade him for Bainbridge. But Mustifa managed to slip out of Derna and join Yusuf's troops on May 12.

The next morning, Yusuf's army counterattacked.

• • •

For five days, Hassan Bey's troops had watched the city from the same hills where Eaton had launched his attack. He had sent spies to try turning the townspeople against Eaton and Hamet, hoping to gain an edge. Well aware of Hassan's preparations, Eaton and his officers found, as Mustifa had before them, that defending a city of Derna's size properly would unfortunately require more troops than they had. They would have to depend on manned outposts along the city's outskirts to alert them to an attack and hope they could respond swiftly and repel whatever came, wherever it might be aimed.

On May 13, Hassan's troops overran an outpost held by 100 of Hamet's Arab cavalrymen and raced toward Derna. The *Argus's* and *Nautilus's* alert gunners opened up. Hamet's two fieldpieces joined in. But the horsemen raced through the shot and shell fire. At the edge of the city, they ran gantlets of musket fire from O'Bannon's infantry and armed Derna sympathizers—among them the sheik who had protected Mustifa so diligently—and charged into the middle of town, straight to the governor's palace, where Hamet and his entourage had encamped.

The attackers intended to storm the palace and capture Hamet, knowing this was the surest way to end the threat to their bashaw. One final surge into the palace, and the expedition and all of Eaton's and Hamet's hopes would perish.

And then a well-aimed shot from one of the ships landed dead among Yusuf's cavalrymen in the palace courtyard, horribly mangling two of them before their shocked companions. The attackers' nerve abandoned them. They wheeled around suddenly and tore off into the countryside, harried by cannon and musket fire. It had been a close call, reminding Eaton and Hamet of their tenuous hold on Derna, but it also was a scalding experience for Hassan's soldiers, who had lost 28 killed and 56 wounded, of whom 11 later died of their wounds. Eaton's troops suffered 14 killed and wounded.

With Hassan rocked back on his heels, Eaton turned to the pressing problem of how to replenish his alarmingly low stocks of bread, rice, coffee, sugar, and ammunition. Hull had no additional supplies and no cash to buy them, owing to Barron's tightfistedness toward Eaton, but Hull was eager to help Eaton if he could. They hit on the desperate contingency of bartering the *Argus*'s prize goods for meat in Derna. "A humiliating traffic, but we have no cash," Eaton noted tersely in his journal. On May 20, Hamet implored Hull to give him $300 to pay off his Arab chiefs, who were threatening to switch sides and join Yusuf's army. Hull didn't have the money. But he loyally offered to turn his cannons on the town and destroy every house if the people of Derna showed ingratitude to Hamet. Finally, touched by Hamet's "very low spirits," Hull stripped his ship of goods and equipment to help him meet the emergency and buy food and supplies.

Hassan's 350 Tripolitans, 200–300 Arab cavalry, and 300 desert Arab foot soldiers began readying for another attack. Worried that he might not be able to fend them off this time, Eaton proposed a preemptive night strike on their camp three miles from town. Hamet's Arabs said they did not fight at night. So they waited.

Hassan also was having trouble inducing his soldiers to attack. After the bloody debacle of May 13, they were wary of charging into the city again. They complained of the way the Americans fought, firing "enormous balls that carried away a man and his camel at once, or rushed on them with bayonets without giving them time to load their muskets." Hassan tried to motivate his soldiers with bribes and bounties: $6,000 to anyone who killed Eaton, twice that sum if he were captured alive, and $30 for every Christian killed. They were unmoved. Hassan's officers began collecting camels to serve as "traveling breastworks." But the Arabs objected to their camels being used in this manner, and the project was abandoned.

In Derna, confidence in Eaton's leadership soared. His officers were inspired to draft and sign a loyalty pledge. "Everything assures us of complete victory under your command. We are only waiting for the moment to win this glory, and to fall on the enemy. . . . We swear that we shall follow you and that we shall fight unto death." O'Bannon, Mann, the remaining Farquhar, Selim Comb, and two other officers signed the pledge. Eaton himself was so pleased with the expedition's success that he took to calling his camp in Derna "Fort Enterprize".

The afternoon of May 21, the sea breeze shifted to the south, and the air became suffocatingly hot and dusty. Then, a towering column of swirling sand rose from the desert. Three miles long, it approached rapidly. "Heated dust, which resembled the smoke of a conflagration . . . turned the sun in appearance to melted copper . . . We were distressed for breath:—the lungs contracted:—blood heated like a fever. . . ." For days, all military plans were held in abeyance while the sirocco blew. The searing desert wind warped the white pine boards of Eaton's folding table, and the covers of his books were seared and wrinkled as though they had lain too close to a roaring fire. Standing water burned fingers when touched. Eaton's troops stopped working on the fortifications because the stones they were using became too hot to handle.

"The heated dust penetrated everything through our garments:—
and indeed seemed to choak the pores of the skin," noted Eaton.
"It had a singular effect on my wound, giving it the painful sen-
sations of a fresh burn." At sea, the blowing sand coated the
Argus's rigging and spars. Hull noted that it was only "with difficulty we could look to windward without getting our Eyes put
out with dust."

While Eaton's army was on the march to Derna, reports about the
expedition's progress, sometimes weeks old because of slow communications, had begun to reach Yusuf's castle, causing growing
alarm. The Americans, the bashaw complained bitterly, had raised
the stakes from tribute to his very throne. He vowed to Cowdery
that he would raise them even higher. "He swore by the prophet
of Mecca, that if the Americans brought his brother against him,
he would burn to death all the American prisoners except me."
Cowdery would be spared, Yusuf said, because he had saved the
life of his sick child. The bashaw communicated the same sentiments to Bainbridge, bellicosely threatening to strike the United
States "in the most tender part." When news of Derna's capture
reached Tripoli, "the greatest terror and consternation reigned,"
noted Marine Second Lieutenant Wallace W. Wormeley, one of
the *Philadelphia* captives. Yusuf convened the Divan, Tripoli's
council of state, in an emergency session, announcing that he
wished to execute the American prisoners. But the Divan had no
stomach for a bloody massacre and postponed taking any action.

If possible, the *Philadelphia* crewmen's treatment worsened. At
the height of the sirocco, twenty-five of them were sent with a cart
into the countryside to gather timber. After working all day in the
dusty, oppressive heat, they were exhausted and thirsty. They

asked their Tripolitan driver for permission to drink at a nearby well. The overseer coldly reminded them that they were Christian dogs and deserved no water. Then he beat them with a heavy club.

The bashaw's spy from Malta arrived in Tripoli on May 19 with more sobering news: The American squadron, he said, intended to pick up Hamet and his army, capture towns all along the coast, and then attack Tripoli itself. "The Bashaw and his people seemed much agitated," Cowdery reported. Yusuf locked Hamet's eldest son in the castle. He also reduced the rations of his domestics and Mamelukes to one meal a day. His money gone, racked by apprehensions, Yusuf confided to Cowdery that if it were possible for him to make peace and give up the *Philadelphia* captives, he would gladly do it. "He was sensible of the danger he was in from the lowness of his funds and the disaffection of his people."

Reports of the Derna triumph were nearly as unwelcome at squadron headquarters in Syracuse. Lear redoubled his planning for a negotiated peace and assisted the ailing Barron in directing his squadron. Barron—or perhaps Lear, for he was making many of the decisions at this point—denied Eaton money, supplies and the 100 Marines he had requested. The Marines might have welcomed the relief from the tedium of blockading and convoying, although they also would have had to sacrifice their generous liberties in the various Mediterranean ports. To Lear's annoyance, Eaton had succeeded despite everything, even though Barron—or Lear, ghostwriting his letters—was actively discouraging his support for Hamet's insurgency.

The first of Barron's two extraordinary letters on this subject had reached Eaton at Bomba in early April. This letter would have compelled many leaders to abandon the expedition on the spot.

But not Eaton, who kept its demoralizing contents to himself and continued on to Derna. "I must withhold my sanction" to any agreement with Hamet, Barron or Lear wrote, unhappy with the convention Eaton and Hamet had signed. "You must be sensible, Sir, that in giving their sanction to a cooperation with the exiled Bashaw, Government did not contemplate the measure as leading necessarily and absolutely to a reinstatement of that Prince in his rights on the regency of Tripoli. . . . I repeat it, we are only favoring [Hamet] as the instrument to an attainment and not in itself as an object. . . ." Once a peace treaty was signed, "our support to Hamet Bashaw must necessarily be withdrawn." This wasn't what Barron had said just months earlier; he had changed the rules. Hamet had become a tool for obtaining a more favorable treaty from the bashaw, a tool that, once used, could be discarded.

As though realizing he might have gone too far in his hard appraisal of Hamet's utility, Barron added that his observations shouldn't "cool your zeal or discourage your expectations." So much depended upon on-the-spot decisions, he said soothingly, "that I must consider myself rather your Counsellor than your director." He extended the wan hope that if enough Tripolitans rallied to Hamet's cause to carry him to Benghazi, Barron might furnish him naval support at Tripoli's gates. Otherwise, he would have to withdraw his cooperation.

Eaton's reply, written two days after Derna's capture, was full of the steely determination and pragmatism that had carried him through fifty days of mutinies and hardships in the Libyan Desert. Scorning Barron's calculating support of Hamet, Eaton predicted that "the Enemy will propose terms of Peace with us, the moment he entertains serious apprehensions of his Brother. This may happen at any stage of the War, most likely to rid him of so dangerous a rival, and not only Hamet Bashaw, but every one acting with him, must inevitably fall victims to our economy." If Yusuf did propose peace and Barron and Lear agreed to it, at the very least, America should place Hamet beyond the bashaw's reach, in a situation comparable to the one from which he was taken.

He accused Barron of parsimony with money, men, and supplies. Barron had disbursed only $20,000, while Eaton's expenses had already reached $30,000. Even so, "we are in possession of the most valuable province of Tripoli." Ready cash now, he said, would tip the scales decisively in Hamet's favor, because Tripoli's failed harvest and Yusuf's levies had drained the land of resources for either brother. "This is a circumstance favorable to our measures, if we will go to the expence of profiting of it—No Chief, whatever may be the attachment of his followers, can long support Military operations, without the means of subsisting his troops." Arab troops in particular would switch loyalties to whichever side paid the most, because they are "poor, yet avaricious, and who being accustom'd to despotism, are generally indifferent about the name or person of their despot, provided he imposes no new burdens." With cash, his army could defeat the bashaw's army at Derna and march to Tripoli, where, with the squadron's help, it would drive out Yusuf. "It would very probably be a death blow to the Barbary System." Conversely, "any accomodation savoring of relaxness would as probably be death to the Navy, and a wound to the National honor."

As Eaton had foreseen, the bashaw had begun extending peace feelers as soon as he learned that his brother was on the march.

Nissen relayed an overture from Sidi Mahomet Dghies, Tripoli's foreign secretary. Act quickly, Nissen warned, because Dghies, the only Divan member opposed to war with America in 1801, was now nearly blind and planning to retire to the countryside, where he no longer would be able to influence Yusuf.

Within days of receiving Nissen's letter, Lear got one written in lime juice from Bainbridge; as the ranking captive, Bainbridge was in daily contact with Yusuf's top officials. Peace was negotiable for $120,000, Bainbridge said.

Lear, too, was stirred to diplomacy by Eaton and Hamet's success. The Spanish consul in Tripoli, Don Joseph de Souza, had forwarded an unspecific proposal in December to which Lear had not responded. In March, with Eaton on the move, Lear replied. Yes, he said, he would entertain reasonable peace proposals. Don Joseph sent on a proposal from Yusuf: $200,000, and the surrender of all Tripolitan prisoners and property. Don Joseph carefully added that it was only "the ground work of a negotiation." The sum was too high, groundwork or not, and as Lear confided to Bainbridge, he was unwilling to open negotiations without "the most unequivocal prospect of its being successfull." He wanted "Peace upon terms which are compatable with the rising Character of our Nation and which will secure a future peace upon honorable and lasting grounds."

But that was before the electrifying victory at Derna. Now Lear knew he had to act without delay. Another factor was Barron's growing realization that his health was not improving and that he soon would have to turn command of the squadron over to Captain John Rodgers. Lear knew the pugnacious Rodgers well enough to see that he might very well send the squadron against

Tripoli. The captain once had declared that "his name should be written in blood on the walls of Tripoli" before he would pay a cent for ransom or tribute. While that attitude might bring Yusuf to the negotiating table, Rodgers would win all the laurels and Lear would be denied the diplomatic triumph. If Lear didn't negotiate now, peace might very well be made through the expedient of war—as Jefferson had intended all along—and with Lear a footnote to Rodgers, as he had been to George Washington.

Lear told Rodgers that while $200,000 was "totally inadmissible," it was "much less extravagant than I should have expected." He was certain Yusuf wished to negotiate; the bashaw was offering unacceptable opening terms only to save face with Tunis, Algiers, and Morocco. When Bainbridge's letter arrived with $120,000 as the price for peace, Lear's certainty grew.

The other Barbary regencies were eager to see the war end. In mid-May, Algiers's dey wrote a letter to Yusuf wildly asserting that he was "sending" Lear to Tripoli to negotiate a treaty, and urging the bashaw to "renew the peace with him . . . as though you were making it with me." Tunis's sapitapa offered to mediate personally, but withdrew the offer when the American consul, George Davis, said—inaccurately, as events would show—that the United States would not agree to either ransom or tribute.

Softened by months of invalidism, Barron now became highly sympathetic to the *Philadelphia* prisoners' plight. While the captives always had aroused his sympathy, their welfare never had taken precedence over a peace with honor. Now it did. "I must contend that the liberty and perhaps the lives of so many valuable & estimable Americans ought not to be sacrificed to points of honor, taken in the abstract." He offered to send Lear to Tripoli on the *Essex* whenever he wished, which, of course, was perfectly agreeable to the consul general. "I conceive it my duty to endeavor to Open and bring to a happy issue, a negociation for peace. . . ."

Barron and Lear now made sure that Hamet and Eaton would not upset the anticipated peace talks by marching to Tripoli. In his second letter to Eaton, on May 19, Barron—again, with Lear probably helping him write it—announced the United States would provide only naval support to Hamet, and absolutely no more supplies, manpower, or money. Barron was pulling the plug. "By our resources and by your Enterprize & valor we have placed him at the post from whence he was driven," Barron observed. But Hamet "must now depend on his own resources & exertions." Without openly ordering Eaton and his men to evacuate Derna, Barron obliquely instructed them to do so, taking "that line of Conduct most prudent to be adopted in the present posture of affairs." He made it clear that he had made up his mind and was not open to argument. "Whatever your ideas touching those intentions, I feel that I have already gone to the full extent of my authority." Lear, Barron told Eaton, was poised to negotiate a peace with Yusuf that also would provide for Hamet, "without sacrificing anything." Writing to Hull at the same time, the commodore said he expected Eaton, his officers, and the Marines to leave Derna on the *Argus*.

Three days later, Barron resigned as squadron commander, and Rodgers took charge, although Eaton would not know this until much later because of the erratic communication medium upon which he and the American command had to rely—warships that happened to be sailing between Derna and Syracuse. It was "a duty which I owe to our Country and to the service in general, but more particularly to the present Squadron." While Barron was commodore, the largest naval squadron ever sent to war by the United States had not once fired on Tripoli's fortifications. Barron ensured that Rodgers wouldn't either, informing him of Lear's plan to negotiate peace, "for which I am persuaded, that the present moment is eminently favorable & the success of which, I entertain sanguine expectations."

It never seemed to have occurred to Barron and Rodgers to follow up on Eaton's success at Derna with a naval strike on Tripoli, which most likely would have ended the war quickly, without ransom or tribute. Even with everything portending success, as it now did, the Barbary War leaders seemed congenitally unable to act decisively, except for Preble and Eaton. The long-awaited gunboats and bomb vessels—Preble had supervised construction of many of them—were due in the Mediterranean within weeks, and would bring the squadron's strength to more than twenty vessels. But the contagion of inaction even infected the normally combative Rodgers, who professed the bizarre belief that it would be somehow dishonorable to attack Tripoli, "persecuting an Enemy . . . [who] felt himself more than half vanquished."

Eaton didn't tell Hamet of Barron's decision to abandon him, knowing their small army would dissolve once the news was known. He buried his anger and gnawing worries in supervising the fortification of Fort Enterprize and monitoring the bashaw's army, swollen to more than 3,000 soldiers—945 cavalry, 1,250 infantry, 350 refugees from Derna, and 500 new recruits.

Eaton's force of 1,000 was barely adequate for defending the city and too small for offensive action. Hull and Eaton estimated they would need another 300 to 400 Christian troops for that. Receiving no more funds from Barron, Eaton fed and equipped his troops by bartering whatever Hull could strip from the *Argus*. Eaton knew there would be no more supplies, no more cash to buy off the Arab sheiks. He kept the knowledge to himself and composed a response to Barron's letter.

Eaton didn't mince words. To leave Hamet "in a more hopeless situation than he left the place" was shameful. Equally dishonorable was to "strike the flag of our Country here in presence of an enemy who have not merited the triumph—at any rate it is a retreat—and a retreat of Americans!" If Barron would invest in Hamet's army what he intended to spend on a purchased peace, he could decisively defeat the bashaw's troops outside Derna. Then nothing would stand between Hamet, Tripoli, and the throne. "The total defeat of his forces here would be a fatal blow to his interests." Conversely, abandoning the expedition would invite tragedy. "You would weep, Sir, were you on the spot, to witness the unbounded confidence placed in the American character here, and to reflect that this confidence shortly sink into contempt and immortal hatred . . . havoc and slaughter will be the inevitable consequence—not a soul of them can escape the savage vengeance of the enemy."

But by the time Eaton penned these lines, Lear already was in Tripoli, and Barron no longer commanded the Mediterranean squadron.

Three frigates from Barron and Rodgers's powerful squadron sailed into Tripoli harbor on May 26. The *Essex* immediately ran up the truce flag, allaying any fears that might have assailed the bashaw and his officers when they saw the *Constitution, President,* and *Essex* and their combined 120 guns in their home waters. The Spanish consul, Don Joseph, came aboard in his mediator role, and the involved diplomatic dance began.

The negotiations were conducted on the *Constitution* over the next several days. Don Joseph and Leon Farfara, a broker and leader of Tripoli's Jewish community, shuttled proposals and counterproposals between Yusuf and Lear, who refused to go ashore until there was a tentative agreement. On May 29, Yusuf reduced his asking price sharply from $200,000 to $130,000. Two days later, Lear made what he said would be his final offer: $60,000 ransom for the *Philadelphia* captives, peace with no price.

The decisive moment was at hand. Was the bashaw serious about peace?

Yusuf sent for Cowdery. Tell Captain Bainbridge, the bashaw said, that their nations were now at peace. When they heard the news, the *Philadelphia*'s officers erupted joyously.

Nissen replaced Don Joseph as mediator during the final negotiations: for some reason, Yusuf had become dissatisfied with the Spanish consul. Lear hadn't yet gone ashore, so Nissen was still carrying on shuttle diplomacy. A snag developed when Lear suddenly stipulated that the *Philadelphia* prisoners must be released before a treaty was signed, a condition the bashaw found unacceptable. Before the disagreement could do any lasting damage to the negotiations, Nissen and Dghies drafted a counterproposal that Lear accepted immediately: sending Bainbridge aboard the *Constitution* as a goodwill gesture. Now they had to persuade Yusuf to agree to the condition. While he was willing, the Divan balked; it had trouble imagining anyone returning voluntarily to captivity. But when Dghies and Nissen stepped up and personally guaranteed Bainbridge's return, the Divan reluctantly assented to send him to the American flagship.

Cowdery raced to the castle dungeon with the glad tidings. The crewmen were ecstatic, and some wept with joy. The war was over.

The captives' flinty Tripolitan drivers ended their celebration by setting them to hard labor, flogging many of them.

Thousands of people greeted Lear at the crowded Tripoli wharf on June 3. Among them were the *Philadelphia*'s officers, released from prison the previous day. "The sight of them so near their freedom was grateful to my soul, and you must form an idea of their feelings; for I cannot describe them." Yusuf's officers escorted the consul general to the castle. With little ceremony, he and Yusuf signed the treaty ending the Barbary War. Tripoli's forts thundered salutes, answered by the U.S. frigates.

America agreed to pay Tripoli $60,000 and hand over 81 Tripolitan prisoners. In exchange, the 297 *Philadelphia* crewmen who had neither turned Turk nor died would go free—a ransom of $277 per man. The United States pledged to withdraw from Derna. Tripoli accepted peace without annual tribute and agreed to release Hamet's family from captivity.

But it would turn out there was more to the latter concession than met the eye.

After they sobered up from celebrating, the *Philadelphia* captives left Tripoli on June 5, happily watching their castle prison of nineteen months and five days recede in their ships' wakes. Two crewmen, however, stayed behind voluntarily: Quartermaster John Wilson, one of the five Americans who had "turned Turk," and John Ridgely, a *Philadelphia* surgeon like Cowdery. Ridgely elected to remain as U.S. agent to Tripoli until a new consul could be sent from America. Cowdery departed after a last audience with Yusuf, who had grown attached to him. "I bid the Bashaw a final adieu, at which he seemed much affected."

An unhappy surprise awaited the four captives besides Wilson who had turned Turk. Wilson understandably had decided to stay in Tripoli instead of returning to the United States with his former shipmates, who despised him for his ill-treatment of them while he was their overseer. The four other converts, however, had chosen to go home. But their decision evidently displeased Yusuf, who might have suspected that the spur behind their conversions was not religious devotion, but a desire to be freed from hard labor and captivity. Instead of being released with their mates, the four were led from the city under guard. They were never seen again.

Fifty years later, when Southern slavery was about to plunge the nation into the Civil War, the abolitionist poet John Greenleaf Whittier wrote about the Tripoli prisoners and their sufferings in "Derne" in a blanket indictment of all slavery. In the stanzas celebrating the captives' release, Whittier declaimed:

> In sullen wrath the conquered Moor
> Wide open flings your dungeon-door,
> And leaves ye free from cell and chain,
> The owners of yourselves again.
> Dark as his allies desert-born,
> Soiled with the battle's stain, and worn
> With the long marches of his band
> Through hottest wastes of rock and sand,
> Scorched by the sun and furnace-breath
> Of the red desert's wind of death,

With welcome words and grasping hands,
The victor and deliverer stands!"

Barron ordered Hull to bring Eaton and his troops to Syracuse, but Eaton refused to leave Derna until Lear concluded his negotiations. Eaton rightly believed that holding Derna was integral to obtaining an honorable peace. "I cannot reconcile it to a sense of duty to evacuate it," he told Hull, who didn't argue. Instead, he cruised off Derna with the *Hornet* and *Argus,* ready to give Eaton supporting fire if needed.

Hassan and Eaton's armies skirmished in several small, sharp actions during the weeks after the May 13 attack. Eaton led thirty-five Americans and Greeks in a raid against an enemy force twice their size on May 28 and defeated it, killing a captain and five men and taking prisoners. A wave of desertions swept Hassan's army. So many troops melted away that Hassan's officers resorted to chaining up the relatives of Arab soldiers to stem the defections. The enemy probed Eaton's lines on June 3 and was firmly repulsed by Eaton, O'Bannon, and the Christian troops. During the prelude to that skirmish, O'Bannon had galloped on horseback through the city as citizens called out to him, "Long live our friends & protectors!"

Hassan's cavalry and soldiers advanced en masse on Derna on June 10 for a decisive battle. Communications being what they were, neither side knew that the war officially had ended a week earlier. This very day, in fact, the treaty was being debated by the Divan in Tripoli. Bainbridge was allowed the rare privilege of observing the proceedings because he had kept his word and returned to Tripoli when he was permitted to boat out to the squadron during the peace talks. When the Divan deadlocked

4–4, Yusuf broke the tie by removing his signet from his robe, pressing it to the document, and exclaiming, "It is peace!" The treaty ratification was announced with a 21-gun salute from the castle ramparts, returned by the *Constitution.*

But the armies facing one another at Derna were unaware of these events. Hamet and his Arab cavalry met the advancing Tripolitans a mile outside Derna. A swirling battle quickly developed, with countless attacks and counterattacks by thousands of troops. From a distance, Eaton watched Hassan's troops attack repeatedly, each time repulsed by Hamet without the benefit of naval gunfire. The *Argus* and *Hornet* were unable to fire over the hills jutting between the shore and the battlefield, try though they did to maneuver into a position where they could support Hamet. But even without supporting fire or reinforcements, Hamet's cavalry drove off the attackers after four hours, killing 40 to 50 enemy and wounding another 70 while losing 50 to 60 men. Eaton's battle report brimmed with paternal pride. "The Bashaw deserves the merit of this victory—I had little to do with its arrangement, and could not render him any assistance in arms but from the fire of a single field piece ." Too late, Hamet had proved himself an able leader.

Eaton's refusal to evacuate Derna reached Rodgers, who feared it might wreck the peace Lear had just made. "A none compliance will make the responsibility his own: nevertheless, the consequence will be his country's," Rodgers wrote tartly to Lear. To "prevent impending mischief," he dispatched the *Constellation* to Derna to fetch Eaton. Yusuf, equally concerned about the progress of the expedition to depose him, insisted that his own representative go along.

Before the frigate left Tripoli, both Rodgers and Lear wrote letters apprising Eaton of the treaty and the need to evacuate Derna immediately. Rodgers bluntly said he wished "no farther hostilities by the forces of the U. States be committed against the said Josuph Bashaw, his subjects or dominions, and that you evacuate and withdraw our forces from Derne, or whatever part of his Teritory this may find you in."

Lear diplomatically gave Eaton's expedition credit for pushing the bashaw into negotiations: "I found that the heroic bravery of our few countrymen at Derne, and the idea that we had a large force and immense supplies at that place, had made a deep impression on the Bashaw." As he would do unfailingly, Lear carefully distinguished between the Americans' bravery in battle and what he regarded as the ill-conceived cooperation with Hamet. In any event, the rump alliance was terminated, and if Hamet withdrew from Derna, the bashaw would free family. It was "all that could be done, and I have no doubt but the U. States will, if deserving, place him in a situation as elegible as that in which he was found."

In this matter, however, Lear was not forthright.

After the second counterattack, Eaton told Hamet about Barron's decision to cut off supplies and money to the expedition and to recall American personnel. Experienced as he was at losing, Hamet immediately grasped his situation's hopelessness, but not without some bitterness. "He answers that, even with supplies, it would be fruitless for him to attempt to prosecute the war with his brother after you have withdrawn your squadron from the coast," Eaton wrote to Barron. "He emphatically says that To abandon him here is not to cooperate with him, but with his rival!"

When the *Constellation* reached Derna, Eaton glumly read the

303

letters from Lear and Rodgers and resigned himself to abandoning Derna and the grand expedition upon which he had pinned such high hopes. But evacuation would be tricky. A withdrawal in the face of a large enemy force invited slaughter unless it were executed with the greatest cunning and skill. Eaton told the *Constellation*'s commander, Captain Hugh Campbell, that he would leave Derna the next day, June 13.

Above all, Eaton well knew, the evacuation had to proceed in the greatest secrecy. If Hassan learned of it, he would attack when Eaton's forces were most vulnerable, and it would be a bloodbath. How would he do it? He hit upon a bold subterfuge: He made everyone, including his own men, believe he was planning an attack. He sent extra ammunition and rations to his Arab troops. He deployed scouts to pinpoint enemy troop dispositions. He ordered his soldiers to shed their heavy baggage so they would be more mobile. But as soon as darkness fell, Eaton stationed Marine patrols in Derna to keep people away from the waterfront. Boats from the *Constellation* slipped up to the docks and embarked the cannoneers, European soldiers, and fieldpieces, then Hamet and his retinue, and finally, Eaton, O'Bannon, and the Marines.

As the last boats pulled away from the wharf, the townspeople and Arab troops rushed the waterfront, "some calling on the Bashaw—some on me—Some uttering shrieks—some execrations," Eaton reported. They descended on Fort Enterprize, stripping it of the tents and horses Eaton had left behind. By daybreak, the Arabs had vanished into the mountains, along with many of the town's inhabitants and "every living animal fit for subsistence or burthen which belonged to the place."

The bashaw's envoy went ashore with letters offering amnesty to the people of Derna, provided they promised to be loyal to Yusuf, but the unhappy citizenry was in no mood for it. They vowed to fight the bashaw's troops. Eaton watched the spectacle with sadness and anger. "This moment we drop them . . . into the hands of this enemy for no other crime but too much confidence in us!" Hamet, he noted glumly, "falls from the most flattering prospects of a Kingdom to beggary!"

Eaton's mission was ended. With little of the rancor that would consume him later, he reported to Rodgers: "Our peace with Tripoli is certainly more favorable—and, seperately considered, more honorable than any peace obtained by any Christian nation with a Barbary regency at any period within a hundred years: but it might have been more favorable and more honorable."

He requested passage home to America.

XVI

AFTERMATH

If War is his object, I shall be obliged to meet it.
—Commodore John Rodgers, referring to Bey Hamouda Pacha of
Tunis, in a letter to George Davis, U.S. chargé d'affaires in Tunis

I fear we stopped too short.
—William Eaton, in a letter to Thomas Dwight

Hamouda Pacha was threatening war. He wanted back the xebec and two Neapolitan prizes that Rodgers had caught as they tried to run the American blockade of Tripoli in early May. Commodore John Rodgers had landed the Barbary crews back in Tunis, but refused to return the vessels. Chargé d'Affaires George Davis had done his best to deflect the bey's litany of demands while Rodgers and Lear ended the Tripolitan war. The impatient bey even had written directly to Jefferson, warning that only the president's previous assurances that he wanted peace with Tunis were preventing war now. Then, for weeks, the bey and Rodgers had exchanged demands, refusals, and threats.

Finally Rodgers had had enough. His natural combativeness was aroused over the prospect of hostilities after all the tedious months of cruising off Tripoli. "If War is his object, I shall be obliged to meet it." He sent the *Congress,* commanded by Decatur, to Tunis Bay to defend U.S. shipping. The bey responded by announcing he would not grant Lear an audience; Rodgers retorted that the bey would have no choice but to receive Lear, and sent more warships to Tunis. Tensions reached the breaking point when the *Vixen* boarded and searched a polacre and a gunboat in Tunis Bay. Rodgers gathered his formidable squadron for a display of power.

In America, the controversial Tripoli treaty was making waves. Navy Secretary Smith boasted that it was better than any treaty negotiated with Tripoli in 100 years. Certainly it was that. "All Europe is giving us national reputation for this," he crowed to Preble. But Smith was enough of a realist to foresee the bitter fight looming in Congress over treaty ratification, sarcastically noting, "Our own good folk [critics of the treaty] will be busy in telling the world that we are, in fact, a very contemptible people." Preble publicly held his tongue, but was among the many who were disappointed with the treaty; privately he lamented "the sacrifice of National honor which has been made by an ignominious negotiation." The $60,000 ransom stuck fast in the craws of treaty opponents, who asked: Need any ransom have been paid, with Eaton occupying Derna and a large U.S. squadron just a day's sail from Tripoli? Anticipating this argument in his letter to Preble, Smith asserted that the *Philadelphia* prisoners' safety alone justified the treaty. Smith said all the returning former captive officers—this wasn't altogether true—were convinced that Yusuf would have massacred them if Lear had not paid their ransom and Rodgers instead had attacked Tripoli. "The Bashaw said again & again that having killed a father & brother he would not have any scruples in killing a few infidels." Smith was rehearsing for the donnybrook ahead.

• • •

Eighteen U.S. Navy vessels crewed by 2,500 men entered Tunis Bay on July 30, 1805. The United States had never before gathered in one place such a naval force. The forest of masts and crowd of canvas presented a menacing sight. Tunisians watched with awe and fear, expecting a devastating bombardment to commence any hour. The vessels deployed in a long line spanning the harbor mouth, boarding and inspecting the papers of all departing and arriving vessels.

Every U.S. warship in the Mediterranean was present: the frigates *Constitution, Constellation, Essex,* and *John Adams;* the brigs *Siren, Vixen,* and *Franklin;* the schooners *Nautilus* and *Enterprise;* the sloop *Hornet;* and eight U.S.-built gunboats, which weeks before had arrived in the Mediterranean. Ten gunboats in all had recently been completed at shipyards along the East Coast, but Gunboat 1 had to turn back to Charleston with structural problems, and Gunboat 7 vanished during the Atlantic crossing and was never seen again.

After letting the Tunisians absorb the sight of his formidable battle group, Rodgers sent Hamouda Pacha a letter reminding him that he had once said if a U.S. squadron entered his harbor, it would mean war. Did he still mean that? he asked provocatively. He gave the Tunisian leader thirty-six hours to decide: peace or war. If there was no reply, Rodgers would assume the bey meant war and offensive and defensive operations would commence.

Hamouda was in a quandary. He fervently wished to avoid a shooting war he undoubtedly would lose. But if he gave in, he would lose face with the other Christian powers paying him tribute, and that could jeopardize the entire Barbary States' system of terror, robbery, and extortion. He tried to buy time by reminding Rodgers that he had sent an appeal to Jefferson. Until he received an answer, he planned no warlike actions and intended to honor his treaty with the United States.

This only irritated Rodgers. He imposed a new deadline for Hamouda to decide how matters stood between Tunis and America. Davis piped up unexpectedly that he thought the ultimatum unreasonable. Rodgers slapped him down, "much astonished" that Davis had failed to understand his intentions. The commodore ordered Davis to prepare to leave Tunis. As the clock ticked down to the new deadline, Rodgers added a new condition and threat: The bey must pledge himself to peace in the presence of both the British and French consuls—so he couldn't later deny having done so—or Rodgers would send his ships to capture Tunisian cruisers at sea.

Hamouda refused.

The *Constitution* fired on a brig attempting to leave Tunis, compelling it to turn back. The *Vixen, Nautilus,* and *Enterprise* began cruising the waters outside the harbor, stopping every vessel in sight. In an extemporaneous demonstration of U.S. destructiveness, the *Vixen's* officers, during an afternoon of relaxation on an island in Tunis Bay, shot several seals and fowl, and then started a fire that got away from them and burned the entire island.

Lear threw the besieged bey a lifeline so that he could extricate himself from his predicament. It perplexed him, Lear noted, that the bey claimed to value the president's friendship, yet refused to meet with Lear, the president's designated representative. The bey grabbed the line and held fast to it. He hadn't realized Lear represented the president; knowing that now, of course he would receive Lear. Rodgers moved back the deadline two days, but it may as well have been two years, for it was clear there would be no shooting war now.

Hamouda now had an inspiration: He would send an ambassador to Washington to personally argue Tunis's reparations claims for the xebec and the prize vessels. The appeal to higher authority accomplished two things: It automatically imposed a cooling-off period, and it tied the hands of Rodgers, who, as a naval officer bound to the chain of command, couldn't very well deny the bey the right to petition higher-ups. He graciously offered passage to the Tunisian ambassador on one of his frigates. Hamouda responded by granting the United States "most favored nation" trade status, meaning it no longer would have to pay the higher duties Tunis imposed on the lesser nations such as Denmark and Naples, but not on the major powers such as Britain and France. Hamouda also asked Rogers to name a new chargé d'affaires, after coolly observing Davis's distress over his countrymen's aggressiveness and Rodgers's displeasure with him. Davis, still smarting from his treatment by Rodgers and Lear, didn't mind leaving. "After such a degradation, I could not return to the duties of my office," he sniffed. Rodgers appointed another ship's surgeon, Dr. James Dodge of the *Constitution.* naval surgeons, because of their learning, evidently were regarded as competent substitute-diplomats; Dodge was the third named in Barbary since the war began. The Tunisian crisis sputtered to an end.

Rodgers was justifiably proud of the diplomatic victory achieved with his show of naval force: ". . . I feel satisfied this lesson has not only changed his [the bey's] opinion of our Maritime strength, but has caused him to discover more distinctly his own weakness in every sense." It was the first time the Mediterranean squadron had followed to the letter the instructions written in 1802 by Smith and Madison of "holding out the olive Branch in one hand & displaying in the other the means of offensive operations." Hamouda later insisted in his correspondence with Jefferson that the confrontation was due solely to "the too martial temper" of Rodgers and to Davis's "equivocal conduct."

Fuming over Lear and Barron's abandonment of his expedition, Eaton sailed to Gibraltar to await a berth on a ship bound for America. Before leaving Syracuse, he had paid off his European troops and said good-bye to Hamet, whom he would never see again. Now Eaton began to brood over the war's disappointing outcome, believing that he and Hamet could have marched to Tripoli and forced Yusuf to free the captives. "I fear we stopped too short," he wrote to Thomas Dwight, a friend in Massachusetts, in June. "I hoped to have stood on to see the temerity of Joseph Bashaw chastized and his perfidy punished. The lesson would have been awful to Barbary—Perhaps another such occasion will never offer."

As Eaton pondered what had happened, his disappointment metastasized into a black anger directed at one villain: Tobias Lear. He began putting his thoughts on paper. He carefully documented the promises made by Jefferson administration officials before he left Washington, and how they had proved chimerical. This web of broken promises was the framework for a letter to Smith, written during Eaton's Gibraltar layover. Page after accusatory page piled up, each sharper in tone than the one before, until he had composed a 5,000-word screed.

Everything changed, he wrote to Smith, when Lear, "a man who had no authorized agency in the war . . . intruded himself" into

Barron's confidence. Thus began Eaton's censorious letter. Barron, he wrote, had initially supported his expedition and was aware that "an understanding Subsisted Between the Commander in Chief and myself that I should go forward And exercise Discretionary measures for bringing Hamet Bashaw forward with all his influence in order To Intercept Supplies to the Enemy from the country and to cut off his escape in the rear." Eaton, Rodgers, and Preble had agreed that after Eaton and Hamet captured Derna and Benghazi, the squadron would transport their army across the Gulf of Sidra to Cape Mensurat, where they would assault Tripoli from the rear while warships attacked from the harbor.

But Barron's illness had left him helplessly under the spell of the "Machiavellian Commissioner." Lear viewed Hamet as only a lever for obtaining a quick negotiated peace. Lear had ordered Eaton's withdrawal from Derna even before he left Malta to begin negotiations. It was Lear who had withheld supplies and reinforcements from Eaton, while Barron's squadron passively cruised off Tripoli, never attacking or planning offensive action. Eaton complained about being denied the 100 Marines he had requested: ". . . it did not require a greater latitude of discretion to indulge them the permission to fight at Derne than to furlough them on parties of pleasure at Catania—and they must have subsisted cheaper on the coast than at any port in Italy." With Derna in American hands, two to three months might have been spent in planning and coordinating a crushing land–sea attack that would have resulted in Tripoli's capture. But Lear instead made a hasty treaty while claiming that offensive operations would have jeopardized the *Philadelphia* captives' lives—a claim Eaton disputed. "Man seldom mediates vengeance when disolution glares him in the face. . . ." He pointed out that awful threats also had been made against the captives before Preble bombarded Tripoli in 1804—and were never carried out. "The terrible bashaw's first care was to provide for his own safety and he uniformly took refuge in his gardens or in his Bomb-proof and all experience has taught us that the more rougly he was handled and the nearer danger approached him the more tractable he has been rendered." He wondered whether Lear had even considered exchanging Derna and its 12,000–15,000 Tripolitan citizens for the 300 *Philadelphia* captives. "Tripoli was in our power and with no verry extraordinary effort it might have been also in our hands."

He derided Lear's professed preference for Yusuf over Hamet. "Was Mr. Lear sent out to co-operate with Joseph Bashaw?" If parricide, fratricide, piracy, and broken treaties are hallmarks of an able ruler, "Mr. Lear has chosen the fittest of the two brothers for his man of confidence." He acidly criticized the Arabs' abandonment at Derna. "This is the first instance I ever heard of a religious test being required to entitle a soldier to his rations." And, in a burst of caustic verse, he sneered at Lear's praise for the Americans' bravery at Derna, "a military compliment from the provisional colonel Lear. A colonel/Who never set a squadron in the field/Nor the division of a battle Knows/More than a spinster." Lear's peace treaty was "a wound on our national dignity" that cried for an official inquiry; from it, honor "recoils and humanity Bleeds," he wrote.

During his weeks-long Atlantic crossing on the *Constellation,* Eaton touched up his fiery, rambling letter. Normally convivial, Eaton spent much of the trip alone in his cabin, or on deck, gazing at the sea.

Eaton and the *Philadelphia* captives received heroes' welcomes in America. Bainbridge had returned on September 10 with 117 fellow crewmen after a court of inquiry presided over by Eaton on the *President* at Syracuse found him blameless for the loss of the *Philadelphia*. Yet, some still hadn't forgiven him for surrendering his ship without firing a shot.

Eaton, however, was embraced without reservations by one and all. Dinner invitations arrived in a flood for the man of the hour, from everyone from President Jefferson to congressmen to old War Department friends. At a testimonial dinner in Richmond attended by Chief Justice John Marshall, Eaton was honored for leading "the Spartan band who spread the glory of the American arms where the American name was not known." Newspapers referred to him as "the modern Africanus," and as a latter-day Alexander or Belisarius. "General Eaton is the inheritor of the mantle of Alexander of Great!" gushed Dr. Francisco Mendrici, who had aided Eaton in Egypt, in a widely quoted panegyric. "The sands of the desert part before him, and the mountains melt away. He conquers all that lies in his path!" Addressing Eaton, Preble warmly added that he had "astonished not only your country but the world." Had he received the money, supplies, and naval support that he requested, "what would you not have done!"

A Senate resolution, never implemented, established a six-square-mile township named Derne in an unspecified location, "as a memorial of the conquest of that city forever"—to be parceled among Eaton, Midshipman Mann, Lieutenant O'Bannon, and the five surviving Marine enlisted men. Massachusetts awarded Eaton 10,000 acres in Maine for his "undaunted courage and brilliant services." Odes were written to him. One, by Federalist poet Robert Treat Paine, was sung at Boston's General Eaton Fire Society gathering to the tune "God Save the King," later famous on this side of the Atlantic as the patriotic hymn "America":

Eaton, a glorious name!
Struck from the flint of fame
A spark whose chymick [chemical] flame
Dissolved their chains.

Eaton reveled in the celebratory dinners and the admiring strangers who bought him drinks in Washington's taverns. It was a welcome release after the long, abstentious months in the desert and at Derna. Eaton made the most of it. In his barroom perorations on the war, he vilified Lear for having denied America a resounding military triumph, and for agreeing to a demeaning ransom when the captives' release might have been obtained without any ransom paid.

Federalist congressmen were listening carefully to Eaton's denunciations, seeing a prime opportunity to strike a blow at the Republicans, ascendant for five years now. They flattered and cultivated "the general," pumping him for information that would help them argue against the Tripoli treaty and give the Republicans a black eye. It promised to be a battle royal. Federalist newspapers already were pillorying the treaty, while the Republican press spun its own tapestry, depicting Hamet as a debauchee "addicted to sordid propensities," and Yusuf as his antithesis, a man inclined to "elevated centiments ."

Eaton's staunchest allies were Senator Timothy Pickering of Massachusetts, the former war secretary who had supported Eaton when he was stationed in Georgia, and Senator William Plumer of New Hampshire. Pickering deplored Lear's treachery; he had "acted contrary to his instructions" and "shamefully betrayed" Hamet. Recalling the mysterious disappearance of the Washington-Jefferson letters six years earlier, Pickering suggested that circumstance alone "will warrant any surmise unfavourable to Lear; while it will account for J's [Jefferson's] solicitudes to vindicate Lear from reproach."

Between consorting with Federalists and deprecating Lear at every opportunity, Eaton swiftly transformed himself into an enemy of the Jefferson administration. He burned the last bridge to his former benefactors when he distributed copies of his diatribe to Smith to newspapers in Boston and Hartford and put it in a pamphlet circulated in Washington. "The effect has been that the Executive has been probed to the core, every syllable of document drawn from him which could throw light on the subject; and, you have the result—Lear will be impeached," he crowed. Eaton also continued to harangue Smith, who was trying to ascertain the United States's obligations to Hamet. There were none, Eaton said, but reminded him that America had deceived Hamet—as well as Eaton himself—by pledging to cooperate with him, then using him as "an instrument" and discarding him. "On entering the ground of war with Hamet Bashaw, Mr. O'Bannon and myself united in a resolution to perish with him before the walls of Tripoli, or to triumph with him within those walls." It was the same bitter story Eaton was telling anyone who would listen in the taverns where he held court nearly every day.

Federalist senators went on the attack over the Tripoli treaty in January 1806, requesting that Jefferson turn over all of his administration's correspondence with Barron, Rodgers, and Eaton, along with Eaton's and Lear's instructions. At the same time, the House examined Eaton's convention with Hamet. Jefferson personally supervised the collection of the letters and papers, listing all official correspondence, instructions, and commissions pertaining to Tripoli and noting cryptically that only $20,000 was to have been spent on Hamet's expedition and that it wasn't known whether he had been reunited yet with his family. He composed a message to Congress that in a disinterested, lawyerly way explained that Eaton's convention with Hamet was intended to "produce effects favorable to both, without binding either to guaranty the objects of the other," with Hamet attacking by land and Barron by sea. The convention never committed the United States to restoring Hamet to Tripoli's throne, argued Jefferson. Thus, when Hamet was unable to carry on alone from Derna, the United States was not obligated to land its own troops or to hire Arab soldiers to fight for him.

But the Federalists interpreted the correspondence to mean that there *had* been an alliance, and it was supposed to have culminated in a land–sea operation before the bashaw's castle. A Senate committee began studying the treaty and the events leading to it. Federalists hoped the panel would take the Republicans down a peg, but it needed Eaton's help. "The present moment were you on the spot would undoubtedly be the most propitious to your obtaining that justice which you have so richly merited from your Country and the World," the committee chairman, Senator Stephen Row Bradley of Vermont, wrote Eaton. Eaton obliged him, as did the former *Philadelphia* captives, whose testimony didn't always jibe with Smith's assertions that they believed their lives were imperiled by American military operations against the bashaw.

The committee's 472-page report, made public in April 1806, came down hard on Lear. The Tripoli treaty was an "inglorious deed," and ran counter to the advice of squadron officers. Hamet could have been placed on Tripoli's throne for a fraction of the $60,000 ransom, and the captives freed without any payment made. Derna never should have been evacuated. Lear was blamed for everything. The consul general, the committee concluded, appears "to have dictated every measure; to have paralised every military operation by sea and land. . . ." The committee didn't blame Barron, ill as he was and, it believed, under Lear's malign influence. The report cited the testimony of Lieutenant John Dent, who said that during the winter of 1804–5 Barron could scarcely "recollect any thing that transpired from one day to another. . . . It was generally believed by the officers in the Mediterranean that Mr. Lear had a great ascendancy over the commodore in all his measures relative to the squadron."

The report rejected Lear's claims that the squadron was unfit for action, and that he had acted to protect the *Philadelphia* prisoners' safety. It included Marine Second Lieutenant Wallace W. Wormeley's testimony that in May 1805 Tripoli was "in the most distressed situation," and Eaton and Hamet, "almost without firing a shot," might have marched from Derna and captured Tripoli without harm to any prisoner. Wormeley said he believed he still would be locked in the bashaw's castle if Eaton hadn't captured Derna.

Despite all the sound and fury, the report didn't stop the Senate from ratifying the treaty on April 12, nor did it damage Lear's employment; he remained North African consul general through 1812. The Jefferson administration shrugged off the indictment of its North African diplomacy as other events crowded in, one upon the other: trouble with Spain over Florida and western Louisiana in the wake of the momentous Louisiana Purchase; violations of American neutrality by England, France, and Spain. Because of the distance-imposed time lag between America and the Mediterranean, the treaty controversy was rapidly receding from public consciousness just when Rodgers and Lear were hearing the worst of it. The withering criticism burnished their long friendship from Santo Domingo days, although their reactions diverged, with Lear more pained than angry, and the feistier Rodgers vowing to defend his character against "base scoundrels."

The Tunisian ambassador, Sidi Soliman Melli Melli, arrived in the United States in November 1805 on the *Congress* with four Arabian horses that he presented to the president as gifts. His seriocomic diplomatic visit began with a quick triumph, when Jefferson agreed to pay restitution for the xebec and two prizes. Melli Melli then spent several months enjoying Washington and being gawked at by the public, who had never seen a Mediterranean Moslem in full regalia. His relaxed morals offended the more Puritan-minded congressmen, but the government, wishing to keep him happy, quietly supplied him with women and a $200-a-week allowance, selling the gift horses to defray the cost. Partly to get him out of town and also to impress upon him America's size and strength, Madison sent Melli Melli on a tour of the Eastern cities, with James Cathcart, the former consul in Tripoli, as his guide and escort. Melli Melli caused a sensation wherever he went, with his flowing robes and entourage. In the meantime, Madison and Smith looked around for suitable restitution for the xebec and two prizes, all liquidated in prize court months earlier. They decided upon the brig *Franklin,* which had brought Eaton home from Gibraltar, and to add cash and gifts totaling $10,000 for the bey, sapitapa, Melli Melli, and his entourage.

319

The *Franklin* turned out to be a poor choice. As Melli Melli correctly pointed out, it had been Tripoli's only U.S. wartime prize, captured in 1802. By coincidence, the bey had come into ownership of it briefly before selling it to some Americans in Trieste. Melli Melli said Hamouda never liked the *Franklin* and would consider it a grave insult to be presented with it again as restitution for the three captured vessels. He refused to accept it, or to sail home on it, which had been the American expectation. He would rather hire a ship instead.

The gifts for the bey and sapitapa were unloaded from the *Franklin* in Boston, the ambassador's embarkation point, while Melli Melli hunted for a merchantman to take him back to Tunis. The complication made Melli Melli quarrelsome, difficult, and intolerable to Cathcart, who was notoriously short-tempered himself. His irksome companion, Cathcart complained, was "a very mean, suspicious, avaricious character; bias'd by nothing but self interest, devoid of every sense of delicacy, and the sooner we get rid of him entirely the better." Melli Melli chartered the *Two Brothers* and, to Cathcart's relief, sailed home in September 1806. The long voyage mellowed his temper and perhaps gave him time to savor his pleasant memories of America and the profusion of gifts riding in the *Two Brothers'* hold: coffee, china, chocolate, furniture, rum, and four brass fieldpieces with cartridges. By the time he reached Tunis, he was full of enthusiasm about his visit to the United States. Satisfied with Melli Melli's report and visibly pleased with the cash and the gifts, the bey reaffirmed Tunis's previous treaty with America.

Lear returned to Algiers, which was reeling from a coup, a civil war, and a war with Tunis. The upheaval had begun in the summer of 1805, when rioters in the city of Algiers burned the "Jewish Directory"—the banking house of Bacris and Busnah—and murdered the Jewish proprietor, Naphthali Busnah. At Busnah's funeral, a mob massacred many of the mourners and wrecked the Jewish quarter. Then, in a continuation of the mayhem, Turkish soldiers assassinated the dey and his prime minister. They made the late dey's principal secretary the new dey. Some Algerian provinces took advantage of the anarchy and seceded, one of them allying with Tunis. Algiers and Tunis went to war. They fought through the winter of 1805–6, while Algiers also was trying to brutally suppress uprisings in Oran. On Christmas Day 1805, Lear witnessed the arrival of a small vessel from Oran bearing a grisly cargo: the heads of 600 Algerian rebels and "a vast number of Ears of the Insurgents. . . . They take off the Heads of the Slain and the Ears of the Prisoners, which they send as a proof of their Victory."

Through all the turmoil, Lear somehow managed to stay on excellent terms with the Algerian government. So highly was Lear regarded by the dey and his officers that when Rodgers paid a last, formal visit to Algiers in May 1806 before leaving for home, the dey permitted Rodgers to wear his sword during his royal audience. The stubborn Rodgers had told the dey's aide he would not see the dey without his sword. It was unprecedented for a Christian to be granted this privilege.

With all the Barbary States now at peace with the United States, Jefferson thought it no longer necessary for twenty warships to patrol the western Mediterranean. The frigates, brigs, and schooners, and the eight gunboats and two new bomb vessels that had joined the squadron in 1805 were ordered to sail home—all but the *Constitution, Siren,* and *Enterprise.*

The Tripolitan war had cost just $3.6 million, but Treasury Secretary Albert Gallatin, who kept an iron grip on the federal purse strings, was still harping on Republican frugality, although Jefferson no longer was. For nine straight years, Gallatin diligently cut the federal debt each year by $2 million to $8 million, so that by 1809, when Madison became president, the $83 million debt in 1801 had been pared to $42 million, despite the expense of the Tripoli War and the $15 million Louisiana Purchase. Even with revenues increasing steadily, Gallatin was not seduced into reckless spending by the prospect of surpluses.

But the thrifty Gallatin and Navy Secretary Smith were becoming strikingly out of step with Jefferson, who had made a sharp turn toward a more Federalist-style government. In December 1806, he asked Congress to build a nationwide system of roads and canals, a national university, and coastal fortifications. It was hard to believe this was the same Jefferson who six years earlier had said the federal government should collect taxes, deliver mail, and maintain a navy to protect trade—and leave everything else to the states. Gallatin, however, had remained true to the Republican creed, as had the Southern Republicans, who were caught up in a retrograde movement to recapture the "Spirit of 1800." They opposed spending money on forts and on more ships. They preferred gunboats because they were cheaper than stone fortifications, and, they wrongly believed, better suited for coastal defense than brigs and schooners.

After protesting that three warships could not possibly protect U.S. Mediterranean trade, Rodgers closed the Syracuse naval hospital, handed command of the shrunken squadron to Captain

Hugh Campbell, and embarked for America in May 1806. Aboard Rodgers's ship was a pair of Barbary broad-tailed sheep. They were for President Jefferson, whose many interests included animal husbandry.

XVII

FULL CIRCLE

*... the weight of misfortune has only increased, and for the first time, am
completely abandoned, and by a great nation...*
—Hamet Karamanli, in a letter to Thomas Jefferson

George Davis reembarked for the Mediterranean in late
1806 with a new title: consul to Tripoli. After his humiliation during the Tunisian crisis of August 1805, he had sailed
home, but it wasn't long before he began to miss the status, privi-
leges, and freedom he had enjoyed in Barbary. The former ship's
doctor reached Gibraltar on September 10, 1806. There he waited
for one of the three remaining U.S. warships to take him the rest
of the way to Tripoli. Growing impatient, he took passage on a
vessel bound for Leghorn. He expected that it would be relatively
simple to find a ship to take him from Italy to Tripoli, but it
wasn't. Early 1807 found him still in Leghorn.

The long layover in Leghorn proved lucky in one respect. Davis
happened to meet Nicholas Nissen there as the former Danish
consul to Tripoli was on his way home. The consul's devotion to the
Philadelphia captives during their nineteen months of imprison-
ment had been rewarded with a formal expression of gratitude from

the U.S. government and a silver urn purchased by the former prisoners. Now Nissen was retiring from the diplomatic corps. He brought Davis up to date on Tripolitan affairs, including the peace treaty, which Davis had not seen. The treaty, he told Davis, contained a secret clause. Nissen knew it did because he had drafted it.

The secret clause was written into the treaty during the last stages of negotiations. With most of the main issues settled, Lear had dutifully raised the question of releasing Hamet's wife and children, prisoners since the bashaw closed the city gates to his brother ten years before. Here he had touched on a tender subject with Yusuf. The bashaw and his Divan were uneasy about relinquishing their only leverage over Hamet, who, after all, had made it as far as Derna with his ragtag army. But Lear knew he couldn't sign a treaty that lacked even this small acknowledgment of Hamet's predicament. The treaty that had seemed such a sure thing suddenly wasn't so certain—until Nissen made a saving suggestion: a clause permitting the bashaw to retain custody of Hamet's family for four years, with their release at the end of that period contingent on Hamet's good behavior. This would technically satisfy Lear's requirement that Yusuf agree to release Hamet's family, while giving Yusuf ample time to quell any lingering dissent in his far-flung provinces that conceivably could foster another Hamet insurgency. And, as Nissen noted to his own government a week after the treaty signing, his proposal vouchsafed to the bashaw and Divan "that I had not tried to deceive them," and incurred a debt on Yusuf's part that might one day be called in by Nissen's successor. Lear, Yusuf, and his Divan signed the clause on June 5, 1805, the day after they had formally affixed their names to the main part of the treaty.

The clause was attached to Article 3, which stipulated that America would stop aiding Hamet's insurgency, withdraw its forces, and persuade Hamet to pull out, and that Yusuf would hand over Hamet's family if those conditions were met. Lear undoubtedly was aware that the four-year moratorium would be a political red flag when the treaty came before the Senate for ratification. He avoided that problem simply by omitting it from the treaty and never explicitly revealing its existence to anyone in Washington. In his report to Madison on the negotiations, Lear said Yusuf had balked at releasing Hamet's family, and they then had agreed the bashaw might wait "a period of time" before doing so, to ensure that his brother wouldn't attempt to revive his insurgency.

Uninformed of the four-year clause, in March 1806 Jefferson's cabinet weighed restoring the blockade to force the release of Hamet's still-captive family. "We will not incline from the fulfillment of that article of the treaty," Jefferson declared. All that prevented the blockade's revival was the president's trenchant observation that it very well might constitute an act of war, which would require congressional approval. The Cabinet stayed its own hand for the moment, but if Tripoli didn't take steps to release Hamet's family, it planned to lay the matter before Congress.

Hamet and his three dozen or so attendants were subsisting on friends' charity and a $200-a-month stipend authorized grudgingly by Rodgers. The commodore had suggested that Hamet emigrate to the United States, but the prospect of crossing the ocean in a boat terrified Hamet and he refused to go. Yet he was miserable in Syracuse. He fired off appeals to Jefferson, Congress, and "the People of the United States of America." To Jefferson, he wrote: ". . . the weight of misfortune has only increased, and for the first time, am completely abandoned, and by a great nation. . . ." In another letter, he implored, "I beg you to send me some token, in order that I may not remain in the dark." To Congress, he said, "I have lost my inheritance; my acquisitions; and my fair prospects are lost also. . . . I had no right to apprehend that my devotion and my complacency would overwhelm me in bottomless ruin." He had a point: According to Eaton, Hamet was forced to leave behind $50,000 worth of possessions in Derna, in addition to losing his army of Arabs. Eaton estimated he was owed $30,000–$40,000. "I trusted to the faith of a great people," Hamet wrote pathetically in his open letter to the American people. His appeals were largely ignored, now that the war was over and he was no longer of any use to the United States. Congress paid him $2,400 as a final settlement in June 1806, when the $200 monthly stipend was terminated. Thus Hamet received a total of $6,800 from the United States: a paltry sum for his contribution at Derna, without which an honorable peace would have been impossible.

Becoming increasingly restless in Leghorn but still without transport to Tripoli, Davis sailed to Syracuse, which, at least, was closer to Tripoli than Leghorn was. Being in Syracuse also afforded him the opportunity to meet Hamet. It wasn't a pleasant meeting. Hamet harangued Davis about needing more money and his family's continuing captivity. Davis didn't reveal what he had learned about the secret treaty clause, wanting to use this knowledge to somehow force Yusuf to free Hamet's family. Instead, he promised Hamet that he would bring up his family's situation during his first audience with Yusuf. Davis also suggested to

Hamet that reconciling with his brother might be the best means of effecting his family's release.

Nine months after leaving the United States, Davis finally reached Tripoli in early May 1807. At his first audience before Yusuf, he raised the subject of Hamet's family, sternly informing the bashaw that his failure to release Hamet's family violated the treaty. He made no mention of the secret clause. Yusuf responded by producing a copy of it and pointing to the four-year grace period. Davis flatly refused to recognize it as a valid part of the treaty. He stuck to that position through nearly a week's worth of talks. By May 12, Davis had worn down the bashaw, who did not wish to renew hostilities with the United States, to the point where he agreed reluctantly to release his brother's family.

But June and July came and went with Hamet's wife and children still in Tripoli. When Davis badgered Yusuf about his failure to carry out his pledge, the bashaw complained that Hamet's supporters in the distant provinces were still giving him trouble. Finally, on August 7, Yusuf cleared Hamet's wife, three sons, and a daughter for departure, but another two months passed before they sailed away on the merchantman *Tartan* to be reunited with Hamet in Syracuse after twelve years.

Davis managed to wring one last concession from the bashaw for Hamet: an unspecified "liberal allowance" to support Hamet's family. Having won this favor from a former enemy, the consul tried his luck with his own government, suggesting that it contribute $1,000 a year. But the United States never gave Hamet another cent.

The Jefferson administration's official position was that it never was aware of the secret clause until Davis reported the successful outcome of his parley with Yusuf in a June 2 letter to Madison. It is entirely possible that is true, given Lear's tendency to operate independently and the vagueness of the only extant mention of the clause, made by Lear in his letter to Madison two years earlier. For the first time, Jefferson publicly acknowledged the provision's existence on November 11, 1807. He made no excuses; he blamed no one. The announcement caused a brief flurry of consternation in Congress, and the president ordered a reexamination of all of Lear's correspondence to determine whether the consul general had reported the clause and it somehow had been overlooked. The inquiry turned up only Lear's allusive reference of 1805, which had been so fleeting that it evidently had escaped the State Department's notice. "How it happened that the declaration of June 5 [1805] had never come to our attention, cannot with certainty be said," Jefferson concluded in a memo to the Senate that ended all discussion of the matter.

Fresh trouble with the Great Powers pushed Barbary affairs into the background. The U.S. Navy may have taught the Barbary States to respect the United States, but not Europe. The warships of Spain, England, and France routinely stopped and searched U.S. merchant ships, sometimes looting and claiming them for prizes. The searches-and-seizures had reached outrageous proportions, but America's Navy, doughty as it had been at times in Barbary, was no match for the European powers' men-of-war with their triple gun decks. Prudence dictated forbearance.

Tensions with Spain lingered over the 1803 Louisiana Purchase and its aftermath. When the Spanish ceded the same territory to France in 1800, France had agreed never to relinquish it to another nation, Spain claimed. But that promise had lasted only until Napoleon needed money for his wars. Spain also was alarmed by America's designs on West Florida, the long corridor stretching across the Deep South from present-day Florida to the Mississippi River. The land-hungry Jefferson administration had all but concluded that the Louisiana Purchase also compassed West Florida. This was an amazing conclusion, considering that Spain clearly possessed the territory and garrisoned thousands of troops there and in western Louisiana. The Americans' specious rationale was that West Florida belonged to the French until their defeat by England in the Seven Years' War (1756–63), which was followed by France's withdrawal from the territory. But since France had never formally ceded West Florida to anyone, the French could still legitimately transfer the territory to the United States as part of the Louisiana Territory. Not unhappy to see trouble come to its bothersome ally Spain, France did nothing to discourage the Americans' interpretation of the Louisiana Purchase.

Besides the disagreement with Spain, there was the recurring problem of being caught in the middle of England and France's long enmity. Both nations, fearful that their rival might gain an advantage by trading with America, stopped and searched U.S. ships for goods that might benefit the other. The British went to the extent of brazenly anchoring two frigates outside New York harbor, boarding every outgoing vessel and sending captured ships and suspected contraband to prize court in Halifax, Nova Scotia. They also impressed U.S. seamen—1,000 a year on the average, infuriating the Jefferson administration—but the fact was that America's merchant fleet couldn't have operated very long without its own complement of several thousand British sailors. For their part, the British felt they were justified in taking seamen who were English to begin with. The British detentions, looting, and impressments happened in the Atlantic, the Mediterranean, the Pacific Ocean, even in China, where the British operated much as pirates.

France had been somewhat chastened by the Quasi-War and didn't tread as heavily on U.S. sovereignty as did Britain. But it clearly was dismissive of U.S. power. Citizen Beaussier, the French chargé d'affaires in Tripoli, exemplified this attitude of maddening condescension soon after the release of the *Philadelphia* captives. He claimed that two crewmen were French, and that France was entitled to compensation from the United States for the nineteen months they were imprisoned. This sent the volatile Commodore Rodgers into a fury. In his acid reply, he upbraided Beaussier for "perjury," and said it was "disgraceful to honor & truth" to think that France would do nothing for the two while they were captives, but now was justified in demanding redress. The claim died a quick death.

Undoubtedly the European warships dwarfed the American frigates, but the aura of invincibility that invested their fleets sometimes had unfortunate results. In August 1806 in the Straits of Gibraltar, several Spanish gunboats without provocation attacked the *Enterprise,* which under Lieutenant Andrew Sterrett had shredded the *Tripoli* five years earlier. The *Enterprise's* current skipper was the tough, competent Lieutenant David Porter, wounded in coastal skirmishes at Tripoli, an alumnus of the *Philadelphia* and destined for future greatness in the War of 1812. Porter tried to avoid a fight even as the gunboats bore in on his schooner with their guns blazing. He hoisted the U.S. colors, thinking the Spanish might have mistaken his ship for a British vessel. The Spanish came on, still firing. Porter tried hailing them. They kept coming, behind volleys of grape and sheeting musket fire. It was abundantly clear that the gunboats intended to board the *Enterprise*. Porter ordered his gunners and Marines to give the Spanish everything they had. The blast of withering fire littered the gunboats' decks with dead and wounded. The *Enterprise* gunners reloaded and began a continuous fire. The gunboats, their decks slick with their crews' blood, slewed about as the casualties piled up. Then they turned and ran for the Spanish shore, with the *Enterprise* now in hot pursuit, cannons booming. Only when the gunboats reached the protection of the Spanish coastal batteries did Porter veer off, hoping he had dispensed "a useful lesson to them," not to provoke neutral vessels, particularly U.S. warships.

With tensions running high between America and the Great Powers, Navy Secretary Smith reduced the Mediterranean squadron from three ships to two to hold down costs and to keep as many warships home as possible for coastal defense. He dispatched the *Chesapeake,* under Captain James Barron, and the sloop *Wasp* to relieve the *Constitution, Enterprise,* and *Siren.* The *Wasp* was to sail by way of England and the *Chesapeake* to go straight to Gibraltar.

James Barron seldom visited the *Chesapeake* in the weeks before she left Hampton Roads. Had he done so more often, he might have noticed her appalling unreadiness for sea. Likewise, he might have taken to heart British demands to turn over three supposed deserters from the HMS *Melampus,* and he might have noted how British hostility toward him spiked when he ignored those demands.

But Barron didn't observe any of those developments, because he wasn't with his ship. Virginia was his home state, and he was well connected there. Not only was his older brother, Commodore Samuel Barron, one of the highest-ranking naval officers, but their father, James Barron, Sr., was a bona fide war hero. As commander of the Commonwealth of Virginia Navy during the Revolution, the elder Barron had intercepted a letter being carried up Chesapeake Bay to Maryland Governor Robert Eden from Lord George Germain, British secretary of state for the colonies. The letter contained a gleaming nugget of intelligence: a British plan to strike in the Southern colonies. Barron immediately alerted all Southern ports and the commanders of the colonists' coastal fortifications. Not long afterward, Sir Peter Parker appeared with a British invasion force off Sullivan's Island, South Carolina. The defenders were ready for him and repelled his attack. The distractions arising from his being the scion of a famous Virginia military family produced fatal results for James Barron and his crew.

At 6:00 A.M. on June 22, 1807, the *Chesapeake* glided out of Hampton Roads with her 370 officers and crewmen still struggling to ready her for sea. The crew had never fired the *Chesapeake*'s 38 guns. They couldn't have if they wanted to. Heaps of lumber clogged the gun deck, few of the powder horns had been filled, and some of the guns were not even secured in their carriages. The disorder evident everywhere made her perilously vulnerable to attack, but battle was the last thing on Barron's mind. He was counting on a peaceful voyage to Gibraltar to give his officers time to put everything in order and train the crew in gunnery. But they already had run out of time.

The *Chesapeake* passed British men-of-war at Lynnhaven Bay on their first day out. Signals flashed among the British warships, and one of them eased into the Atlantic ahead of the American frigate. That afternoon, 10 miles off Cape Henry, Barron spotted the British ship, the 50-gun HMS *Leopard*. She didn't appear to be going anywhere in particular, but, in fact, to be waiting for the *Chesapeake*. The commander, Captain Salisbury Pryce Humphries, sent over an officer. He presented Barron with the orders Humphries intended to carry out: to search the *Chesapeake* for three deserters. As Barron scrawled a reply—he knew of no such men; his recruiters were instructed not to enlist British deserters—Barron's officers noticed that the *Leopard* had opened her gun ports and the cannons' tampions had been removed. They excitedly reported these ominous developments to Barron. The captain instructed Master Commandant Charles Gordon to send his men to quarters quietly. But before they could clear the gun decks or strike a match, the *Leopard* fired a broadside. As the *Chesapeake* crew frantically tried to clear for action, four more broadsides followed. Then, before his stunned crew could fire a single shot, Barron struck his colors. Three Americans were dead, and eighteen were wounded, including Barron. It had all taken just twenty minutes.

Barron chivalrously offered to surrender his frigate as a prize, but Humphries was interested only in the alleged deserters. His officers removed the three and a fourth man, while Humphries deplored the loss of life and wished matters "might have been adjusted more amicably." The *Leopard* then sailed away. The *Chesapeake* limped back to Hampton Roads. She would never see Mediterranean duty, nor would the *Wasp*.

The surprise attack revived the fierce hatred of England that had propelled America into the Revolution. If the Royal Navy thought nothing of shooting up an American ship a half day's sail from her home port, what was to stop it from landing British troops and reasserting the Crown's hegemony over its former colony? War fever crackled up and down the East Coast and westward into the settlements beyond the Alleghenies. Invasion rumors flew through the seaports. A mob in Norfolk attacked an English sailor. British warships fanned the growing anger and fear by anchoring inside the Virginia Capes and firing indiscriminately at every passing American vessel. Decatur began fitting out four old gunboats to defend the southeast Virginia ports against anticipated British attacks.

Jefferson closed all U.S. seaports to British ships. In England, U.S. Ambassador James Monroe demanded that the British government apologize and agree to stop its impressment of American seamen. The British were willing to apologize, but unwilling to end impressment. With one significant exception, Jefferson's Cabinet and the American people were ready to go to war. A U.S. House committee described the *Chesapeake* attack as "circumstances of indignity and insult, of which there is scarcely to be found a parallel in the history of civilized nations." "Instant and severe retaliation" was wholly justified.

But Jefferson didn't want to fight. Instead, he chose a curious form of reprisal: terminating all U.S. foreign trade and retreating into isolation. Congress approved the infamous Embargo on Christmas Day 1807. Actually Secretary of State Madison's idea, the Embargo ended all foreign trade and communication; only outbound foreign vessels and authorized U.S. coastal traders were permitted to leave American seaports.

Later in life, Jefferson seemed to have second thoughts about the Embargo, admitting it cost the United States $50 million in annual exports, while war would have cost only one-third that amount. The strategy rested on the faulty premise that withholding U.S. goods from Europe would hurt Europe more than America. U.S. merchants, however, foresaw that the Embargo would ruin *them,* while having only a slight effect on England and France, the nations it was designed to hurt the most. America's bread-and-butter agricultural staples, which were highly dependent on foreign markets, took a severe beating. Wheat tumbled from $2 a bushel to 7 cents. Warehouses bulged with unsold, unshipped tobacco and cotton. One of the few bright spots was America's finished-goods industry—furniture, clothing, utensils—which thrived as never before in the absence of foreign competition.

The Embargo was impossible to enforce once merchants decided to violate it with impunity whenever they could. Smugglers operated successfully from the East Coast's multitude of bays, inlets, and estuaries. A surprising amount of American goods managed to reach Canada and the West Indies despite vigorous blockading by U.S. naval vessels. The Embargo overshadowed Jefferson's last year as president and his entire second term.

Smith instructed Campbell to bring home the three warships remaining in the Mediterranean. With foreign trade shut down, there was no reason to maintain a Mediterranean squadron. Campbell emptied the Malta storehouses and filled the holds of the *Constitution, Hornet,* and *Enterprise* with the stockpiles. The depots at Syracuse, Leghorn, and Gibraltar were liquidated. In the fall of 1807, the three warships left Barbary.

America's Mediterranean naval presence, begun in 1801 with

Commodore Richard Dale's tiny squadron, had ended. It would be eight years before the U.S. Navy would return.

The *Chesapeake*'s mortified officers requested a court of inquiry. They wanted to clear their names of any "disgrace which must be attached in the late premature surrender . . . without their previous knowledge or consent. . . ." They accused Barron of negligence and failing to resist. Had they not begun proceedings, the Navy Department, shocked by Barron's failure to put up a fight, surely would have. Smith relieved Barron of his command and gave it to Captain Stephen Decatur, Jr.—perhaps the origin of the captains' tragic blood feud.

The court of inquiry threw the book at Barron. His guns were unready and ill-equipped. The Marines were supplied cartridges that didn't fit their weapons. During the forty minutes that elapsed before the *Leopard* actually opened fire, Barron had failed to call his crew to general quarters. But most damning of all was the court's conclusion that he struck his flag without a fight; damage to the ship and the crew's injuries did not warrant the surrender.

With these findings, the court-martial outcome was foreordained. Barron's fellow officers found him guilty of negligence of duty and suspended him from the naval service for five years.

Captain Edward Preble died on August 25, 1807, in the city of his birth, Portland, Maine, ten days after his forty-sixth birthday. Preble's shaky health had collapsed during a recurrence of the ulcers and assorted stomach ailments that had prevented him from sailing with the first two Mediterranean squadrons. The naval establishment and the nation mourned his death.

The burning of the *Philadelphia* and the naval assaults on Tripoli had made Preble one of the war's larger-than-life figures. His actions were celebrated in paintings and a two-act New York musical, *Tars from Tripoli*. Congress had struck a gold medal stamped with a relief of the August 3, 1804, bombardment, "a testimony to your Country's estimation of the important and honorable services rendered by you. . . ." Before Smith was talked out of stepping down as Navy secretary early in Jefferson's second term, Preble was the rumored successor. Jefferson felt the loss personally, for he and Preble were friends. Once, when Preble sent the president a cask of Mediterranean wine—Jefferson was a wine connoisseur—Jefferson, concerned that the gift might be construed as a sort of bribe, reciprocated by sending Preble a polygraph, a primitive copier consisting of two connected pens.

Preble was buried in Portland with military honors and bells tolling throughout the city before Washington learned of his death. When it did, flags were lowered to half mast on all frigates in the Navy Yard and at the Marine garrison. Beginning at 12:30 P.M. on September 1, a cannon was fired in the Navy Yard every five minutes until 17 minutes before sunset, when 17 minute guns were fired. To this day, Preble's name endures on the hulls of naval vessels and on buildings and monuments along the East Coast.

Another man who missed Preble keenly was William Eaton. He and the commodore were faithful correspondents who agreed on matters of great importance to both: the imperative of using military force against Barbary, and in their opinions about Lear, the Barrons, and Rodgers. While both became national celebrities as a result of their Tripoli exploits, Preble's fame was the more lasting, although Eaton had reveled in the public adulation as the more modest Preble never had.

Eaton's celebrity, however, was on the wane in 1807, with the Barbary War eclipsed by the *Chesapeake* affair and the Embargo, and Eaton himself having fallen from official and public favor. It was a hard landing after the halcyon days of 1805 and 1806, when testimonial dinners followed one after another and Congress had awarded him a brigadier general's pension. Eaton had tarnished his reputation with heavy drinking, boasting, and his relentless vilification of Lear and the Jefferson administration. Senator Plumer had warmly embraced Eaton when he and other Federalists were trying to sink the Tripoli treaty, but now was disgusted with him. Eaton was "an imposter . He is continually vaunting of the glory of his expedition . . . And yet if the state of that little affair is examined it will be found trivial in its operations and not affording a single prospect of success."

One of the few places where Eaton remained a hero was in his hometown, Brimfield, Massachusetts. His loyal neighbors chose him to be justice of the peace of Hampshire County in 1806. They elected him to the Massachusetts legislature in the spring of 1807. He might have passed a quiet middle age among old friends who appreciated him had it not been for Aaron Burr.

Vice President Burr's meteoric political career flamed out in July 1804, when he killed Alexander Hamilton at Weehawken, overlooking the Hudson River. He could never run for president, nor would Jefferson—who had thoroughly distrusted Burr even before the duel—tolerate him as a running mate. The month before the duel, the 12th Amendment's ratification had meant the vice president would run as part of a ticket, rather than the office automatically going to the presidential runner-up. With Governor George Clinton of New York as his 1804 running mate, Jefferson crushed Federalist Party candidate Charles Cotesworth Pinckney in the Electoral College, 162–14.

While high political office was closed to him forever, Burr still was arguably the most brilliant lawyer in the land, a man of vast personal charm who might have amassed a fortune and salvaged his name. However, Burr wasn't interested in ordinary bourgeois success; his aspirations were Napoleonic. At the head of an army of disaffected frontiersmen, he was certain he could seize the Spanish-occupied Southwest and Mexico, maybe grab Florida, and, in the process, dismember all the U.S. territories west of the Alleghenies for his personal aggrandizement.

For this grandiose vision to become hard fact, Burr needed generals, and his recruitment of them proved to be the riskiest aspect of his plan. General James Wilkinson was the first to sign on for the Southwest invasion, at least. He was the key to that scheme because he commanded the U.S. Army units in New Orleans that patrolled the Southwest frontier. A friend of Burr's from their Revolutionary War service, Wilkinson also happened to be a Spanish spy—he was listed as Spy No. 13 in the Spanish government's books—and he was as oleaginous as Burr himself. Burr recruited Andrew Jackson, who hated the Spanish, for his plan to seize Texas and Florida. And he attempted to enlist a third general: William Eaton.

At first Eaton was enthusiastic about reprising his Derna desert march with an expedition to Mexico, but he was never entirely comfortable with the plan. The more Burr talked, the more Eaton's uneasiness grew, and Burr just couldn't stop talking. He told Eaton about detaching the western United States. Then, he rashly confided an even more outrageous adventure: marching on Washington. At this point, Eaton rode to Washington to warn Jefferson personally. During their meeting, Eaton suggested that the president appoint Burr to a remote ministerial post in Europe to get him out of the way. Jefferson could have saved himself and his government a lot of trouble had he done so, or if he had heeded the warnings also given by Jackson, who quit the scheme when he learned Burr didn't plan to stop with Mexico, Texas, and Florida, but intended to abscond with the U.S. territories west of the Allegheny Mountains as well. Inexplicably, Jefferson did nothing.

It wasn't until fall 1806, as Burr gathered his invading "army"— about 100 men and women volunteers—on an island in the Ohio River, that Jefferson at last listened to Eaton's warnings, but only when they were repeated by Postmaster General Gideon Granger. Jefferson issued a nationwide warning that a Western insurgency was afoot. Before long, Burr was run to ground in Mississippi. But sympathizers set him free, and he fled deeper into West Florida. In February 1807, Burr was recaptured in present-day Alabama and brought to Richmond for trial.

With so many of the nation's leading men attending Burr's treason trial in Richmond in August 1807—so many that the proceedings were moved from the courthouse to the Virginia House of Delegates—it seemed that the stage was set for Eaton's triumphal rebirth as a patriotic whistle-blower. But fortune no longer smiled on Eaton.

Supreme Court Chief Justice John Marshall was the presiding judge, an incomparable stroke of luck for Burr, caught red-handed as he was plotting revolution. A staunch Federalist and avowed enemy of Jefferson, Marshall gave Burr wide latitude in leading his defense team and examining witnesses.

As a result, when Eaton took the witness stand, he faced Burr, the best courtroom attorney in the country. Eaton testified that while he knew of no "overt act" by Burr that was treasonous, "concerning Colonel Burr's expressions of treasonable intentions, I know much." Then Burr went to work on Eaton. When Eaton tried to describe how he warned Jefferson of Burr's scheme, Burr goaded him with insinuations. Perhaps Eaton, too, had been involved, he suggested. Burr pushed Eaton until he exploded: "You spoke of *your* riflemen, *your* infantry, *your* cavalry!" In his anger, Burr's barbed suggestions about Eaton's involvement melded confusedly with villainous portrayals of Wilkinson, and Eaton blurted out, "From the same views you have perhaps mentioned *me!*" The outburst did Eaton no credit and did not help prosecutors.

Outside the courtroom, Eaton was an all-too-familiar figure in Richmond's taverns. During the four months between his grand-jury testimony and Burr's treason trial, everyone heard Eaton's oft-repeated and embellished stories and his rants against Lear, while having plenty of opportunity to witness his heavy drinking and womanizing. "The once redoubted Eaton has dwindled down in the eyes of this sarcastic town into a ridiculous mountebank, strutting about the streets under a tremendous hat, with a Turkish sash over colored clothes when he is not tippling in the taverns," wrote Harman Blennerhassett, a Burr co-defendant. It went unrecorded whether Eaton performed his sword-twirling trick for his audiences; he had had scant opportunity to use his scimitar while crossing the North African desert and during the Derna fighting. Eaton's behavior wrecked any chance he might have salvaged from his testimony against Burr of securing a government position.

Amazingly, Burr was acquitted. Embittered, Eaton returned to Massachusetts, shocking the Massachusetts legislature by denouncing Chief Justice Marshall in a vituperous floor speech. The Federalists, his former allies, shunned him, and Brimfield ousted him from local office in 1808.

Eaton kept to his home and sold some of his Maine acreage to pay his bills. He was held in such low esteem that few would receive him at all, former President John Adams and his son, John Quincy, being notable exceptions. Reclusive, suffering from gout and rheumatism, and drinking heavily, Eaton learned over Christmas 1810 that his beloved stepson, Navy Lieutenant Eli Danielson, who had accompanied him in Egypt as a young midshipman, had been killed in a duel. The sad news sent him into a depression, and he took to his bed.

On June 1, 1811, the indomitable adventurer died. He was only forty-seven.

Eaton's disgrace and obscurity were compassed in the single line in which the Massachusetts *Columbian Centinel* reported his death: "Gen. Eaton, the hero of Derna and the victim of sensibility was entombed at Brimfield on Wednesday last."

Algiers began to act like the piratical Algiers of old. In November 1807, Algerian frigates captured three American merchantmen— the *Eagle* and *Mary Ann* of New York, and the *Violet* of Boston. Captain Ichabod Shiffield and his *Mary Ann* crew didn't go easily. As they approached Algiers as prisoners on their own vessel, the Americans threw four of their Algerian captors overboard, made captives of the rest, and sailed for Naples.

When Lear demanded the release of the *Eagle* and *Violet,* the dey complained that the United States had fallen two years behind in its tribute payment of naval stores. Lear paid the dey cash to square the overdue account, and the dey released the two vessels. But then he demanded $18,000 indemnity for the prize crew carried off by the *Mary Ann*. Lear paid that, too, certain that if he did not, Algiers would only send out its corsairs to seize more U.S. merchantmen.

Preble, Eaton, and Rodgers had taught Tripoli and Tunis to respect U.S. power, but Algiers had managed to avoid a direct confrontation with the Jefferson administration and the U.S. Navy. As the years passed with no evidence of American naval power in the Mediterranean, Algiers, with Britain's encouragement, grew confident that it had nothing to fear from the new republic across the ocean.

XVIII

EPILOGUE

Algiers, July 1812

"My policy and my views are to increase, not to diminish the number of my American slaves; and not for a million dollars would I release them."
—Hadji Ali, Algiers's dey, to U.S. Consul M. M. Noah

If our small naval force can operate freely in the sea, Algiers will be humbled to the dust . . .
—Consul General Tobias Lear, in a letter to
Secretary of State James Monroe

Laden with military stores to satisfy the United States' tributary obligations, the *Alleghany* disgorged muskets, shot, gunpowder, timber for masts, and cable onto Algiers's waterfront. The 1795 treaty had withstood the Tripolitan war and Algerian revolts and regime changes. It was the only U.S. agreement that still required annual tribute payments. Over the treaty's life, the United States had paid Algiers $500,000 or more in tribute, gifts, and military stores: $21,600 worth of military supplies each year, $17,000 in biennial gifts to the dey's officers, and $20,000 each time a new consul arrived in Algiers. Even in 1795, the weapons and ship supplies Algiers demanded had cost more than $21,600, and with inflation over the next seventeen years the stores' value had soared. This partly explained why the United States often fell behind in its tribute deliveries and then offered to square accounts with cash.

Hadji Ali, the aged, fierce dey, watched as the military stores were trundled from the *Alleghany*'s hold to Algiers's wharf. Hadji had been listening to Great Britain's blandishments and was poised to turn the clock back twenty years on Algiers–U.S. relations. The British foreign minister recently had written Hadji a letter pledging England's warm friendship and protection. While Algiers was threatened by no nation at the moment, Britain, which within weeks would be at war with America, implied that England's future enemy might become Algiers's, too. The British minister blustered that "the American flag would be swept from the seas, the contemptible navy of the United States annihilated, and its maritime arsenals reduced to a heap of ruins." Hadji believed him. If Hadji had to choose allies in the coming war, there was no question that it would be England and her mighty navy. And he knew he had to exploit every means at hand to keep his throne. This policy had enabled him to rule longer than any of the deys who had come along after Mustafa Hamouda was deposed in 1805. The janissaries had assassinated Mustafa's successor, Hamet Bashaw, in 1808, and the new dey, Ali Cogia, was deposed five months later by Barbary's favored method of effecting a succession: the silken strangulation cord. Hadji had ruled since then. In the interests of prolonging his tenure and his life, Hadji stopped the unloading of the *Alleghany*.

He complained that the shipment of tribute contained too little gunpowder and cable, and ordered it sent back. In its place, he demanded an instant substitution payment of $27,000 cash. He brusquely informed Lear that as soon as he paid it, he must pack up and leave Algiers. This came as a rude shock to Lear, who hadn't foreseen expulsion, although he had been conscious of the steady erosion of respect for America during the Navy's long absence from the Mediterranean, going on five years now. Lear tried desperately to avert the diplomatic breach that now confronted him, while arguing that $27,000 wasn't what the treaty stipulated as annual tribute. Hadji smoothly explained that he observed the briefer Ramadan year, not the Gregorian 365-day year. Since 1795, the additional Ramadan calendar days and weeks had added up, and they now must be reckoned with. Pay the $27,000 now, the dey warned, or he would seize the *Alleghany* and enslave its crew and every American in Algiers. If Lear paid, the Americans would have three days to leave. Lear wangled a two-day extension, but nothing more. Lacking $27,000 in ready cash, he was forced to borrow from the Bacri money house—it had survived David Coen Bacri's beheading a year earlier—and agreed to pay a stiff 25 percent premium.

Lear, his wife and son, and three other American residents of Algiers sailed away on the *Alleghany* on July 25. The ship happened to reach Gibraltar simultaneously with the news that America had declared war on England. The British instantly took possession of the brig, clapped the crewmen in irons, and sent them to England on a prison ship. Lear and his family were permitted to sail to Cadiz and then home. As he sat down to write his report to Secretary of State James Monroe, Lear predicted that America one day would avenge Algiers's abusive treatment and rid itself of tribute "and an imperious and piratical depredation on their commerce. If our small naval force can operate freely in the sea, *Algiers will be humbled to the dust. . . .*"

Before there could be any U.S. retaliation against Algiers, America had to face Britain, the world's supreme naval power, with more than 600 warships to the U.S. Navy's 17. In addition to this seemingly insurmountable disadvantage, the U.S. Navy was burdened with the memory of the Revolutionary War, when the British had destroyed or captured 34 of the Continental Navy's 35 ships, while losing only 5 of their own. And John Paul Jones, dead twenty years now, was responsible for two of the British losses, the *Drake* and *Serapis*. But in 1812, the United States had far better ships and the leadership of "Preble's Boys," the Barbary War's junior officers who had risen to commands in the fleet: Isaac Hull, Stephen Decatur, Jr., William Bainbridge, James Lawrence, Isaac Chauncey, David Porter, Charles Stewart, and Thomas Macdonough. As the U.S. Navy's "super frigates" entered the Atlantic to face the daunting British war fleet, Algerian cruisers prowled the Mediterranean for U.S. merchantmen. Weeks after Lear's departure from Algiers, the *Edwin* was snapped up.

On August 12, the *Edwin,* a brig from Salem, Massachusetts, with Captain George C. Smith and ten crewmen aboard, was captured between Malta and Gibraltar. At about the same time, Algerians stopped a Spanish ship and removed an American, a Mr. Pollard, and he became Algiers's twelfth American prisoner. They would be the last; the war kept the U.S. merchant fleet home for nearly three years. The Madison administration authorized M. M. Noah, the U.S. consul in Tunis, to offer up to $3,000 ransom per man. Hadji spurned the offer. "My policy and my views are to increase, not to diminish the number of my American slaves; and not for a million dollars would I release them." Britain, desperate for fresh seamen, offered to buy two of the *Edwin* crewmen, and Hadji sold the British the two most unproductive prisoners for $2,000 apiece.

Washington threw a naval ball on December 28, 1812, presided

over by First Lady Dolley Madison. Hundreds of candles illuminated the battle flags of two British warships, the HMS *Guerriere*
and the HMS *Alert,* captured during the halcyon first months of
the war. At midnight, as the orchestra struck up "Hail Columbia,"
a midshipman appeared as if by magic, striding purposefully
across the room toward Mrs. Madison. The naval officers and
their wives broke into loud cheers when they saw what he was carrying. The midshipman laid the object at the First Lady's feet. She
picked it up and unfolded it. It was a third British battle flag,
belonging to the HMS *Macedonian.* The triumph belonged to
Captain Stephen Decatur, Jr., and the *United States.* The idea for
the dramatic presentation of the battle flag to the First Lady was
Decatur's, too. Like his frigate's performance in the Atlantic,
Decatur's bit of theater was a smashing success.

A blend of dash, raw nerve, and perfectly calibrated instincts,
Stephen Decatur had first burst into the public consciousness as
the electrifying hero of the *Philadelphia* and the Battle of the Gunboats. He became the U.S. Navy's youngest captain at twenty-five.
Because of his striking good looks, competence, and aura of success, a legend had grown up around him. By 1812, Decatur, for
whom cities and towns would be named, was a national celebrity.
Arguably the Navy's best combat officer, he had made a brilliant
marriage to intelligent, beautiful Susan Wheeler. They were an
extremely well-matched, well-connected Washington couple, with
the Madisons among their close friends. Nothing, it seemed, was
impossible for Stephen Decatur.

Decatur had met the *Macedonian* in the middle of the Atlantic
about 500 miles west of the Canary Islands on October 25,
1812. The 38-gun British frigate was commanded by Captain

John Carden, a peacetime friend of Decatur's. Because Carden was somewhat of a martinet, the *Macedonian* had a reputation as a crack warship. But not only was Carden outgunned by the 44-gun *United States,* whose 42-pound carronades could wreak havoc at close range, he was facing a gunnery zealot in Decatur, as Carden well knew. Decatur believed gunnery alone could win battles—without need for boarding parties. He and Carden even had debated the subject over dinner and drinks one night in Norfolk. Carden had been happy to point out that Decatur's view ran counter to established doctrine. While it was true that believing in the primacy of gunnery placed him in the vanguard of naval theory at the time, Decatur was so sure he was right that he put his belief into practice by drilling his *United States* crew in rapid firing and target practice until they were lethally quick and accurate.

Decatur proceeded to demonstrate his crew's deadly skill against Carden's ship when they met in the Atlantic. His gunners, firing two shots for every one shot fired by the *Macedonian's* gun crews, flattened the British frigate's mizzenmast. When the *United States* got within carronade range, the gunners raked the British frigate's hull and turned the decks into scenes of appalling slaughter. By the time Carden offered Decatur his sword, there were 105 British killed and wounded, compared with just 12 American casualties.

Decatur brought the prize into New London in January 1813, but then couldn't put to sea again, as British cruisers were blockading Long Island Sound. After fruitless maneuvering and waiting in vain for an opening to escape to sea, he went to New York in 1814 to take over the frigate *President,* his unluckiest command ever.

He encountered the same problem in New York that he had in Long Island Sound: British warships blocked the harbor continually. Months passed without a break in the blockade. And then, in January 1815, a storm drove the British ships out to sea. Seizing his chance, Decatur set out in the *President*. Disaster befell her immediately; she struck a sandbar and hung there for nearly two hours before the crew got her off, with a damaged keel and sprung masts. Decatur tried to return to port, but the tide was against him, and he hugged the Long Island shoreline, waiting for the tide to turn.

British warships, however, returned before the tide. The battered *President* was compelled to fight. While her maneuverability was crippled, there was nothing wrong with her gunnery. In a two-hour running battle with the 40-gun *Endymion,* the American gunners mauled the British frigate at long range, forcing her to break off the fight. But the *President* still was far from port, and three British warships overtook her before she made it safely home. With one-fifth of the President's crew dead or wounded and three of her five lieutenants gone, Decatur reluctantly struck his flag.

Decatur and his crew were imprisoned in Bermuda until a peace treaty was signed, but that was only a month coming. Upon returning to New London, Decatur expected to be court-martialed for losing the *President.* But he needn't have worried; he was as popular as ever. He and his crew received heroes' welcomes. The U.S. Navy thought so highly of Decatur that even with a court of inquiry pending, he was offered his pick of choice assignments: any shore billet he wished, command of the *Guerriere*—the British frigate Captain Isaac Hull had captured off Boston in 1812—and a squadron that would sail very soon to the Mediterranean, or command of the new 74-gun man-of-war *Washington* and a second squadron that would be sent to the Mediterranean later. Decatur wasn't willing to wait. He accepted command of the ten-ship squadron and the flagship *Guerriere*.

Madison was sending the fleet to the Mediterranean to settle up with Algiers. Hadji Ali had declared war in 1814, betting that the British would drub the Americans. On February 23, 1815, just five days after news of the Treaty of Ghent reached Washington, Madison recommended that Congress declare war on Algiers, whose opportunism cried for reprisal.

The U.S. Navy was battle-tested, formidable, and ready for a fresh fight. Its 17-ship fleet of 1812 by 1815 had ballooned to 64 ships mounting 1,500 guns. Algiers hadn't been idle, either. Its navy had 5 frigates, 6 sloops of war, and a schooner, for a total of 12 ships carrying 360 guns. Its harbor forts were defended by another 220 cannons. That would have been enough to repel the American squadron of 1801, when Commodore Dale entered the Mediterranean with 4 ships, or to give pause to Preble in 1804, when the *Constitution* was the only American frigate in the sea. But the U.S. Navy had sloughed off its awkward adolescence while fighting the world's most powerful navy. The fleet's officers and crews were competent, its frigates big and fast.

Nineteen ships in two squadrons were to go to the Mediterranean under Decatur and Captain William Bainbridge, who had atoned for surrendering the *Philadelphia* by defeating the heavy frigate HMS *Java* off Brazil on December 29, 1812. Decatur's ten ships sailed from New York on May 20, 1815; Bainbridge was to follow from Boston six weeks later.

Aboard the *Guerriere* was the new Barbary consul general,

William Shaler, who was authorized to negotiate peace, as were Decatur and Bainbridge. But the squadron's officers and men hoped to serve Algiers hot iron and steel first.

The squadron reached Gibraltar on June 15, minus the brig *Firefly*, forced to turn around with a sprung mast. There was no time to rest and refit at Gibraltar. There were reports that the Algerian squadron, returned to the Mediterranean from cruising in the Atlantic, had just sailed for Cape de Gatt on Spain's southern coast. Decatur went after the Algerians.

Lookouts sighted several sails off Cape de Gatt the next night. Decatur flashed the signal to the *Macedonian,* his one-time Britsh prize, and several smaller ships to give chase. By the following morning, the *Constellation* had spotted a large frigate flying the penndant of Algiers's admiral, Reis Hammida. The *Constellation, Guerriere,* and sloops-of-war *Epervier* and *Ontario* closed in.

Hammida's flagship was the 44-gun *Meshuda*—but not the Tripolitan cruiser of that same name that Commodore Dale had trapped in Gibraltar in 1801. Decatur signaled his harriers to raise British flags, hoping to lure the frigate closer with the false colors of an ally. But the *Constellation* bumblingly raised the Stars and Stripes instead. The *Meshuda,* well-crewed and a fast sailer, bolted for the Algerian coast with the four American warships in pursuit.

Through strenuous sailing, tacking, and trimming, the *Constellation* tried to make up for her blunder, slowly closing the distance to the flying *Meshuda.* Soon, the *Constellation* was within range with her bow guns, and opened fire. The *Meshuda* veered off to the northeast and raced flat-out for Cartagena, Spain. But she couldn't shake her three other pursuers. The *Guerriere, Epervier,* and *Ontario* boxed her in expertly.

As a boy, Hammida had arrived penniless in Algiers from his birthplace in the rugged Jurjura Range of Adrar Budfel—the "Mountain of Snow," where he was reared among the Berber Kabyle tribe. He signed on as a sailor and succeeded beyond his wildest dreams. Through brains, drive, and ability, he had risen through the ranks of the Algerian navy to become grand admiral. Now, hemmed in by four warships crewed by battle-hardened veterans, he faced a supreme test.

Using all of his cunning, Hammida tried to break out of the trap, but the Americans foiled him. Badly wounded when the *Constellation* raked the *Meshuda*'s quarterdeck, he continued to give orders while propped on a divan, bleeding. Then the *Ontario* crossed the *Meshuda*'s bow, and the *Guerriere* gave her two broadsides that wreaked awful carnage. Hammida was cut in half with a 42-pounder.

Master Commandant John Downes boldly brought his 18-gun *Epervier* in close and blasted the *Meshuda* with nine broadsides, and the Algerians struck their flag. Thirty Algerians, including the grand admiral, lay dead on the *Meshuda*'s decks. Four hundred six of their fellow crewmen, many of them wounded, became American prisoners. Enemy fire killed only one American and wounded three others; a bursting gun on the *Guerriere* was deadlier, killing three crewmen and wounding seven. Just two days after reaching the Mediterranean, Decatur's squadron had sliced off the Algerian navy's head.

Two days later, June 19, the squadron spotted a warship off Cape Palos. It took to its heels, spurring the Americans to action. The *Epervier, Spark, Torch,* and *Spitfire* gave chase, and soon were in a running gun battle with what they could see was an Algerian brig.

In shoal water off the Spanish coast, she ran aground. Some of the crew took to their boats and headed for shore, and the Americans sank one of them. Navy crewmen seized the 22-gun *Estedio*. Twenty-three bodies were strewn about her decks, and eighty crewmen were taken prisoner. The prisoners and prize were sent to Cartagena. The squadron turned back toward Algiers to confront the dey.

Months earlier, Omar the Terrible had succeeded Hadji, and his short tenure had been rocky. Locusts ravaged the countryside, and Omar had inherited wars with America and Holland. On June 28, nine U.S. warships massed outside Algiers harbor, and Omar knew that his tribulations were just beginning.

Decatur raised a white flag and the Swedish pennant, a signal for the Swedish consul, John Norderling, to whom the expelled Lear had entrusted U.S. affairs, to boat to the *Guerriere* under a flag of truce. Norderling was accompanied by the captain of the port. Decatur asked the captain where the Algerian squadron had gone. When the captain smugly replied that it undoubtedly was in a safe port somewhere, Decatur informed him the *Meshuda* and *Estedio* were now American prizes. The port captain didn't believe him—until Decatur produced a *Meshuda* prisoner, a lieutenant, who described the captures of the *Meshuda* and *Estedio,* and Hammida's gory death. Decatur recorded the port captain's reaction to the news: "The impression made by these events was visible and deep."

Norderling delivered a letter to the dey from President Madison, announcing that America was at war with Algiers, yet expressing a desire for peace, but not on the old terms of tribute and bribes: ". . . peace, to be durable, must be founded on stipulations equally beneficial to both parties, the one claiming nothing which it is not willing to grant the other; and on this basis alone will its attainment or preservation by this government be desirable." A second letter, drafted by Decatur and Shaler, stated they would negotiate only on equal terms and would not obligate the United States to pay any tribute.

The dey invited them ashore to negotiate, but Decatur and Shaler said negotiations must be conducted on the *Guerriere*. They formally outlined to Norderling and the port captain the treaty terms that would be acceptable to them: abolition of tribute forever; release by both parties of all American and Algerian prisoners; $10,000 compensation for the *Edwin* and other confiscated American property; and freedom for any Christian slave who managed to escape to an American warship. Captives in any future U.S.–Algerian war would be prisoners of war, and not slaves.

Omar did not want to fight the American squadron, but knew if he conceded all of Shaler and Decatur's demands without receiving anything in return, he might well feel the silk strangulation cord tightening around his own throat. He said he would agree to the terms if the *Meshuda* and *Estedio* were returned. Shaler and Decatur did not object. As far as they could see, the vessels would be of no use to the United States; it was doubtful whether they would even survive an Atlantic crossing. They would return the vessels, they said, but not as part of the treaty. Omar had to sign the treaty before he would get back his ships.

The dey requested a three-hour truce to think about it. Decatur emphatically said no. "Not a minute; if your squadron appears in sight before the treaty is actually signed by the Dey; and the prisoners sent off, ours would capture them." Only when a boat left shore flying a white flag and with the *Edwin*'s crew aboard would

Decatur suspend hostilities, he said. As the dey was chewing over this uncompromising response, American ships spotted an Algerian corvette in the distance, filled with Turkish soldiers from Tunis. Decatur ordered the squadron into action. The corvette and the Americans' preparations evidently were witnessed by the dey's officers as well, because at that moment a boat set out across the harbor, with a white flag fluttering. The *Edwin* prisoners were aboard.

Omar agreed to all of Decatur and Shaler's conditions. Six weeks after the squadron's departure from New York, and sixteen days after its arrival in the Mediterranean, Decatur had brought the war to an end.

The treaty was the best made with Algiers by a Christian nation in more than 200 years. "It has been dictated at the mouths of our cannon," Decatur proudly wrote to Navy Secretary Benjamin W. Crowninshield on July 5, and "has been conceded to the losses which Algiers has sustained and to the dread of still greater evils apprehended."

Lieutenant John Shubrick was given command of the *Epervier* and dispatched to Washington with the new treaty and the *Edwin* captain and crew. The sloop-of-war passed Gibraltar on July 12 and never was seen or heard from again. The ship and crew might have perished in a hurricane that blew up in the western Atlantic about the time the *Epervier* would have reached the East Coast. Lost were the *Epervier* crew, the *Edwin* crewmen and captain, and Master Commandant William Lewis and Lieutenant B. J. Neale, who had recently married sisters and had been granted home leave to visit them.

• • •

Algiers wasn't the only Barbary State that had been seduced by
Britain's cocky predictions of victory over America during the
recent war. Early in 1815, the American privateer *Abellino* had
brought several English prizes into Tunis and Tripoli, supposed
neutrals in the war. The prizes should have been secure in the neutral ports, but Tunis and Tripoli had permitted British cruisers to
retake them—two from Tunis and two from Tripoli—over the
protests of U.S. consuls. Decatur learned of the violations only
when he reached Barbary; the Madison administration had been
unaware of the neutrality violations when Decatur embarked from
New York, so he had no instructions to guide him. The commodore took it upon himself to square matters.

The squadron entered Tunis harbor July 26. Through U.S.
consul M. M. Noah, Decatur demanded that the bey pay him
$46,000 in reparations. If he failed to do so within twelve hours,
the U.S. squadron would go into action against him. As the bey
and his officers conferred, an adviser reminded the bey that
Decatur was the brash young officer of eleven years earlier who
had burned the *Philadelphia.* Then Noah led the bey to a window
and pointed out the *Guerriere* and *Macedonian* in the harbor. Both
had once belonged to the supposedly invincible Royal Navy, he
said—until America had taken them from Britain. The bey
studied the ships through his telescope, and thoughtfully stroked
his beard with a tortoiseshell comb, turning over in his mind this
new evidence of U.S. power. Then he paid the $46,000.

Decatur's next stop was Tripoli, where he said reparations
would cost $30,000. Yusuf, still the bashaw after twenty years,
refused curtly. He manned his batteries and assembled 20,000
troops for action. Then the news arrived of the capitulation of
Algiers and Tunis, and Yusuf had a swift change of heart. He sent

Decatur a counterproposal of $25,000. Decatur said this was acceptable, but only if Yusuf also would release ten Christian captives. This met the bashaw's approval. Decatur, who had a long memory, selected two Danes and a Sicilian family of eight for release: the Danes to repay Denmark for Nicholas Nissen's services, and the Sicilians for the Two Sicilies' loan of the gunboats to Commodore Preble all those years ago. To celebrate the renewal of American–Tripolitan amity, the *Guerriere's* band played "Hail Columbia" on the Tripoli quay.

Decatur transported the grateful Danes to Naples and the Sicilians to Messina, and sailed on alone to Spain. Lookouts sighted seven Algerian warships one day. Decatur cleared the *Guerriere* for action, savoring the prospect of a good fight should the Algerians not have learned of the new treaty or chose to disregard it. The Algerians wisely let the *Guerriere* pass unmolested.

Bainbridge's squadron reached Gibraltar on September 29, after Decatur already had settled affairs with Algiers, Tunis, and Tripoli. Together, he and Decatur headed the most powerful U.S. Mediterranean squadron until that time: eighteen ships, including Bainbridge's 74-gun ship-of-the-line *Independence,* where a future naval hero, David Farragut, was serving his apprenticeship as a fourteen-year-old midshipman. But the squadron's business was finished in Barbary, and most of the warships sailed for America on October 7.

In Washington, everyone applauded the peace dictated at "cannon's mouth." President Madison laid the new Algerian treaty before the Senate for ratification on December 6, and it won swift approval, with no objections to the terms Decatur and Shaler had dictated: favored-nation status, no tribute, the release of American captives. Congress expressed its gratitude to the squadron by appropriating $100,000 as indemnification for the *Meshuda* and *Estedio,* to be distributed to the naval crews who captured them.

Britain tried to capitalize on Decatur's success in the fall of 1815. Lord Exmouth sailed to Algiers with six men-of-war, two frigates, three sloops-of-war, a bomb ship, and several transports. Omar, by then regretting the peace he had made with America, was unwilling to concede anything. Exmouth wound up agreeing to pay nearly $400,000 to free 12,000 Neapolitan and Sardinian captives.

This wasn't exactly what the Admiralty had in mind when it dispatched Exmouth to the Mediterranean. But the British treaty did wonders for Omar's confidence after his unhappy encounter with Decatur, so much so that when Shaler presented him the next April with the Senate-ratified 1815 treaty, Omar rejected it. Decatur had returned the *Meshuda,* but the dey still hadn't gotten back the *Estedio.* Therefore, Omar said, the treaty was void. He waved off Shaler's explanation for the brig's absence: U.S. consuls still were negotiating her release with Spain, where she was floating in Cartagena harbor.

Shaler lowered the U.S. consular flag and went aboard the *Java,* where Captain Oliver Hazard Perry prepared for a night attack on Algiers, supported by the frigates *United States* and *Constellation* and the 18-gun sloops-of-war *Erie* and *Ontario.* The five warships drew up in front of the mole, with boats ready for 1,200 volunteers to launch an amphibious assault. The alarmed dey declared a truce and invited Shaler to return. The squadron withdrew. But then, in a letter to President Madison, Omar proposed a return to the 1795 treaty—to annual tribute payments.

• • •

The British government was so incensed with the outcome of Lord Exmouth's negotiations in Algiers that it sent him back as joint commander of a powerful Anglo–Dutch fleet with Dutch Admiral van Cappellen. On August 27, 1816, the warships assembled outside Algiers harbor. Whether by accident or design, an Algerian gun fired on them. The English and Dutch replied with a massive bombardment. When the firing stopped, the British and Dutch had discharged 34,000 rounds and inflicted 883 casualties, all but wiping out the Algerian navy and wrecking the city fortifications and residential areas. Exmouth and van Cappellen forced the dey to free 1,200 prisoners and to agree to abolish Christian slavery forever.

While Algiers was still rebuilding its shattered navy and city, Commodore Isaac Chauncey and the 74-gun man-of-war *Washington,* accompanied by six warships, appeared in Algiers harbor in October. More menacing Christian warships was the last thing the dey and his officers wished to see after Exmouth's devastating attack. Shaler, who had witnessed the bombardment and whose home was heavily damaged, reassured Omar that for the moment the squadron was only making a show of force, but it would return. Shaler sailed with Chauncey and the squadron to Gibraltar to await orders from the State Department.

They returned to Algiers in December 1816. The Spanish finally had handed over the *Estedio,* so Omar no longer had a good reason to reject the 1815 treaty. Shaler delivered a letter from President Madison to the dey. The United States would fight before it would pay Algiers tribute again, the president wrote. "It is a principle incorporated into the settled policy of America, that as peace is better than war, war is better than tribute." Should there have been any mistaking Madison's message, Chauncey and Shaler added their own ultimatum. With both the *Meshuda* and *Estedio* in Algiers's possession again, all outstanding debts were canceled and the 1815 treaty now must be accepted. "The undersigned believe it to be their duty to assure his Highness that the above conditions will not be departed from; thus leaving to the Regency of Algiers the choice between peace and war. The United States, while anxious to maintain the former, are prepared to meet the latter."

With his navy in shambles from the Anglo–Dutch attack, Omar had no choice but to sign the treaty. He imposed a single condition: that Shaler sign a statement that Omar had agreed to the treaty only to avoid war with the United States. Shaler's affidavit extended Omar's tenuous reign less than a year: He was assassinated in September 1817.

The treaty, America's last with Algiers, renounced tribute forever. It was signed on December 23, 1816, thirty-one years after Algiers captured the *Dauphin* and the *Maria*.

Never again would the Barbary States trouble America.

Yusuf and Hamet reconciled briefly in 1809, when the bashaw gave his brother a government position in Derna. For reasons unknown, but most likely a combination of Hamet's sloth and treachery, he soon incurred Yusuf's displeasure. By 1811, he and his family once again were on the run to Egypt. They never returned to Tripoli. Hamet was not heard from again.

The last act of Hamet's story unfolded in 1832, when a man named Mahommed Bey presented himself to the American consulate in Alexandria, claiming to be Hamet's eldest son. He requested aid for his destitute family in Cairo. There is no record that he received any.

In 1835, Yusuf's son Muhammad attempted to assassinate his father and seize power. After forty years of rule, Yusuf lost control of Tripoli, and it erupted into civil war. The French and British consuls sought the intervention of the Ottoman Empire, which still claimed Tripoli as a regency. The sultan dispatched twenty-two ships and 6,000 troops. Ottoman soldiers arrested Muhammad and his fellow conspirators and snatched the reins of government from Yusuf, who had survived the coup. The Turks ruled Tripoli until Italy occupied it in 1911 and renamed it Libya.

France invaded Algiers in 1830, but was unable to gain complete control until 1848. In 1851, the French also seized Tunis.

Stephen Decatur's seagoing days ended when he returned to the United States from his triumphant expedition to Algiers, Tunis, and Tripoli, more of a hero than ever. Baltimore gave him a silver dinner service, and Philadelphia awarded him a plate dinner service worth $1,020, raised through $10 subscriptions. Amid the rounds of banquets that took him up and down the East Coast, Decatur made the now-famous toast at a dinner in Norfolk: "Our country!" Decatur said, raising his glass. "In her intercourse with foreign nations may she always be in the right; but our country, right or wrong." He stowed away his sea chest forever, joining Captains John Rodgers and David Porter on the Board of Navy Commissioners. His days were filled with paperwork and meetings. With his wife Susan, he built a home and reentered the high-powered Washington social whirl. Yet Decatur missed the sea. "What shall I do?" he wrote a friend in 1818. "We have no war, nor sign of a war, and I shall feel ashamed to die in my bed."

That wouldn't happen. After serving his suspension from the Navy, James Barron submitted an application to command the new 74-gun man-of-war *Columbus*. Decatur reminded his fellow commissioners of Barron's negligent command of the *Chesapeake* in 1807, and also noted that Barron had not sought a ship during the War of 1812, when his services might have been welcomed. Now that the war was over, he was suddenly anxious to return. Barron explained that he was abroad in 1812 and had wanted to return, but lacked money for passage home. Decatur brushed aside his excuse, saying it only demonstrated that he was unresourceful. He blocked Barron's application.

Barron stewed over his rejection. He wrote a letter on June 19, 1819, accusing Decatur of publicly claiming that "you could insult me with impunity." Decatur denied it. In October Barron had another grievance: Decatur had forwarded their correspondence to mutual friends in Norfolk with the purpose of alienating them from Barron. Decatur acknowledged sending on the letters, but not the malevolent intent. The men exchanged thirteen letters in all, Barron's becoming progressively more acerbic; he always believed he had been scapegoated for the *Chesapeake* incident, and now he had a target for his bitterness.

Finally Barron challenged Decatur to a duel, and Decatur, a veteran of several affairs of honor, accepted. They met at Bladensburg, the site of the disastrous 1814 defense of Washington, on March 22, 1820. They agreed to fire at eight paces, a relatively short distance that was a concession to Barron's nearsightedness. Before taking up their pistols, both men urinated; it was commonly believed that an empty bladder reduced the chance of infection if one was hit. They stepped off the eight paces. Decatur already had decided to aim for Barron's hip, not wanting to kill him but knowing he must wound him in order to end the affair.

The men turned and fired simultaneously. Barron was hit in the thigh, Decatur in the right side. Decatur's wound was mortal, Barron's was not. Decatur died in agony at his home before the next sunrise. The U.S. Navy's brightest spirit, who perhaps more than anyone, had molded its fighting tradition, was gone.

Did the United States chastise the Barbary States, as Jefferson so fervently desired, and did it earn Europe's respect? It depends on whether the year is 1805 or 1815.

During the 1801–5 Tripolitan war, the necessary ingredients for lasting peace never coalesced at one time or place: a large force, an aggressive commander, and skilled diplomacy. Morris and Barron demonstrated the futility of assigning a strong naval force to a weak commander. Preble showed that without adequate firepower, a fighting commodore could not deliver a decisive blow. Only when Rodgers took over Barron's squadron and brought it before Tunis with Lear on hand was it used as Jefferson, Madison, and Smith had envisioned, "holding out the olive Branch in one hand & displaying in the other the means of offensive operations."

But in 1815, the United States was a battle-hardened naval power, and Decatur was able to parley at "cannon's mouth" and finally win the respect both of Barbary and Europe. What better evidence could there be of Europe's respect than England's attempt to imitate Decatur's success in Algiers?

More importantly, America demonstrated, as Jefferson had hoped, that it was different from Europe and on principle would not truckle to extortionist despots. Jefferson was proven right: Facing down terror worked; Europe showed its new respect by imitating the American example before Barbary's harbor fortresses. It was yet another manifestation of America's revolution against the established order, another assertion of "American spirit," whose most passionate advocate was Jefferson.

By sending American ships and fighting men to their first war on foreign soil, fought for the principle of sovereign trading rights, Jefferson was making a statement of national character: the American belief that nations as well as people had a right to freedom from tyranny. America didn't pay obeisance to English kings, and it certainly wouldn't bow to Islamic deys, beys, and bashaws who used their navies as instruments of terror to extort tribute and fill their dungeons with "Christian dogs."

In the Mediterranean, America learned the practicalities of waging a distant war: operating from foreign bases, making short-term alliances, and using local insurgents and indigenous troops—the basic tenets that would serve it in conflicts in the late twentieth and early twenty-first centuries. Had the United States been unable to use Sicily, Malta, and Gibraltar as resupply and headquarters ports, it would have been virtually impossible to sustain its convoys and blockades, and the hemorrhaging of Mediterranean trade would have continued; as it was, 35 American ships and 700 sailors were captured by the Barbary corsairs between 1784 and 1815. Without Neapolitan gunboats, Preble couldn't have taken the war to Tripoli's harbor in 1804. Hamet and his Tripolitan and Arab supporters made possible Eaton's bold invasion. Without Salvador Catalano, Decatur's "special ops" mission to burn the *Philadelphia* might have run aground on one of Tripoli harbor's notorious shoals.

The fighting U.S. Navy that stopped Britain in 1812 was forged in the Mediterranean under Preble. The brief Quasi-War with France had blooded it, but the rising generation of junior officers needed more seasoning. The "super frigates" served as the war colleges of Decatur, Bainbridge, Porter, Stewart, and Hull— "Preble's Boys." When they finished their education in the Mediterranean, they were ready to test themselves against the world's preeminent naval power, and then to return to Barbary in 1815 as seasoned veterans eager to punish Algiers.

The Barbary War convinced Congress and the American people that the U.S. Navy and Marine Corps were indispensable. Aided by low casualties—little more than 30 killed—and the emergence of a pantheon of war heroes, the seafaring services were safe from Congress's budget ax. Preble, Decatur, Eaton, and O'Bannon entered the American lexicon, and their stories were still being told by candlelight in farmhouses fifty years later. If congressmen needed a better argument, they only had to look to the prosperous Mediterranean trade made possible by U.S. Navy convoys. While the Navy's future was now secure, the Marine Corps periodically was targeted by government cost-cutters; it escaped extinction during the post–World War II downsizing campaign largely because of its demonstrated readiness at the outbreak of the Korean War, when its "Fire Brigade" stopped the invading North Koreans at the Naktong River.

The punitive expeditions of 1815 and 1816 ended Algiers's long reign as a major Mediterranean power. The old Ottoman regency no longer struck terror into England, France, Spain, and the United States. Finally, after 400 years, trade in the Mediterranean became truly free.

It happened sooner rather than later because of Thomas Jefferson. "I very early thought it would be best to effect a peace through the medium of war," Jefferson wrote to John Adams when they debated the respective merits of war and tribute.

Jefferson's unshakable faith in the supreme revolutionary principle—freedom from tyranny wherever it might be found, and in whatever form—caused the western Mediterranean to be swept clean of the marauding corsairs.

No longer would merchant ship captains anxiously scan the flat horizon for the long-prowed ships of plunder flying under lateen sails.

Jefferson and his fighting sailors and Marines had freed America and Europe from The Terror.

NOTES

Prologue

xvii. "Curly-haired and fair": *Naval Documents Related to the United States Wars with the Barbary Powers*, 6 vols. (Washington: U.S. Government Printing Office, 1939), vol. 1, portrait facing p. 582.

xvii. "Canvas rustled above him": Ibid., p. 540.

xvii. "The *Enterprise* was sailing": Ibid., p. 535.

xviii. "Above the *Enterprise's*": Ibid., p. 503.

xviii. "The Enterprise was the third": Henry B. Culver, Forty Famous Ships (New York: Garden City Publishing Co. Inc., 1938), pp. 181–4.

xviii. "Later, after she was": Howard I. Chapelle, *The History of the American Sailing Navy* (New York: Bonanza Books, 1935), p. 101.

xviii. "By then, she": Culver, p. 181.

xviii. "Before the *Enterprise*": *Naval Documents*, vol. 1, p. 534.

xix. "The *Tripoli* edged closer": Ibid., pp. 537-9 (*National Intelligencer* story); A. B. C. Whipple, *To the Shores of Tripoli: The Birth of the U.S. Navy and Marines* (New York: William Morrow and Company Inc., 1991), pp. 79–80; Glenn Tucker, *Dawn Like Thunder: The Barbary Wars and the Birth of the U.S. Navy* (Indianapolis: The Bobbs-Merrill Company, Inc. 1963), pp. 141–6.

xxi. "'The carnage on board'": *Naval Documents*, vol. 1, p. 537.

xxi. "While the *Enterprise's* doctor": Ibid., pp. 538–9 (*National Intelligencer* story).

xxi. "Sterrett did a damage": Ibid., p. 537.

xxv. "'Holding out the olive Branch'": *Naval Documents*, vol. 2, p. 130.

Chapter I: The "Pacifist" President

1. "'Peace, commerce & honest'": Paul Leicester Ford, ed., *The Writings of Thomas Jefferson,* 10 vols. (New York: G. P. Putnam's Sons, 1892–9), vol. 8, pp. 2–5.

1. "a soft voice": Nathan Schachner, *Thomas Jefferson: A Biography* (New York: Thomas Yoseloff Ltd., 1951), p. 661; Ford, vol. 8, pp. 3–4.

2. "the disgruntled president": David McCullough, *John Adams* (New York: Simon & Schuster, 2001), p. 565.

2. "'a wise and frugal'": Ford, vol. 8, pp. 3–4.

2. "Jefferson issued the": *Naval Documents,* vol. 1, p. 486.

3. "'The motives pleading'": John P. Foley, ed., *The Jeffersonian Cyclopedia*, 2 vols. (New York: Russell & Russell, 1900), p. 83.

4. "Two members of Jefferson's": *Thomas Jefferson papers at the Library of Congress.* June 11, 1801, letter to Wilson Cary Nicholas.

4. "James Madison, Jefferson's": *The Papers of James Madison. Secretary of State Series* (Charlottesville: University Press of Virginia, 1986), pp. 1–2.

4. "The other late arrival": Henry Adams, *The Life of Albert Gallatin* (New York: Peter Smith, 1879), p. 1.

5. "'Shall the squadron'": *Thomas Jefferson notes on Cabinet meetings, May–June 1801* (Library of Congress).

6. "The Navy now floated": William M. Fowler, Jr., *Jack Tars and Commodores: The American Navy, 1783–1815* (Boston: Houghton Mifflin Company, 1984), p. 60.

6. "the $83 million": E. James Ferguson, ed., *Selected Writings of Albert Gallatin* (Indianapolis and New York: The Bobbs-Merrill Company Inc., 1967), pp. 208–9.

8. "'Jihad' is derived": Robert Wuthnow, ed., *Encyclopedia of Politics and Religion* (Washington: Congressional Quarterly, 1998), pp. 425–6.

8. "As Islam exploded": Ibid.

8. "Jihad's new interpretation": Ibid.

8. "Their refusal to pay": McClintock and Strong, *The Cyclopedia of Biblical, Theological, and Ecclesiastical Literature* (World Wide Web), vol. VI, p. 417.

8. "The Barbary States stuck": Muhammad Abdel Haleem, *Understanding the Qur'an: Themes and Style* (London, New York: I. B. Tauris, Publishers, 1999), pp. 61–3.

Chapter II: The Dreadful Corsairs

9. "The Moors were": Jamil M. Abun-Nasr, *A History of the Maghrib* (Cambridge, England: Cambridge University Press, 1971), p. 7.

9. "the Maghrib, the 'land of sunset'": Ibid., p. 1.

10. "During one expedition": Charles-André Julien, *History of North Africa* (New York: Praeger Publishers, 1970), p. 13.

10. "the first Barbary corsairs": Tucker, pp. 48–9.

11. "King Roderick": Stanley Lane-Poole, *The Barbary Corsairs* (New York: G. P. Putnam's Sons, 1901), p. 14.

11. "The Moors, as the": Stanley Lane-Poole, *The Moors in Spain* (New York: G. P. Putnam's Sons, 1911), pp. vii–ix.

11. "In 1800, U.S. libraries": Henry Adams, *History of the United States during the Administrations of Thomas Jefferson and James Madison* (New York: A & C Boni, 1930), vol. 1, p. 61.

12. "In 1491, at": Lane-Poole, *The Moors in Spain,* pp. 270–1.

12. "Most Granadan Moors preferred": Ibid., p. 272.

12. "While a few refugees": John B. Wolf, *The Barbary Coast: Algiers Under the Turks, 1500–1830* (New York: W. W. Norton & Co., 1979), pp. 5–6; Will and Ariel Durant, *The Story of Civilization,* 11 vols. (New York: Simon & Schuster, Inc., 1935–75), vol. 6, pp. 217–8, 696.

13. "The 'little war'": Ellen G. Friedman, *Spanish Captives in North Africa in the Early Modern Age* (Madison, Wis.: University of Wisconsin Press, 1983), p. xiv.

13. "The escalating raids": Wolf, pp. 4–5; Julien, p. 242; Lane-Poole, *Barbary Corsairs,* pp. 8–10.

13. "Spanish Christians believed": Lane-Poole, *Moors in Spain,* pp. 273–80.

14. "Charles signed the edict": Ibid.

14. "Given command of": Ibid.

14. "Between 1492 and 1610": Ibid.

15. "In 1580, the Holy": Friedman, p. xxii.
16. "The shipyards of Tunis": Wolf, p. 143; Lane-Poole, *Barbary Corsairs*, pp. 219–21.
16. "Hundreds of English": Samuel C. Chew, *The Crescent and the Rose: Islam and England during the Renaissance* (New York: Octagon Books Inc., 1965), p. 350.
16. "they brought with them": Wolf, p. 145.
17. "Coming upon a": Lane-Poole, *Barbary Corsairs*, p. 225.
17. "It was usually over": Ibid., p. 193.
17. "Murad Reis, a legendary": Ibid., pp. 226–33.
17. "800 raiders": Ibid.
17. "Corsairs appeared off": Ibid.
17. "Between 1613 and 1622": Wolf, p. 190.
17. "Four hundred English ships": Lane-Poole, *Barbary Corsairs*, p. 266.
18. "During six months": Chew, p. 358.
18. "Between 1628 and 1634": Lane-Poole, *Barbary Corsairs*, p. 233; Louis B. Wright and Julia H. Macleod, *The First Americans in North Africa: William Eaton's Struggle for a Vigorous Policy Against the Barbary Pirates, 1799–1805* (Princeton, N.J.: Princeton University Press), p. 11.
18. "The Spanish abetted": Friedman, pp. 10–11.
18. "Gibraltar's nine watchtowers": Ibid., p. xvii.
18. "Even when privateers": Ibid., p. 34.
18. "Long stretches of": Ibid., pp. 48–9.
18. "Spain and Italy": Ibid., p. 165; Colin McEvedy, *The Penguin Atlas of Ancient, Medieval and Modern History,* 3 vols. (Baltimore: Penguin Books Inc., 1967), vol. 3, p. 37; 1999 Europe population figures.
19. "the habitual 'climate of fear'": Friedman, p. xxv.
19. "In 1616 alone": Julien, p. 306.
19. "Wrote Diego de Haedo": Lane-Poole, *Barbary Corsairs*, p. 205.
19. "Algiers's lavish public": Julien, pp. 106–7.
20. "The Algiers skyline sprouted": Wolf, pp. 94–7.
20. "The hazards of": Ibid., p. 148.
20. "expensive, ornamented fountains": Ibid., p. 97.
21. "The youngest, handsomest": Friedman, pp. 68–9.
21. "Algiers's 'zoco'": Ibid., pp. 56–7.
21. "Father Dan happened": Lane-Poole, *Barbary Corsairs*, p. 133.
21. "True, some corsair captains": Friedman, pp. 72–4.
22. "Christians usually were": Ibid., pp. 55–6.
22. "'Our beds were nothing'": Chew, p. 381.
22. "Ships docking in": Lane-Poole, *Barbary Corsairs*, p. 252.
22. "Surgeons were another": Friedman, pp. 69–70.
23. "Chained naked to": Lane-Poole, *Barbary Corsairs*, pp. 214–5.
23. "One was Germaine": Friedman, pp. 68–9.
23. "Two thousand slaves": Ibid., pp. 66–7.
24. "Slaves were bastinadoed": Gardner W. Allen, *Our Navy and the Barbary Corsairs* (Hamden, Conn.: Archon Books, 1905), p. 21.
24. "Jean de Matha": Friedman, pp. 91–101.
24. "The sight of the": Ibid., p. xxv.
24. "The pashas allowed": Ibid., pp. 91–101.

25. "During eighty-two redemption": Ibid., pp. 145–6.
25. "between 1520 and 1830": Wolf, pp. 151–2.
26. "Admiral Lambert appeared": Ibid., pp. 90–1.
26. "English Admiral Robert Blake": Wolf, pp. 220–1.
27. "Dutch Admiral Michiel De Ruyter": Tucker, p. 56.
27. "British Admiral Edward Spragg": Wolf, p. 215.
27. "The four janissary": Abun-Nasr, p. 175.
28. "In 1682, Admiral Abraham Duquesne": Wolf, pp. 259–60.
29. "the French king Louis XIV sent": Ibid.
30. "In 1712 Holland sent": Lane-Poole, *Barbary Corsairs,* pp. 258–69.
31. "Algiers's population, thinned": Julien, p. 320.

Chapter III: The New Nation and Barbary
32. "'An ambassador from America!'": McCullough, p. 337.
33. "In October 1784": Mary A. Giunta, ed., *The Emerging Nation: A Documentary History of the Foreign Relations of the United States under the Articles of Confederation: 1780–1789,* 3 vols. (Washington: National Historical Publications and Record Commission, 1996), vol. 2, p. 503.
33. "'Our sufferings are beyond'": Ibid., p. 767.
33. "Jay already had instructed": Ibid., p. 553.
34. "the Dutch, Danes": Ibid., pp. 564–5.
34. "The men warmed": *The Works of John Adams,* 10 vols. (Freeport, N.Y.: Books for Libraries Press, 1969), vol. 8, pp. 372–3.
35. "In 1698, during another": Whipple, pp. 292–3.
36. "an average of 100": Julian P. Boyd et al., ed., *The Papers of Thomas Jefferson,* 25 vols. (Princeton, N.J.: Princeton University Press, 1950–), vol. 18, p. 371.
36. "Mediterranean markets consumed": Curtis P. Nettles, *The Emergence of a National Economy, 1775–1815* (New York, Evanston, London: Harper & Row, Publishers, 1962), p. 57.
36. "Richard Harrison": *Emerging Nation,* vol. 2, p. 115.
36. "'It is not [in] their Interest'": Ibid.
36. "In 1782 Livingston": Ibid., p. 58.
37. "He warned that": *Works of John Adams,* vol. 8, pp. 374–6.
37. "The shipyards had": Nettles, p. 50.
38. "France and Britain": Gordon C. Bjork, *Stagnation and Growth in the American Economy 1784–1792* (New York, London: Garland Publishing Inc., 1985), p. 167.
38. "More than 50,000 slaves": Schachner, p. 217.
38. "Rice exports told": Nettles, pp. 46–50.
38. "Adams ambitiously proposed": Ibid., p. 66.
38. "Jefferson estimated British": Ibid., p. 63.
38. "The French, however, lacked": Samuel Eliot Morison, *The Oxford History of the American People,* 3 vols. (New York: New American Library, 1972), vol. 1, p. 369.
39. "American tobacco, flour": Ibid., p. 370.
39. "The *Empress of China*": Gorton Carruth, *What Happened When: A Chronology of Life & Events in America* (New York: Signet, 1991), p. 151.
40. "The novelty wore off": Boyd, vol. 9, p. 358.
41. "the 47th Surah": T. B. Irving, trans., *The Qur'an* (Brattleboro, Vt.: Amana Books, 1986), pp. 288–9.

41. "By first extending": Haleem, pp. 61–3.
41. "Jefferson gloomily estimated": Boyd, vol. 9, p. 500.
41. "which meant going": Ibid., pp. 357–9.
42. "Adams observed that": *Works of John Adams,* vol. 8, pp. 406–7.
43. "Adams was certain": Ibid.
43. "Jefferson replied with": Boyd, vol. 10, pp. 123–5.
45. "Adams conceded there": *Works of John Adams,* vol. 8, pp. 410–2.
46. "The Confederation Congress's": Morison, vol. 1, p. 363.
46. "'It seems almost Nugatory'": Dorothy Twohig, ed., *The Papers of George Washington, Confederation Series,* 6 vols. (Charlottesville, Va., and London: University Press of Virginia, 1997), vol. 5, pp. 106–7.
46. "'I should not be angry'": *Emerging Nation,* vol. 2, pp. 967–8.
47. "'If we act properly'": Ibid., p. 863.
47. "'We ought to begin'": Boyd, vol. 7, p. 511.
47. "'These pyrates are contemptibly'": Boyd, vol. 2, pp. 542–3.
48. "Morocco's seizure of": Whipple, p. 25.
48. "'It is not surprising'": *Emerging Nation,* vol. 2, p. 520.
49. "he impulsively displayed": Ibid., p. 503.
49. "'to show them'": Tucker, p. 65.
49. "The envoy and": *Emerging Nation,* vol. 2, p. 841.
49. "John Lamb, a Norwich": Ibid.
49. "Lamb passed along": Boyd, vol. 18, pp. 374–5.
49. "Richard O'Brien, master": *Naval Documents,* vol. 1, p. 6.
50. "'If there were'": *Emerging Nation,* vol. 2, p. 178.
50. "Lord Sheffield expanded": Boyd, vol. 18, pp. 373–4.
50. "Jefferson appealed to": Ibid., p. 431.
51. "Jefferson raised the sum": Whipple, pp. 26–7.
51. "But Hamilton's actions so": Schachner, pp. 182–4.
52. "In his secret idealistic": Thomas Jefferson, *Autobiography of Thomas Jefferson* (New York: Capricorn Books, 1959), pp. 77–9; Boyd, vol. 10, pp. 560–2.
53. "Jefferson was subtler": *Autobiography of Thomas Jefferson,* p. 78.
53. "Lafayette first presented": Boyd, vol. 10, pp. 562–3.
54. "'There is betwen'": Gottschalk, ed., *Letters of Lafayette to Washington, 1777–1799* (Philadelphia: American Philosophical Society, 1976), p. 315.
54. "In 1787 Virginia": Boyd, vol. 10, pp. 564–5.
54. "Congress 'declined an engagement'": *Autobiography of Thomas Jefferson,* p. 79.

Chapter IV: "A Good Occasion to Build a Navy"
55. "Nearly four million": Nettles, p. 77.
56. "Revolutionary War debt": Ibid.
56. "Trade continued to lag": Ibid., p. 396.
57. "The occasion was": Boyd, vol. 18, pp. 423–4.
57. "Besides being at war": Ibid., p. 428.
58. "Spain's peace had cost": Ibid., p. 426.
58. "they boiled down to": Ibid., p. 431.
58. "'For this, we'": Foley, p. 83.
58. "'to repel force'": Boyd, vol. 18, pp. 410–3.
58. "a Senate resolution": Ibid.

59. "His 'Proposal to Use Force'": Ibid., p. 416.

60. "Logie, the London": Ibid., pp. 374–5; Tucker, p. 72.

61. "'Money is the God'": *Naval Documents,* vol. 1, p. 3.

61. "When the Americans complained": John Foss, *Journal of the Captivity and Sufferings of John Foss, Several Years a Prisoner of Algiers* (Newburyport, Maine: A. March, Middle-Street, 1798), pp. 1–12.

62. "'All my hopes'": Ibid., p. 57.

63. "Yellow fever had cut": McCullough, p. 446.

63. "'Everyone is getting'": Ford, vol. 9, pp. 236–7.

63. "Philadelphia's sultry summers": McCullough, p. 446.

64. "'As we passed'": Foss, p. 14.

64. "The prisoners used gunpowder": Ibid., p. 20.

65. "'every article that'": Ibid., p. 29.

65. "Sherief was the worst": Ibid., pp. 20–1.

66. "The captives were required": Ibid., pp. 31–3.

66. "The Algerians' 'tenderest mercies'": Ibid., Frontispiece.

66. "Fourteen slaves caught": Ibid., p. 25.

67. "Turks who committed": Ibid.

67. "the Merchant Marine Act": Tucker, p. 79.

67. "While U.S. ports": Carruth, p. 169.

68. "The navy debate began": *Annals of Congress, Third Congress, 1st Session* (Library of Congress), pp. 438–9.

69. "Benjamin Goodhue": Ibid., p. 441.

69. "Fisher Ames": Kenneth J. Hagan, *This People's Navy: The Making of American Sea Power* (New York: The Free Press, 1991), p. 30.

69. "Britain, said John Nicholas": *Annals of Congress, Third Congress, 1st Session,* p. 439.

70. "Madison asserted that": Hagan, p. 31.

70. "British interference was not": *Annals of Congress, Third Congress, 1st Session,* pp. 440–1.

70. "The House passed": Fowler, p. 20.

71. "The ships, Knox concluded": Tucker, pp. 79–81.

71. "Given the job": Allen, p. 50.

71. "Since the United States": Allen, p. 51; Fowler, p. 18; Tucker, pp. 81–2; Whipple, p. 44.

71. "Humphreys rhapsodized to": Tucker, p. 87.

72. "the Continental Navy had": Barbara W. Tuchman, *The First Salute* (New York: 1988), pp. 47–8.

72. "The cobbled-together fleet": Whipple, p. 293.

72. "The last Continental warship": Fowler, p. 8.

72. "Knox parceled out": Hagan, p. 34.

72. "Then Knox also made": Hagan, pp. 32–3.

72. "Finally, he had insisted": Fowler, pp. 24–5.

73. "The *Constitution,* 'Old Ironsides'": Tucker, pp. 82–7.

73. "The unlucky *Chesapeake*": David S. and Jeanne T. Heidler, ed., *Encyclopedia of the War of 1812* (Santa Barbara, Denver, Oxford: ABC-CLIO, 1997), p. 296.

73. "Not able to afford": Hagan, p. 34.

74. "The carronade was": Tucker, p. 84.

74. "Copper bottoms repelled": Ibid., p. 33.
74. "The British Royal Navy": William N. Fowler, Jr., *Rebels Under Sail: The American Navy During the Revolution* (New York: Charles Scribner's Sons, 1976), pp. 253–4.
74. "The 44-gun super frigates": Fowler, *Jack Tars,* pp. 127–30.
74. "Each day, they stood": Ibid., pp. 133–6.
75. "Quitting watch before relief": *Naval Documents,* vol. 1, pp. 482–3.
75. "David Humphreys and Joel Barlow": Tucker, 91–4.
75. "The dey opened": Michael L. S. Kitzen, *Tripoli and the United States at War: A History of American Relations with the Barbary States, 1785–1805* (Jefferson, N.C., London: McFarland & Company Inc., 1993), p. 19; Tucker, p. 91.
76. "The *Fortune* was": Foss, p. 66.
76. "the British replied": Kitzen, pp. 21–2.
76. "On top of everything": Allen, p. 53.
77. "A Spanish privateer": Foss, pp. 66–70.

Chapter V: "Will Nothing Rouse My Country?"

78. "The Senate ratified": Hagan, pp. 36–7.
78. "Another reason for": Robert J. Allison, *The Crescent Obscured: The United States and the Muslim World, 1776–1815* (New York, Oxford: Oxford University Press, 1995), p. 23.
79. "Knowing that the Republicans": Hagan, p. 37.
80. "In just one year": Ibid., p. 30.
80. "'A naval power'": Ibid., pp. 38–9.
80. "The French envoys": Carruth, p. 172.
81. "Pinckney's forceful reply": Hagan, p. 40.
81. "a French privateer": Tucker, p. 88.
81. "Congress created a": Hagan, pp. 41–3; Fowler, *Jack Tars,* p. 36; Moskin, p. 27.
82. "During the Revolutionary War": Moskin, p. 33.
82. "Congress amended the": Schachner, p. 602.
82. "Then came the Sedition": Carruth, pp. 173–4.
83. "The 20-gun *Montezuma*": Fowler, *Jack Tars,* pp. 36–7.
83. "Two squadrons cruised": Ibid., p. 39.
84. "In the Leeward Islands": Fowler, pp. 44–5.
84. "In February 1800": Ibid., pp. 54–7.
84. "France captured 159": Ibid., p. 52.
85. "The Navy had 33 ships": Ibid., p. 43.
85. "'He was like'": Samuel Edwards, *Barbary General: The Life of William Eaton* (Englewood Cliffs, N.J.: Prentice-Hall Inc., 1968), pp. 68–9.
85. "O'Brien had arrived:" Allen, p. 21; Whipple, pp. 52–3.
86. "Bobba surely was cheered": Tucker, p. 110.
86. "Bobba, however, was": Tucker, pp. 102–3.
86. "Betsy Robeson, the twenty-year-old": Kitzen, pp. 25–7.
87. "Described in later years": Tucker, p. 24.
87. "He said later in": Whipple, p. 177.
88. "'He endured fatigue'": Tucker, pp. 247–8.
88. "Wayne assigned Eaton": Edwards, pp. 27–39.
89. "Eaton trapped and arrested": Ibid., pp. 52–3.

90. "Eaton raised the": Tucker, p. 113.

91. "'Not much shall be feared'": *Naval Documents*, vol. 1, p. 317.

92. "Snatching a whip": Edwards, p. 76.

92. "The articulate Eaton": Tucker, p. 115.

92. "The bey sent away Famin": Edwards, p. 76.

92. "O'Brien and Cathcart": Allison, p. 185.

92. "'The United States set out'": Wright and Macleod, p. 41.

92. "Congress must 'send a'": Ibid., p. 47.

93. "Bobba Mustapha expected": Edwards, p. 63.

93. "'I don't pray often'": Wright and Macleod, p. 45.

93. "The shadow fell on Denmark": Ibid., pp. 66–7.

93. "Eaton came to": Allen, p. 71.

93. "But the Danes got": Wright and Macleod, pp. 66–7.

94. "At Cathcart's first meeting": Tucker, p. 118.

94. "McDonough bargained the bashaw": Ibid., pp. 124–5.

94. "Cathcart paid, borrowing": Allison, p. 169.

94. "O'Brien and Eaton wisely": Ibid., pp. 170–2.

95. "In a letter to President Adams": *Naval Documents*, vol. 1, pp. 322–3.

95. "In July 1800": Ibid., p. 372.

95. "But in unmistakable language": Ibid., pp. 394–5.

96. "The *George Washington*'s cargo": Allison, p. 175.

97. "Besides its 130 crewmen": Allen, pp. 75–80.

97. "The Americans took pleasure": Ibid.

98. "Throughout the meal": Tucker, pp. 34–5.

98. "Two months after leaving": Allen, pp. 75–80.

98. "'The sending to Constantinople'": Hagan, pp. 55.

98. "'I would have lost'": *Naval Documents*, vol. 1, p. 398.

99. "Tunis's bey, Hamouda Pacha,": Ibid.

99. "'He seldom robs'": Ibid., p. 431.

99. "Bainbridge returned to the": Wright and Macleod, p. 61.

99. "'He was a large'": Edwards, p. 84.

100. "One of Bobba's officers": *Naval Documents*, vol. 1, p. 411.

100. "Sweden had agreed": Ibid., p. 404.

100. "'I have every reason'": Ibid., p. 420.

101. "Consuls and agents": *Papers of James Madison*, pp. 3–5.

Chapter VI: War and Early Triumph

102. "The bashaw set the": *Naval Documents*, vol. 1, p. 420.

102. "In two years": Kola Folayan, *Tripoli During the Reign of Yusuf Pasha Qaramanli* (Ile-Ife, Nigeria: University of Ife Press, 1979), p. 27.

103. "America's $60,000 treaty": Ibid., p. 29.

103. "More aggravating than": Ibid., pp. 33–4.

104. "In letters to": Ibid., p. 35.

104. "'If the United States'": *Naval Documents*, vol. 1, p. 430.

104. "'. . . it would strike'": *Papers of James Madison*, p. 92.

105. "But the fact was": Jefferson Notes on Cabinet Meetings, *The Thomas Jefferson Papers at the Library of Congress*, May–June 1801.

105. "Off Sicily, Tunisian pirates": *Naval Documents,* vol. 1, p. 479.

106. "The squadron was to": Ibid., p. 463.

106. "'It is hopeful that'": *Papers of James Madison,* pp. 199–200.

107. "Moslem absolutism, the literature": Allison, p. 37, pp. 48–9.

107. "Moreover, Europeans believed": Ibid., pp. 61–4.

108. "'One great object'": *Naval Documents,* vol. 1, p. 463.

108. "The cruise, Madison said": *Papers of James Madison,* p. 209.

108. "Sterrett was said": Alexander Laing, *American Sail: A Pictorial History* (New York: Dutton, 1961), p. 42; Tucker, p. 142.

109. "Even while readying": Schachner, p. 688.

109. "The Reduction Act also": Fowler, *Jack Tars,* p. 60.

110. "Truxtun, however, wanted": Ibid., pp. 65–6.

110. "The three-year delay": Jefferson letter to Congressman Wilson Cary Nicholas, June 11, 1801, *Jefferson Papers at the Library of Congress.*

111. "From the quarterdeck": Tucker, pp. 133–4; Edwards, p. 97.

111. "Already friction had": Whipple, p. 74.

112. "Dale gave Sterrett": *Naval Documents,* vol. 1, p. 497.

112. "Three days after Sterrett's": Ibid., p. 501.

112. "Murad Reis was actually": Tucker, pp. 121–2.

113. "The American flag": Wright and Macleod, p. 89.

113. "No, he told Dale": *Naval Documents,* vol. 1, p. 501.

113. "Dale gave Bobba Mustapha": *Papers of James Madison,* p. 213.

114. "'The squadron under my'": *Naval Documents,* vol. 1, pp. 531–3.

114. "'The shore along'": Ibid., p. 587.

115. "Flowering hibiscus, olives": Tucker, pp. 221–4

115. "Hamet the Great": Ibid., pp. 225–8.

116. "He led a revolt": Folayan, pp. 17–20.

117. "When Hamet returned": Tucker, pp. 225–8.

117. "Eaton sent a circular": *Naval Documents,* vol. 1, p. 528.

117. "Murad unbent his": Ibid, pp. 541–2.

117. "Murad, happily rid of": Tucker, p. 147.

118. "Commodore Richard Dale's first": Ibid., pp. 546–7.

118. "The furious bashaw": Donald Barr Chidsey, *The Wars in Barbary: Arab Piracy and the Birth of the United States Navy* (New York: Crown Publishers Inc., 1971), p. 76; *Naval Documents,* vol. 1, p. 539 (*National Intelligencer*).

119. "Sterrett was awarded": *Naval Documents,* vol. 1, pp. 539–40.

119. "The victory inspired a play": Allison, p. 187.

119. "In a congratulatory letter": Christopher McKee, *Edward Preble, A Naval Biography, 1761–1807* (Annapolis, Md.: *Naval Institute Press,* 1972), pp. 91–2.

120. "Sterrett's promotion, however": *Jefferson Presidential Papers,* Microfilm, Reel 33.

Chapter VII: The War That Wasn't

121. "Dale perversely interpreted": *Naval Documents,* vol. 2, p. 54.

122. "The Essex convoyed": Ibid.

122. "Dale complained there": Ibid., vol. 1, p. 553, 560.

122. "'I don't expect'": Ibid., vol. 1, pp. 603–4.

122. "As early as August": Ibid., p. 560.

123. "'There never was'": Ibid., pp. 610–11.
123. "En route to Toulon": Ibid., p. 620.
123. "He sailed from Malaga": Ibid., vol. 2, pp. 27, 44.
124. "But before his recall": Ibid., pp. 142–3.
124. "Thinking ahead to when": Ibid., vol. 1, pp. 565–6.
125. "Richard Valentine Morris": Tucker, pp. 153–4.
125. "Navy Secretary Smith": *Naval Documents*, vol. 2, p. 103.
126. "Smith disliked ultimatums": Ibid., p. 76–83.
126. "The bashaw was sending": Ibid., p. 66.
126. "Algiers had sent twelve": Ibid., pp. 155, 173.
127. "'I never was at Sea'": Ibid., pp. 161–2.
127. "Holding out the'": Ibid., p. 130.
128. "Soliman now announced": Ibid., pp. 179–83.
128. "He invited Simpson": Ibid., p. 276.
129. "Morris put a watch": Ibid., pp. 275–6, 280.
129. "Handwritten letters and": Tuchman, p. 7.
129. "The Navy Department sent": Ibid., p. 136.
129. "Belying his unyielding": *Naval Documents*, vol. 2, p. 309.
130. "Congress, which supported": Schachner, pp. 711–2.
130. "Two corsairs had slipped": *Naval Documents*, vol. 2, p. 176.
130. "Firing cannon salutes": Ibid., pp. 176, 201.
131. "Eaton tried to open": Ibid., p. 201.
131. "On October 11": Ibid., pp. 279, 288.
131. "Richard O'Brien, the U.S.": Ibid., p. 349.
131. "'Let me at this time'": Ibid., p. 232.
132. "It was so late": Ibid., pp. 296–7.
132. "Morris confided to Cathcart": Ibid., p. 291.
132. "O'Brien had learned": Ibid., p. 289.
132. "'This year has proved'": Ibid., p. 213.
132. "Sweden made peace": Ibid., pp. 305–6.
133. "Young Wadsworth thought": Ibid., pp. 273–4.
133. "The forecastle captain's wife": Ibid., p. 387.
133. "It was so widespread": Whipple, p. 309.
133. "Lawson, who had never": *Naval Documents*, vol. 2, pp. 293–5.
134. "He displayed his": Ibid., pp. 293–95, 299.
135. "Carmick was returning": Ibid., p. 300.
135. "'Yesterday we left Livonine'": Ibid., p. 310.
135. "Cochran tried to pick": Ibid., p. 362; Whipple, p. 90.
136. "Congress empowered the president": Edwards, p. 111.
136. "Congress also authorized": *Naval Documents*, vol. 2, pp. 51–2.
136. "Early in 1803": Ibid., p. 346, 362, 366.
137. "'Sunday: One and a'": Ibid., pp. 49–50.
137. "'Government may as well'": *Naval Documents*, vol. 2, p. 229.
137. "He also was angry": *Naval Documents*, vol. 2, pp. 166–9.
138. "'I beleive you'": Ibid., p. 145.
138. "'Our operations of the'": Ibid., pp. 248–9.
139. "The United States risked": Ibid., pp. 196–7.

139. "'intolerable abuse and'": Ibid., pp. 248–9.

139. "A Barbary consul:" Ibid., p. 353.

139. "'Nothing of importance'": Ibid., p. 327.

139. "Finally, in February 1803": Ibid., p. 306.

Chapter VIII: Frustration

140. "Morris's squadron delivered": Ibid., pp. 86–7.

140. "The bey instructed Eaton": Ibid., pp. 134–5.

141. "He told Eaton": Charles Prentiss, *Life of the Late William Eaton* (Brookfield, Mass.: Merriam & Co., 1813), pp. 214–5; *Naval Documents,* vol. 2, p. 354.

141. "The brief rapprochement": *Naval Documents,* vol. 2, p. 163, 166.

141. "The frigate, he said": Ibid., p. 269.

141. "'It is false'": Ibid., p. 305.

142. "'I will indemnify myself'": Ibid., pp. 344–6.

142. "Morris insisted the *Paulina*": Ibid., pp. 351–4.

143. "Yet it was true": Prentiss, pp. 238–9.

143. "Eaton had added": Wright and Macleod, pp. 102, 122.

144. "The torrent of vituperation": Prentiss, p. 241; Edwards, p. 122; Tucker, p. 167.

144. "Cathcart reported what happened": *Naval Documents,* vol. 2, p. 369.

144. "Eaton found a buyer": Ibid., pp. 354–5.

144. "The commodore sent the bey": Ibid., p. 369.

144. "'Had I commanded'": Ibid.

145. "'It is unprecedented'": Prentiss, p. 239.

145. "'I presume it would'": *Naval Documents,* vol. 2, p. 396.

145. "'His character does not'": Ibid., p. 301.

145. "The snub prompted": Ibid., pp. 379–81.

146. "Given sailing orders": Ibid., p. 387.

146. "Dale, the Navy's senior": Ibid., pp. 330, 337.

147. "He was ordered to": Ibid., p. 405.

147. "Over Cathcart's protests": Ibid., pp. 398–9.

147. "While the *New York*": Allen, p. 125; Tucker, p. 171.

148. "'Twelve months pass'd'": *Naval Documents,* vol. 2, p. 417.

148. "While dining at a": Tucker, pp. 182–3.

149. "Rodgers displayed the same": *Naval Documents,* vol. 2, pp. 408–9.

149. "Days later, the *Enterprise*": Ibid., p. 416.

150. "Five days after": Ibid., pp. 425–6.

151. "A few days later": Ibid., p. 430.

151. "Thirty-five miles northwest": Ibid., pp. 530–1.

151. "At 8:00 P.M., Porter": Ibid., pp. 435–7.

152. "Fifty officers, sailors": Ibid., pp. 435–7, 530–1.

153. "Yusuf boasted to Nissen": Ibid., pp. 439–40.

153. "Sailing into Tripoli harbor": Ibid., p. 449.

154. "the squadron spotted a 22-gun": Ibid., pp. 465–6.

155. "The *New York* pulled": Ibid., p. 495.

155. "The trigger-happy French": Ibid., pp. 509, 521–2.

156. "'You will upon receipt'": Ibid., p. 457.

157. "Jefferson and his": Edwards, pp. 128–30.

157. "Eaton had observered": Prentiss, p. 244.

157. "The Cabinet met": McKee, pp. 112–4.

157. "Morris was court-martialed": *Naval Documents*, vol. 2, pp. 528–31.

158. "Algerian corsairs attacked": Whipple, p. 311.

158. "In February 1803, he": Ray W. Irwin, *The Diplomatic Relations of the United States with the Barbary Powers, 1776–1816* (Chapel Hill, N.C.: The University of North Carolina Press, 1931), pp. 129–30.

Chapter IX: The *Philadelphia* Disaster

160. "The commodore had teamed": *Naval Documents*, vol. 3, pp. 61–2.

161. "Unfortunately for Bainbridge": Ibid., p. 174.

161. "Born a year": H. A. S. Dearborn, *The Life of William Bainbridge, Esq., of the United States Navy* (Princeton, N.J.: Princeton University Press, 1931), pp. vi–7.

162. "He evidently could be": Allen, p. 86.

162. "He got within": Dearborn, p. 55; *Naval Documents*, vol. 3, p. 172.

162. "A boat was lowered": *Naval Documents*, vol. 3, p. 172.

163. "Wind and waves": Ibid.

163. "At 4:00 P.M., after attempting": Ibid., p. 174.

164. "Cannon, arms and ammunition": Ibid., pp. 171–2.

164. "The sailor manning": William Ray, *Horrors of Slavery: Or, The American Tars in Tripoli* (Troy, N.Y.: Oliver Lyon, 1808), p. 77; J. Robert Moskin, *The U.S. Marine Corps Story* (New York: McGraw-Hill Book Co., 1977), pp. 56–7.

164. "Bainbridge sent an officer": Ray, p. 77.

165. "The practical-minded sailors": Ibid., p. 78.

165. "The greedy Tripolitans": *Naval Documents*, vol. 3, p. 529.

165. "the Tripolitans shoved": Ray, p. 78.

165. "Seated on a small": Ibid., pp. 81–2.

165. "'He counted us'": *Naval Documents*, vol. 3, pp. 529–30.

166. "The crew was marched": Ray, pp. 84–5.

166. "they witnessed a melancholy": *Naval Documents*, vol. 3, pp. 529–30.

166. "An even more demoralizing": Ibid., pp. 14, 173.

166. "but only a few hundred": Whipple, p. 315.

167. "'Had I not sent'": *Naval Documents*, vol. 3, pp. 171–4.

167. "'A just comparison'": Ibid., p. 177.

167. "'I have zealously served'": Ibid., p. 174.

167. "Bainbridge's torment moved": Ibid., p. 169.

167. "Busy convoying, Preble": Ibid., p. 175; McKee, p. 179.

168. "'This affair distresses me'": *Naval Documents*, vol. 3, p. 256.

168. "He feared that": Ibid., p. 175.

168. "'Would to God'": Ibid., p. 256.

168. "To his brother": McKee, p. 181.

168. "'I have not the smallest'": *Naval Documents*, vol. 3, p. 280.

168. "'Keep up a good heart'": Ibid., p. 335.

169. "Preble discovered months' worth": *Naval Documents*, vol. 3, pp. 351, 385–6.

169. "Jefferson's political enemies": Allison, pp. 29–30.

169. "'This accident renders'": *Jefferson Presidential Papers* (Library of Congress), Microfilm, Reel 30.

169. "Congress established a": Ibid., p. 523.
170. "'I have never been'": Ford, vol. 8, p. 301.
170. "So while the president": *James Madison Presidential Papers* (Library of Congress), vol. 27, p. 35.
170. "On May 8, 1803": Whipple, p. 96.
170. "Besides being instructed": *Naval Documents,* vol. 2, p. 468.
171. "Off Cape de Gatt": *Naval Documents,* vol. 2, p. 507.
171. "James Simpson, the U.S.": Ibid., p. 514.
172. "Algiers's dey was": Ibid., vol. 3, pp. 132, 361–2.
172. "Rodgers objected to it": Ibid., pp. 46–7.
173. "The American merchantman *Hannah*": Ibid., pp. 23, 62–3.
173. "Finally, the emperor arrived": Ibid., p. 106.
173. "He made a show": Ibid., pp. 107–8.
173. "The delighted emperor": Ibid., p. 110.
174. "'a small man'": Ibid., p. 126.
174. "The emperor suspended": Ibid., pp. 164–5.
174. "As the two nations": Ibid., pp. 19, 118, 126–7, 153.
174. "Many were built": Ibid., pp. 461, 466.
174. "The morning after": Ray, pp. 83–4.
175. "While the crewmen": Ibid., p. 104.
176. "'Rough-bearded men'": John Greenleaf Whittier. *The Complete Poetical Works of John Greenleaf Whittier* (Boston: Houghton Mifflin Company, 1892), pp. 410–1.
177. "John Morrison, a": Ray, pp. 114–5.
177. "'Behave like Americans'": *Naval Documents,* vol. 3, p. 312.
177. "A janissary cut off": Ray, p. 96.
178. "The officers were excused": *Naval Documents,* vol. 3, pp. 530–2.
178. "the midshipmen attended": Ibid., p. 256.
178. "The captain even": Dearborn, pp. 66–7.
179. "blindness was a relatively": Whipple, p. 128.
179. "With happier results": *Naval Documents,* vol. 3, pp. 531–2.
179. "a sailor cut his": Ibid.
179. "Nelson's '. . . Answer was'": Ibid., p. 357.
179. "The first convert": Ibid., pp. 530–1.
179. "Wilson became one": Allison, p. 120.

Chapter X: A Daring Counterstroke
180. "The Danish consul": *Naval Documents,* vol. 3, pp. 266–7.
180. "Lear opened an account": Ibid., pp. 310, 369; Allen, pp. 163–4.
181. "He first tried": Dearborn, p. 60.
181. "After experimenting with milk": Ibid.; Whipple, p. 121.
181. "The censor's eyes": *Naval Documents,* vol. 3, pp. 526–7.
181. "Bainbridge suggested to Preble": *Naval Documents,* vol. 3, p. 253.
182. "'I shall hazard much'": Ibid., p. 258.
182. "Lieutenant Charles Stewart swore": Ibid., pp. 426–7.
182. "A month after": Ibid., p. 236.
182. "By mid-December, he had": Ibid., p. 273.
183. "Preble and Decatur now": Ibid., p. 304.

183. "The *Mastico* was": Ibid., pp. 351, 374.

183. "They turned up": Ibid., p. 334.

184. "Preble had shifted": Ibid., p. 257.

184. "Before the *Mastico's* capture": Ibid., p. 292.

184. "Yusuf's agent at Malta": Ibid., pp. 385, 378.

184. "But Preble decided": Ibid., p. 311.

185. "Who was the": Irvin Anthony, *Decatur* (New York, London: Charles Scribner's Sons, 1931), pp. 4–33.

186. "Decatur helped equip": Ibid., pp. 35–41.

187. "He settled his first": Ibid., pp. 103–4.

187. "Decatur and Macdonough": Ibid., p. 121.

188. "Decatur had assembled": *Naval Documents,* vol. 3, p. 389.

188. "'We shall astonish'": Ibid., pp. 381–2.

189. "'It will be well'": Ibid., pp. 375–7.

189. "The strike force arrived": Ibid., pp. 399, 415–6.

189. "The *Intrepid* was small": Ibid., p. 417.

189. "When they weren't busy": Anthony, p. 129; Whipple, p. 133.

189. "The most recent": *Naval Documents,* vol. 3, p. 258.

190. "The *Intrepid* slowly": Ibid., p. 416.

190. "Decatur launched the mission": Ibid. p. 418.

190. "Decatur divided his force": Anthony, pp. 124–5.

191. "A voice in the": Ibid., p. 132.

191. "The *Philadelphia's* officer": Ibid., pp. 416–7; Anthony, pp. 130–3.

192. "The enemy's bloodcurdling": *Naval Documents,* vol. 3, pp. 417–9.

192. "The frigate went up": Ibid., p. 415.

193. "Morris described the sight": Whipple, p. 319.

193. "With seamless precision": *Naval Documents,* vol. 3, p. 414.

193. "Thirty *Siren* crewmen": Ibid.

194. "At daybreak, they": Ibid., pp. 414–5.

194. "The *Philadelphia* burned": Tucker, p. 283.

194. "The commodore signaled impatiently": *Naval Documents,* vol. 3, p. 444.

194. "'Their conduct in the'": Ibid., p. 413.

194. "'the most bold'": Irwin, p. 135.

195. "'The American commander'": Allison, p. 193.

195. "'.. . it is the only'": *Naval Documents,* vol. 3, p. 525.

195. "Congress Decatur commended": Ibid., pp. 427–8.

195. "A silent play": Allison, p. 190.

195. "Francis Scott Key": Victor Weybright, *Spangled Banner: The Story of Francis Scott Key* (New York: Farrar & Rinehart Inc., 1935), pp. 137–43.

195. "Key's new, forgettable": Ibid., pp. 143–50.

196. "Susan Decatur made": *Naval Documents,* vol. 3, pp. 421, 230–1; Allen, pp. 174–5.

197. "The night of the": Ray, p. 110.

197. "The commotion also": *Naval Documents,* vol. 3, p. 532.

197. "At daybreak the next": Ray, p. 110.

197. "'The Turks appeared'": *Naval Documents,* vol. 3, p. 421.

197. "when the soldiers tried": Ray, p. 111.

198. "'I have seen the Sea'": *Naval Documents,* vol. 3, p. 256.
198. "Six weeks after": Ibid., p. 532.
198. "One reason for": Ibid., p. 474.
198. "'people who handle'": Ibid., p. 489.
198. "the bashaw forbade": Ibid., p. 536.

Chapter XI: Preble's Fighting Squadron
199. "In Tripoli, gun crews": *Naval Documents,* vol. 4, pp. 293–4.
200. "Since taking command": Ibid., vol. 2, p. 508.
200. "Cathcart had tried": Ibid., vol. 3, p. 459.
200. "Prime Minister Sir John Acton": Ibid., vol. 4, pp. 100–1.
200. "Preble mounted all": Ibid., p. 130.
201. "He had sent": Ibid., pp. 183–92, 255.
201. "'It is from thence'": Ibid., p. 275.
201. "Tobias Lear said": Ibid., p. 471.
202. "*It must be dreadful*": Ibid., p. 79.
202. "Almost alone, Bainbridge": Ibid., vol. 3, pp. 329–30.
202. "'A harassing bombardment'": Ibid., vol. 4, pp. 264–5.
203. "The Philadelphia prisoners": Ray, p. 119.
203. "The captives were driven": Ibid., pp. 121, 145.
203. "Stephen Decatur led Lieutenants": *Naval Documents,* vol. 4, p. 295.
204. "Trippe boarded another": Ibid., pp. 296–7.
204. "For the rest": Ibid., footnote.
205. "'I find hand to hand'": Ibid., p. 346.
205. "Decatur overtook an": Anthony, pp. 144–5.
206. "As a souvenir": *Naval Documents,* vol. 4, pp. 347–8. (Excerpt from *Life of Stephen Decatur* by Alexander Slidell Mackenzie, U.S.N.)
206. "The *Constitution* bombarded": Ibid., pp. 296–7.
206. "Preble, expecting more": Anthony, pp. 146–7.
207. "'I always thought'": *Naval Documents,* vol. 4, p. 346.
207. "Forty-four Tripolitans perished": Ibid., pp. 297–8.
208. "Blake's gunboat never": Ibid., pp. 385–6.
208. "they ascribed the Americans'": Ray, pp. 123–4.
208. "A few days after": *Naval Documents,* vol. 4, pp. 297–8.
208. "'They did not abate'": Ray, pp. 124–7.
209. "Two days after": *Naval Documents,* vol. 4, p. 62.
209. "'The conduct for sometime'": Ibid., vol. 2, pp. 474–7.
209. "Preble was determined": McKee, p. 176.
209. "The commodore had": *Naval Documents,* vol. 4, pp. 323, 495–6.
210. "The *Siren* chased": Ibid., pp. 234, 255.
210. "'a deep designing'": Ibid., vol. 3, p. 70.
210. "When he was fourteen": McKee, pp. 6–7.
210. "was a midshipman": Ibid., pp. 10–12, 18.
210. "he went back to sea": Ibid., pp. 20–9.
211. "He then had": Fowler, *Jack Tars and Commodores,* p. 49.
211. "he contracted malaria": Whipple, p. 106.
211. "A husky six-footer": McKee, frontispiece, p. 80.

211. "Preble was known": Ibid., p. 35.

211. "criminal charges were": Ibid., pp. 46–7.

212. "In a letter": Ibid., p. 138.

212. "Unlike Morris, Preble": Ibid., pp. 133–4; *Naval Documents,* vol. 3, p. 225.

212. "on October 4, 1803, five": *Naval Documents,* vol. 3, p. 105.

212. "On November 16, 1803": Ibid., p. 225.

212. "Preble kept all": Ibid., pp. 103–4.

213. "Thus, when Robert Quinn": Ibid., vol. 4, pp. 218–9, 227.

213. "The meeting took": Anthony, pp. 109–11.

214. "And then, without warning": *Naval Documents,* vol. 4, pp. 352, 298–9.

215. "The bashaw hunkered": Ibid., pp. 299–300.

215. "Besides the casualties": Ibid.

Chapter XII: A Destructive Scheme

217. "Whenever Barron arrived": *Naval Documents,* vol. 4, pp. 114–5.

218. "While he regretted": Ibid., p. 301.

218. "Preble's pride was": Ibid., p. 377.

218. "Weeks later, when": Ibid., pp. 63–4.

218. "The *John Adams*": Ibid., pp. 300–1.

219. "Since the failed parley": Ibid., p. 222.

219. "Preble offered $80,000": Ibid., pp. 389, 397.

219. "Yet he couldn't resist": Ibid., p. 397.

219. "Stephen Decatur had exulted": Ibid., p. 243.

220. "Preble had declared": Ibid., vol. 3, p. 210.

220. "Enemy gunners opened up": Ibid., vol. 4, p. 301.

220. "Preble decided to resume": Ibid., pp. 302, 481.

220. "Yet the nervous": Ibid., p. 64.

221. "For three hours": Ibid., pp. 302–3.

221. "Inside the city": Ibid., pp. 64, 476, 480–2.

221. "Bainbridge was nearly": Ibid., pp. 302–3.

221. "Preble brought the *Constitution*": Ibid., pp. 472–3, 476, 504.

221. "A few days later": Ibid., pp. 302–4.

222. "Preble suggested a": Ibid., p. 495.

222. "Beaussier reported that": Ibid., 496–7, pp. 480–2.

222. "The American fire": Ibid., p. 65.

222. "There were so many": Ray, p. 135.

223. "Preble once again": *Naval Documents,* vol. 4, pp. 304–5, 504.

223. "Preble's reckless sorties": Ray, p. 142.

223. "When Somers asked": *Naval Documents,* vol. 4, p. 508.

224. "'No place presents'": Ibid., p. 49.

225. "In Malta in May": Ibid., p. 136.

225. "Preble himself demanded": Ibid., vol. 3, pp. 112–3, 156.

225. "A decade later": Allen, p. 140; Tucker, p. 338.

225. "'many remarkable fine'": *Naval Documents,* vol. 3, p. 210.

225. "'I have an excellent'": Ibid., p. 439.

226. "Somers impulsively removed": Anthony, pp. 150–1.

226. "The *Intrepid* was loaded": *Naval Documents,* vol. 4, pp. 305–6.

226. "'like so many planets'": Ibid., p. 352.
226. "The huge concussion": Ibid., pp. 360, 509.
227. "The *Nautilus* showed": Ibid., p. 507.
227. "there was no sign": Ibid., p. 306.
227. "Without any basis": Ibid., pp. 306–7.
228. "The bashaw and his": Ibid., p. 65.
228. "Preble chased down": Ibid., pp. 307–8.
228. "Barron cruised off": Ibid., p. 513.
228. "President Jefferson took time": McKee, pp. 314–5.
229. "With $1,245 they raised": *Naval Documents,* vol. 6, p. 497.
229. "the monument was vandalized": Wright–Macleod, p. 194.
230. "Its inscription reads": Taken from the monument.
230. "In Portland, Maine": Tucker, p. 333.
230. "In 1938, the": Lieutenant (jg) Arthur P. Miller, Jr. *"Tripoli Graves Discovered"* (U.S. Naval Institute Proceedings, April 1950), pp. 373–7.
231. "In April 1949": Ibid.

Chapter XIII: Plotting a Regime Change

233. "'The Secretary of War'": Edwards, p. 127.
233. "This proposal was": *Naval Documents,* vol. 1, p. 494.
233. "'The subjects in'": Ibid., p. 569.
233. "'does not accord'": Ibid., vol. 2, p. 245.
234. "'We have no'": Ibid., vol. 4, p. 153.
234. "Madison permitted up to": Ibid.
234. "Thin, pale, and": Karl Schuon, ed., *The Leathernecks* (New York: Franklin Watts Inc., 1963), p. 34.
234. "he had moved": *Naval Documents,* vol. 2, p. 486; vol. 3, p. 222.
235. "Eaton said that organizing": Ibid., vol. 5, p. 37.
235. "Eaton dispatched his": Edwards, pp. 128–31.
235. "Bainbridge, Murray, Morris": Tucker, pp. 229–31.
236. "Significantly, Preble, the": *Naval Documents,* vol. 3, pp. 259–60, 486.
236. "Eaton complained to": Ibid., vol. 4, p. 120.
236. "'If my project'": Ibid., vol. 5, p. 35.
236. "Hull's verbal orders": Ibid., p. 20.
237. "'How Glorious would'": Ibid., p. 305.
237. "Founded in 332 B.C.": *Funk & Wagnalls New Encyclopedia* (USA: Funk & Wagnalls, 1983), vol. 1, p. 372.
237. "The Americans gazed": P. J. Vatikiotis. *The History of Egypt* (Baltimore: The Johns Hopkins University Press, 1969), p. 31.
237. "Napoleon's lightning invasion": Ibid., pp. 30–1.
238. "'Let the Franks'": Ibid., pp. 38–9.
238. "But the shrewd Napoleon": Ibid., p. 44; Felix Gilbert, Eugene F. Rice, Jr., Richard S. Dunn, Leonard Krieger, Charles Breunig, Norman Rich, ed., *The Norton History of Modern Europe* (New York: W. W. Norton & Company, Inc. 1971), p. 816.
238. "In 1801 they": Vatikiotis, p. 50.
239. "While waiting for the": *Naval Documents,* vol. 5, p. 171.
239. "They started up": Wright–Macleod, p. 151.

239. "A striking blue-eyed": Prentiss, p. 446.

239. "he was fluent": Edwards, p. 5.

239. "He also happened": Ibid., pp. 5–6.

239. "he had mastered": Ibid., p. 11.

240. "These traits had": Ibid., p. 27.

240. "'Egypt has no'": *Naval Documents*, vol. 5, p. 191.

240. "'Wild Arabs' roved": Ibid., p. 186.

240. "Eaton's party hunted": Ibid., pp. 186–7.

241. "'They kissed our'": Ibid., pp. 190–2.

241. "Eaton impressed the": Ibid., p. 174.

241. "Cairo's viceroy, Khorshid": Vatikiotis, p. 37.

241. "They were escorted": *Naval Documents*, vol. 5, pp. 188–9.

242. "'it was more like'": Ibid.

242. "He cemented their": Ibid., pp. 185–6.

242. "The viceroy's envoy": Ibid., p. 192.

242. "Eaton sent a letter": Ibid., p. 180.

243. "'Thus you must'": Ibid., p. 268.

243. "'I cannot but'": Ibid., p. 252.

243. "Bring plenty of money": Ibid., pp. 277–9.

243. "Less than halfway": Ibid., pp. 303–4.

244. "Eaton began to notice": Ibid., p. 314.

244. "'There is more'": Tucker, p. 366.

244. "Turkish guards suddenly": *Naval Documents*, vol. 5, pp. 301, 304.

245. "'Tents were pitched'": Ibid., p. 333.

245. "The governor and": Ibid., p. 304.

245. "Hamet had decided": Ibid., p. 349.

245. "if even 100": Ibid., p. 214.

246. "The envoy was": Ibid., pp. 349–50.

246. "He 'is now'": Ibid., p. 360.

246. "Yusuf had halted": Ibid., p. 100.

247. "'His people thought'": Ibid., p. 131.

247. "Yusuf presided over": Ibid., p. 206.

247. "Hull opened a": Ibid., p. 349.

247. "Eaton got another $7,000": Ibid., pp. 348, 408.

247. "'Cash will do'": Ibid., p. 553.

247. "There were Greeks": Tucker, p. 369.

248. "Of the 400": Edwards, p. 170; *Naval Documents*, vol. 5, pp. 371, 388.

248. "Selim Comb, a Turk": *Naval Documents*, vol. 5, pp. 398–9.

248. "Leitensdorfer was born": Prentiss, pp. 419–24.

249. "Under his new": Ibid.

250. "His adventures with Eaton": Ibid.

251. "'Convention between the'": *Naval Documents*, vol. 5, pp. 367–8.

251. "'I cannot but'": Ibid., p. 354.

252. "'We found the impediments'": Ibid., p. 384.

Chapter XIV: America's Lawrence
253. "As befitted a": Whipple, pp. 203–4.

253. "The army trekked": *Naval Documents*, vol. 5, p. 399.

253. "It was the same": Tucker, p. 376; McEvedy, vols. 1–2.

254. "During World War II": Edwards, p. 15.

254. "In March and April": Tucker, pp. 371–4.

254. "'General Eaton's instincts'": Edwards, p. 185.

254. "'Wherever General Eaton'": Edwards, pp. 3, 6.

255. "They refused to": *Naval Documents*, vol. 5, p. 405.

255. "The Arab cavalry fired": Ibid., p. 410.

255. "Arabs stole all": Edwards, pp. 1–3.

256. "They drew water": *The Leathernecks*, p. 36; Whipple, p. 200.

256. "explored a valley": *Naval Documents*, vol. 5, p. 423.

256. "Eaton examined scattered": Ibid., p. 482.

256. "'with Greek inscriptions'": Ibid.

256. "The camel drivers again": Ibid., vol. 4, pp. 433–4.

257. "Eaton responded to the": Ibid.

257. "Fifty drivers returned": Ibid., vol. 5, p. 435.

257. "The tribesmen thought": Ibid., pp. 444, 448, 454.

257. "'Despondency sat in'": Ibid., p. 456.

258. "'The services of'": Ibid., p. 459.

258. "'Joseph Bashaw's forces'": Ibid., p. 464.

259. "'They were astonished'": Ibid., p. 472.

259. "O'Bannon was a": Tucker, p. 356.

259. "On the *Adams*": *Naval Documents*, vol. 2, p. 335.

260. "'O'Bannon [is] one'": *The Leathernecks*, p. 36.

260. "Eaton's volcanic relationship": *Naval Documents*, vol. 5, p. 475.

260. "Absent several days": Ibid., p. 478.

261. "The proclamation began": Ibid., pp. 467–9.

261. "He leads you'": Ibid., pp. 469–70.

262. "'I shall be'": Ibid.

262. "By early April": Ibid., p. 478.

262. "'If they preferred'": Ibid., p. 490.

263. "Eaton and O'Bannon": Ibid., pp. 490–1.

263. "Eaton then made": Ibid.

263. "Eaton began to berate": Edwards, pp. 6–8.

264. "The standoff ended": *Naval Documents*, vol. 5, pp. 490–1.

264. "Later, O'Bannon scolded": Edwards, pp. 6–8.

264. "Christians and Arabs": *Naval Documents*, vol. 5, p. 498; *The Leathernecks*, p. 36.

264. "Captain Selim Comb": *Naval Documents*, vol. 5, p. 481.

264. "Halting on April 9": Ibid., p. 495.

265. "the hungry Marines": *The Leathernecks*, p. 37.

265. "The women strung": *Naval Documents*, vol. 5, p. 503.

265. "Hamet killed a": Ibid., p. 509.

265. "now reduced to eating": Ibid., p. 512.

265. "'In an instant'": Ibid., p. 498.

265. "The bitter Arabs": Ibid., p. 512.

265. "Eaton and the Christians": Ibid.

266. "Hull had reached": Ibid., p. 493.

266. "The *Argus* and *Hornet*": Ibid., p. 443.
267. "Before his men": Ibid., p. 533.
267. "Yusuf had established": Folayan, p. 42.
267. "A tent was": *Naval Documents,* vol. 5, p. 389.
268. "He returned empty-handed": Ibid., p. 443.
268. "'They said that'": Ibid., p. 505.
268. "The increasingly flustered": Ibid., p. 509.
268. "Ten thousand, the": Ibid., p. 523.
268. "The next morning": Ibid., p. 540.
269. "But Barron's squadron": *Naval Documents,* vol. 6, pp. 30–1.
270. "If he had three": Ibid., vol. 5, p. 94.
270. "Only Preble's August 3": Ibid., pp. 58–9.
270. "He owed Tunis": Ibid., p. 52.
271. "Barron would blockade": Ibid., vol. 4, p. 153.
271. "'without any price'": Ibid., pp. 155–6.
271. "Should 'adverse events'": Ibid., p. 153.
271. "a Cabinet meeting": Jan. 8, 1805, Cabinet meeting notes. *Presidential Papers Microfilm: Thomas Jefferson Papers* (Washington, D.C., 1974), Reel 32.
271. "Jefferson, however, confided": *Naval Documents,* vol. 5, p. 465.
272. "On November 14": Ibid., p. 141.
272. "By December 27": Ibid., p. 221.
272. "April found him": Ibid., p. 536.
273. "'.. . I should place'": Ibid., p. 116.
273. "he appears as": Ray Brighton, *The Checkered Career of Tobias Lear* (Portsmouth: Portsmouth Marine Society, 1985), p. 2.
273. "Lear often signed": Ibid., p. 152.
273. "In May 1786": Ibid., pp. 96, 121–3.
274. "In December 1799": Ibid., pp. 161–3.
275. "But unfortunately, Jefferson,": Schachner, p. 578.
275. "Washington expressed outrage": James Flexner, *Washington: The Indispensable Man* (Boston: Little, Brown and Company, 1974), p. 346.
275. "John Marshall, the": Brighton, pp. 171–3.
276. "Historian Ray Brighton": Ibid., p. 175.
276. "Lear and Jefferson": Ibid., p. 172.
276. "his unlucky business speculation": Ibid., pp. 169–73.
276. "Jefferson and Madison made": Ibid., pp. 32, 329–30.
276. "Two years later": Ibid., p. 193.
276. "Within weeks of": Ibid., p. 181.
277. "He also systematically": Edwards, p. 144; Brighton, p. 237.
277. "So he took cover": *Naval Documents,* vol. 5, p. 182.
277. "'poor effeminate refugee'": Ibid., pp. 136–7.
277. "America had three": Ibid., p. 83.
278. "'He writes to the'": Ibid., vol. 6, p. 1.
278. "'I confess that'": Ibid., vol. 5, p. 486.
278. "Barron confessed to Lear": Ibid., vol. 6, p. 22.
278. "An attack was": Ibid.

Chapter XV: Derna and Peace

280. "Bananas, dates, grapes": Tucker, p. 397.
280. "whose cultivation dated": Richard Carrington, *East From Tunis* (London: Chatto and Windus, 1957), pp. 209–10.
280. "Derna was the administrative": Magali Morsy, *North Africa 1800–1900* (London, New York: Longman Group Limited, 1984), p. 100.
281. "What he learned": *Naval Documents,* vol. 5, pp. 540–1.
281. "'I thought the Bashaw'": Ibid., p. 528.
281. "Before boating ashore": Ibid.
282. "They were landed": Ibid., p. 542.
282. "Eaton had offered": Ibid.
283. "The *Argus, Hornet*": Ibid., pp. 547, 553–5.
283. "O'Bannon took charge": Ibid., p. 528.
284. "The assault force": Ibid., vol. 6, p. 121.
284. "O'Bannon and his": Schuon, p. 38.
284. "The Americans turned": *Naval Documents,* vol. 5, pp. 547–8.
284. "A little after": Ibid., pp. 553–5.
284. "just two dead": Ibid., p. 548; Schuon, pp. 35, 38.
284. "In years to come": Moskin, pp. 36, 87.
284. "O'Bannon later accepted": Merrill L. Bartlett and Jack Sweetman, *The U.S. Marine Corps: An Illustrated History* (Annapolis, Md.: Naval Institute Press, 2001), p. 31; Karl Schuon. *U.S. Marine Corps Biographical Dictionary* (New York: Franklin Watts Inc., 1963), p. 163.
284. "O'Bannon resigned his": Moskin, p. 62.
285. "He moved to Kentucky": Whipple, p. 274.
285. "He died on": Schuon, p. 163.
285. "The headstone over": U.S. Marine Corps Web archive.
285. "The sheik said": *Naval Documents,* vol. 6, pp. 4–5.
285. "Eaton threatened him": Ibid., pp. 10–1.
285. "'Neither persuasion, bribes'": Ibid., vol. 5, pp. 553–5.
285. "But Mustifa managed": Ibid., vol. 6, p. 14.
286. "He had sent spies": Allen, p. 241.
286. "On May 13, Hassan's troops": *Naval Documents,* vol. 6, pp. 12–3.
286. "a well-aimed shot": Ibid., p. 14.
287. "'A humiliating traffic'": Ibid., p. 29.
287. "Hamet implored Hull": Ibid., p. 28.
287. "They complained of": Ibid., p. 59.
288. "Hassan tried to motivate": Ibid., p. 45.
288. "Hassan's officers began": Ibid., p. 15.
288. "'Everything assures us'": Ibid., pp. 28–9.
288. "Eaton himself was": Ibid., p. 15.
288. "'Heated dust, which'": Ibid., p. 29.
288. "The searing desert": Ibid., p. 47.
289. "Hull noted that": Ibid., p. 29.
289. "'He swore by'": Ibid., p. 14.
289. "The bashaw communicated": Ibid., vol. 5, p. 505.
289. "'the greatest terror'": Ibid., vol. 6, p. 373.

289. "Yusuf convened the": Ibid., p. 43.
289. "At the height": Ibid., p. 45.
290. "'The Bashaw and'": Ibid., p. 27.
290. "Yusuf confided to Cowdery": Ibid., p. 46.
290. "or perhaps Lear": Ibid., p. 377; Brighton, pp. 242–3.
291. "'I must withhold'": *Naval Documents*, vol. 5, pp. 438–40.
291. "Barron added that": Ibid., p. 441.
291. "'the Enemy will propose'": Ibid., p. 553.
292. "He accused Barron": Ibid., p. 550.
292. "'This is a circumstance'": Ibid., pp. 550–3.
293. "Act quickly, Nissen warned": Ibid., pp. 421–2.
293. "Within days of": Ibid., p. 438.
293. "In March, with Eaton": Ibid., vol. 6, pp. 159–63.
293. "Don Joseph sent on": Ibid., p. 1.
293. "he was unwilling": Ibid., vol. 5, pp. 462–3.
293. "The captain once": Ibid., vol. 6, pp. 145–6.
294. "Lear told Rodgers": Ibid., p. 1.
294. "In mid-May, Algiers's dey": Ibid., pp. 17–8.
294. "Tunis's sapitapa offered": Ibid., p. 7.
294. "'I must contend'": Ibid., pp. 22–3.
295. "'I conceive it'": Ibid., p. 24.
295. "'By our resources'": Ibid., pp. 24–6.
295. "It was 'a duty'": Ibid., p. 32.
296. "Barron ensured that Rodgers": Ibid., pp. 31–2.
296. "The long-awaited gunboats": Ibid., vol. 5, p. 395.
296. "who professed the bizarre": Ibid., vol. 6, p. 98.
296. "swollen to more": Ibid., p. 107.
296. "Hull and Eaton": Ibid., vol. 5, pp. 555–6.
297. "To leave Hamet": Ibid., vol. 6, pp. 59–61.
297. "Three frigates from": Ibid., pp. 50–2.
298. "On May 29, Yusuf": Ibid., pp. 159–63.
298. "Tell Captain Bainbridge": Ibid., p. 69.
298. "A snag developed": Ibid., p. 104.
299. "The captives' flinty": Ibid., p. 71.
299. "'The sight of them'": Brighton, p. 254.
299. "With little ceremony": *Naval Documents*, vol. 6, p. 80.
299. "After they sobered": Ibid., p. 82.
299. "Two crewmen, however,": Ibid., p. 93.
300. "'I bid the Bashaw'": Ibid., p. 96.
300. "Instead of being": Allen, p. 157.
300. "'In sullen wrath'": *The Complete Poetical Works of John Greenleaf Whittier*, p. 412.
301. "'I cannot reconcile'": *Naval Documents*, vol. 6, pp. 84, 89.
301. "So many troops": Ibid., p. 59.
301. "During the prelude": Ibid., p. 61.
301. "Bainbridge was allowed": Dearborn, pp. 83–4.
301. "When the Divan deadlocked": Ibid.

302. "A swirling battle": *Naval Documents,* vol. 6, p. 62.
302. "'The Bashaw deserves'": Ibid., p. 122.
302. "'A none compliance'": Ibid., p. 83.
303. "Before the frigate": Ibid., pp. 87, 91.
303. "'I found that'": Ibid., p. 22.
303. "It was 'all that'": Ibid., p. 92.
303. "'He answers that'": Ibid., p. 63.
304. "He made everyone": Ibid., pp. 116–7.
304. "As the last boats": Ibid.
305. "The bashaw's envoy": Ibid., p. 117.
305. "Hamet, he noted glumly": Ibid.
305. "'Our peace with'": Ibid.

Chapter XVI: Aftermath
306. "The impatient bey": *Naval Documents,* vol. 6, p. 185.
306. "'If War is his'": Ibid., p. 143.
306. "The bey responded": Ibid., pp. 146, 194.
307. "Tensions reached the": Ibid., p. 196.
307. "All Europe is'": Ibid., p. 284.
307. "'Our own good folk'": Ibid.
307. "privately he lamented": Ibid., p. 364.
307. "Smith said all": Ibid., p. 284.
308. "Every U.S. warship": Ibid., pp. 198–9.
308. "Ten gunboats in all": Ibid., p. 330.
308. "but Gunboat 1": Ibid., p. 39.
308. "Rodgers sent Hamouda Pacha": Ibid., p. 202.
309. "Davis piped up": Ibid., pp. 204–5.
309. "The *Constitution* fired": Ibid., p. 36.
309. "In an extemporaneous": Ibid., p. 211.
309. "It perplexed him": Ibid., pp. 206–7.
310. "Hamouda responded by": Ibid., p. 257.
310. "'After such a'": Ibid., p. 308.
310. "Rodgers appointed another": Ibid., p. 234.
310. "'. . . I feel satisfied'": Ibid., p. 240.
311. "'holding out the'": Ibid., vol. 1, p. 620.
311. "Hamouda later insisted": Ibid., vol. 6, p. 256.
311. "Before leaving Syracuse": Ibid., p. 153.
311. "'I fear we'": Ibid., p. 122.
311. "'Everything changed, he": Ibid., pp. 213–4.
312. "Eaton, Rodgers, and Preble": Ibid., p. 146.
312. "But Barron's illness": Ibid., pp. 213–8.
313. "Normally convivial, Eaton": Edwards, p. 236.
313. "Bainbridge had returned": *Naval Documents,* vol. 6, p. 275.
314. "At a testimonial": Wright–Macleod, pp. 188–9.
314. "'General Eaton is'": Edwards, p. 191.
314. "'astonished not only'": *Naval Documents,* vol. 6, p. 296.
314. "A Senate resolution": Ibid., vol. 5, p. 545.

314. "Massachusetts awarded Eaton": Ibid., vol. 6, p. 376.

315. "'Eaton, a glorious'": Allison, p. 200.

315. "Federalist newspapers already": Ibid., pp. 197–8.

315. "Pickering deplored Lear's": Brighton, p. 271, Letter to Fisher Ames.

316. "He burned the last": *Naval Documents*, vol. 6, p. 398.

316. "'The effect has'": Ibid.

316. "There were none": Ibid., p. 315.

316. "'On entering the'": Ibid.

316. "Federalist senators went": Ibid., p. 343.

316. "Jefferson personally supervised": *Presidential Papers Microfilm: Thomas Jefferson Papers* (Washington, D.C., 1974), Reel 35. Jefferson notes.

317. "He composed a message": *Naval Documents*, vol. 6, pp. 344–5.

317. "'The present moment'": Ibid., p. 349.

317. "The committee's 472-page": Ibid., pp. 391–3.

318. "Lieutenant John Dent, who said": Ibid., p. 377.

318. "Marine Second Lieutenant Wallace W. Wormeley's": Ibid., pp. 373–4.

319. "The withering criticism": Ibid., pp. 436, 512–3.

319. "The Tunisian ambassador": Ibid., p. 36.

319. "His seriocomic diplomatic": Ibid., p. 308; Wright–Macleod, p. 187.

319. "Madison sent Melli Melli": *Naval Documents*, vol. 6, p. 428.

319. "They decided upon": Ibid., pp. 441, 448.

320. "As Melli Melli correctly": Ibid., p. 462.

320. "'a very mean'": Ibid., p. 457.

320. "the profusion of gifts": Ibid., pp. 498–9.

320. "Satisfied with Melli Melli's": Ibid., p. 508.

321. "The upheaval had begun": Wright–Macleod, p. 187.

321. "Turkish soldiers assassinated": *Naval Documents*, vol. 6, p. 298.

321. "On Christmas Day": Ibid., p. 326.

321. "So highly was Lear": Ibid., p. 432.

321. "The frigates, brigs": Ibid., p. 431.

322. "The Tripolitan war": Ibid., pp. 30–1.

322. "For nine straight": Ferguson, ed. *Selected Writings of Albert Gallatin*, pp. 208–9.

322. "Even with revenues": Adams, *History of the United States*, vol. 3, p. 345.

322. "Jefferson, who had": Ibid., p. 355.

322. "In December 1806": Ibid., p. 347.

322. "After protesting that": *Naval Documents*, vol. 6, pp. 430, 433, 465.

Chapter XVII: Full Circle

324. "George Davis reembarked": *Naval Documents*, vol. 6, p. 482.

324. "The consul's devotion": Ibid., p. 79.

325. "Now Nissen was retiring": Ibid., pp. 103–4.

325. "The treaty, he told": Ibid., p. 496.

325. "The treaty that had": Ibid., pp. 81–2.

325. "'that I had not'": Ibid., p. 105.

326. "The clause was attached": Ibid., pp. 81–2.

326. "In his report": Ibid., p. 161.

326. "'We will not incline'": *Presidential Papers Microfilm: Thomas Jefferson Papers,* Reel 35.
326. "The commodore had suggested": *Naval Documents,* vol. 6, p. 246.
327. "... the weight of'": Ibid., pp. 209–10, 350.
327. "'I have lost'": Ibid., pp. 575–6.
327. "According to Eaton": Ibid., p. 178.
327. "'I trusted to'": Ibid., pp. 263–4.
327. "Congress paid him": Ibid., p. 178.
327. "Davis didn't reveal": Ibid., pp. 516–7, 519.
328. "At his first audience": Ibid., p. 522; Wright–Macleod, p. 185.
328. "When Davis badgered": *Naval Documents,* vol. 6, p. 551.
328. "they sailed away": Ibid., p. 570.
328. "Davis managed to": Ibid., p. 585.
329. "For the first time": Brighton, pp. 272–3.
329. "When the Spanish": *Adams,* vol. 2, p. 58.
330. "The Americans' specious": Ibid., p. 72.
330. "The British went": Ibid., vol. 3, pp. 92–3.
330. "They also impressed": Ibid., p. 97.
331. "The British detentions": *Naval Documents,* vol. 6, pp. 532–3.
331. "He claimed that": Ibid., p. 128.
331. "In August 1806": Ibid., p. 475.
332. "He dispatched the *Chesapeake*": Ibid., p. 523.
332. "James Barron seldom visited": Ibid., p. 536.
333. "Not only was": Tucker, pp. 342–3.
333. "At 6:00 A.M. on": Walter Lowrie, Walter S. Franklin, ed., *American State Papers. Documents, Legislative and Executive, of the Congress of the United States.* 6 vols. (Washington: Gales and Seaton), *I-Foreign Relations,* vol. 3, pp. 6–7.
334. "Barron's officers noticed": *Naval Documents,* vol. 6, pp. 536–40.
334. "Humphries deplored the loss": Ibid., p. 536.
335. "War fever crackled": Schachner, p. 840.
335. "A mob in Norfolk": Ibid.
335. "British warships fanned": *Naval Documents,* vol. 6, pp. 543–4.
335. "Jefferson closed all": Schachner, p. 877.
335. "Jefferson's Cabinet, with": Schachner, pp. 840–9; *American State Papers, I-Foreign Relations,* vol. 3, pp. 6–7.
335. "Congress approved the Embargo": *Naval Documents,* vol. 6, p. 583.
335. "The infamous Embargo": Schachner, p. 862.
335. "Later in life, Jefferson": Ibid., p. 885.
336. "America's bread-and-butter": Ibid., p. 876.
336. "Smugglers operated successfully": Ibid., p. 871.
336. "Campbell emptied the": *Naval Documents,* vol. 6, pp. 546–7.
337. "The *Chesapeake*'s mortified officers": Ibid., p. 540.
337. "The court of inquiry": Ibid., pp. 563–7.
337. "Barron's fellow officers": Tucker, p. 343.
338. "His actions were celebrated": Allison, pp. 194–5.
338. "Congress had struck": *Naval Documents,* vol. 6, p. 427.
338. "Preble was the rumored": Ibid., p. 297.

338. "Once, when Preble": *Presidential Papers Microfilm: Thomas Jefferson Papers,* Reel 33.

338. "Preble was buried": *Naval Documents,* vol. 6, pp. 554–5.

338. "He and the commodore": Ibid., p. 297.

339. "Congress had awarded": Edwards, p. 247.

339. "Eaton was 'an imposter'": Wright–Macleod, p. 193, Plumer's journal.

339. "His loyal neighbors": Ibid., pp. 194, 196.

340. "With Governor George Clinton": Schachner, p. 790.

340. "At the head": Buckner F. Melton, Jr., *Aaron Burr: Conspiracy to Treason* (New York: John Wiley & Sons, 2002), pp. 53–4.

340. "General James Wilkinson": Ibid., pp. 56, 122.

340. "Burr recruited Andrew Jackson": Ibid., pp. 107–11.

341. "At this point, Eaton": Ibid., p. 97.

341. "It wasn't until": Ibid., pp. 131–2, 135.

341. "Before long, Burr": Ibid., pp. 140, 157, 163.

342. "Eaton testified that": Ibid., p. 202.

342. "'The once redoubted Eaton'": Francis F. Beirne, *Shout Treason: The Trial of Aaron Burr* (New York, Hastings House Publishers, 1959), p. 177.

343. "Embittered, Eaton returned": Wright–Macleod, p. 196: Edwards, p. 254; Whipple, p. 274.

343. "Reclusive, suffering from": Whipple, p. 274; Tucker, p. 443; Edwards, pp. 263–9.

343. "Eaton's disgrace and": Wright–Macleod, pp. 196–7.

343. "In November 1807": *Naval Documents,* vol. 6, p. 577.

343. "When Lear demanded": Brighton, p. 283.

344. "Lear paid the dey": *Naval Documents,* vol. 6, p. 583.

344. "But then he demanded": Allen, p. 275.

Chapter XVIII: Epilogue

346. "The British foreign": Allen, p. 276.

346. "'the American flag'": Edgar Stanton Maclay, *A History of the United States Navy, From 1775 to 1898* (New York: D. Appleton and Company, 1893), vol. 2, p. 6.

346. "The janissaries had assassinated": Irwin, p. 170; Brighton, pp. 291–2.

346. "He complained that": Irwin, pp. 171–2.

347. "Lear wangled a": Allen, pp. 276–7; Brighton, p. 296.

347. "As he sat down": Allen, pp. 277–8.

347. "America had to face": Fletcher Pratt, *Preble's Boys: Commodore Preble and the Birth of American Sea Power* (New York: William Sloane Associates, 1950), p. 44.

348. "the British had destroyed": Ibid.

348. "The *Edwin,* a brig": *American State Papers, I-Foreign Affairs,* vol. 3, pp. 748–9.

348. "'My policy and'": Allen, pp. 279–80.

348. "Washington threw a": Pratt, pp. 85–6.

349. "By 1812, Decatur": Ibid., p. 98.

349. "Decatur had met": Ibid., p. 99.

350. "Decatur brought the prize": Ibid., pp. 99–104.

351. "And then, in January": Ibid., pp. 104–6.

352. "Hadji Ali had": Allison, p. 209.

352. "On February 23, 1815": *American State Papers, I-Foreign Affairs,* vol. 3, p. 748.

352. "Its 17-ship fleet": Maclay, vol. 2, p. 6.

352. "Its navy had 5": Ibid., pp. 7–8.

352. "Aboard the *Guerriere* was": Allen, p. 292.

353. "Lookouts sighted several": Maclay, vol. 2, pp. 9–10.

354. "As a boy": Tucker, pp. 454–5.

354. "Badly wounded when": Maclay, vol. 2, pp. 11–3.

354. "Two days later": Ibid., pp. 13–4.

355. "Omar the Terrible": Anthony, pp. 248–51.

355. "On June 28": *American State Papers, I-Foreign Affairs,* vol. 4, p. 6.

355. "'.. . peace, to be durable'": Allen, p. 285.

356. "A second letter": Ibid., p. 286.

356. "The dey invited": Ibid., pp. 286–7.

356. "He said he would": *American State Papers, I-Foreign Affairs,* vol. 4, p. 6.

357. "American ships spotted": Maclay, vol. 2, p. 15.

357. "'It has been dictated'": Anthony, pp. 249–51.

357. "Lieutenant John Shubrick": Allen, p. 289; Maclay, vol. 2, pp. 16–7; Anthony, p. 251.

358. "Early in 1815": Maclay, vol. 2, p. 17; Anthony, pp. 252–4.

358. "Decatur learned of the": Allen, p. 289.

358. "Through U.S. consul": Maclay, vol. 2, p. 17–8; Anthony, p. 253; Allen, p. 290.

358. "Decatur's next stop": Maclay, vol. 2, pp. 18–9; Anthony, p. 254; Allen, pp. 290–91.

359. "Lookouts sighted seven": Maclay, vol. 2, pp. 19–20.

359. "Bainbridge's squadron reached": Maclay, vol. 2, p. 20; Anthony, pp. 258–60; Allen, pp. 292–3.

359. "In Washington, everyone applauded": Allen, p. 292; *American State Papers, I-Foreign Affairs,* vol. 4, p. 4.

360. "Lord Exmouth sailed to": Maclay, vol. 2, p. 21.

360. "when Shaler presented": Ibid., pp. 21–2.

360. "The alarmed dey": Allen, p. 296.

361. "The British government": Julien, p. 328.

361. "Exmouth and van Cappellen": Wolf, p. 331.

361. "'It is a principle'": Allen, p. 339.

362. "Chauncey and Shaler added": Ibid., pp. 299–300.

362. "He imposed a single": Ibid., p. 300; Wright–Macleod, p. 206.

362. "Yusuf and Hamet": Allen, p. 265.

362. "The last act": Tucker, p. 437.

363. "In 1835, Yusuf's son": Whipple, p. 338.

363. "Baltimore gave him": Anthony, pp. 270–1.

363. "'Our country!' Decatur said": Ibid., p. 265.

363. "He stowed away": Pratt, p. 110.

363. "After serving his": Ibid., p. 112.

364. "He wrote a letter": Ibid; Anthony, p. 287.

364. "In October Barron had": Ibid., pp. 287–90.

364. "They agreed to fire": Ben Birindelli, *The 200 Year Legacy of Stephen Decatur, 1798–1998* (Gloucester Point, Va.: Hallmark Publishing Company Inc. 1998), p. 68.

364. "Decatur already had": Ibid.; Anthony, p. 308.

365. "Decatur died in agony": Birindelli, p. 68.

366. "35 American ships": Allison, p. 110.

367. "little more than 30": Allen, pp. 333–5.

367. "their stories were still": Adams, *History of the United States,* vol. 2, p. 436.

BIBLIOGRAPHY

Abun-Nasr, Jamil M. *A History of the Maghrib*. Cambridge, England: Cambridge University Press, 1971.

Adams, Henry. *History of the United States during the Administrations of Thomas Jefferson and James Madison*. 4 vols. New York: A & C Boni, 1930.

Adams, Henry. *The Life of Albert Gallatin*. New York: Peter Smith, 1943.

Adams, John. *The Works of John Adams*. 10 vols. Freeport, N.Y.: Books for Libraries Press, 1969.

Allen, Gardner W. *Our Navy and the Barbary Corsairs*. Hamden, Conn.: Archon Books, 1905.

Allison, Robert J. *The Crescent Obscured: The United States and the Muslim World, 1776–1815*. New York, Oxford: Oxford University Press, 1995.

Anthony, Irvin. *Decatur*. New York, London: Charles Scribner's Sons, 1931.

Bartlett, Merrill L.; Sweetman, Jack. *The U.S. Marine Corps: An Illustrated History*. Annapolis, Md.: Naval Institute Press, 2001.

Beirne, Francis F. *Shout Treason: The Trial of Aaron Burr*. New York: Hastings House Publishers, 1959.

Birindelli, Ben. *The 200 Year Legacy of Stephen Decatur, 1798–1998*. Gloucester, Va.: Hallmark Publishing Company, 1998.

Bjork, Gordon C. *Stagnation and Growth in the American Economy, 1784–1792*. New York, London: Garland Publishing Inc., 1985.

Brighton, Ray. *The Checkered Career of Tobias Lear*. Portsmouth: Portsmouth Marine Society, 1985.

Brodie, Fawn M. *Thomas Jefferson: An Intimate History*. New York: W. W. Norton & Co. Inc., 1974.

Carr, Caleb. *The Lessons of Terror*. New York: Random House, 2002.

Carrington, Richard. *East from Tunis*. London: Chatto and Windus, 1957.

Carruth, Gorton. *What Happened When: A Chronology of Life & Events in America*. New York: Signet, 1991.

Chapelle, Howard I. *The History of the American Sailing Navy*. New York: Bonanza Books, 1935.

Chew, Samuel C. *The Crescent and the Rose: Islam and England during the Renaissance*. New York: Octagon Books Inc., 1965.

Chidsey, Donald Barr. *The Wars in Barbary: Arab Piracy and the Birth of the United States Navy*. New York: Crown Publisher Inc., 1971.

Churchill, Winston S. *A History of the English-Speaking Peoples*. 4 vols. New York: Dodd, Mead & Company, 1962.

Culver, Henry B. *Forty Famous Ships.* New York: Garden City Publishing Co. Inc., 1938.

Dearborn, H. A. S. *The Life of William Bainbridge, Esq. of the United States Navy.* Princeton, N.J.: Princeton University Press, 1931.

Dupuy, R. Ernest and Trevor N., eds. *Harper Encyclopedia of Military History.* New York: HarperCollins Publishers, 1993.

Durant, Will and Ariel. *The Story of Civilization.* 11 vols. New York: Simon and Schuster, Inc., 1935–1975.

Edwards, Samuel. *Barbary General: The Life of William H. Eaton.* Englewood Cliffs, N.J.: Prentice-Hall, Inc., 1968.

Ellis, Joseph J. *American Sphinx: The Character of Thomas Jefferson.* New York: Alfred A. Knopf, 1997.

Ferguson, James, ed. *Selected Writings of Albert Gallatin.* Indianapolis, New York: The Bobbs-Merrill Company Inc., 1967.

Flexner, James Thomas. *Washington: The Indispensable Man.* Boston, New York, Toronto, London: Little, Brown and Company, 1974.

Folayan, Kola. *Tripoli During the Reign of Yusuf Pasha Qaramanli.* Ile-Ife, Nigeria: University of Ife Press, 1979.

Foley, John P., ed. *The Jeffersonian Cyclopedia.* 2 vols. New York: Russell & Russell, 1900.

Ford, Paul Leicester. *The Writings of Thomas Jefferson.* New York: G. P. Putnam's Sons, 1897.

Foss, John. *Journal of the Captivity and Sufferings of John Foss, Several Years a Prisoner in Algiers.* Newburyport, Maine: A. March, Middle-Street, 1798.

Fowler, William M., Jr. *Jack Tars and Commodores: The American Navy, 1783–1815.* Boston: Houghton Mifflin Company, 1984.

Fowler, William M., Jr. *Rebels Under Sail: The American Navy during the Revolution.* New York: Scribner, 1976.

Friedman, Ellen G. *Spanish Captives in North Africa in the Early Modern Age.* Madison, Wis.: The University of Wisconsin Press, 1983.

Funk & Wagnalls New Encyclopedia. USA: Funk & Wagnalls, 1983.

Garraty, John A.; Carnes, Mark C., eds. *American National Biography.* New York: Oxford University Press, 1999.

Gilbert, Felix; Rice, Eugene F., Jr.; Dunn, Richard S.; Krieger, Leonard; Breunig, Charles; Rich, Norman. *The Norton History of Modern Europe.* New York: W. W. Norton & Company, Inc., 1971.

Giunta, Mary A., ed. *The Emerging Nation: A Documentary History of the Foreign Relations of the United States Under the Articles of Confederation: 1780–1789.* Washington: National Historical Publications and Record Commission, 1996.

Gottschalk, Louis Reichenthal, ed. *The Letters of Lafayette to Washington, 1777–1799.* Philadelphia: American Philosophical Society, 1976.

Hagan, Kenneth J. *This People's Navy: The Making of American Sea Power.* New York: The Free Press, 1991.

Haleem, Muhammed Abdel. *Understanding the Qur'an: Themes and Style.* London, New York: I. B. Taurus, Publishers, 1999.

Heidler, David S. and Jeanne T., eds. *Encyclopedia of the War of 1812.* Santa Barbara, Calif., Denver, Oxford: ABC-CLIO, 1997.

Irving, T. B., transl. *The Qur'an.* Brattleboro, Vt.: Amana Books, 1986.

Irwin, Ray W. *The Diplomatic Relations of the United States with the Barbary Powers, 1776–1816.* Chapel Hill, N.C.: The University of North Carolina Press, 1931.

Jefferson, Thomas. *Autobiography of Thomas Jefferson.* New York: Capricorn Books, 1959.

Jefferson, Thomas. *The Papers of Thomas Jefferson.* 25 vols. Princeton, N.J.: Princeton University Press, 1950–.

Jefferson, Thomas. *Presidential Papers Microfilm: Thomas Jefferson Papers.* 65 reels. Washington, 1974.

Jefferson, Thomas. *The Writings of Thomas Jefferson.* Washington: The Thomas Jefferson Memorial Association, 1903.

Julien, Charles-André. *History of North Africa.* New York: Praeger Publishers, 1970.

Kitzen, Michael L. S. *Tripoli and the United States at War: A History of American Relations with the Barbary States, 1785–1805.* Jefferson, N.C., London: McFarland & Company, Inc., 1993.

Laing, Alexander. *American Sail: A Pictorial History.* New York: Dutton, 1961.

Lane-Poole, Stanley. *The Barbary Corsairs.* New York: G. P. Putnam's Sons, 1901.

Lane-Poole, Stanley. *The Moors in Spain.* New York: G. P. Putnam's Sons, 1911.

Leckie, Robert. *The Wars of America.* New York: Harper & Row, 1981.

Lowrie, Walter; Franklin, Walter S., eds. *American State Papers. Documents, Legislative and Executive, of the Congress of the United States.* Washington: Gales and Seaton, 1832.

MacGregor, David R. *Fast Sailing Ships: Their Design and Construction, 1775–1895.* Annapolis, Md.: Naval Institute Press, 1973.

Maclay, Edgar Stanton. *A History of the United States Navy, From 1775 to 1898.* New York: D. Appleton and Company, 1893.

Madison, James. *The Papers of James Madison.* Secretary of State Series. Charlottesville, Va.: University Press of Virginia, 1986.

McCarthy, Justin. *The Ottoman Turks: An Introductory History to 1923.* London, New York: Addison Wesley Longman Limited, 1997.

McCullough, David. *John Adams.* New York: Simon & Schuster, 2001.

McEvedy, Colin. *The Penguin Atlas of Ancient, Medieval and Modern History.* 3 vols. Baltimore, Md.: Penguin Books Inc., 1967.

McKee, Christopher. *Edward Preble, A Naval Biography, 1761–1807.* Annapolis, Md.: Naval Institute Press, 1972.

Melton, Buckner F., Jr. *Aaron Burr: Conspiracy to Treason.* New York: John Wiley & Sons, Inc., 2002.

Miller, Arthur P. "Tripoli Graves Discovered." *U.S. Naval Institute Proceedings,* April 1950.

Morison, Samuel Eliot. *The Oxford History of the American People.* 3 vols. New York: New American Library, 1972.

Morsy, Magali. *North Africa 1800–1900.* London, New York: Longman Group Limited, 1984.

Moskin, J. Robert. *The U.S. Marine Corps Story.* New York: McGraw-Hill Book Co., 1977.

Naval Documents Related to the United States Wars with the Barbary Powers. 6 vols. Washington: U.S. Government Printing Office, 1939.

Nettles, Curtis P. *The Emergence of a National Economy, 1775–1815.* New York, Evanston, London: Harper & Row, Publishers, 1962.

Pratt, Fletcher. *Preble's Boys: Commodore Preble and the Birth of American Sea Power.* New York: William Sloane Associates, 1950.

Prentiss, Charles. *Life of the Late William Eaton.* Brookfield, Mass.: Merriam & Co., 1813.

Ray, William. *Horrors of Slavery: or, The American Tars in Tripoli.* Troy, N.Y.: Oliver Lyon, 1808.

Schachner, Nathan. *Thomas Jefferson: A Biography.* New York, London: Thomas Yoseloff Ltd., 1951.

Schuon, Karl, ed. *The Leathernecks.* New York: Franklin Watts, Inc., 1963.

Schuon, Karl, ed. *U.S. Marine Corps Biographical Dictionary.* New York: Franklin Watts, Inc., 1963.

Tryckare, Tre. *The Lore of Ships.* New York: Holt, Rinehart and Winston, 1963.

Tuchman, Barbara W. *The First Salute.* New York: Alfred A. Knopf, 1988.

Tucker, Glenn. *Dawn Like Thunder: The Barbary Wars and the Birth of the U.S. Navy.* Indianapolis: The Bobbs-Merrill Company, Inc., 1963.

Twohig, Dorothy, ed. *The Papers of George Washington.* Charlottesville, Va., London: University Press of Virginia, 1997.

Vatikiotis, P. J. *The History of Egypt.* Baltimore: The Johns Hopkins University Press, 1969.

Weybright, Victor. *Spangled Banner: The Story of Francis Scott Key.* New York: Farrar & Rinehart Inc., 1935.

Whipple, A. B. C. *The Seafarers: Fighting Sail.* Alexandria, Va.: Time-Life Books, 1978.

Whipple, A. B. C. *To the Shores of Tripoli: The Birth of the U.S. Navy and Marines.* New York: William Morrow and Company, Inc., 1991.

Whittier, John Greenleaf. *The Complete Poetical Works of John Greenleaf Whittier.* Boston, New York: Houghton Mifflin Company, 1892.

Wolf, John B. *The Barbary Coast: Algiers Under the Turks, 1500–1830.* New York, London: W. W. Norton & Co., 1979.

Wright, Louis B.; Macleod, Julia H. *The First Americans in North Africa: William Eaton's Struggle for a Vigorous Policy against the Barbary Pirates, 1799–1805.* Princeton, N.J.: Princeton University Press, 1945.

INDEX

ABOUT THE AUTHOR

JOSEPH WHEELAN was a reporter and editor for The Associated Press for 24 years in Cheyenne, Wyoming; Denver; Little Rock; and Raleigh, North Carolina. While news editor in the AP's Denver and Raleigh bureaus, Wheelan directed team, feature and investigative reporting projects and supervised daily news coverage. He also reviewed dozens of books for the AP and, among other things, wrote about the Korean War and the continuing battle by its veterans to obtain government benefits for cold-weather injuries.

Before joining the AP, he was a reporter and state editor for the *Casper (Wyo.) Star-Tribune.* Wheelan is a graduate of the University of Wyoming and the University of Colorado-Denver.

He and his wife, Pat, a research scientist, have two grown daughters and live in Cary, N.C.